Institutional and Organizational Analysis

What explains the great variability in economic growth and political development across countries? Institutional and Organizational Analysis has developed since the 1970s into a powerful toolkit, which argues that institutions and norms rather than geography, culture, or technology are the primary causes of sustainable development. Institutions are rules that recognized authorities create and enforce. Norms are rules created by long-standing patterns of behavior, shared by people in a society or organization. They combine to play a role in all organizations, including governments, firms, churches, universities, gangs, and even families. This introduction to the concepts and applications of Institutional and Organizational Analysis uses economic history, economics, law, and political science to inform its theoretical framework. Institutional and Organizational Analysis provides a framework for understanding why the economic and political performance of countries worldwide has not converged and reveals lessons for business, law, and public policy.

ERIC ALSTON is Scholar in Residence in the Finance Division and Faculty Director of the Hernando de Soto Capital Markets Program in the Leeds School of Business at the University of Colorado Boulder. He also serves as a research associate with the Comparative Constitutions Project.

LEE J. ALSTON is the Ostrom Chair, Professor of Economics and Law, and Director of the Ostrom Workshop at Indiana University. He is a research associate at the NBER. Alston is a former president of the International Society for New Institutional Economics and the Economic History Association.

BERNARDO MUELLER is a lecturer at the Department of Economics at the University of Brasília. He is the co-author of *Brazil in Transition: Beliefs, Leadership, and Institutional Change*, along with Lee J. Alston, Marcus André Melo, and Carlos Pereira.

TOMAS NONNENMACHER is the Patricia Bush Tippie Chair of Economics and Co-director of the Center for Business and Economics at Allegheny College. He is an affiliated faculty at the Ostrom Workshop.

New Approaches to Economic and Social History

SERIES EDITORS

Marguerite Dupree (University of Glasgow)
Debin Ma (London School of Economics and Political Science)
Larry Neal (University of Illinois, Urbana-Champaign)

New Approaches to Economic and Social History is an important new textbook series published in association with the Economic History Society. It provides concise but authoritative surveys of major themes and issues in world economic and social history from the post-Roman recovery to the present day. Books in the series are by recognized authorities operating at the cutting edge of their field with an ability to write clearly and succinctly. The series consists principally of single-author works – academically rigorous and groundbreaking – which offer comprehensive, analytical guides at a length and level accessible to advanced school students and undergraduate historians and economists.

A full list of titles published in the series can be found at:
www.cambridge.org/newapproacheseconomicandsocialhistory

Institutional and Organizational Analysis

Concepts and Applications

ERIC ALSTON
University of Colorado

LEE J. ALSTON
Indiana University

BERNARDO MUELLER
University of Brasília

TOMAS NONNENMACHER
Allegheny College

CAMBRIDGE
UNIVERSITY PRESS

CAMBRIDGE
UNIVERSITY PRESS

University Printing House, Cambridge CB2 8BS, United Kingdom

One Liberty Plaza, 20th Floor, New York, NY 10006, USA

477 Williamstown Road, Port Melbourne, VIC 3207, Australia

314–321, 3rd Floor, Plot 3, Splendor Forum, Jasola District Centre,
New Delhi – 110025, India

79 Anson Road, #06–04/06, Singapore 079906

Cambridge University Press is part of the University of Cambridge.

It furthers the University's mission by disseminating knowledge in the pursuit of
education, learning, and research at the highest international levels of excellence.

www.cambridge.org
Information on this title: www.cambridge.org/9781107086371
DOI: 10.1017/9781316091340

First published 2018

Printed in the United States of America by Sheridan Books, Inc.

A catalogue record for this publication is available from the British Library.

Library of Congress Cataloging-in-Publication Data
Names: Alston, Eric C., 1982– author.
Title: Institutional and organizational analysis : concepts and applications / Eric
Alston [and three others].
Description: Cambridge, United Kingdom ; New York, NY : Cambridge University
Press, 2018. | Series: New approaches to economic and social history | Includes
bibliographical references and index.
Identifiers: LCCN 2018011066| ISBN 9781107086371 (hbk) | ISBN
9781107451254 (pbk)
Subjects: LCSH: Social institutions. | Institution building. | Social structure.
Classification: LCC HM826 .A57 2018 | DDC 306–dc23
LC record available at https://lccn.loc.gov/2018011066

ISBN 978-1-107-08637-1 Hardback
ISBN 978-1-107-45125-4 Paperback

To Sarah, Mary, Suely, Shannan, and our parents

Contents

Figures

Tables

Acknowledgments

Our intellectual debts are many. We owe a special debt to John Wallis for his overall insightful comments and for prompting us to revisit the distinction between norms and institutions. For comments, we thank Doug Allen, Martin Andersson, Jeremy Atack, Andy Baker, Eduardo Brondizio, Charles Calomiris, Federica Carugati, Alan Dye, Thráinn Eggertsson, Gustavo Franco, Patrick Francois, David Gerard, Thomas Ginsburg, Victor Goldberg, Regina Grafe, Avner Greif, Stephen Haber, Anne Hanley, Murat Iyigun, Gary Libecap, John Londregan, Dean Lueck, Shannan Mattiace, Noel Maurer, Terry Moe, Joel Mokyr, Aldo Musacchio, Larry Neal, Douglass North, Guilherme de Oliveira, Sonja Opper, Samuel Pessoa, James Robinson, Kenneth Shepsle, William Summerhill, Richard Sylla, Gustavo Torrens, Stefan Voigt, James Walker, Barry Weingast, and the participants at the following seminars and conferences: Lund University, Institute of Behavioral Science (University of Colorado), Ostrom Workshop (Indiana University), Vanderbilt University, the Society for Institutional and Organizational Economics, George Mason University's Antonin Scalia Law School, the Coase Institute Workshop, and Columbia Law School. We thank President Rafael Correa for hosting separately Eric and Lee J. Alston and for invaluable discussions with him. We especially thank Larry Neal for his encouragement early in the project. At Cambridge University Press, we thank early reviewers and especially Michael Watson for not losing faith in us. For an incredible job on editing, we thank Patty Lezotte of the Ostrom Workshop. For research assistance and comments, we thank Timothy Larsen. We are also indebted to the numerous students at Allegheny College, University of Brasília, University of Colorado, University of Illinois, and Indiana University. Our students gave us invaluable feedback on earlier versions of this material. We are incredibly indebted to our spouses and partners – Sarah, Mary, Suely, and Shannan – who patiently listened and supported our obsessive talking and thinking about institutional and organizational analysis.

Abbreviations

ADA	Americans for Democratic Action
AFSCME	American Federation of State, County and Municipal Employees
CIA	Central Intelligence Agency
CRP	Center for Responsive Politics
DPA	Drug Policy Alliance
EPA	Environmental Protection Agency
FC	fixed costs
FTC	Federal Trade Commission
GDP	gross domestic product
IMF	International Monetary Fund
INCRA	National Institute for Colonization and Agrarian Reform
IOA	Institutional and Organizational Analysis
IRS	Internal Revenue Service
MPB	marginal private benefit
MPC	marginal private cost
MPP	Marijuana Policy Project
MSB	marginal social benefit
MSC	marginal social cost
MST	Landless Peasant Movement (Movimento Sem-Terra)
NCIA	National Cannabis Industry Association
NFL	National Football League
NORML	National Organization for the Reform of Marijuana Laws
NUMMI	New United Motor Manufacturing, Inc.
OB	office bloc
PC	party column
PMR	pure majority rule
PT	Workers' Party
SENPLADES	National Planning and Development Secretariat
UDHR	Universal Declaration of Human Rights
VC	variable costs

Introduction

Why isn't the whole world developed? How can we explain the great variability in economic and political performances across countries? Finding answers to these questions is one of the enduring challenges in social science. While a small number of countries have reached high levels of economic prosperity and political openness, most have experienced short bursts of growth followed by economic and political volatility, often involving violence. The explanation for this uneven development provided by Institutional and Organizational Analysis (IOA) emphasizes the role of institutions and norms as fundamental determinants of economic and political development. Institutions are rules that recognized authorities create and enforce. Norms are long-standing patterns of behavior, shared by a subset of people in a society or organization. These factors play a role in all organizations, including governments, firms, churches, universities, gangs, and even families. In this book, we present an overarching framework and a set of concepts for institutional and organizational analysis, the tools used to analyze the evolution and effects of institutions, and a set of case studies drawn from economic, legal, and political history.[1]

---

[1] This book is not an overview of the entire literature on institutional and organizational analysis, which is now far too big to summarize in a single volume, but is our attempt at defining the major concepts at play in the literature and integrating them into a unified framework. For broad contributions and surveys to institutional analysis, see Acemoglu and Robinson (2006); Alston, Eggertsson, and North (1996); Brousseau and Glachant (2002, 2008); Drobak and Nye (1997); Eggertsson (1990); Engerman and Sokoloff (2012); Furubotn and Richter (1991, 2005); Galiani and Sened (2014); Gibbons and Roberts (2013); Greif (2006); Hodgson (1988, 2003); Klein and Sykuta (2010); Ménard and Shirley (2005); North (1990, 2005); North and Thomas (1973); North, Wallis, and Weingast (2009); Parisi and Fon (2009); Posner and Parisi (1997); Richter (2015); and Williamson (1985, 1996).

The book is in three parts, each presenting a different level of institutional analysis. In Part I, we analyze how the institutions and norms of society determine property rights, which provide the incentives for organizations and contracts and ultimately shape economic performance. In Part II, we analyze the determinants and impact of the laws of society and their enforcement, which over-all determine political performance. In Part II, we take constitutional-level rules as fixed, treating them as the umbrella under which organizations and actors interact to shape and enforce laws. Taken together, Parts I and II analyze the normal operation of the economic and political systems and the interaction among institutions, property rights, technology, and economic perfor-mance. The system is not static; there are new technologies and growth, but the underlying belief system and political system remain unaffected. In Part III, we analyze broader explanations of the divergent development trajectories of nations around the world. We consider in detail the circumstances under which beliefs become malleable and change and how those changes, frequently orche-strated by leadership, can lead to transitions to different economic and political trajectories. At this scale, we analyze longer stretches of time, allowing for differences in fundamental core beliefs that in turn can transform the development path of a society. In Part III, we also analyze the determinants of constitutions that emerge through a process in which beliefs shape constitutions and, under some circumstances, the constitutional-making process shapes beliefs.

Examples of Institutional and Organizational Analysis

The interpretation and implementation of institutions is dynamic, shaped by other institutions, norms, individuals, and organizations. This means that the effect of institutions and norms on behavior is difficult to generalize and often requires a more granular consideration of the behavior within a given social group that a rule is trying to influence. In order to familiarize the reader with the benefits of a mode of analysis that focuses on the specific rules in play in a given context, we provide a series of illustrative examples in this section. Each example can be situated in one of the parts of our book, empha-sizing the analytical toolkit that we develop throughout.

The Decline of Littering in the United States

Casual disposal of one's refuse became widely recognized as a social problem in the period following World War II, although some jurisdictions note laws reaching as far back as 1897 (Frisman, 2008). Nonetheless, the effect of the institutions prohibiting littering is not clear, because the practice of littering persisted for decades after the enactment of such laws. Why might legal enforcement be ineffective in restraining a practice like littering? Careful consideration of the different ways in which institutions and norms incentivize behavior provides a compelling explanation for the eventual decline in littering in the United States.

In first considering institutions as a potential solution to the problem of littering, it is important to remember that institutions depend upon a recognized authority for their enforcement. In the case of laws (or ordinances) prohibiting littering, the enforcement authority is the police. In order to enforce the consequences for littering, police must either witness the act of littering, engage in an investigation to determine the identity of the litterer after the fact, or rely on the testimony of eyewitnesses who saw the littering occur.[2] Each of these possible means of enforcement fails to provide a cost-effective deterrent to the practice for obvious reasons. Littering laws are difficult to enforce because it is hard to catch someone in the act of littering and hard, after the fact, to determine who did the littering. Thus, the deficiencies of enforcement of the minor crime of littering suggest that laws prohibiting littering are unlikely to affect the behavior of individuals inclined to do so.

Absent such an analysis, one could look at the decline in littering subsequent to the enactment of laws prohibiting the behavior, and infer that the laws caused the eventual decline in the practice. However, given the preceding analysis, it is unlikely that laws whose enforcement costs outweighed the marginal social benefit of deterring individual acts of littering had their intended effect. Instead, while the decline in the practice of littering in the United States has been quite substantial (a 61 percent decrease between 1969 and 2009 by one estimate

---

[2] In today's world, cameras that capture many acts like littering are increasingly found in cities like London, where nearly every aspect of public behavior is recorded, often from multiple angles. Our example of littering sets aside the case of technological shocks to enforcement costs, because the change in practices surrounding littering in the United States occurred well before such public surveillance was affordable for common law enforcement purposes.

[Schultz and Stein, 2009]), this change has occurred gradually. As importantly, this change occurred over the same period when public attitudes regarding the importance of a healthy environment increased significantly. While many states passed laws explicitly designed to address the problem of littering from the 1950s to the 1970s, it is more likely that these laws were an expression of the underlying change in beliefs regarding the environment. These same beliefs led to a change in norms; where littering was previously quite commonplace, the increased social costs of littering had two important implications for individual behavior. Individuals likely held the underlying belief regarding the value of a clean environment. Even if some individuals did not hold such a belief, the likelihood that members of their social group did hold such a belief increased significantly, which meant an individual who littered in view of anyone was more likely to bear costs such as ostracism or direct criticism of their behavior. Over time, this increased likelihood of either individually valuing the environment more than the convenience of littering, or one's social group doing so, led to more and more individuals adopting the norm against littering, regardless of the legal penalties associated with the action. The example of littering displays how careful analysis of the incentives created by different rules, and the comparative costs of the enforcement of rules (both individually and in comparison to other rules in society), provides a deeper understanding of an important social change than a cursory analysis of legal change and subsequent behaviors.

Land Reform in Brazil

Rural conflict and the struggle for land permeate Brazilian history. In the nineteenth century, slavery and the coffee boom consolidated the ownership of land in the hands of a small elite, and the highly concentrated pattern of land ownership has persisted to the present day. The coexistence of unproductive *latifundia* with large numbers of landless peasants has resulted in recurring violence, conflict, and deforestation, promoting economic uncertainty and social disruption. As Brazil returned to democracy in the mid-1980s after decades of authoritarian rule (1964–1984), the level of rural violence and unrest further increased, as landless peasants organized and initiated systematic invasions of underused properties. The new government adopted land redistribution as a flagship policy and symbol of the return to democratic ideals. The redistribution consisted of the compensated yet forced expropriation of unproductive farms and the creation of settlement projects. The Brazilian government gave land, credit, and technical support to landless peasants. Despite the prominence of land reform policies in the political agenda, landowners resisted politically and physically. The upshot was a steady increase in the number and severity of rural conflicts throughout the 1990s and 2000s. The number and audacity of the invasions, and the ruthlessness of the reaction by landowners and police, kept land reform as a constant fixture in the media and in political and electoral debate. Although each new instance of rural violence prompted renewed promises of greater government action, the violence and conflicts just seem to get worse every year.

Critics maintained that the government's land reform effort was insufficient and the solution was to invest more resources and redistribute enough land to diffuse the source of the conflicts. Nevertheless, as each new president upped the ante and adopted higher targets for the number of families settled and higher land reform budgets, the level of tension and number of invasions just seemed to get worse.

The problem with this way of looking at the issue of rural conflicts in Brazil is that it focuses on the upfront manifestations of the actions of players, but does not consider the institutional foundations that determine the players' incentives and constraints. Conflicts should not be understood as a game played in physical space, where the player that grabs the land and defends it most successfully is the winner (Alston, Libecap, and Mueller, 1999a, 1999b, 2000). Instead, it is a game played in institutional space, where the players engage in violence, not for its direct effect on the opponent, but strategically, for the indirect effect that results from the institutional rules that mediate land reform in Brazil. The key insight to understand rural violence is that Brazilian society (public opinion and the majority of voters) is strongly in favor of redressing historical wealth inequalities through redistributive land reform. This has become a valence issue in Brazilian politics despite the fact that Brazil is overwhelmingly urban and few voters are directly affected. Politicians, especially the office of the president, which is directly in charge of land reform, understand these preferences and respond accordingly, promising to further the cause. There are, however, organized interests that oppose the reforms, especially landowners and agricultural producers. They strive in Congress, in the courts, and in the field to undermine land reform efforts. The upshot is a balance where neither side has overwhelming influence, so that the struggle continues.

In the 1980s and early 1990s, very little land got effectively redistributed because politicians responded to the pressure for redistribution by creating the structure for land reform (a program, ambitious targets, and political visibility), yet did not allocate sufficient funding. Formally, landless peasants should register with the land reform agency and wait to be called when land became available. The agency would seek out land that fit the legal criteria for being expropriable according to the constitution (unproductive and/or bad title) and would then proceed through the process of taking the land and establishing settlement projects. Because this process turned out to be woefully slow, organized landless peasants realized that rather than waiting their turn, they could expedite things by preemptively invading land. Landless peasants did not invade randomly, but rather, they targeted properties, which the peasants knew fit the criteria for land reform redistribution. The landless did not intend to grab the land for keeps; rather, the strategy was to create a commotion that the media noticed and would have the effect of embarrassing and pressuring the land reform agency and politicians to prioritize that specific case. Every time this strategy succeeded, it had a demonstration effect that led to further invasions. Very soon, invasions became the main route for land redistribution.

Although the invasions were not strictly legal, they worked because of a constitutional provision that land must fulfill its social function, that is, the function of being productive. In a way, all the invasions did was to expedite something that the government should be doing anyway. If this recognition of the legitimacy of the invasions was the only claim to legality, then it would be hopeless for landowners to resist, and redistribution would proceed quickly and with little violence. However, landowners also had a legal recourse in the case of invasion. They could appeal to their local courts asking for a reintegration of possession, which often involved a warrant for the police to remove the interlopers. The courts might be aware of the land reform aspects of the invasion, but this was not in their jurisdiction, as land reform is a federal matter. Instead, they treated the issue as any other case of wrongful appropriation: if the plaintiff could prove rightful ownership, the judge would usually grant the eviction of the squatters.

With conflicting institutions legitimizing the opposing claims from each side, and without a clear rule of which institution should trump the other, the result was uncertainty and ultimately conflict and violence. The example illustrates the importance of institutional and organizational analysis. Under the standard diagnostic that conflicts arise out of insufficient political will to pursue land reform, the obvious solution would be to simply invest more resources and more effort to settle more families. The application of more resources escalated violence. An institutionally driven analysis, on the other hand, would have suggested a focus on resolving the legal contradictions that prompted each side to persist in the pursuit of land through violence. This might not fully resolve an issue that reflects deep historical cleavages in Brazilian society, but it would have resulted in less conflict, suffering, and waste.

Beliefs and Empire: Understanding the Decline of Portugal in the Sixteenth Century

The rise and fall of the Portuguese Empire in Asia during the fifteenth and sixteenth centuries illustrates the importance of beliefs and their interaction with institutions in affecting economic performance, a major theme we address in Part III of this book. During the fifteenth century, the Portuguese achieved considerable technological breakthroughs in nautical technologies and gradually managed to extend their reach down the coast of Africa and sail around the Cape of Good Hope to reach India in 1498. The Dutch and the English would only manage to follow suit almost one hundred years later. During this time, the Portuguese were poised to dominate the lucrative trade that supplied spices and other Asian goods to Europe satisfied by a dispersed caravan trade that ferried the goods by land and sea to the Middle East, where they traded with Mediterranean merchants. However, although the Portuguese had such a huge head start, they never quite managed to make the most of the new trade opportunities. Throughout the one hundred years prior to the Dutch and the English, the caravans remained the main suppliers of Asian goods to Europe. When the

Dutch and English finally arrived, they almost immediately displaced the Portuguese, who thereafter were minor players in an area where they once seemed set to reign supreme.

What explains the success of the Portuguese during the fifteenth century in tackling the myriad intricacies and impediments to developing the technology, knowledge, and organization required to brave the unknown and establish a route that no nation had sailed before? And, given this success, why did they not capitalize on the opportunities that these accomplishments had set at their feet? It seems clear that the proximate cause of the failure to reap the potential gains from the sea route to Asia was the decision to base their strategy on violence (redistribution) instead of commerce. Rather than using their maritime and military superiority to arbitrage the price differential of goods in Asia and Europe and drive the caravans out of business, they chose instead to prioritize the charging of duties, tolls, taxes, rights of transits, and other forms of veiled or outright extortion, leaving commerce as a secondary consideration. Previously, a variety of local bosses, princes, and caliphates charged fees and the Portuguese simply used their naval might to usurp many of these sources of revenue, especially on sea routes to the Persian Gulf. Correspondingly, during the reign of the Portuguese, caravans continued to carry the bulk of Asian supply to Europe, while the arrival of the Dutch and the English in the seventeenth century practically drove the caravans to a halt.

Many historians have ascribed the failure of the Portuguese to a culture and religion that was not conducive to trade and commerce (Hall, 1985; Jones, 1981; Landes, 1998). A different interpretation came from economic historians who faulted instead the "structures" of trade by the Portuguese. We can interpret the structures as institutions. This view, often associated with Steensgaard (1974), argued that the *Estado da India* – the Portuguese enterprise in Asia, manned by a viceroy, captains, diplomats, priests, down to the lowest soldiers – captured the rents and did not effectively pursue the king's interest as mandated.

In Part III of this book, we focus on the interaction of beliefs and institutions. Beliefs, as defined here, are a derivative of culture and refer to the agents' understanding of how institutions affect outcomes. Under this definition, it makes no sense to discuss whether beliefs *or* institutions were responsible for the rise and fall of the Portuguese

Empire; the Portuguese chose institutions consistent with their beliefs, the two go hand-in-glove. Those with power chose institutions purposefully to accomplish desired ends, given their beliefs of how the world works. If the expected outcomes materialize, this reinforces the beliefs. If they do not, then the belief becomes fragile and is displaced. There is thus a coevolution of beliefs and institutions.

Coevolution of beliefs, institutions, and organizations best explains the rise and fall of the Portuguese in the fifteenth and sixteenth centuries (Mueller and Leite, 2016). Mueller and Leite single out two specific dimensions of Portuguese medieval beliefs to explain the sequence of events.[3] The first, *patrimonialism*, is the belief that it is the state and not the individual or private sector that is the engine of wealth and progress. If something is to be accomplished, it is the state that will be the driving force. Consequently, the path for individual advancement is through capture and rent-seeking. A characteristic of this belief is thus a blurred boundary between public and private interests. The second dimension is a belief in the dishonor of manual labor, prudence and commerce, and the virtue of chivalry, just war, crusades, and violence. This was a common belief in many European medieval societies and was especially strong in Portugal, where the aristocrat or *fidalgo* (translated as "son of somebody") perceived themselves as born warriors and even the king would go off to the crusades.

It is straightforward to see how these beliefs and the institutions they spawned can make sense of both the rise and the fall of the Portuguese Empire. Portuguese success in developing and employing the technology and organization that enabled their unprecedented expansion was the result of a long process financed and managed by the state. While most nations were financially impoverished by the wars of the fifteenth century, Portugal experienced a level of centralization and financial solvency that allowed the state to lead the way, for example, through the leadership of Prince Henry the Navigator and the School of Sagres. For these accomplishments, a belief in the predominance of the state and the centralized institutions that

---

[3] It is common for scholars who analyze the interaction of beliefs and institutions to try to single out main dimensions or traits that characterize the beliefs, although beliefs are typically quite complex and nuanced. See Alesina and Giuliano (2015) for an extensive review of this literature and for several examples of the beliefs identified in different historical circumstances.

accompanied the process, were appropriate and successful. Similarly, a belief that prioritizes the virtue of crusades, war, and conquest also contributed towards that success. Both patrimonialism and a belief in violence were conducive to institutions that promoted the crusades and the voyages of expansion. In contrast, the Dutch and the English reached Asia many decades later, spurred by very different beliefs and institutions. Their enterprise was primarily commercial, and the institutions and organizations that they developed, such as the trading companies and their rules, had different incentives with different outcomes.

While patrimonialism and violence had served the Portuguese well in the fifteenth century, as they sought to develop the knowledge and organization to conquer their enemies and nature, these beliefs were not as beneficial in the new setting that the Portuguese encountered in the sixteenth century. In Asia, those beliefs proved to be poor guides for how to best capitalize on the opportunities that their earlier achievements had made possible. The choice of violence instead of commerce as the defining strategy of the Portuguese enterprise in Asia paid off handsomely in the first couple of decades of Portuguese presence. It gave the Portuguese a dispersed foothold in the region and much wealth in the form of plunder and taxes. Gradually, violence ran into decreasing returns as the local people and organizations learned how to avoid or minimize Portuguese exploitation. As this happened, and the proceeds from the enterprise systematically failed to live up to the Portuguese king's expectations, the Crown made many attempts to reform the *Estado da India* and the rules that sought to incentivize its agents and restrain their opportunism. Portuguese historian Vitorino Godinho (1965) describes this period as one of shifting beliefs, marked by the tensions and contradictions of the incomplete transition from the medieval to the modern era in Portugal. That is, there was a perception that a new world order held opportunities that necessitated different beliefs and institutions, but the attempted conversion was always incomplete and insufficient. The Portuguese state never quite managed to develop a commercial enterprise or to give room for a strong mercantile class to arise. Similarly, the aristocrat never fully became a merchant, adopting thrift and prudence, nor did the merchant avoid becoming a warrior (Godinho, 1965: 62, vol. I). So, although the Portuguese navigated the passage to Asia, they never navigated the passage from a medieval to an early capitalist order, and the poor results of the enterprise reflected this mismatch.

The century-long struggle by the king to reform the *Estado da India*, and the set of institutions within it, are clear manifestations of how hard it is to break free from a combination of beliefs and institutions. Beliefs are sticky, as are the institutions that they spawn, even when it is clear that the status quo is inadequate and that there are better viable alternatives. The king tried to reign in opportunistic behavior by: limiting stints in Asia to three years; having only two fleets set sail per year; and careful control of cargo space, routes, and stops on the return trips. Nevertheless, the private interests in *Estado da India*, especially the captains, but even the lowly soldiers, managed to appropriate or dissipate much of the wealth it plundered or created.

Towards the end of the sixteenth century, the king tried a regime of freedom of trade (but having to disembark and pay taxes in Lisbon); then a share system with a German contractor; followed by a similar deal with an Italian syndicate; and finally an attempt at a Portuguese East India Company. None of these reforms worked, as the interest rooted in *Estado da India* sabotaged the new organizations and institutions. Similarly, the failure to change the organizations and institutions reinforced the beliefs that patrimonialism and violence were appropriate understandings of how the world works. Thus, the perverse combination persisted even in the light of the more promising example provided by the Dutch and the English. Part III of the book explores in detail how the persistence of poor and less-developed countries across the world, beside a smaller group of countries that thrives and prospers, is related to similar entrenched dynamics of interrelated beliefs and institutions.

Overview of the Book

In Part I: From Institutions to Economic Outcomes, we combine standard neoclassical economics with the concepts of the IOA to explain linkage from institutions and norms to economic performance. The framework, presented in Figure I.1, maps how the institutions and norms of society affect de jure and de facto property rights (Chapter 1), transaction and transformation costs (Chapter 2), and technology and organizational/contractual choice (Chapter 3).

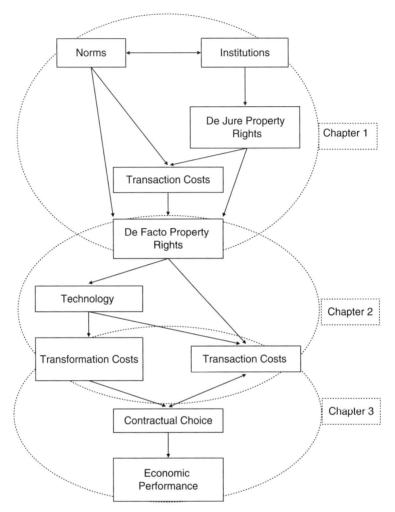

Figure I.1 Institutions and economic performance

In Part I, we take institutions and norms as given and analyze how institutions affect economic performance. Part I provides the reader with the same concepts that we use in different contexts in Parts II and III. The concepts, when tied together, yield a toolkit for understanding economic, political, and social outcomes. Our focus in Part I is on economic performance, but these concepts have broad explanatory value, as illustrated in Parts II and III.

Institutions are "the humanly devised constraints that shape human interaction" (North, 1990: 3). Ever since North's (1990) pathbreaking work, scholars working in IOA have classified institutions as formal and informal (Williamson, 2000; Ostrom, 2005; Acemoglu and Robinson, 2012). We depart from this tradition in order to highlight the different ways that institutions and norms arise and incentivize behavior.[4] We define an institution as a rule that recognized entities (individuals or organizations) devise and enforce.[5] Norms are long-standing patterns of behaviors shared by a subset of people in a society or an organization (e.g., governments, firms, universities, churches, and families).[6] Consistent with being widely held is the expectation that violating the norm will lead to consequences, even if the specific means and nature of enforcement are unclear. Because they are long-standing, are perceived as valid and are expected to be enforced, norms generate *behavioral beliefs* about how people will act in given situations, reducing uncertainty.

Institutions and norms can affect one another, leading us to place an arrow between them in Figure I.1. If institutions are inconsistent with norms, and norms are widely held, then the institutions are less likely to have their desired impact on outcomes. If institutions don't lead to an expected outcome, there may be a change in *core beliefs*. In contrast to behavioral beliefs, core beliefs are beliefs about the expected effect of institutions on outcomes.[7] Authorities and institutions can influence the adoption and sustainability of norms, but norms are generally stickier than institutions, meaning that those with power can change institutions more readily than norms.

To illustrate the difference and interaction between institutions and norms, consider plagiarism at colleges. Most colleges have institutions (rules) forbidding plagiarism on papers. These rules appear in student handbooks and apply to students of the college. The institutions define

---

[4] We credit Wallis (2018b) for leading us down this road.
[5] The enforcer of the rule may be a separate entity from the individual or organization who devises the rule. Note that while it is common to use the word "institution" to refer to an organization (e.g., an institution of higher education), we use a more specific definition.
[6] Norms derive from culture and, by some, are part of culture. We adopt Mokyr's (2017) view of culture, which emphasizes how individual-level determinants of decisions can have significant aggregate effects when shared by a sufficient number of individuals in society.
[7] The analysis of core beliefs plays a central role in Part III of the book.

plagiarism, when it is forbidden, and specify sanctions. A norm against plagiarism has many of the same characteristics, except that there is no explicit sanction or method of enforcement. Violating a norm against plagiarism might generate feelings of guilt by the violator and ostracism for the violator by observers. Norms and institutions certainly differ – a college's institution prohibiting plagiarism generally only applies to students, whereas the norm against plagiarism also applies to faculty – but they often overlap significantly. When institutions are consistent with generally held norms, institutions become much easier for the governing body to enforce.

Constitutions, which we analyze in Part III but take as given in Parts I and II, typically sit at the top of a society's hierarchy of institutions, followed by other laws of society, followed by rules created by economic and social organizations. The comparative permanence of a constitution establishes the hierarchy of institutions: constitutional rules are less mutable than ordinary law. Because of this primacy in the rule structure, constitutions serve two primary functions. First, in defining fundamental government structures and enforcement mechanisms, constitutions provide the rules about making all other rules, as well as rules for self-amendment. In addition, constitutions express fundamental principles of societal organization, including the blend of rights and duties each individual in society holds against one another and the government itself. This characteristic legal hierarchy extends from the public legal system to the realm of contracts.

The laws of society define the distribution of de jure property rights. These include the rights to use, sell, derive income from, and bequeath an asset. De jure property rights are the formal rights stipulated by the laws of society and enforced by the government or other entity. Laws can never perfectly define rights and the government can never perfectly enforce them, leading to a divide between de jure and de facto rights. De facto rights are the combination of the enforced de jure rights and the abilities that people exercise through extra-legal means.

The value of property rights to the toolkit of institutional analysis extends considerably further than the examination of production in an economy, a point that we develop in greater detail in our later chapters. For example, a set of institutions and norms define the de jure and de facto property rights of committee chairs in the US Congress (Shepsle and Weingast, 1987). Their powers go well beyond the institutions; norms developed to clarify the powers of committee chairs. In this context, the outcomes of the process are legislative, as opposed to economic, but the relevant actors in the process have clear abilities to shape the legislative process. Similarly, property rights have been identified as integral to economic development beyond a certain level, given the role they play in incentivizing investment in improvements to property, as well as creating the possibility for transfer to occur in the first place (de Soto, 2000).

The standard neoclassical theory of production takes technology as given, but in Figure I.1, the technological possibilities are endogenous, determined by de facto property rights. Patent and trademark law affect the type of technology available and who gets to use it. Laws restricting the use of certain technologies limit property rights of producers and can lead to technical regress.[8] More than laws can influence technology. Norms can determine whether an inventor of a new technology is likely to be lauded or killed by his neighbors. The norms and beliefs associated with the Enlightenment incentivized the technology developed during the Industrial Revolution (Mokyr, 2012).

Because the costs to the government of establishing and maintaining de jure property rights are positive, individuals and organizations will spend resources on establishing and maintaining de facto rights. For example, the government hires police to patrol the streets and maintain law and order, but most people make additional investments by locking their houses and cars. These resources represent transaction costs. Transaction costs exist whenever an individual, a firm, a government, or any other organization makes the effort to establish and maintain property rights. They appear twice in Figure I.1, both as a determinant of de facto property rights and as a determinant of contractual choice. Transaction costs are a key tool in the institutional and organizational analysis toolkit, and our goal is to provide a framework for classifying them and understanding their interaction.

The neoclassical theory of production models firms as profit-maximizing entities that make decisions about inputs and outputs at

---

[8] See Higgs (1996) for an example of technical regress in salmon fisheries.

the margin. While we do not abandon the marginal analysis central to the neoclassical model, the underlying assumption of zero transaction costs means there is no reason to study organizations.[9] Economic activity is organized in many ways, going well beyond discrete choices such as partnerships versus corporations or the firm versus the market. We use the phrase "contractual choice" in Figure I.1 as shorthand for the many institutional and organizational decisions that actors make in structuring economic activity. The choice of contract is always done on a comparative basis, with each contractual arrangement using different technologies and exhibiting different transformation and transaction costs.[10]

In a world without transaction costs, it is of no consequence how society organizes its resources. Central planning, a state-sponsored monopoly, a large corporation, small independent partnerships, market transactions, or any number of other organizational forms could organize production. Economic actors would take the initial allocation of property rights and bargain to the most efficient outcome (Coase, 1937, 1960). However, the economic world is one filled with transaction costs, making the organization of society's resources a critical determinant of growth. Institutions fundamentally shape property rights, transaction costs, technological and contractual choice, and economic performance.

In Part II: From Economic Outcomes to Political Performance, we present a framework for studying the process of what James Buchanan called "ordinary" or "post-constitutional" politics. Figure I.2 starts with economic performance and constitutions and ends with formal institutions, completing the cycle begun in Figure I.1. In Figure I.2, we take constitutional rules as exogenous and show them as an umbrella over the political process. Legislative

---

[9] While the tools of institutional and organizational analysis can be applied to any type of organization (e.g., universities, churches, or families), the focus of Part I is economic organizations. Part II of the book focuses on political organizations.

[10] For example, in the postbellum US South, plantation owners negotiated a variety of contracts with their workers: wage, sharecropping, and tenant contracts. The distribution of property rights, the production technology available at the time, the costs of supervising labor, and the costs of monitoring the use of capital determined contract choice (Alston and Higgs, 1982). A new technology, like the mechanized cotton harvester, disrupted the organization of production, changing the ways farm owners hired labor and incentivized their workers (Alston and Ferrie, 1999).

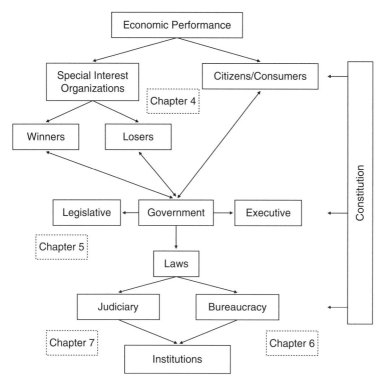

Figure I.2 Determinants of institutions

decision making occurs in the shadow of constitutional rules, defined in a constitution and interpreted by the judiciary.[11] In this framework, actors operate under the umbrella of existing constitutional rules, societal norms, and beliefs. The outcomes of the process are the institutions of society and their enforcement. The institutions can be made at different levels in a federal system and by different branches of government. In the United States, the legislatures pass bills, the judges make common law, and the administrative agencies make administrative law. The flowchart starts with economic performance and then examines the roles of special interest groups and citizens in the political process (Chapter 4), the functioning and exchanges between legislatures and executives (Chapter 5), bureaucracies (Chapter 6), and the judiciary (Chapter 7).

---

[11] This assumes that the Constitution is binding and the judiciary independent to interpret legislation.

The normal functioning of the economic system is a process of creative destruction that creates winners and losers (Schumpeter, 1942). The losers have an incentive to lobby for rule changes that protect them from market changes, while the winners seek to protect their gains and lobby for additional rules that favor their interests. Winners and losers can be concentrated enough to overcome the collective-action problems in lobbying (Olson, 1965; Buchanan and Tullock, 1962). One group is often concentrated while the other is not, leading to an unbalanced distribution of political power. Free trade might hurt a small group of inefficient domestic producers while helping a large number of consumers, but the concentrated "losers" have a strong interest in protecting their property rights at the expense of the dispersed "winners." Actors do not only respond to past changes in economic performance but also look forward, lobbying for rules that advance their economic interests.

A given set of demands from citizens and special interest groups filter through the legislative and executive branches. The output of this process is a set of institutions (laws), interpreted and enforced by the judiciary and bureaucracy. Different methods of organizing the rule-making process will yield different outcomes. For instance, many small competing parties within a parliamentary system will yield different rules than a strong two-party presidential system. Or, strong presidential systems will lead to different outcomes than weak presidential systems. The institutions governing the political process are important. For instance, the institutions and norms that govern the committee system in the US Congress determine who has gatekeeping powers and can bring bills to the floor of Congress. The organizational structure of government is not destiny, as political actors will, if they are able, bargain towards outcomes that are mutually beneficial.

Bureaucracies administer laws. In the United States, federal agencies not only have the power to adjudicate and enforce the laws of Congress, but can also promulgate new rules. The bureaucracies consist of agents with their own interests, creating a principal-agent problem between the legislature and the agency. Employees within the bureaucracy have interests in how they enforce the rules. In the United States, most employees of the Environmental Protection Agency (EPA) want to protect the environment, and, given the often vaguely worded laws they are charged to enforce, have great leeway in using their own judgment. Members of Congress, knowing this, may attempt to starve the EPA of resources, hoping to force the agency to prioritize its efforts and reduce its capabilities. Special interest groups also approach the bureaucracy directly, lobbying for changes in agency rules, adjudication, and enforcement.

The judicial branch of government plays many different roles. It judges the constitutionality of laws, adjudicates disputes, and, in a common law system, creates law via precedent. The institutions and norms governing the judicial system determine (1) whether judges are independent of the executive and legislative branches, (2) the powers of judges to make and interpret the law, and (3) the incentives to bring cases to the legal system. For instance, it matters a great deal for the rule of law whether the courts that interpret the constitutionality of legislation are independent of the executive and legislative branches. If the courts are not independent, then the laws of society can change in ways that are not bound by higher-level constitutional rules. If courts are truly independent, the executive and legislative branches will enact legislation "in the shadow" of the court, knowing that the court could overturn legislation it deems unconstitutional. The dismal economic growth history of Argentina since 1945 is a good example of the impact on economic performance from a Supreme Court that has not been independent (Alston and Gallo, 2010). The institutional characteristics of the judiciary, including its independence, reputation, and structure, greatly determine the extent to which a given judiciary can achieve its intended functions, which include overseeing the constitutionality of legislation and government actions, and ensuring a range of desirable outcomes associated with the orderly and impersonal administration of the legal system.

In Part III: The Dynamics of Economic and Political Development, we turn from a model of incremental change to explore the dynamics of major political and economic transitions. We survey existing contributions of the IOA that help in understanding the dynamics of economic and political development around the world over lengthy periods. We then introduce four new concepts to understand both incremental institutional change within the same developmental trajectory as well as critical transitions, a shift to a new developmental trajectory. In Figure I.3, we map out the elements of this framework. At the top

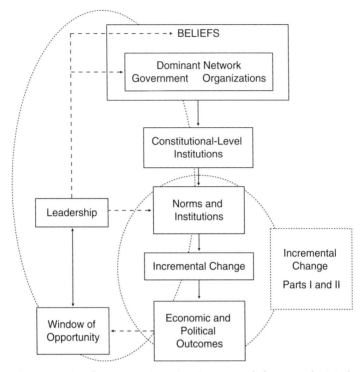

Figure I.3 Development trajectories: Incremental change and critical transitions

of Figure I.3 are beliefs and the dominant network, which we discuss in detail in Chapter 8. The dominant network includes government and other organizations that have the capability to shape and enforce institutions. Because of the plethora of organizations "at the table," our view of power is expansive; it includes all of the organizations that can influence the outcomes of the political process. It consists of both economic and political interests, though government plays an especially important role as coordinating activity under the umbrella of a constitution.

Institutions are nested within a set of core beliefs, which do not change often. Core beliefs are subjective beliefs about how fundamental institutions will affect outcomes. Like norms, culture influences institutional choices, but *changes* in core beliefs come about through shocks or *ex ante* anticipation by leaders of downstream crises.[12] For example, since World War II, the reactions by Germans to financial crises have been to impose austerity measures. Why? Most likely because of their fear of inflation, which brought Hitler to power. Until outcomes explicitly make clear that austerity is not working, the Germans will stick with the belief that austerity is the right solution for financial crises.

At times, institutions will codify norms and other times, institutions displace norms if they are not firmly rooted as an equilibrium. Because norms typically precede institutions, given the inherited nature of most norms, norms will not typically displace institutions. In some instances, norms can influence or prompt institutional change (e.g., women's suffrage, civil rights, gay marriage, or marijuana legalization). In other instances, norms and institutions can be orthogonal.

Governments coordinate and enforce rules under the shadow of a belief structure. Given a certain power structure, those in power choose institutions to best match their expectations of how institutions will affect outcomes. This is dependent on their set of beliefs. Following North (2005), we consider beliefs as the subjective view of actors of how the world works. For the purposes of tractability, we depart from North by taking a narrower definition of beliefs in order to understand the underlying determinants of the constitutions and institutions of a society. In our framework, core beliefs are the expected views of actors on how institutions will affect economic and political outcomes. When outcomes match expectations, we will see marginal changes in laws and norms. Societies stay more or less on the same developmental trajectory, with incremental institutional changes as depicted at the bottom of Figure I.3 and in more detail in Parts I and II of the book.

A window of opportunity for significant change in underlying beliefs and institutions occurs when actual or expected outcomes diverge dramatically from those initially expected. Examples of this include the threat of invasion by another country, an economic crisis, or a natural disaster. During such moments, leaders have an opportunity to shape underlying beliefs and constitutional-level institutions. However, in the event that leaders do not step forward to take advantage of these windows of opportunity, the moment can pass without

---

[12] We develop this more explicitly in Part III.

any change in beliefs or fundamental institutions. Alternatively, leaders can create a window of opportunity by convincing others that future outcomes will be dire unless beliefs about extant institutions change.

We define "constitutional moments" as a specific moment within a critical transition when the new core beliefs prompt those in power to establish new institutions. At constitutional moments, the dominant organizations revamp the rules under which political and economic organizations interact and contract. The process begins with a window of opportunity depicted in Figure I.3. Leadership involves taking advantage of the window to coordinate beliefs among the organizations in power in such a way as to generate new core beliefs among the dominant network.[13] As such, it is a loop beginning with business as usual and ending with a constitutional-level institutional change. The process typically involves changes to the constitutional structure itself, through amendments or the drafting of a new constitution. However, fundamental changes to the governance structure can at times be wrought extra-constitutionally.

Deep changes in economic and political trajectories entail more than a single "constitutional moment" or critical juncture. Indeed, they require reinforcing institutional changes to alter and solidify core beliefs. We flush out the dynamics of the transition to a new trajectory. We identify contributions of the IOA that help identify the benefits that "superior" institutional sets can offer in expectation to members of the dominant network during a potential critical transition. Namely, successfully moving to a superior institutional set creates the possibility for transactions of greater magnitude and complexity given the same underlying resource set for a given society. These comparatively superior institutions also provide resilience in the face of shocks, and sometimes prevent the need for major institutional change from ever arising. The iterative process of institutional deepening requires multiple loops around the circuit to shape and deepen beliefs, the dominant network, constitutional-level institutions, and the supporting norms, institutions, and organizations. The process ends in a new developmental trajectory (new system of incremental change in which beliefs are again in alignment with the outcomes of the economic and political systems). We conclude in

---

[13] Large changes in economic or political outcomes can also change the organizations in the dominant network, who may hold different beliefs.

Chapter 9 with four illustrative case studies of critical transitions: (1) United States, 1783–1789: Transitioning from "States Rule" to the United States of America; (2) Argentina, 1912–1955: Budding Belief in Checks and Balances to Redistributive Populism; (3) Brazil, 1985–2014: Belief in Social Inclusion to Fiscally Sound Social Inclusion; and (4) Ecuador, 1998–2017: From a Neoliberal Belief to a Belief in Inclusive Politics.

From Institutions to Economic Outcomes

Introduction to Part Topics

In Part I of this book, we examine the links between society's rules and the organization of economic life.[1] We do this by linking several elements that contribute to *social order*: institutions, norms, property rights, organizations, and transaction costs. In Part I, we take the institutions and norms of society as given and examine how they determine property rights and transaction costs, which in turn affect the choice of technologies and methods of organizing economic activities.[2] This is a comparative task. Actors choose organizational and contractual forms that provide the maximum net benefits relative to feasible alternatives.

The research agenda for the first part of this book was succinctly described in 1973 by Douglass North and Robert Thomas. They linked transaction costs and property rights to economic performance in the following way:

If exclusiveness and the enforcement of accompanying property rights could be freely assured – that is, in the absence of transactions costs – the achievement of growth would be simple indeed. Everyone would reap the benefits or bear the costs of his actions ... [In] the real world of positive transactions costs, the problems of achieving growth are more complicated, and they become still more uncertain when we recognize that adjustments must inevitably occur between the initial creation of a set of property rights and the operation of the system once those rights have been established. Property rights are always embedded in the institutional structure of a society, and the creation of new property rights demands new

---

[1] This part of the book draws heavily on Ronald Coase's fundamental insights about "the significance of transaction costs and property rights for the institutional structure and functioning of the economy" (Nobel Prize in Economic Sciences, 1991).

[2] In Part III, we expand our analysis to the examination of critical transitions between social orders, adding the elements of leadership and beliefs.

institutional arrangements to define and specify the way by which economic units can co-operate and compete. (North and Thomas, 1973: 5)

In Chapter 1, we begin our analysis with how institutions and norms
shape property rights. Institutions and norms have a particular "grammar," and we use the work of Ostrom (2005) and Wallis (2018b) to
explain their logic. Institutions shape property rights, a broad term
used to describe the rights, privileges, and other relationships associated with property. We distinguish between de jure property rights,
the "formal legally enacted laws supported by the states' power of
violence and punishment" and de facto property rights, which are
additionally "supported by the force of etiquette, social custom, [and]
ostracism" (Alchian, 1977: 129). Property is a social construct. We do
not possess property in a social vacuum, so property rights define our
ability to use different aspects of an asset within society. The costs of
specifying and enforcing property rights – known as transaction costs –
are fundamentally important for resource allocation. In a world of
positive transaction costs, it is not a straightforward matter to
rearrange property rights, so who has the rights will matter a great
deal for resource allocation.

   In Chapter 2, we turn to a description of transaction costs as the costs
of "transfer, capture, and protection" of property rights. This definition of transaction costs includes any costs associated with organizing
human activity, regardless of whether the activity occurs in hierarchies
or the price mechanism. Coase (1937) and Coase (1960) are the foundation of this analysis and are two sides of the same coin; Coase (1937)
shows that if transaction costs are zero, the particular method of
organizing production is irrelevant to economic efficiency, and Coase
(1960) shows that if transaction costs are zero, the initial distribution
of property rights within a society is irrelevant to economic efficiency.[3]
The true lesson of Coase is that since transaction costs are never zero,
the organization of economic activity and the distribution of property
rights matter to economic efficiency.

   Transaction costs are a key determinant of organizational and
contractual choice. We use the language of North, Wallis, and
Weingast (2009: 15) to describe organizations as a collection of
individuals "pursuing a mix of common and individual goals

---

[3] This is known as the "Coase Theorem," even though Coase encouraged
    economists to study the world of positive transaction costs.

through partially coordinated behavior." Individual behavior in every organization is shaped by rules embedded in norms and institutions. Setting up rules incurs fixed transaction costs, and these rules and their enforcement in turn determine the marginal transaction costs of establishing and maintaining property rights within the organization and with other individuals and organizations. While organizations consist of individuals and do not have their own objective functions, many economic models have simplifying assumptions about organizational objectives, such as "firms maximize profits" and "governments maximize social welfare." These simplifying assumptions are useful when the goal is to study broader patterns of social behavior or to study particular questions of firm behavior. Since the field of Institutional and Organizational Analysis (IOA) is more interested than neoclassical economics in explaining behavior within and among organizations, it generally has a richer set of assumptions about organizational behavior, focusing on the incentives of individuals within organizations and the behavior those incentives elicit.

Examples of organizations include a group of coworkers coordinating on where to have lunch, a family coordinating the upbringing of its children, a religious group coordinating its worship and outreach activities, and a firm coordinating its production and sales. In a workplace, we can be members of many organizations. For example, in universities, faculty might have appointments in more than one university and more than one department at a university. They might be members of faculty unions and professional organizations, some of which may have competing agendas. Students enrolled at the university might identify most strongly with an organization within the university, such as a sports team, a club, or a sorority. We consume the services provided by organizations, such as firms, schools, and governments. Our relationship with some of these organizations, such as a church or a local government, can involve long-standing relationships, while our relationship with others, such as an online retailer or an airline, can be short-lived arm's-length transactions. Our membership in and attempts to influence the behavior of organizations is fluid. What determines who belongs to organizations, how long they last, the extent of their activities, who controls those activities, and who reaps the rewards? These are central research questions within the IOA. In Chapter 3, we delve most deeply into one organizational form, the firm. In Part II of this book, we analyze another organization, the government.

In Chapter 3, we focus on how transaction costs shape the structure of contracts and organizations. We treat the "price mechanism" and "hierarchies" as the endpoints on a spectrum of contractual choices and provide a theoretical justification for and examples of different intermediary forms, such as long-term contracts, sports leagues, joint ventures, and franchising. The conceptual literature builds on the material from Chapters 1 and 2 and reviews several frameworks for understanding the relative merits and costs of organizational and contractual choice, including classical and neoclassical; agency; governance; and new property-rights theories. In Chapter 3, we also discuss why firms take on different ownership structures and what factors influence firms to go hybrid, that is, choose a non-standard form of contracting.

Two examples give the flavor of the importance of institutional analysis of the sort we study in Part I. The first comes from Coase's (1974) study of lighthouses, a service that he shows had been repeatedly held up as a classic example of a public good. Since the services of a lighthouse are both non-excludable (the light is visible from any ship at sea) and non-rivalrous (one ship's use of a lighthouse's services does not diminish other ship's use), the public good argument is that lighthouses should be provided by the government, because the private sector would undersupply a much-needed service. Coase showed that it was possible both theoretically and in practice to have lighthouse services provided by a non-governmental agency. In order to do this, however, the government needed to grant and enforce another property right to lighthouse owners. Governments gave private lighthouse owners the right to some of the revenue from ships docking at nearby ports. This bundling and unbundling of property rights – the operator of the lighthouse gained the right to certain fees but had the duty to provide certain services – shows how property is a social construct and that when the costs of establishing and maintaining property rights are low enough, many alternative contractual forms can achieve a desired outcome.[4]

---

[4] See van Zandt (1993) and Bertrand (2006) for additional institutional details about the role of government in supporting the offering of lighthouse services.

Our second example comes from Helper and Henderson's (2014) comparison of the management practices of General Motors and Toyota. GM was once the dominant firm in American automobile manufacturing, with more than 40 percent of the market share. However, by 2009, GM's market share fell to 20 percent and it declared bankruptcy in the midst of the financial crisis. Scholars and pundits offered many explanations for GM's decline, including "high legacy labor and healthcare costs," but Helper and Henderson point to the differences in how the two companies contracted with both their employees and their suppliers. Their explanation for GM's decline was that GM's management practices were "predicated on a view of workers, suppliers, and even white collar employees as commodities whose work could be fully controlled by experts through the use of careful specifications and the spot market, while Toyota's practices were critically dependent on joint problem solving across boundaries of all kinds, and thus on the existence of strong relational contracts" (Helper and Henderson, 2014: 55). One example of the differences in management practices between the two firms was Toyota's use of the "andon cord," a cord that an assembly line worker could pull once in order to summon help and a second time to shut down the entire production line. Giving employees the power to shut down the line required tremendous trust in them by management, as "shutting down the line for a popular model could cost $10,000 in lost profits per minute" (Helper and Henderson, 2014: 57). In a relationship organized around norms of trust and reciprocity, such a mechanism could be very powerful. But it could not work in a relationship organized around bullying and hostility.

Starting in 1984, GM had first-hand exposure to Toyota's management practices through NUMMI (New United Motor Manufacturing, Inc.), a joint venture that Toyota ran at an unproductive (and mothballed) GM plant. Toyota agreed to rehire all of the former GM employees, and after instituting its management practices, the plant quickly became as productive as Toyota's Japanese plants. GM, however, was slow to adopt Toyota's practices. Helper and Henderson point to two obstacles. First, GM needed to "understand the nature of the cluster of techniques that drove Japanese success" (Helper and Henderson, 2014: 67). One anecdote of this failure of inspiration is from a report by a GM employee who was ordered to "go there [NUMMI] with cameras and take a picture of every square inch. And whatever you take a picture of; I want it to look like that in our plant. There should be no excuse for why we're different than NUMMI, why our quality is lower, why our productivity isn't as high, because you're going to copy everything you see" (quoted in Helper and Henderson, 2014: 55). The GM manager's first inclination was to copy Toyota technology, but the differentiating factors were the contractual and organizational structures.

GM's second obstacle to adopting Toyota's techniques was switching from an adversarial to a relational contracting framework with its employees and suppliers. This was hard to do. For example, the exact circumstances under which the andon cord should be pulled could not be specified in a contract. Toyota workers pulled the andon cord when they saw a problem on the production line and supervisors interpreted it as a sign of something seriously amiss. In a less cooperative and trusting relationship, pulling the cord could be used to avoid work or as a negotiating tactic by workers, while supervisors could punish the worker who pulled the cord, even if it was done appropriately (Gibbons and Henderson, 2012). GM ultimately was able to move to a management system like Toyota's, but it took many years to make the change, indicating how difficult it is for one organization to adopt the institutions and norms of another.

Why can't efficient production technologies be transferred from more efficient to less efficient firms? Why can't citizens in countries with underperforming economies demand that their governments adopt and implement the rules of their more successful neighbors? Surely, all else equal, firms want to produce more efficiently and governments want their citizens to be more prosperous. Our answer for why persistent differences in performance exist focuses on the norms and institutions that govern social and economic interaction and, in particular, the costs of changing and maintaining that system of norms and institutions. In Part I, we begin this analysis by examining how norms and institutions affect the organization of economic activity.

1 | *Institutions and Property Rights*

Introduction and Opening Case: Institutions and Norms in Yucatán, Mexico

Economic models often assume away the laws of government, the norms of society, and the structure of organizations, but no economic activity would occur without a legal, social, and organizational framework. Laws, norms, and organizations are elements that contribute to *social order* and structure individuals' efforts to coordinate, cooperate, and compete at levels ranging from the family to international trade. This chapter provides an introduction to institutions, which include laws, policies, and any other rules devised and enforced by a recognized authority. Institutions are defined by Douglass North (1990: 3) as "the humanly devised constraints that shape human interaction" and by Elinor Ostrom (2005: 3) as "the prescriptions that humans use to organize all forms of repetitive and structured interactions." Institutions, together with the other elements of a social order, define property rights, the set of decisions that individuals can make about resources.

An example from Mexican economic history illustrates the interaction between institutions, norms, and organizations. During the henequen boom in Yucatán, the relationship between hacendados and the Maya workforce took a distinct form, described by American "muckraking" journalists as a system of debt peonage. While it is not surprising to learn that indigenous Maya worked in a coercive environment, the specific mechanics of the debt peonage contract are hard to explain without understanding the details of the institutions, norms, and culture of Yucatán. Henequen, a fiber extracted from the long leaves of the henequen agave and used to make twine for the McCormick binder, was Mexico's most important agricultural export at the time.[1] The number of acres under henequen cultivation grew from 6,500 to 790,000

---

[1] The information on labor contracting in Yucatán is drawn from Alston, Mattiace, and Nonnenmacher (2009) and Mattiace and Nonnenmacher (2014).

between 1860 and 1916, making Mérida, the state capital, an island of prosperity in a vast sea of henequen. Henequen plants lived twenty years, the first six of which were unproductive, making henequen a long-term investment. Harvesting, weeding, and planting occurred year-round, and workers quickly processed the leaves in a rasping mill located on-site. Many henequen haciendas had an internal trolley system that hauled workers to the fields and the cut leaves to the rasping mill. Supervisors assigned fieldworkers acres to weed or bundles of leaves to cut as a day's task, but workers had the ability to shirk along many margins, including cutting too many leaves from a single plant, putting too few leaves in a bundle, or failing to weed properly.

Mexico's Constitution of 1857 was the law of the land during the henequen boom. It outlawed slavery, going so far as to free any slave that stepped foot onto Mexican soil. A worker could not "be compelled to render personal services without due compensation and without his full consent." Especially for its time, the enumeration of rights in the 1857 Constitution was exhaustive. The constitutional rules were not, however, the rules on the ground. An elite, which consisted of the thirty most prosperous henequen families (the *Casta Divina* [Divine Caste]), ruled the Yucatán. Political power was closely intertwined with economic power. Maya who were not attached to a hacienda were subject to a military draft and corvée service for road building and public works. At the local level, hacendados made rules of their own, enforceable through violence, and local political bosses supported those rules. Maya had little recourse to the courts, which the ruling elite controlled.

Two social norms structured labor relations between Maya workers and hacendados. The first was a norm that Maya workers had a relatively expensive wedding at an early age. This norm seems to have its roots in Maya culture, but its specific manifestation during this period was in the form of a Catholic wedding officiated by the local priest. Neither the workers nor their families could afford to pay for the wedding, so the hacendado for whom they worked lent them the money. While the hacendado recorded the loans on the books of the hacienda, in practice, they were never repaid and can be thought of as gifts from the hacendado to the young couple and their parents. This brings up the second norm, a norm of reciprocity. Workers reciprocated the hacendados' gifts by staying on the hacienda and providing loyal-like behavior. Some workers fled and some paid off their debts, but most were born, worked, and died on the same hacienda. Hacendados provided additional paternalistic benefits to workers, including protection from military and work drafts, medical care for the sick, care for the elderly, and land to plant a garden. Given the coercive political and social environment that the hacendados themselves helped to create, Maya workers often found staying tied to a hacienda through debt peonage to be the best of a bad set of choices. Only by understanding the specific social, political, and economic environment can we understand this unique contractual mechanism of loans with no expectation of repayment. This chapter introduces some of these concepts, focusing on institutions, but we touch upon other elements that contribute to creating social order, including norms, organizations, values, preferences, and beliefs, to show their effect on economic outcomes.

Institutions

A myriad of rules that can arise in many different ways shape human behavior. Governments create and enforce some rules, like speeding laws, while other rules, like the "golden rule," have their roots in many ancient religions. Our goal in this section is to provide a classification of rules, distinguishing between rules that are an element of an institution or a norm. We make this distinction by examining how a rule is made and enforced. We define an institution as a rule that recognized entities purposefully devise and have the recognized right to enforce. Rules define what a designated party must, must not, or may do under a certain set of conditions and assign sanctions for non-compliance. Rule makers purposefully devise institutions, and the rule maker must be recognized as having the authority to do so. This authority is usually achieved through a collective-action process, governed by complementary institutions and norms. For example, citizens of a country recognize the government's authority to create laws, and employees of a firm recognize management's authority to make operating rules. Finally, entities, often not the rule maker, are assigned the rights or duties to monitor conduct and impose sanctions. Additional institutions and norms also govern the actions of the enforcement entities. For example, parents are recognized as having the right to punish their children to enforce household rules, but laws put limits on punishment. The law in many US states allows parents to use "moderate physical discipline" but forbids punishment that would result in "substantial harm" to a child. Additional rules govern the actions of police, plaintiffs, and courts.

We distinguish between institutions and norms.[2] A norm consists of a rule and a pattern of enforcement, both of which arise after repeated interactions in a path-dependent process. While individuals and organizations can attempt to shape norms through means such as education and religion, norms emerge over time. The process can be referred to as spontaneous order, which is generally used to describe the order that emerges from individual interactions in the market, any one of which lacks a centralized motive to create this order. Individuals follow the rule from an institution or a norm for many of the same reasons. First, following the rule helps them choose between multiple equilibria, such as driving on the right or left side of the street. Second, following or not following the rule can cause internal feelings of satisfaction or guilt. And, third, other parties provide inducements, either by rewarding rule-followers or punishing rule-breakers. For institutions, the rule-making entity may assign another entity the right or duty to enforce the institution. In contrast, the mechanisms that lead to norm-following emerge over time.[3] Constitutions, laws, organizational rules, and contracts are subcategories of institutions. Social norms and conventions are subcategories of norms. The dividing line between institutions and norms becomes blurred when institutions codify pre-existing norms of behavior.

Rules assign rights and place constraints on human behavior by specifying what a defined set of individuals must, must not, and may do in certain situations and prescribe penalties for non-compliance.

---

[2] In order to highlight the difference between deliberately constructed institutions and norms of behavior, we break with the definitions that categorize both formal rules and informal norms as institutions (North, 1990; Ostrom, 2005). Doing so aligns our definitions more closely with Wallis (2018b). Hadfield and Weingast (2012: 473) define society as being organized under a legal order if "an identifiable entity . . . deliberately supplies a normative classification scheme that designates some actions as 'wrongful' [that induces actors to] forego wrongful actions to a significant extent."

[3] See Hadfield and Weingast (2013) for examples of laws that are enforced via distributed means, such as Medieval Iceland, where courts announced penalties but enforcement occurred through collective punishment. These examples fit into our definition of an institution, as the entities enforcing the rule were widely recognized as having the authority to do so.

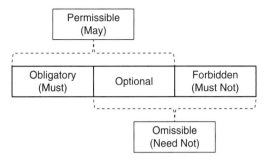

Figure 1.1 Deontic classification
Source: Based on McNamara (2006).

We borrow from Crawford and Ostrom's (1995) grammar of institutions, known as ADICO, to define the elements of rules.[4]

A: Attributes: To whom does the rule apply?
D: Deontic: Does the rule permit, oblige, or forbid an action?
I: Aim: To which action is the rule assigned?
C: Conditions: When and where is the rule applied?
O: Or else: What are the consequences for not following the rule? Who enforces the rule?

The deontic, which specifies whether an action is obligatory, permitted, or forbidden, is a central element of a rule. As shown in Figure 1.1, those actions that are not forbidden are permissible, and those actions that are not obligatory are omissible. Actions that are optional are neither obligatory nor forbidden. The representation of the deontic in Figure 1.1 hides the reciprocal nature of the deontic: granting one person the right to take a specific action requires additional rules about the duties of other members of society. We will address the social relations involved in the deontic further in Chapter 2.

An institution, adopted by many colleges and universities, is an honor code that prohibits plagiarism. Students, faculty, and other stakeholders recognized higher education organizations (universities and colleges) as having the authority to define and enforce the honor code, making the honor code an institution. The institution's rule states that: "Students at University of XYZ (Attribute) are forbidden

---

[4] Crawford and Ostrom (1995) have a more nuanced interpretation of the deontic and "or else" statements that we combine into a simpler description of "or else."

(Deontic) from presenting someone else's work as their own without proper acknowledgement (Aim) on papers and tests turned in for a grade (Condition). Doing so will result in an honor code hearing and sanctions as described in the Student Handbook (Or else)." These rules are limited to whom and for what activities they apply. University of XYZ's honor code only applies to students at University of XYZ for work turned in for classes at that university. They do not apply to faculty at University of XYZ or students at ABC College. Honor codes describe the responsibilities of witnesses for reporting incidents of suspected cheating. It may be a violation of the honor code not to report suspected violations of the honor code.

A web of institutions and norms combines to influence social behavior. One way to sort out this web is to follow the creation of a new rule. For instance, in the United States, in order to become a law, a bill must pass through committees, both houses, and a conference committee, and then be signed by the president into law. An agency is charged with enforcing the law and the Supreme Court can rule on its constitutionality. All of these stages of the rule-making and enforcement process occur in linked arenas that have their own sets of institutions and norms that shape behavior.

Institutions range from the constitutional to the contractual level. Following Ostrom (2005), we limit ourselves to three levels of rules – constitutional, collective choice, and operational – all of which can occur at different levels of societies and in different organizations. Operational rules directly shape day-to-day behavior. Collective-choice institutions determine the process by which recognized entities make operational institutions. At the highest level, constitutional-level institutions specify the structure of an organization and the process by which institutions can be created and challenged. An organization, such as a college or university, may have a set of constitutional-level institutions in the form of a charter that describes its organizational structure, how that structure can be changed, and how new institutions can be created (McCubbins, Noll, and Weingast, 1989). Collective-choice institutions, in the form of student and faculty handbooks, structure the operation of the university. Operational institutions govern the day-to-day decision making at the university and include grading policies and the contracts with food and cleaning services. Constitutional-level institutions may be included in a formal constitution, but may also be a set of laws and principles that have the equivalent of constitutional standing. Such is the case for Great Britain, which has no codified constitution.[5]

An example of a constitutional-level institution is the Third Amendment to the US Constitution, which prohibits the quartering of troops during a time of peace without the permission of the owner. If a property owner believed that an agent of the government violated this constitutional institution, the property owner must appeal to the court system to protect her rights. The constitutionality of laws can be reviewed by the courts in countries with judicial review. While the deontic in the Third Amendment is clear – unauthorized quartering during times of peace is forbidden – the "or else" points to a process of judicial review rather than an explicit penalty associated with the violation of the deontic. This enforcement mechanism is part and parcel of the social order. A country with no formal or informal means of enforcing constitutional provisions has constitutional institutions in form but not in function.[6]

Some institutions devised by a recognized authority are not enforced because they are either difficult to enforce or the agency charged with enforcement chooses not to enforce them. We call these *institutions-in-form*, and distinguish between institutions-in-form and *institutions-in-use*, which are regularly enforced by a recognized authority.[7] "Enforced" does not mean that sanctions are automatically and costlessly imposed. Instead, it means there is a party assigned to enforcing the rule and

---

[5] Another way to conceptualize rules is Hart's (2012) distinction between primary and secondary rules in the law. Primary rules "are concerned with the actions that individuals must or must not do" and secondary rules "specify the way in which the primary rules may be conclusively ascertained, introduced, eliminated, varied, and the fact of their violation conclusively determined" (94).

[6] Although there are many constitutions worldwide that are enforced in a manner inconsistent with the notions of constitutionalism we have developed thus far, this is not to argue that such constitutions serve no purpose whatsoever. "Constitutions have a wide array of functions, and some of these functions are likely to be shared across both authoritarian and democratic regimes. A very central function of formal rules including constitutions is simple coordination. All regimes need institutions and need to coordinate on what institutions will play what role. Laying out the structures of government facilitates their operation because it prevents continuous renegotiation. A written constitutional text can thus minimize conflict over basic institutions for any regime. Furthermore, we know that certain institutions can facilitate coordination within the core of the governing elite itself" (Ginsburg and Simpser, 2013: 3).

[7] Those laws that are "on the books" but not enforced are also called dead letter laws.

a probability that violating a rule will lead to a sanction. If you steal your neighbor's car, you may never be accused, you may be prosecuted but found not guilty of a crime, or you may be prosecuted, found guilty, and sentenced to pay a fine or serve a term in jail. Laws prohibiting theft are rules-in-use if there is an expectation that agents of the government will enforce the penalties in a predictable manner. When the costs of establishing and protecting property rights are positive – as we will see in the next chapter is always the case – enforcement of rules cannot be perfect.[8]

The intended purpose of sanctions is well developed in the legal scholarship on retribution and deterrence: if one person murders another, societies have identified a value in punishing the murderer, but ideally, the nature of that punishment signals to other social actors that future murders will be similarly penalized. The extent to which punishment on its own right has social value absent from its deterrent effect is a matter of considerable scholarly debate, but evidence suggests that for many social actors, retribution has value. Sanctions can have additional intended purposes, depending on the nature of the dispute or crime committed. For contractual violations, as well as torts (a harm committed against an individual or their property), sanctions can also restore the harmed party, compensating her for the harm. Finally, incarceration carries the additional purposes of incapacitating and rehabilitating a given criminal, to the extent a given prison system is actually capable of accomplishing this.

Laws prohibiting usury illustrate the difference between institutions-in-use and institutions-in-form. Limits on interest rates go at least as far back as the Code of Hammurabi (1750 BC), which set the maximum interest rate that could be charged and the maximum length of time a debtor could be sentenced to debt slavery. Islamic, Christian, and Jewish traditions all have some form of a prohibition against usury, but charging interest or its equivalent has been widespread among people of all three faiths. In Islam, the interest ban has been ignored or circumvented via alternative arrangements, such as the use of a "double sale." A double sale involves the borrower selling the lender an item and then immediately buying it back and promising to

---

[8] In many cases, people know or suspect that a rule exists but do not know the exact content of the rule. You may know that murder and theft are crimes in your jurisdiction, but not know the penalties for these crimes. Marginal changes in penalties may therefore cause little change in behavior of would-be criminals.

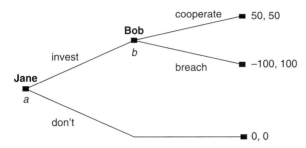

Figure 1.2 Investment game with no contract enforcement

pay the lender the initial sale price plus a premium at a specified time in the future.[9] Merely knowing that Islam prohibits interest might make a student of Islamic banking think that no lending occurs. But knowing that alternatives exist might make students of Islamic banking think that there are no differences between Islamic and Western modes of banking. Neither of these suppositions is correct: arrangements that imperfectly mirror interest rates have existed in Islamic banking, but the differences between Islamic and Western institutions are important and have led to differing evolutions in their banking sectors (Kuran, 2011).

Institutions that support trade are among the most important for economic development. Contract law provides for the third-party enforcement of agreements through the judicial system by setting penalties for failing to fulfill contractual obligations. Figure 1.2 illustrates a simple investment game in which the investor (Jane) can invest or not invest, and the agent (Bob) can cooperate or breach. The payoffs to Bob and Jane are the monetary gain they will receive from the combination of actions. For instance, if Jane invests and Bob breaches, Jane loses $100 and Bob earns $100. Assume initially that Jane and Bob seek only to maximize their monetary payoffs and that there are no mechanisms in place to enforce that agreement. If this interaction took place on a farm, Jane could buy a mule and a plow, while Bob could cooperate by using that equipment to farm the fields. Breaching the agreement could involve Bob appropriating Jane's investments and selling them or using them to farm elsewhere.

---

[9] See Kuran (2011) for additional examples and a list of court cases in which these agreements were upheld.

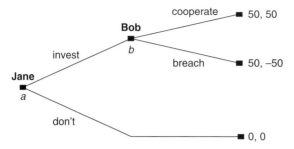

Figure 1.3 Investment game with perfect expectation damages

Sequential move games, such as the one described in Figure 1.2, are solved via backward induction. At decision node *b*, Bob's optimal strategy is to breach, earning him a payoff of $100 versus $50 from cooperating. Bob will therefore breach. Knowing this, Jane will not invest at decision node *a*. The lost $100 in social surplus is a deadweight loss.

Courts in the United States traditionally require the elements of offer, acceptance, and consideration for a legally binding contract to be formed. In this case, Jane offers to provide the equipment if Bob promises to farm the land with it. Bob can either accept or reject that offer. The provision of the farming equipment by Jane can act as consideration, the inducement to the contract. One way to encourage cooperation is to penalize Bob for breaching by making him pay perfect expectation damages, which state that if Bob breaches the contract, he must pay Jane enough money to put her in the position she would have been in had the promise been fulfilled. The payoffs from perfect expectation damages are shown in Figure 1.3. If Bob breaches, he must pay Jane $150 to give her a total payoff of $50, which is what Jane would have received had Bob cooperated. These damages give Jane the incentive to invest and Bob the incentive to cooperate. The set of strategies (invest, cooperate) in Figure 1.3 is a Nash equilibrium, as neither player has an incentive to change his or her strategy given the strategy of the other player.

In a world in which contracting is costly, the size of damages awarded to the injured party matters. A fortunate or unfortunate contingency may raise the opportunity cost of performance so that it is inefficient to perform. If damages awarded by the courts are too high, then promisors will complete too many contracts. If damages are too low, then promisors will complete too few contracts. By setting damages correctly, courts can encourage optimal performance and breach of contracts.[10]

Rewriting the payoffs in Figure 1.2 to transfer $150 from Bob to Jane when Bob breaches presupposes a legal system that can costlessly and flawlessly interject itself into private agreements to establish and enforce property rights.[11] Among the many factors influencing the enforcement of contract law are the accessibility and funding of the courts; the training, honesty, and diligence of judges; the rules of evidence; the laws regulating the organization of the legal profession; and the norms of legal reasoning (Hadfield, 2005). Rewriting the payoffs also presupposes that using the judicial system to settle disputes is an accepted practice and that Jane and Bob both have the expectation of having the rules applied in an equitable manner.

It is important to note that our definition of rules encompasses both rules and standards as they are typically distinguished in the legal literature. A good example is a speed limit: drivers traveling at a speed greater than the stated limit of 65 mph are typically subject to a fine and additional penalties on their driving records. However, some jurisdictions have instead employed a standards-based approach, such as Montana, where for a period the standard was that a person was to drive reasonably given the nature of the road and the ambient conditions. A rule is precise as compared to a standard. Individuals charged with driving at 79 mph in a 65 mph zone do not have a lot of room for argument before the enforcing court or officer that their behavior was actually legal. If the radar machine identifies a car as travelling at a specific velocity, it is well accepted that the precise machine did not somehow "get it wrong." In contrast, a motorist in Montana under the "reasonable" standard could employ a variety of arguments to the enforcers as to why 79 mph was reasonable given the weather conditions and level of traffic on the road. Ostrom's ADICO definition of

---

[10] For a fuller discussion of the economics of precaution and reliance, see Cooter and Ulen (2011).

[11] An assumption necessary for Figure 1.2 to make sense is that a social order exists that protects Jane's property rights enough for her to be able to make a decision to invest or not, but does not protect her property rights enough for her to contract successfully with Bob. The student of Institutional and Organizational Analysis (IOA) should look at every game tree or matrix and ask what assumptions about the social order are necessary to generate the required distribution of property rights.

a rule is clearly one that incorporates standards as we define them. It is the aim (I) that is vaguer in a standard (drive safely) than a bright-line rule (don't drive faster than 65).

This distinction between rules and standards is an important institutional tool for legislators and policymakers when considering the benefits of each. Rules tend to be more easily enforced than standards, but by this same token, remove discretion from the enforcer in terms of their ability to determine whether a given individual's conduct violated the social rules animating the particular broader standard. Therefore, these examples also highlight the importance of the role of the enforcer. In many jurisdictions, the police don't pull people over at 66 mph, despite the bright-line nature of the rule in play. Relatedly, in Montana, the imprecise standard was ultimately overturned by the courts because it gave enforcers far too much discretion in choosing who to pull over, which led to discriminatory outcomes in terms of policing practices.

Norms

The payoffs listed in Figures 1.2 and 1.3 associated with the investment example show the monetary gains or losses from participating in the game. But economic actors respond to more than monetary payoffs; they may therefore follow strategies that, on the surface, do not look rational. A strong preference for acting in a cooperative manner could overcome Bob's incentive to breach and Jane's hesitance to invest in Figure 1.2. Similarly, a norm of cooperation might lead to the cooperative outcome. A social norm of cooperation is followed when there is a chance of being observed by others. Being observed would generate a feeling of contempt by the observer towards the violator. That contempt may lead to punitive actions (shunning, confronting, physically accosting) by the observer and feelings of shame by the violator.[12] In order to avoid the disutility from this combination of external or

---

[12] Elster (2007) also includes moral norms, quasi-moral norms, and legal norms in his taxonomy of norms. These differ in the mechanism that encourages compliance. Moral norms are entirely internalized. Quasi-moral norms are followed because the potential violator observes others following it. We classify legal norms under institutions, as they have specified sanctions and designated enforcers.

internal sanctions, the potential norm-violator may choose to cooperate rather than breach.

Norms can govern behavior "contrary to nature," reciprocity, retribution, cooperation, distribution, work, and consumption. Norms of
behavior "contrary to nature" include prescriptions against incest and
cannibalism. Norms of reciprocity and retribution guide the exchange
of benefits and harms. Norms of cooperation prescribe the degree to
which people cooperate in situations like a prisoner's dilemma game.
Distribution norms determine what is considered a "fair" distribution
of society's resources. Work norms guide how hard and in what manner one works. Consumption norms indicate what types of goods and
services are expected to be consumed by members of a particular group.
This list is far from exhaustive, but gives a sense of the many ways in
which norms can affect behavior.

In any situation, individuals can choose the set of norms upon which
they will draw. Employers can appeal to a work norm (a job well done
is its own reward) or norms of distribution (if the company is not
profitable, it cannot afford pay raises). Workers' appeals to norms
are reflected in many union slogans, such as cooperation (Workers of
the world, unite!), reciprocity (A fair day's wage for a fair day's work),
or distribution (Eight hours for work, eight hours for sleep, eight hours
for what we will). If employers invoke a norm of distribution to share
the losses of a poor harvest, a norm of reciprocity can be invoked
by workers to share the wealth of a bountiful harvest. The same
norm may be drawn upon to advocate for opposite policies. The anti-
welfare slogan "Entitlement Nation" and the anti-Wall Street slogan
"The 99%" both appeal to a norm of fairness.

Norms vary in their expansiveness and their importance. Norms can
apply to multiple cultures (incest and cannibalism are forbidden in
most societies); a single society (the nineteenth-century Corsican code
of honor [Elster, 2007: 362]); a religious group (the Christian day of
rest is Sunday, the Jewish day of rest is Friday to Saturday sundown);
a school (students at XYZ College "work hard and play hard"); or
a business (everyone works late when a big project is due the next day).
Norms can also vary in their importance. A "contrary to nature" norm
forbidding cannibalism is more substantive than a fleeting consumption norm regarding fashion. The consumption norm of spending a lot
on a wedding is fairly widespread, but the sanctions for violating the
norm vary. Walking on the right side of the sidewalk or the right side of

the grocery aisle is a norm, but it is neither that important nor is it universally followed, as shoppers swerve from side to side as they find items or text on their phones.

Individuals

While institutions and norms are the rules of the game, individuals are the players. Individuals are the foundational unit of analysis in economics. Methodological individualism holds that only individuals, not organizations, have goals or aims and that changes in social outcomes are due to the actions of individuals.[13] We highlight four characteristics of individuals that differ from the typical textbook presentation: their rationality, preferences, values, and beliefs.

A typical microeconomics textbook models individuals as rational egoists who maximize their material well-being subject to a set of constraints.[14] In these models, individuals can gather and evaluate information about alternatives in a costless manner. The strong assumptions regarding the availability and processing of information led Herbert Simon (1961) to posit that economic models should be built on a weaker version of rationality. Actors who are *boundedly rational* are "intendedly rational, but only limitedly so" (xxiv). Bounded rationality assumes that there are limits to humans' ability to gather and process information. For this reason, individuals may regret actions ex post that seemed optimal ex ante. Actors use tools such as satisficing behavior, rule following, and incomplete contracts in order to compensate for their bounded rationality.

Individuals possess a complex set of preferences, values, and beliefs that complicate the modeling of utility as a monotonic transformation of material outcomes. Preferences and values are normative statements. Preferences describe an individual's tastes for "consumption and personal affairs" while values describe an individual's tastes for the ordering of "society and social relations (often thought of as ethics and ideology)" (Mokyr, 2017: 8).[15] Preferences and values can come from

---

[13] See Rutherford (1994) for a discussion of methodological individualism and holism.

[14] See Ostrom (2005) for a discussion of the assumptions of rational egoists.

[15] Values can be internalized social norms, but can also be preferences for a particular element of social order, such as religious values being more or less important.

norms that have been completely internalized, but can also be independent of norms. Beliefs are positive statements that "pertain to the state of the world, including the physical and metaphysical environments and social relations" (Mokyr, 2017: 8). Preferences and values describe how an individual thinks the world should work, while beliefs describe how an individual thinks the world does work.

A student might prefer that other students in a class not cheat on an exam. That student may simultaneously believe that cheating is rampant. The phrase "believe what you want" implies that people's preferences, values, and beliefs are intertwined. Limited government advocates believe that smaller government will generate prosperity and also prefer tax cuts. Big government advocates believe that government intervention is required to fix basic faults in the market economy and also prefer expansive regulatory policy. We return to the importance of beliefs in the Enforcement versus Equilibrium section below.

An individual's preferences, values, and beliefs are partially learned – organizations such as families, churches, schools, and governments work hard to socialize children into certain patterns of behavior – and are partially evolved – certain characteristics have been selected for over time. Detailing the source of preferences is a core question in the field of evolutionary psychology and well beyond the scope of this book.[16] There is a difference between a norm, which is an action or set of actions that society expects or permits in a given situation, and the impulse that undergirds that behavior. You may feel a desire to exact revenge on someone who has recklessly cut in front of you in traffic. The impulse for revenge is an intuitive response to perceived harm that may be learned or may be genetic. The norms and laws of society shape the form of the revenge.[17]

Models based on narrowly defined self-interest can make accurate predictions in certain arenas of economic action, most notably in situations that loosely reflect the assumptions of perfect competition.

---

[16] For an overview of this literature, see Haidt (2012).

[17] Some authors distinguish between social and moral norms. For instance, according to Elster (2007), agents follow a moral norm even when they have no opportunity for being observed, as not following the norm would engender feelings of guilt in an individual. Self-imposed sanctions are automatic, but often require investment by society to instill (Posner and Rasmusen, 1999). We categorize moral norms as part of preferences.

However, situations in which the social order encourages behavior other than competition are often difficult to explain using a model based on the rational egoist assumption.[18] Donating to charitable organizations; working harder than required; unwavering loyalty to a sports team, country, or brand; voting for policies that hurt your material interests; and automatic acceptance or subversion of authority all require explanations that go beyond the maximization of material well-being. Humans are competitive by nature, but also are willing cooperators, particularly when the social order in place encourages cooperation. For this reason, we use a broad definition of rationality – choosing the best means possible to achieve the chooser's ends – rather than one focused narrowly on material well-being.[19]

While individuals have beliefs, values, and preferences, those elements, when shared by a group, make up that group's culture. Mokyr (2017: 8) defines culture as: "a set of beliefs, values, and preferences, capable of affecting behavior, that are socially (not genetically) transmitted and that are shared by some subset of society." In explaining the origins of the Industrial Revolution, Mokyr argues that at the time of the Enlightenment, a culture of "open science" among scholars, engineers, and other elites encouraged them to share information in the public realm. Elites within this culture shared the belief that scientific discoveries and their application could be the source of continual improvement in the human condition.[20]

Organizations

Families, firms, religious organizations, colleges, and governments are all organizations. Organizations form when individuals join together

---

[18] Gode and Sunder (1997) show that even "zero intelligence traders" reach efficient outcomes when markets are designed appropriately, eliminating the need for a rational egoist assumption to explain competitive outcomes. The assumption that humans are "strong reciprocators" and punish non-cooperative behavior "even at a net cost to the punisher" is an alternative to the rational egoist assumption (Fehr and Gintis, 2007: 45).

[19] Using this definition, if you feel obligated to reciprocate someone's generosity by buying her a gift, you would do so by buying and delivering the gift at the lowest cost and by the most appropriate manner (Posner, 1998).

[20] We return to beliefs in Part III, where we analyze a society's core beliefs about the link between institutions and outcomes. Core beliefs are part of social order and form an umbrella over those in power who make the institutions.

to achieve a set of common objectives. North, Wallis, and Weingast (2009) distinguish between adherent organizations and contractual organizations. An adherent organization is "characterized by self-enforcing, incentive-compatible agreements among its members," while contractual organizations "utilize both third-party enforcement of contracts and incentive-compatible agreements among members" (North, Wallis, and Weingast, 2009: 16). The state is an adherent organization, as no exogenous party enforces the constitution. A group of mafia bosses that comes to an understanding about splitting territory or a group of basketball players playing a pick-up game are also adherent organizations, since in neither case is there an overarching organization that enforces the rules. A corporation, on the other hand, is a contractual organization, as it relies on the state to enforce some of its agreements.

Organizations are interesting to the Institutional and Organizational Analysis (IOA) because they create and enforce the bulk of the institutions studied by the discipline. Organizations have two sets of related issues that we will examine. First, they have their own set of institutions and norms that govern their members' behavior. Second, they "impact and interact with the broader world around them" (Greif and Kingston, 2011: 19). Analyses of the internal workings of organizations use tools from sociology, psychology, labor economics, and the modern theory of the firm. The goal is to understand the functioning of organizations that compete against one another in market settings. Since a variety of organizational forms (each with its own set of institutions and norms) are available to achieve a particular goal, one would expect competition among organizational forms that leads to efficient organizational choice. In Chapters 2 and 3, we examine this topic further. Organizations can impact the broader world by shaping preferences through education or advertising. They can also be players in the political process, seeking to shape legislation or coordinate to achieve large-scale institutional change. The influence of organizations in shaping political outcomes is examined in Parts II and III.

Enforcement versus Equilibrium Behavior

In a simple formulation of this framework, organizations and individuals enforce the extant institutions perfectly and costlessly. Property rights are therefore perfectly defined. Thinking about institutions as having clearly defined and enforced sanctions is a good first step towards understanding their effect on behavior. If the severity of a sanction associated with an institution is increased, we expect the quantity demanded of the prohibited activity to decrease. Under this view, if the government raises the fine for speeding, the quantity of speeding will decrease. An alternative *Equilibrium* framework notes that many patterns of behavior within organizations and societies persist with very little monitoring or enforcement of sanctions.[21] Greif and Kingston (2011: 25) note that "it is ultimately the behavior and the expected behavior of others rather than prescriptive rules of behavior that induce people to behave (or not to behave) in a particular way."

Though many patterns of behavior are influenced by institutions or norms, those patterns can be explained as equilibrium outcomes. The use of language is a matter of convention. Without a mutual understanding of what words mean and how grammar should be used, communication would be impossible (Lewis, 1969). We use the words on this page in the ways that we do because we expect our readers to share a similar understanding of their use and meaning. Driving on the right side of the road in the United States is a law and a social norm, but it is the expectation in equilibrium that others will stay to the right that is the greatest inducement to drive on the right. It is a law, because driving on the left side of the road will cause the police to pull the offender over and fine him, and it is a social norm because other members of society who observe the behavior feel and express alarm at the violator's actions. But, even without the law or the social norm, people would still find a means to coordinate their behavior to a single side of the road. Take the example of the simple game shown in Figure 1.4 of a one-period simultaneous move game. Two drivers are speeding towards one another on a narrow dirt road and need to swerve either left or right to avoid an accident.

There are three Nash equilibria in the game: both drivers choose right, both drivers choose left, and both drivers randomize and go right 50 percent of the time and left 50 percent of the time. Without more information about the vehicles, the players, or the history of driving,

---

[21] This framework builds on the literature on conventions. A convention is a "pattern of behavior that is customary, expected and self-enforcing" (Young, 1996).

Driver B

		Left	Right
Driver A	Left	1, 1	0, 0
	Right	0, 0	1, 1

Figure 1.4 Rules of the road

there is no clear way to settle on one of the three equilibria. Staying to the right or left is an arbitrary decision, and the convention concerning which side of the road to drive on has changed over time. The dominant convention in much of continental Europe switched from the left to the right at the time of the French Revolution, but the process of switching was protracted, including switches by Hungary and Czechoslovakia during German occupation during World War II and ending with Sweden in 1967 (Young, 1996). A convention of everyone driving on the right side of the road needs no enforcement. It is a Nash equilibrium, a focal point (Schelling, 1960), and the outcome of a path-dependent series of events. Once drivers have the expectation that other drivers will swerve right, then swerving right is the focal point equilibrium.

Any institution or norm is embedded within other competing and complementary institutions and norms that will affect individuals' behavior. Higher expected penalties for not following a rule may increase compliance, but the effect of a change in a rule on the rest of the social order is not always clear. For instance, suppose a university raises the penalty for being found guilty of cheating on an exam from failure of the exam to automatic expulsion from the university. The university administrators anticipate that this increase in the penalty will lower the quantity of cheating. But raising the penalty may have other effects. Raising the penalty may signal to would-be cheaters that infractions are caught infrequently. Would-be cheaters may therefore cheat more, knowing that the chances of getting caught are so low. Additional effects may increase cheating further. Suppose there is a consensus on campus that the new set of sanctions is "too strong." Behavior will therefore change on a number of margins. Raising the penalty may cause students to not report observed infractions to the formal system. It may cause faculty members who observe cheating to adjudicate outside of the formal system to avoid having their students expelled. It may also cause the organization charged with hearing cases of cheating to be less likely to find an accused student guilty. Looking simply at the increase in the fine, one would expect cheating to fall. But if the increased fine causes the formal process to break down, then the equilibrium level of cheating may actually increase. University administrators may tout the reduction in cheating due to the increased penalty, but what they may be observing is not less cheating, only less reporting of cheating.

Workplace rules offer another example of competing and complementary institutions. Workplace rules often enumerate a list of activities that are forbidden or a minimum level of effort that is required. But "for the organization to work well, it is not enough for employees to accept commands literally. In fact, obeying operating rules literally is a favorite method of work slowdown during labor-management disputes, as visitors to airports when controllers are unhappy can attest" (Simon, 1991: 32). In a workplace, where a great deal of initiative is required by employees, institutions can only set a minimal baseline of behavior. The true determinant of work effort is not the institution but the norms of behavior and the expectation that any one worker has about her coworkers' levels of effort.

De Jure and De Facto Property Rights

Were institutions perfectly enforced, individuals would always follow the prescriptions of what they must, must not, or may do, thereby defining individuals' property rights. One framework in the legal scholarship for understanding what the word "property rights" means is that it consists of a bundle of legal relationships, often called a "bundle of sticks" or a "bundle of rights," that can be separated, combined, altered, traded, and described both individually and collectively. The law of property is not about our relationship with objects but about our relationships with other people, and those relationships change over space and time. This framework for studying the component parts of property traces back to Hohfeld (1913, 1917), who argued that property was composed of four dyads: rights-duties, privileges-no rights, power-liability, and immunity-disability.[22] Hohfeld's framework allows legal scholars to break the legal relationships associated with property into their component parts to clarify their exact form. When we begin to list these relationships, we see quite quickly that a piece of property includes a long list of abilities and restrictions that both the "owner" of the property and other members of society possess (Alchian, 1965; Barzel, 1997). An owner of a piece of land might have the ability to sell, lease, or subdivide it, while society may have the ability to regulate, tax, or take it for public use.

Suppose that you own a house and the land on which it is located. The property may be zoned single-family residential, so building an apartment or commercial building is forbidden. The property may contain wetlands or an historical building, the regulation of which may diminish your ability to build. You may be restricted to whom you sell your property.[23] You may be restricted in your right to rent out your house.[24] If you are allowed to rent out your house, there may be laws controlling how much rent you can charge.[25] Surface and subsurface rights to land can be separated; one person can own the right to build on a piece of land, while another owns the right to mine for coal on it.[26] Other people may have the right to enter your property without your explicit permission.[27] The courts may find that certain activities on your property are forbidden because they interfere with your neighbors' enjoyment of their property.[28] You

---

[22] See Schlag (2015) for a modern interpretation of Hohfeld. The legal relationships described by Hohfeld are the outcomes of rules and the deontics contained therein.

[23] Mexico had a law for many decades limiting foreigners from purchasing property within 50 km of the coast (http://latino.foxnews.com/latino/money/2013/04/24/mexico-loosens-restrictions-on-foreigners-buying-property/).

[24] The apartment rental service Airbnb has faced regulatory pressure in certain cities (www.nytimes.com/2012/12/01/your-money/a-warning-for-airbnb-hosts-who-may-be-breaking-the-law.html).

[25] For decades, the market for apartments in New York City has served as a case study for the perverse effects of rent regulation (www.nytimes.com/2013/07/28/magazine/the-perverse-effects-of-rent-regulation.html).

[26] *Peevyhouse* v. *Garland Coal & Mining Company*, 375 US 906 (Oklahoma, 1962).

[27] In some US states, hunters are allowed to enter unposted private land without permission (http://scholarship.law.duke.edu/cgi/viewcontent.cgi?article=1238&context=dlj).

[28] In *Sturges* v. *Bridgman* ((1879) LR 11 Ch D 852), a famous nuisance case, a doctor argued that his neighbor's confectionary disturbed his medical practice.

may be limited in your ability to hang your laundry to dry, host concerts in your backyard, or install a new water heater.[29]

To give a flavor of Hohfeld's framework, suppose that local regulations grant you the privilege to use the water in a pond on your property to irrigate crops. Under Hohfeld's framework, your neighbor has a corresponding "no right"; that is, if you have the privilege to use the water, your neighbor has no right for you not to irrigate your crops with pond water. However, a privilege to use the stream does not mean your neighbor has a duty to not interfere with your collection of water. If your neighbor collects the water first, that means that you cannot collect that same water. Alternatively, you may have the right that your neighbor cannot take water from the pond without your permission. If so, your neighbor has the corresponding duty not to take your water. Your right and your neighbor's duty mean exactly the same thing. This symmetry highlights the social nature of property. You may, through contract, exchange some of your rights and privileges with your neighbor, perhaps selling her some of your water or collectively deciding to set aside some water for conservation purposes. Once we view property as a "bundle of sticks," those individual sticks in that bundle can be rearranged via contract.

In practice, the property rights associated with water are very complicated.[30] The rights to water in the eastern and western United States are roughly divided by the riparian and prior appropriation doctrines governing their use. The riparian doctrine allows landowners located next to a watercourse to use that water so long as the water is used on the adjoining land and does not interfere with their neighbors' use. This allocation of property rights to water seems most appropriate "where precipitation and streams are plentiful and more-or-less uniformly spread" (Libecap, 2007: 283). In the arid West, water is both scarcer and more unevenly distributed than in the eastern United States, and often must be transported great distances to its final use. Because of

---

Even though the confectioner had operated on the premise for more than twenty years, the court ruled in favor of the doctor due to the nature of the residential neighborhood in which the confectionary was located.

[29] Local bans on line drying laundry exist across the country, and the desire to be free of its unsightliness has led to murder: "One man shot and killed another last year because he was tired of telling the man to stop hanging his laundry outside" (www.nytimes.com/2009/10/11/us/11clothesline.html).

[30] See Libecap (2007) for a more thorough description of property rights in water in the American West.

this, a riparian system of rights has several disadvantages as compared to prior appropriation in areas of greater water scarcity. In areas of comparative plenty, the "reasonable" use standard underlying the riparian doctrine is typically sufficient to govern different adjacent users' behavior and so results in fewer disputes. In a water-scarce environment, such a comparatively vague standard, especially untethered to clear appropriative priority of water users, would be much more likely to result in significant legal disputes. Instead, prior appropriative states rely on a more stringent requirement typically known as "beneficial" use.

Similarly, the adjacency requirement of riparian water use limits transportation of water in a way that would have hindered development along the western frontier, where in many contexts the most productive mining or agricultural land was not necessarily immediately adjacent to a source of water. The doctrine of prior appropriation allows for such transportation by assigning property rights to water according to the order in which users put it to beneficial use, even if the water is used far from the water source. Under the appropriation doctrine, you can have a stream running right through your property but not have the right to use the water in it.[31] This allocation of property rights allows for greater trade in water rights, although current law in most states still hinders trade (Culp, Glennon, and Libecap, 2014).[32]

While rights and privileges are distinct concepts, we generalize and use the term "de jure property rights" to describe all of the legal relationships included in property: rights, privileges, powers, immunities, and their correlatives. There are many entitlements that can be analyzed using the property-rights framework. Real property refers to land and anything attached to it. Personal property includes items that can be tangible (cars, iPhones, and books) or intangible (stocks, patents, and copyrights). Scholars can also use the property-rights framework to analyze other entitlements, such as human rights and political rights. The Bill of Rights in the US Constitution and the

---

[31] Until 2016, households in Colorado were not legally permitted to collect rainwater (www.denverpost.com/2016/08/05/colorado-household-rain-barrel-law-takes-effect-tuesday/).

[32] Moreover, this rights specification further required the definition of water users' rights to construct irrigation canals over public lands and the private property of others.

Universal Declaration of Human Rights (UDHR) both define rights that are held by individuals and duties held by governments. The US Constitution's Second Amendment includes the right to "keep and bear arms," and the First Amendment includes the right to "peaceably assemble."[33] The UDHR includes the "right to a nationality" and "the right to marry and to found a family."

A danger in using the "bundle of sticks" metaphor is that it might leave the impression that "property rights are purely ad hoc assemblages of rights and privileges" that can be separated and combined in an infinite number of combinations (Merrill and Smith, 2011: S89). This would be true if the costs of separating and assembling those rights and privileges were zero. Merrill and Smith argue that in a world in which these costs are not zero, property rights take some standard forms. We will return to the costs of arranging property rights in the next chapter during our discussion of transaction costs, but give three insights here.

The first insight is that the most important right that owners of property have is the right to exclude others.[34] This right of exclusion makes the owners of property the residual claimants – they control any property rights not enumerated in the law and receive any benefits not controlled by others. Property owners therefore have the incentive to invest in and develop their property in ways that no one else does. Second, the costs of figuring out what rights are bundled together and who owns those rights would be "staggering" in a world in which every piece of property had a unique set of rights associated with it. To minimize these costs, the institutions governing property generally fall into one of several categories. New and exotic property-rights schemes do arise, but they are often difficult to manage. A sign stating "Keep Out!" is much easier to understand than a sign stating "Keep Out! Unless . . ." followed by a long list of exceptions. Third, these rights against the world are asymmetric. While the "bundle of sticks" framework suggests that property rights can be arranged on a case-by-case basis between every member of society, doing so is

---

[33] These "rights" are framed in the US Constitution as restrictions on the government. The underappreciated Ninth Amendment states that citizens' rights are not limited to those listed in the Bill of Rights: "The enumeration in the Constitution, of certain rights, shall not be construed to deny or disparage others retained by the people."

[34] This paragraph draws on Merrill and Smith (2011).

much more costly than lumping all rights, such as the right of exclusion, together.

We have discussed property rights in this section using a legal framework, but economists define rights more broadly. Given that the complete delineation and enforcement of de jure property rights is impossible and that someone must be the residual controller of those undefined and unenforced property rights, many uses to property fall outside of the legal boundaries. Many of those uses may be limited by social norms that are not consistent with laws, but uses may not be fully limited by laws or norms. Because institutions and norms are hard to enforce, owners of property have the ability to use it in ways that fall outside of their bounds. We therefore define a de facto property right as the ability to make a decision about resources, including human, physical, or intellectual capital, both in the present and in the future. A de facto property right gives an individual or an organization the ability to "possess, use, improve, exclude, destroy, sell, transform, donate, bequeath, lease, mortgage, consume, or develop an asset" (Allen, 2006: 4). These de facto rights can overlap with the rights as defined by the state, the de jure property rights. But de facto property rights can exist without the state or state enforcement, as shown by Umbeck (1981) and Ellickson (1991). They are also generated by organizations and individuals at all levels of society. We will use this expanded definition of property rights in Chapter 3 when we define transaction costs.

Another justification for property rights is natural law. An eighteenth-century Enlightenment version of property advocated by Quesnay was that property rights "were deeply embedded in a set of natural laws that had been worked out by the creator and were clearly discoverable in the light of human reason" (Rothbard, 1995: 369). De facto and de jure property rights can, and often do, overlap with natural property rights, but one can possess one right without the others. This is especially the case given that the definition of natural rights requires elaboration by an authority, whose pronouncements as to which rights are "natural" can change over time.

Examining the property rights associated with slavery shows the overlap between natural, de jure, and de facto rights. Doing so also allows us to see how the costs of enforcing institutions drive a wedge between de jure and de facto rights. As defined by the Catholic Church's position, the natural right to own slaves has changed over the centuries, depending on economic, political, and social forces. The position laid out in Vatican II in 1965 is that slavery is an infamy that poisons society. During the nineteenth century, the church's position was more mixed, ranging from a description of slavery by Cardinal John Henry Newman as "a condition of life ordained by God in the same sense that other conditions of life are" to the condemnation of the slave trade by Pope Gregory XVI as "absolutely unworthy of the Christian name" (see Noonan, 2005). A clear, "natural" right to one's own person did not exist for slaves during the era in which slavery flourished.

In the US South, slaves were considered to be the legal property of their owners. The laws of individual states dictated the specific rights of slaves. Some laws, such as how slavery passed from mother to child, were similar across all states. Other laws, such as the penalty for killing a slave, varied widely. In North Carolina, the ruling in *State* v. *Mann* (1829) stated that owners had the right to punish their slaves in any way they deemed necessary, including killing them (Tushnet, 2003). In other jurisdictions, slaves had greater protection under the law from physical abuse. Some slave codes allowed slaves to live away from the owner's property and contract with others for their services. Other codes forbade a slave from contracting.

While slaves were the legal property of their owners and strictly limited in their de jure rights, they did possess some de facto rights. These rights to make decisions over the use of resources arose because slaves were not automatons, allowing their owners the ability to control their every action. Slaves were human actors whose work effort needed to be incentivized, monitored, and enforced. An uncooperative slave could engage in work slowdowns, petty theft, sabotage, and any number of "weapons of the weak" (Scott, 1985). Slaves were given the ability to use land, their free time, and even to purchase their freedom, even when legal rights did not exist. Even negative incentives, such as whippings, were only required because slaves had the ability to make decisions about work effort. Owning another person de jure does not imply having complete de facto property rights over that person.

Conclusion

If de facto property rights were undefined, any attempt to use or improve an asset could immediately be thwarted or appropriated by other individuals. Institutions and norms are central elements in the definition of property rights. They are ubiquitous, although their specific form varies considerably from place to place. Just as an absence of institutions and norms would beget chaos, their ubiquity indicates the value they provide in facilitating social order. While the grammar of any one rule can be analyzed in isolation, a web of institutions, norms, organizations, and individuals shapes the way in which any particular rule is promulgated, perceived, and enforced. These elements define and determine the distribution of de facto property rights. It is never the case that de facto property rights are perfectly defined; there are always costs associated with their establishment and protection. These costs, called transaction costs, are discussed in the next chapter and are the next major building block of the IOA.

2 | Property Rights and Transaction Costs

Introduction and Opening Case: Intellectual Property Rights

As an undergraduate at the London School of Economics, Ronald Coase (1992: 715) asked: Why does "management" exist if "the pricing system provided all the coordination necessary"? The ubiquitous role of management seems to have no purpose in a world in which the price mechanism can coordinate economic activity at zero cost. His answer was that there must be costs to organizing economic activity that differ across different forms of organization.[1] Rather than model a frictionless world of "blackboard economics," Coase urged economists to examine a world in which transaction costs are positive and have a significant impact on organizational and institutional choice.[2]

In Chapter 1, we defined de facto property rights as the "ability to freely exercise a choice over an asset." In a simple neoclassical economic model, all assets are viewed as having clearly defined rights. Land, labor, and capital are inputs into the production function; televisions, video games, and hamburgers are outputs. When a neoclassical firm (with assumed zero transaction costs) hires a unit of labor, it does not have to ask the questions: "What quality of worker did I hire? Will he steal from me? How much will I have to monitor him? Can I fire him?" The de facto property rights to all inputs and outputs are established and maintained effortlessly, with no measurement or enforcement issues. But, in reality, all transactions involve more than just a clean transfer that ends when the parties exchange goods and payments. And all economic activity requires that parties monitor and

---

[1] Coase (1937, 1960) argued that in a world without transaction costs, "there is no economic basis for the existence of the firm" and that "the institutions which make up the economic system have neither substance nor purpose" (1988: 14).
[2] A search of EconLit found that more than 1,000 books or articles had the words "Coase" or "transaction costs" in their title since 2000.

58

enforce de facto property rights. Owners of property rights in land, labor, hamburgers, and video games constantly establish and defend their rights.[3]

An example of the costs of establishing and maintaining property rights comes from intellectual property law. Intellectual property law is a set of rules that provide rights and protections for owners of intellectual property, thereby rewarding inventors and artists for their work. Intellectual property rules define how inventors and artists can establish legal rights over intellectual property, what the rights entail, and how the rights can be protected. The traditional argument for government-supported protection of intellectual property is based on the non-excludability of information. New information is hard to generate but easy to copy, and the incentive to generate new information falls if competitors can immediately copy and sell it. The costs and benefits of establishing rights to intellectual property differ from country to country. These variations lead to systematic differences in the types of investments that inventors make in acquiring knowledge and the methods used to protect that knowledge.

A patent is one type of intellectual property, granted for a "new and useful process, machine, manufacture, or composition of matter, or any new and useful improvement thereof" (35 US Code § 101). There are costs for filing a patent and costs for responding to infringements on that patent.[4] Inventors must weigh the benefits (patent strength and length) with the costs (patent fees and legal costs) to determine whether to file for a patent and how much effort to make in protecting it. An alternative to filing a patent is to rely on secrecy. Keeping an innovation secret is more likely in cases where it is hard to reverse engineer the final product. Where patenting is costly or weak, one would expect greater reliance on secrecy and greater innovation in industries in which secrecy is feasible.

Evidence from two nineteenth-century world's fairs supports the hypothesis that patent laws shape the direction of innovative activity. Comparing thirteen European countries with patent lengths from zero to twenty years, Moser (2005: 1231) finds that inventors in countries without patents focused their activities "in industries

---

[3] For the remainder of the book, when we use the term "property rights," we mean de facto property rights.

[4] See Khan and Sokoloff (2001) and Khan (2005) for a history of the development of the patent system in the United States.

where secrecy was an effective alternative to patent grants." Inventors in Switzerland and Denmark, two countries without patent protection, focused their attention on scientific instruments, food processing, and dye stuffs, which are difficult to reverse engineer, while generating fewer innovations in engines and manufacturing, which are easily copied and rely on patent protection. The Netherlands abolished its patent laws in 1869, leading to a large increase in innovations in food processing mirrored by a large drop in innovations in textiles and manufacturers, consistent with a shift to industries that could rely on secrecy to protect innovations.

The costs to inventors of establishing and maintaining patent rights involve retaining lawyers, filing a patent, monitoring competitors, and suing for patent infringement. These must be weighed against alternative methods of protecting investments in innovation, such as the use of secrecy. All of the resources expended in establishing and maintaining property rights, whether through the patent system, secrecy, or other methods, are called transaction costs. This chapter expands our conceptual toolkit to include the link between property rights and transaction costs, beginning with the definition of transaction costs and then moving to a comparison of hypothetical zero and infinite transaction cost worlds with the real world of positive, but finite, transaction costs.

Defining Transaction Costs

Suppose that you are a high school student seeking to borrow your parents' car on a Friday night. You have agreed to perform a series of chores in exchange for the right to use the car. Your use of the car is most likely limited in many ways. Those limits may involve a specific time frame (you have to be home by midnight), an injunction against drinking and driving, a set of friends you may take in the car, or a set of places that you can go. Your rights to the car, even if they are not explicitly limited, are certainly implicitly limited. Your relationship with your parents is likely to be important to you, and acting irresponsibly with their property will affect your long-term relationship. Your parents could monitor the use of their car by having you call them with updates through the evening, installing a tracking device, or sitting in the back seat while you drive around.

Transaction costs are the "resources used to establish and maintain [de facto] property rights. They include the resources used to protect and capture (appropriate without permission) property rights, plus any deadweight costs that result from any potential or real protecting and capturing" (Allen, 1991: 3).[5] They are the costs of organizing society's resources and can be borne by individuals, governments, firms, or any other organization in society.[6] Transaction costs accompany every actual transaction. However, the transaction costs facing any potential transaction also greatly determine a variety of transactions that never occur. If they are high enough, all forms of trade break down.

Every transaction involves transaction costs. Coase (1988) notes that commodity exchanges are often used as examples of perfectly competitive markets with low transaction costs. However, even trades that occur within these organizations have transaction costs, because there are rules that structure the transfer and protection of property rights that are designed and enforced by the exchanges and the government. Coase concludes that "for anything approaching perfect competition to exist, an intricate system of rules and regulations would normally be needed" (9). The efforts made to write and enforce rules and regulations that establish and maintain de facto property rights are all transaction costs.[7]

While transaction costs occur with any economic activity – within a market, a firm, a family, a government, or any other organization – they exist only in a social setting. Robinson Crusoe, until the appearance of the cannibals and Friday, did not bear any transaction costs,

---

[5] This definition is similar to that of Barzel (1989: 2), who defines transaction costs as the costs of "transfer, capture, and protection" of economic property rights. See Allen (2000) for a comparison of the "property rights" and the "neoclassical" definitions of transaction costs. See Lueck and Miceli (2007) for a concise accounting of a transaction cost-centered view of property rights from a legal perspective.

[6] Transaction costs can be both broader and narrower than the costs of exchange, leading Cheung (1989: 77) to argue that they are "institutional costs including those of information, of negotiation, of drawing up and enforcing contracts, of delineating and policing property rights, of monitoring performance, and of changing institutional arrangements."

[7] Hirschman (1984: 94) makes a similar point about social norms and the economic system, arguing that if the capitalist system extinguishes "morality and public spirit, the universal pursuit of self-interest being all that is needed for satisfactory performance," it will find that "the system will undermine its own viability which is in fact premised on civic behavior and on the respect of certain moral norms to a far greater extent than capitalism's official ideology avows."

because he did not have anyone with whom to trade or from whom he needed to protect his property rights. Dahlman (1979: 148) provides a commonly cited set of transaction costs: "search and information costs, bargaining and decision costs, policing and enforcement costs." This list is a good starting place for categorizing and understanding transaction costs, but we emphasize that these costs are transaction costs only in the context of establishing and protecting rights in a social setting. When Robinson Crusoe arrived on the island, he faced information costs, such as figuring out where to make a shelter or how to tame wild goats. He also faced transportation costs, such as moving supplies from the shipwreck back to shore. These costs are not transaction costs, however, as they did not involve establishing and protecting property rights in relation to other actors (Demsetz, 1967).

Consider all the ways in which the owners of property rights seek to protect their rights. The state may protect property rights by spending resources on a legislature, police, courts, and other organizations. Society charges these organizations with making and enforcing rules. Enforcement can come through ex ante efforts by the police to prevent trespass and ex post use of the police and court systems to identify and punish trespassers and compensate homeowners. If you as the homeowner deem the state's protection to be insufficient, you can expend your own resources by building a wall around your yard or posting a "Trespassers Will Be Shot!" sign. You may opt to live in a neighborhood with only close friends and family, where the norm is to leave your doors unlocked but be wary of strangers. You and your neighbors may organize a "Neighborhood Watch" group or jointly hire a private security guard. After the trespass has occurred, you may sue the trespasser or take justice into your own hands by privately punishing the trespasser. These various means of establishing and maintaining property rights can be complements or substitutes in production.

In a dispute resolution sense, transaction costs are any of the costs incurred in preventing and resolving disputes. Efforts made to avoid disputes are as much transaction costs as efforts made to resolve disputes. Some costs are incurred up front and some ex post, but each is a type of transaction cost. Transaction costs determine the extent to which dispute resolution is even possible and how many resources are expended in resolving a dispute. In the event that dispute resolution is too costly, many wrongs will go un-righted in society. Or, individuals or organizations undertake many costly precautions to prevent the wrongs from occurring in the first place because the costs to the aggrieved party of legally resolving the dispute after the fact are too high, or the certainty that they will be able to successfully prevail is too low, or both. Thus, the costs of legal dispute resolution can in turn determine the optimality of private protection and enforcement of rights. If you think your ability to receive compensation for trespass in court is highly uncertain, or more costly than building a protective fence around your yard, then you are more likely to invest in ex ante prevention measures. Ultimately, this calculus depends on how much you value a higher level of protection of your property and a weighing of the comparative costs of additional protection.[8]

Living within a social setting means that we give up some of our property rights in order to secure others. For instance, most members of modern states pay taxes. The state spends some of the taxes on providing services that protect our property rights. Rather than evicting trespassers ourselves, we call the local police to perform this task. Rather than use private violence to resolve a dispute about the limit of a patent, we use patent law and the court system to clarify property rights. But a government that is powerful enough to protect property is also powerful enough to limit property rights in ways that its citizens may not want. Governments establish and protect our property right to money by establishing money as legal tender, regulating the banking sector, and having a competent police force. Governments establish and protect some rights to use money but limit others. We cannot spend our dollars on illicit drugs, nuclear bombs, or state secrets, nor can we build a big bonfire and burn them.[9] Note that gaining and losing property rights happens at different organizational levels, even ones voluntarily entered. A gated community may provide a private security service to protect your property, but may also limit the color you paint your house and the volume at which you play your stereo system. In this case, individuals must weigh the desired and undesired limits on property rights from joining the community.

---

[8] Changing the medium of dispute resolution will cause future actors to adjust their conduct, ideally to reduce the likelihood of disputes occurring in the first place. Nonetheless, the potential for dispute that arises with all our rights to property and our persons is closely tied up with other private and public costs associated with protecting and enforcing these rights.

[9] http://codes.lp.findlaw.com/uscode/18/I/17/333.

In order to categorize the transaction costs and benefits from establishing and maintaining property rights, we present a framework that uses concepts from standard cost-benefit analysis.[10] Total costs consist of fixed costs (FC) and variable costs (VC). Those costs borne by the parties directly involved in the transaction are private costs. Those costs borne by other members of society are external costs. In a truly transaction-costless world, all of these costs, not just private variable costs, would be zero. Just like in a standard cost function, variable and fixed costs can rise or fall as new methods of establishing and defending property rights are adopted.

Some examples of different categories of transaction costs are:

• External Fixed: Costs of establishing a constitutional and legal framework, regulatory and enforcement organizations, traditions, and social norms.
• External Variable: Costs of providing additional police protection, adjudicating court cases, community enforcement of norms.
• Private Fixed: Costs of incorporating and organizing a firm or a commodity exchange.
• Private Variable: Costs of monitoring and enforcing private agreements.[11]

We begin our graphical analysis of transaction costs by assuming there are only private costs and benefits of establishing and protecting property rights. To provide a graphical analysis of transaction costs and property rights, we place "established and maintained property rights" on the x-axis and "costs and benefits" on the y-axis. Doing so allows for a familiar marginal cost-benefit analysis. In Figure 2.1, the marginal private cost (MPC) curve indicates the cost of marginally improving one's property rights. Total transaction costs are variable plus fixed costs. The area under the MPC curve indicates variable transaction costs. Variable transaction costs will be zero when the MPC runs along either the x- or y-axis or when there is no marginal benefit to establishing or protecting property rights. The marginal

---

[10] We will delve much more deeply into specific transaction costs in Chapter 3. Our goal here is to introduce a framework for understanding transaction costs using a familiar set of tools.
[11] Furubotn and Richter (2005: 51) also distinguish between the fixed transaction costs "made in setting up the institutional arrangements," and variable transaction costs "that depend on the number or volume of transactions."

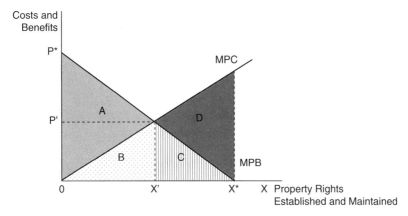

Figure 2.1 De facto property rights and private transaction costs

private benefit (MPB) curve indicates the private benefits from a marginal improvement in property rights. We assume that this curve is downward sloping.[12]

Where the MPB curve hits the x-axis at X*, there are no additional benefits from further establishing or maintaining property rights. The level or property rights X* can be achieved either when the marginal private transaction cost curve lies along the x-axis or, as shown in Figure 2.1, by expending private variable costs of B+C+D. At the point zero on the x-axis, property rights are undefined. If the point (0, P*) were the equilibrium, then the MPC curve would lie along the y-axis. At this equilibrium, private variable transaction costs are zero because there would be no marginal effort made to establish and protect property rights. When property rights are undefined, no economic activity would occur, as any investment made or good acquired could be taken by anyone else in society. While this extreme is unlikely to be reached, in some institutional settings the costs of establishing and maintaining property rights are so high that very little economic activity occurs. Depending on the elasticity of the MPB curve, the equilibrium level of private variable transaction costs, indicated by area B, can rise or fall as MPC rotates up or down.[13]

[12] Anderson and Hill (1975), Eggertsson (1990), and Allen (2014) use similar frameworks to discuss the costs and benefits of transactions and property rights.
[13] As we will see shortly, statements of the "Coase Theorem" that indicate zero transaction costs implicitly assume that the MPC curve runs along the x-axis and that private fixed costs are zero.

In neoclassical theory, total cost as a function of output is derived from a cost minimization problem. Suppose that the output is the protection of your property from trespassers, which you can do by either building a fence or getting a dog. In the transaction cost minimization problem, you will use the combination of fences and dogs that protects property rights at the lowest cost. If dogs and fences are perfect substitutes and one of them is free to acquire and maintain, then the costs of protecting property rights are zero. Just like a firm that has a choice between lower and higher cost methods of production, actors choose between lower and higher cost methods of establishing and maintaining property rights. To say that the MPC lies along the x-axis means that there is one zero-cost method to marginally increase property rights.

Were there only private transaction costs, individuals would choose the optimal form of organization and continue to expend additional effort on establishing and enforcing their property rights as long as the marginal private benefit exceeded the marginal private cost. In Figure 2.1, this point is achieved at (X', P'), where the net private benefit of establishing and maintaining property rights is area A, and the private variable cost is area B. Were the marginal cost zero, private actors would achieve additional net private benefits equal to areas B and C. Transaction costs will increase with a shift out of the MPB curve. As an economy grows, the MPB curve will shift out and more resources will be expended on establishing and maintaining property rights, all else equal. Innovations and new institutional arrangements alter the cost and benefit functions. A new technology or institutional innovation may lower or raise the MPC curve, changing the equilibrium level of property rights. All else equal, a shift down in the MPC curve will lead to more secure property rights and an increase in social wealth.

Focusing on just private decisions misses the external costs and benefits of establishing and maintaining property rights. The state or other members of society incur external costs, like the costs of courts and police.[14] More secure property rights can also lead to external

---

[14] In the best-case scenario, resources spent on courts and police lower private transaction costs. The state may be able to take advantage of economies of scale in the provision of police protection or contract enforcement. In the worst-case scenario, state action raises the private cost and lowers the private benefits of establishing and maintaining property rights. The state may impose regulations

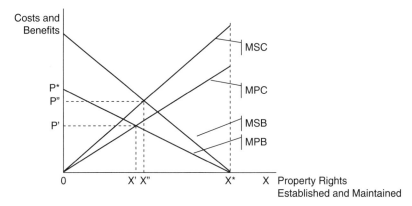

Figure 2.2 De facto property rights and social transaction costs

benefits, such as a patent system leading to more jobs or improved health for other members of society. In Figure 2.2, we add external costs to private costs to get the marginal social cost (MSC) curve. We also add external benefits to private benefits to get the marginal social benefit (MSB) curve. Depending on the relative size of the shift in each curve, incorporating external costs and benefits into the analysis can either increase or decrease the socially optimal level of property rights.[15]

Transaction Costs and Information

Let us now turn our full attention to the term "transaction costs" and begin our analysis of their characteristics. Why do transaction costs exist? Why is it not costless to establish and maintain the ability to use, derive income from, and alienate your property? Remember that all the costs of establishing and maintaining property rights are transaction costs, whether they are borne by the individuals involved in a transaction or a third party. From an individual's perspective, only private transaction costs matter, but from society's perspective, we must consider all of the relevant costs.

---

on establishing new businesses, tax transactions so that they are forced into an underground economy, or arbitrarily take property without due process.

[15] We note that societies are not ever at the societal optimum because of distributive reasons and political transaction costs of rearranging rights and making side-payments. We discuss the political transaction costs in Part II.

Transaction costs vary based on the characteristics of the property right under consideration and on the institutions and organizations that govern those property rights. Transaction cost analysis is therefore always comparative, and practitioners must compare the costs of establishing and maintaining property rights under different governance structures. This comparative analysis is examined in more detail in Chapter 3, where we study the choice of using hierarchies, prices, and hybrids to direct economic activity. While some transaction costs are simply protecting rights from obvious attempts at appropriation – building a fence to keep out trespassers – other transaction costs are subtle, relying on informational differences between relevant parties. Here, we will provide a brief introduction to transaction costs associated with information asymmetries.

In Chapter 1, we defined the concept of bounded rationality as actors being "intendedly rational but limitedly so." This notion of rationality means that "human beings are limited in knowledge, foresight, skill, and time" (Simon, 1957: 199). The assumption of opportunism – self-interest seeking with guile – is often paired with the assumption of bounded rationality, particularly in the work of Williamson (1975, 1985, 1996). Williamson (1985) distinguishes between simple self-interest seeking and opportunism. Under the assumption of simple self-interest seeking, "initial positions will be fully and candidly disclosed upon inquiry, state of the world declarations will be accurate, and cxccution is oath- or rule-bound" (Williamson, 1985: 49). This view of self-interest seeking is consistent with neoclassical theory. Williamson adds the concept of opportunism to highlight the times in which declarations are not accurate and execution is not oath- or rule-bound. Under the assumption of opportunism, Williamson (1990: 12) argues that "agents are allowed to disclose information in a selective and distorted manner. Calculated efforts to mislead, disguise, obfuscate and confuse are thus admitted." The assumptions of bounded rationality and opportunism make humans complex and contracting difficult.

Given bounded rationality, all complex contracts are unavoidably incomplete. Given opportunism, contract-as-promise unsupported by credible commitments is hopelessly naive. Taken together, the following organizational imperative obtains: organize transactions so as to economize on bounded rationality while simultaneously safeguarding against the hazards of opportunism. (Williamson, 1990: 12)

Two important components of any exchange are figuring out the property rights under consideration and then making sure the parties deliver their end of the bargain. For instance, the costs of specifying and monitoring property rights in a contract for labor services can vary widely. Two simple examples of labor contracts are piece-rate and wage contracts. In a piece-rate contract, the worker gets paid based on the level of measured output generated. Alternatively, a flat-wage contract pays the worker for the number of hours worked. At a shoe store, pay could be based on either the number of shoes sold or the number of hours worked.[16] In both cases, the employer typically wants more than the measured output or the physical presence of the employee. The experience of the customer in the store, mentoring junior sales associates, making sure records are kept in order, and organizing the inventory are all additional tasks that the employer requires.

If the employer offers a wage contract, the employer would like to hire employees well suited to working in a shoe store who provide good effort at selling shoes. If the employer offers a piece-rate contract, the employer would like the worker to do more than just sell the maximum number of shoes. In both cases, the employer would like to contract for a certain type of laborer and labor effort: well-suited employees who will provide good effort. However, the employer knows neither the type of worker being hired, nor how much or what type of effort the worker will provide. These both involve information asymmetries, where the parties know different things about the property rights being exchanged. Two categories of information asymmetries are adverse selection and moral hazard.

In adverse selection, one party to an exchange knows things that are (1) relevant to the second party and (2) costly for the first party to transmit or the second party to discover. Adverse selection is also known as a hidden attribute problem. An example of adverse selection from the insurance market is when healthy people hold off on buying insurance until their status changes to unhealthy. If this is the case, then insurance companies would need to raise rates to reflect the much higher risk in the pool, high enough, in fact, that most healthy people will be unwilling to purchase insurance. This logic is developed in Akerlof's (1970) "lemons" paper, which argues that when transaction

---

[16] Other contractual options are available, including a combination of these two.

costs of establishing property rights are high, the market for goods with diverse quality can break down so that only low-quality goods are exchanged.

Note that the effects of adverse selection would be eliminated if either (1) healthy people could costlessly signal their good state or (2) insurance companies could costlessly screen their customers for the state of their health. The costs of signaling (Spence, 1973) and screening (Stiglitz, 1975), along with the lost opportunities for trade due to those costs, are transaction costs.[17] In the case of the labor market, potential employees obtain appropriate educational certificates and other résumé enhancers in order to signal their suitability for a particular type of job. Employers can screen applicants using education, but also by designing employment contracts that encourage workers to reveal their type.[18]

In moral hazard, one party to the exchange may take actions that (1) affect the second party's valuation of the exchange and (2) are costly for the second party to monitor or enforce. Moral hazard is also known as a hidden action problem. An example of moral hazard from the insurance market is when people with insurance act in a more risky manner than when they did not have insurance. An uninsured motorist, who bears all of the cost of an accident, is more likely to drive carefully than an insured motorist who only bears part of the cost of an accident. Moral hazard can occur in any type of employment contract. In a flat-wage contract, the employee will get paid regardless of work effort. The cost of shirking is low, causing the worker to shirk more. In a piece-rate contract, the worker gets paid based on the number of units produced. The incentive to cheat is high, perhaps by replacing high- with low-quality output. A contract to pick apples based solely on the bushels picked will cause workers to cheat by picking unripe, overripe, and damaged apples in order to produce as many bushels as possible. Monitoring the effort of the wage worker and the output of the piece-rate worker are transaction costs.

---

[17] Akerlof, Spence, and Stiglitz were jointly awarded the Nobel Prize in Economic Sciences in 2001.

[18] An example of a screening device used in labor markets is placing new workers in a probationary period with low initial pay. Employers use a probationary period to incentivize applications from only people who think they can pass it and gain a more permanent employment status.

The "Coase Theorem"

Let us delve for a while into the absurd world of zero transaction costs and show how it leads to no effects of legal rules and no roles for organizations.[19] We will then add transaction costs into the mix of total costs that economic actors must consider and show how legal rules and organizational choice can have an effect on outcomes. Coase was critiquing economists who failed to consider transaction costs. He argued that the zero-transaction cost world "is the world of modern economic theory, one which I was hoping to persuade economists to leave" (1988: 174). One statement of the "Coase Theorem" that fits into the property-rights paradigm is: "When property rights are complete, all gains from trade are maximized and the distribution of income is determined by the initial assignment of rights" (Allen, 1991: 3).

Let us begin by supposing that there is a factory located next to a house. The production process for one of the factory's outputs generates a lot of smoke that pollutes the neighbor's air. Coase (1960) summarized three options that economists would usually propose in such a situation. First, the factory could be liable for the harm done to the neighbor. Second, the smoke from the factory could be taxed in order to reduce its ill effects. Finally, zoning regulations could be used to limit factories from locating near residential neighborhoods. Coase thought that all of these policies "are inappropriate, in that they lead to results which are not necessarily, or even usually, desirable" (20).

Coase's alternative was to recognize the reciprocal nature of the harm. Allowing the factory to pollute helps the factory while harming the neighbor. Forbidding the factory from polluting helps the neighbor but harms the factory. Coase argued that we should be clear about who has the relevant property rights and whether mutually beneficial trades could be made to reach an efficient allocation of society's resources.

---

[19] We follow Coase (1988) in putting the term "Coase Theorem" in quotation marks. Indeed, he called it the "so-called 'Coase Theorem'" (see also McCloskey, 1998). Putting the "Coase Theorem" in quotation marks is done to remind the reader that Coase's point was not to analyze a zero-transaction cost world, but to highlight the importance of transaction costs on institutions and organizations.

There are many ways to describe the property rights to pollute or to clean air; let us choose two rules and think about the differences in outcomes between them.

- Factory's rights: The factory has the privilege to generate a fixed amount of pollution at the specified location.[20]
- Neighbor's rights: The neighbor has the right to enjoy unpolluted air at the specified location.[21]

Assume that the factory and the neighbor are the only actors, that is, emissions from the factory harm no birds and global warming is not an issue. Assume that the factory will generate a fixed level of pollution. Under Factory's rights, the neighbor can only enjoy unpolluted air if she can induce the factory to stop polluting. Under Neighbor's rights, the factory can only pollute if it can induce the neighbor to give up her right to unpolluted air.

In a world of costless transacting, both de jure rules lead to completely defined property rights. In this world, if the legal rule is Neighbor's rights, then the factory will not skirt the law by polluting in small amounts or at night, hoping the neighbor will not notice. The neighbor's ability to enjoy unpolluted air is complete. Under Factory's rights, the factory does not need to worry that the neighbor will sabotage the plant or try to get regulations passed that will limit the factory's ability to pollute. The factory's ability to pollute is complete. The only way the factory will give up the right to pollute is if it receives sufficient compensation to do so. Table 2.1 describes the payoffs to the factory and the neighbor from the factory polluting or not polluting. Suppose the payoff to the factory is $300 when it pollutes and $0 when it does not, and that the payoff to the neighbor is $200 when the factory does not pollute and $0 when it does.[22] All

---

[20] Note that using Hohfeld's (1917) terminology, under Factory's rights, the factory has the privilege to pollute and the neighbor has no right that the factory not pollute. However, the factory does not have the right to pollute the neighbor's property, nor does the neighbor have the duty to accept the factory's pollution. The neighbor could, for instance, build a giant fan and blow the pollution back onto the factory's property. See Merrill and Smith (2011) for more on this topic. Under Neighbor's rights, the factory has the duty not to pollute.

[21] In each case, an "or else" of a fine or other sanction for violating the privilege or right is required.

[22] We assume that these payoffs perfectly capture the factory's and the neighbor's preferences on all margins, including money, health, aesthetics, and the

Table 2.1 *Net benefits to factory and neighbor*

	Pollution	No pollution
Factory's net benefit	$300	$0
Neighbor's net benefit	$0	$200
Social surplus	$300	$200

else equal, the factory prefers to pollute and the neighbor prefers that the factory not pollute. The social surplus from pollution is $100 greater than from no pollution, so from society's perspective, the factory should pollute.

The question that the "Coase Theorem" explores is: In a world of costless transacting, does it matter to economic efficiency which rule is chosen? Let us consider three scenarios to show that the allocation of property rights to pollution and clean air does not affect economic efficiency. First, suppose that Olivia is the owner of the factory and lives in the neighboring house. If Olivia decides not to pollute, then she harms the profitability of her factory. But if Olivia decides to pollute, she reduces the benefits of living in her home. Given the payoffs in Table 2.1, Olivia should pollute. Since she is the only party involved, the reduction in her net benefits from living in her polluted home is more than offset by the extra net benefits from allowing the factory to pollute. She will always choose the option that maximizes the social net benefits, regardless of the legal rule.

In the second zero-transaction cost scenario, suppose that Olivia decides to retire, sell off the factory to new owners, and remain living in the neighboring house. The price that the new owners pay for the factory will be determined in part by whether the ability to pollute is included in the sale. Potential buyers would be willing to pay more for the factory if it includes the ability to pollute. Because of the increased profitability of polluting, the purchasers of the factory will be willing to compensate Olivia enough to make her willing to transfer the ability to pollute to them.

In the third zero-transaction cost scenario, suppose that Olivia never owned the factory, lives in the neighboring house, and the rule is

environment. For instance, the neighbor may have slight health effects from the factory smoke or a reduction in utility from having her house dirtied from the factory.

Neighbor's rights. Now we have the situation of the "No Pollution" column in Table 2.1. Olivia enjoys clean air and receives a payoff of $200. The factory is restricted in its ability to pollute and receives a payoff of $0. This seems to be a bad outcome, because society's net benefits are not maximized. But if transaction costs are zero, Olivia and the factory will make a trade that makes both parties better off. The factory could offer Olivia $250 for the right to pollute. Olivia's new payoff would be $250 and the factory's would be $50. This brings us back to the social welfare maximizing outcome that the factory pollutes. This is the important insight of the "Coase Theorem," that when transaction costs are zero, bargains can be made to achieve the highest social benefit, regardless of the initial legal rule.[23]

Critiques of the "Coase Theorem" are legion.[24] While no formal proof or disproof of the "Coase Theorem" exists, the critiques and defenses of the "Coase Theorem" have shown that appropriate definitions of the terms "de facto property rights" and "transaction costs" go a long way towards clarifying the logic of the theorem.[25] Importantly, Coase was not interested in the zero-transaction cost world, but in a world in which transaction costs are positive.

To illustrate the effects of positive transaction costs, let us return to the scenario in Table 2.1. These numbers indicate that the "efficient" outcome is for the factory to pollute. This outcome will indeed happen in a zero-transaction cost world, regardless of the distribution of property rights. But in a world of positive transaction costs, what is efficient may change. Once we recognize that all economic activity requires that property rights be established and maintained and that every means of establishing and maintaining property rights incurs transaction costs, what is efficient is no longer obvious from just looking at the numbers in the table. Suppose that

---

[23] Note that if transaction costs are zero and the payoffs were flipped, that is, Olivia receives a higher payoff from no pollution than the factory receives from pollution, the two parties will always bargain to the efficient outcome of no pollution.

[24] For example, see Wellisz (1964), Calabresi (1965), Mishan (1967), Marchand and Russell (1973), Starrett (1972), and Posin (1990).

[25] Allen (1998, 2000, 2014) has argued that these critiques can be countered with the definitions of de facto property rights and transaction costs that are used above. See Medema and Zerbe (2000), Zelder (1998), and Medema (1999) for additional discussion of the "Coase Theorem."

transaction costs are infinite, meaning that neither party has the ability to establish or maintain property rights. In that case, if the rule is Factory's rights, the factory will choose to pollute. But the factory's right to pollute is not secure either. The neighbor may decide to take a sledgehammer to the factory's equipment, damaging it and its ability to produce. Chaos would ensue as individuals and firms failed to establish and maintain de facto property rights. Just like the world of zero transaction costs, the world of infinite transaction costs is a strange one. If all transaction costs are infinite, how did the factory get built in the first place? How did the neighbor come to own her house? In an infinite transaction cost world, these things could not happen.

Let us now assume that the rule is Neighbor's rights, that transaction costs exist, but are not infinite, and that the neighbor and the factory want to come to an agreement to grant the factory the ability to pollute. The cooperative surplus is $100. As long as the cost for the factory of establishing and maintaining the ability to pollute is less than $100, then a transfer of property rights will occur. Suppose that the cost to the factory of establishing the right to pollute is $50. In this case, the trade will still go through. Only when the transaction costs exceed the cooperative surplus would no trade occur.

We might be tempted to label situations in which the right to clean air stays in the hands of the neighbor as inefficient, but it is only inefficient compared to a zero-transaction cost world. Doing so is the equivalent to saying that using a scrubber is inefficient compared to hiring unemployed Martians to suck up the smoke at a cost of zero dollars. Unemployed Martians do not exist (we think, but given our bounded rationality, we cannot be sure) and neither does a world of zero transaction costs. Transaction costs are the reality of organizing economic activity. When doing economic analysis, Coase urged us to compare two real alternatives, not compare one world in which transaction costs exist with another world in which they do not.

Remember that our definition of transaction costs involves any costs borne by any individual or organization in society to establish and protect property rights. To determine the correct method of protecting property rights from society's perspective, we must include both the private costs borne by the factory and the neighbor and the external costs of establishing and protecting property rights borne by other organizations and individuals in society. These external costs include the government's cost of judges, police, and establishing a legal code and the costs of enforcing norms of behavior. Imagine the factory and the neighbor interacting on the frontier, far from any formal state power. The lowest cost method of establishing and enforcing property rights may be to have local control governed by norms rather than state power. Claiming that private efforts to establish and protect property rights are inefficient in such a scenario would be to ignore the legal costs of doing so. These legal costs can be substantial, but so too can their benefits, and settlers on the frontier seek to legalize their property rights as areas become settled. This was the finding of Alston, Libecap, and Mueller (1999b) in their study of the development of property rights in the Brazilian Amazon, our next case study.

Case Study: Titles and Land Conflict in the Brazilian Amazon

By their nature, frontiers are spaces where individuals or non-governmental organizations specify and enforce institutions. Given the low value of land on a frontier, the private and social costs of establishing and protecting de jure property rights often far outweigh their benefits. Since land is plentiful and competition is low, claiming land is often enough to establish de facto property rights. As frontiers develop, they integrate into the larger economy, a stage that often encourages landowners to seek government defined and defended property rights. Demand for a clear title with government protection is based on the difference in land value with and without the title. Title affects value in two ways. First, security of title reduces uncertainty and therefore increases investment in improving the property. Second, security of title encourages additional entrants into the market.

The process by which de jure property rights evolve has played out on frontiers across time and space. We often think of frontiers in geographical terms: the West in the United States, the Amazon in Brazil, or New South Wales in Australia (Alston, Harris, and Mueller, 2012). But technological advances, such as in biotechnology or computers, can also create spaces in which de jure property rights are unclear. Delimiting the breadth of intellectual property rights for the electromagnetic telegraph in the United States is an example of such a space. Samuel Morse's patent for the telegraph stated that it covered all forms of communication via "electro-magnetism, however developed for marking or printing intelligible characters, signs, or letters, at any distances."[26] His detractors claimed that this interpretation of his patent would grant Morse control over any subsequent discovery related to communications. The case dragged on for years and highlighted the distinction between "scientific discovery and technological innovation" (Hochfelder, 1999: 1). Sorting out how broadly Morse's patent extended was an important early question in intellectual property rights, and the case continues to be cited today.[27]

De jure property rights over physical or intellectual assets do not appear overnight in a clear and costless manner. Competing claims often exist due to a tension between de jure and de facto rights, but also because de jure rights are specified by different government offices and even different governments. Sorting out these conflicting claims is part of the transaction costs of establishing property rights. The Brazilian Amazon has long been an area with unclear de jure property rights. Initial Portuguese attempts to establish de jure property rights to land in Brazil date back to 1532, when the colony was divided into fourteen sections and granted as *captaincies* (Alston, Libecap, and Mueller, 1999b: 33). Even though the captaincies were enormous and the requirements for maintaining them were low, the system of ownership did not stay in place long, as there was very little demand for the land. Four grantees never claimed their captaincies and the Portuguese revoked the system in 1548. The next major system offered settlers large, relatively unencumbered grants, called *sesmarias*. The only condition for maintaining the sesmarias was that the land be cultivated. This requirement that land be used productively to maintain property rights has been invoked frequently throughout Brazilian history, but has been "consistently unenforceable."

Since independence but especially post-1960, the Brazilian government has encouraged development of the Amazon by: allowing squatters to possess unclaimed public land; selling land at low prices; issuing land grants; planned colonization; and the expropriation of private property. During the 1970s, INCRA, the National Institute for Colonization and Agrarian Reform, "concentrated on creating planned

---

[26] *O'Reilly* v. *Morse*, 56 US 15 How. 62 (1853).

[27] See Mossoff (2014) for an analysis of the continuing influence of Morse's patent defense today.

colonization projects in the Amazon" (Alston, Libecap, and Mueller, 1999b: 56). INCRA could not keep up with the flow of migrants and did a poor job of titling land or even surveying and recording it. When the government switched strategies in the late 1970s "to focus on large-scale agricultural projects instead of colonization, most settlers and squatters in the Amazon were left with uncertain tenure to the land they occupied. Much of the land was unsurveyed and untitled and had competing claimants." In the mid-1980s, "INCRA inaugurated a new model of land redistribution based on the expropriation of private properties." Settling people far from markets was bound to fail, but, unused private land "could be expropriated and assigned to small settlers with a greater likelihood of success" (Alston, Libecap, and Mueller, 1999b: 56).

Settlers on a geographical frontier are heterogeneous. Some may operate more successfully in an environment in which de jure rights are not clearly defined, while others have the ability to operate successfully in the legal world. Early settlers on a physical frontier are often young and have low human and physical capital endowments. They may have limited wealth and political experience, but may be comparatively good at the physical labor needed to clear land, at bargaining with neighbors informally to cooperatively protect property rights, and using violence on the occasion that cooperation fails (Alston, Libecap, and Mueller, 1999b: 85). Later settlers may have more human and financial resources. They may be better suited to navigating the bureaucratic hurdles needed to secure de jure property rights, interact with police, or obtain financing to improve their land.[28] Alston, Libecap, and Mueller (1999b) use survey data to test which characteristics make settlers more likely to move, and find that older and wealthier settlers are prone to stay, while younger settlers are more prone to move. Initially locating on the edge of the frontier and subsequently selling to more established settlers is a means by which younger settlers can acquire the experience and capital necessary to develop permanency.

---

[28] A similar pattern of the evolution of property rights happens on technological frontiers. Innovators of new technologies can develop and defend their property rights early on, but often sell out to big firms that are better equipped to navigate mass marketing and patent law (http://blogs.wsj.com/moneybeat/2015/03/16/the-hottest-question-in-pharma-which-company-will-be-next-to-sell/).

Alston, Libecap, and Mueller (1999b: 111) find that settlers in the region around Tucumã, Pará, had four ways in which they could establish property rights over land in the 1980s. On the more legal end of the spectrum, settlers could acquire a legal or a provisional title. On the other end of the spectrum, they could squat on land or purchase the informal rights of a squatter. Their survey results indicate that settlers estimated the increase in land value from having the most recognized title (from INCRA or a private developer) to be around 36 percent over the land value from having less recognized property rights. Regression results based on census data support the finding that having title had a positive effect on land values. The process of moving from no de jure property rights to legal title often involved a period of squatting on land, which was often strategically done to force INCRA to respond. Once on the land, settlers would establish their informal rights by clearing the boundaries of their claim, having sales receipts notarized, paying land taxes, and hiring topographers to map their borders (Alston, Libecap, and Mueller, 1999b: 112). Legal title to the land required that "claimants generally must organize collectively, travel to a local agency office, and formally request surveys and documentation of their land claims" (Alston, Libecap, and Mueller, 1999b: 111). Legal title "reduces private enforcement costs, provides security and collateral for long-term investment in land improvements, and promotes the development of land markets" (Alston, Libecap, and Mueller, 1999b: 110).

As this example illustrates, economic actors weigh the costs and benefits of the available methods of acquiring and maintaining property rights. For many settlers, their investments in establishing property rights resulted in a government-issued title, significantly increasing the value of land and switching some transaction costs of enforcing those rights from individuals to the government. Transaction costs determine whether and how actors establish and maintain property rights. Clearer rights enforced by the government means less use of private violence to establish and maintain property rights. Ultimately, a greater security of rights leads to greater investments in land and infrastructure and higher levels of economic growth.

Conclusion

Transaction costs are everywhere and shape all human interaction, through the expenditure they require, the transactions they shape, and the transactions they prevent from ever occurring. We are constantly establishing and maintaining our ability to enjoy our assets, put them to productive use, and trade them. The resources devoted to engaging in and preventing stealing, shirking, cheating, and rent-seeking are examples of transaction costs. Because these costs are positive, de facto property rights are never perfect. Property rights can be established and maintained at many levels of society. When governments create and enforce laws, they are defining de jure property rights. But laws can never cover the entirety of human interaction, nor can laws ever be perfectly enforced. De facto property rights are therefore always different than de jure rights. Nonetheless, the form of de jure and de facto property rights and the specific balance between the two are important determinants of the level of economic development that society experiences (de Soto, 1989, 2000).

The worlds of zero and infinite transaction costs are equally absurd. In a zero-transaction cost world, the world of the so-called "Coase Theorem," firms and individuals establish, maintain, and trade rights at zero cost. In this world, you do not have to worry about theft, the government rezoning your land, your employee shirking on the job, or buying a lemon when you agreed to a peach. Conversely, in a world of infinite transaction costs, any investment could be immediately appropriated, any employee could baldly shirk, and the quality of any traded good would always be in question. We live in a world of positive, but finite, transaction costs. This world is filled with individuals seeking to achieve their ends at the lowest possible means, which implies that individuals economize on both production and transaction costs. Different organizational structures and institutional environments will generate different costs of establishing and defending property rights. This comparative assessment of organizational and contractual choice is the topic of the next chapter.

3 | *Organizations and Contracts*

In this chapter, we examine the organization of production at the micro level, focusing on the comparative costs and benefits of choosing alternative organizational and contractual forms. Transaction costs drive organizational and contractual choice. In a world in which all transaction costs are zero, production could be organized in many alternative ways. A firm that needed an intermediate part could produce the part itself, purchase it in the spot market, or form a joint venture with a supplier. The means of production could be owned by the government, the customers of the firm, or the suppliers of capital. Employees could be compensated with a flat wage, a piece-rate contract, or a share contract. But in a world of positive transaction costs, the way in which we organize economic activity matters.

Theories that explain the arrangements among economic actors can be understood within a framework of property rights and transaction costs. Different theories focus their attention on different transaction costs, making assumptions, sometimes sweeping, about the extent and importance of other types of transaction costs. Central questions of these theories include: what determines the extent of a firm's activities, how are agreements within and among firms structured, and who reaps the rewards? We draw on the toolkit from the last two chapters to provide some answers. In this chapter, we delve most deeply into one organizational form, the firm. In Part II of this book, we analyze another organization, the government.[1]

In this chapter, we model economic actors as taking social institutions and norms as given and focus on the choice of organization and decision making within organizations.[2] Neoclassical Economics has

---

[1] There are many ways to organize economic and social activity. See, for instance, Ostrom (1990) and Smith (2000) for alternative methods of governing the commons and semicommons.

[2] Williamson (2000) distinguishes among four levels of institutional analysis. The top two levels are the embedded norms and the institutions of society, the topics

traditionally focused on how individuals make decisions on the margin, for example, comparing the cost and benefits to a firm from hiring an extra worker. This focus on marginal decisions has often led neoclassical economics to be described as the "science of choice."[3] The firm itself is a black box, with the transformation of inputs into outputs modelled with a production function. By opening up the black box of the firm and analyzing the inner organization of production, Institutional and Organizational Analysis (IOA) moves the discipline's focus from study of choice to the study of contract (Williamson, 2002).

Case Study: Oil Production and Unitization

Oil production and unitization illustrate the choice of organizational form. The question concerning organization is whether oil extraction should be managed by individual landowners or whether the field should be unified and managed by a single producer. Oil fields in the United States are often located under the property of multiple landowners. Since oil fields are not uniform, oil is migratory, and measuring the quality of a tract is difficult, establishing property rights to oil while it is in the ground is costly.[4] Because of these difficulties, the common law rule regarding oil ownership has been the rule of capture: property rights to oil are established upon extraction. In a system of competitive drilling in which landowners drill and extract oil on their property, the incentive is to pump oil out very quickly. If you control the right to extract oil on a tract and decide not to exercise that right, your neighbor may capture oil located under your property. To make matters worse, new oil fields often have low extraction costs, as subsurface pressure pushes oil to the surface. Excessive drilling and extraction reduces this natural pressure, leading to early depletion of the field, higher extraction costs, and lower aggregate production.

These factors lead to a classic prisoner's dilemma problem. Competitive drillers would be collectively better off if they limited

---

of the previous two chapters. The bottom two levels are governance and resource allocation, the topics of this chapter.

[3] See Backhouse and Medema (2009) for a survey of definitions of economics in a variety of introductory textbooks.

[4] These costs have fallen over time due to improvements in measurement technology.

and coordinated oil extraction, but each has an individual incentive to extract at a faster rate.[5] One solution to the prisoner's dilemma is to unitize the oil field. Unitization and competitive drilling are alternative organizational forms. Under competitive drilling, each landowner decides how much to drill and extract. Under unitization, the drilling and extraction rights are delegated to a single firm that manages the entire field, with each landowner receiving an agreed-upon portion of the net revenues. Unitization contracts are often for the life of the field, at least with the known technology of the day, and involve shutting down certain wells while extracting oil from those wells that maximize the yield from the reservoir. The organizational question is whether a unitization agreement can be reached that transfers extraction rights from the hands of individual landowners into the hands of the unit operator. The collective net revenues under unitization are almost certainly greater than under competitive drilling, but unitization was not a common organizational choice in the United States.[6]

While the transfer of extraction rights to a unit operator seems to be wealth-enhancing, the transaction costs to reorganizing rights are high. The distribution of information across those with rights to oil affects strategic behavior. Prior to production, little is known about the potential productivity of a particular tract. As production on a tract ramps up, more information about the characteristics of an oil field becomes available. Given the high level of subjectivity in interpreting the data, it is difficult to transfer this information to others. Property owners have an incentive to overestimate the oil under their properties in order to get a larger share of the revenue

---

[5] Losses due to overdrilling were estimated at 23 percent of the total value of production in 1914 (Libecap, 1989: 94). These costs include the drilling and maintenance of too many wells, the loss in productivity from overdrilling, the costs of excess storage capacity, and the costs of the loss of oil due to fire and evaporation. The rule of capture was consistently upheld in the courts, even if judges thought it a poor rule. For instance, in *Barnard* v. *Monongahela Natural Gas Co.*, 65 A. 801, 802 (Pa. 1907), the judge ruled that if someone drills a well next to the property line with his neighbor in order to extract natural gas, then the neighbor "must protect his own oil and gas. He knows it is wild and will run away if it finds an opening and it is his business to keep it at home. This may not be the best rule; but neither the Legislature nor our highest court has given us any better."

[6] Estimates of unitization range from 0.4 percent in the United States in 1947 to 38 percent in Oklahoma and 20 percent in Texas in 1975 (Libecap, 1989: 96).

from the unitized field. Parties also have an incentive to hold out from a unitization agreement, as lower extraction rates elsewhere will help keep a holdout's production costs down.[7]

Government rules, most importantly those that determine when unitization takes place and what percentage of a field has to agree to unitization, shape the organization of production. Wiggins and Libecap (1985) found that negotiations to form a unit that began prior to production averaged six months, while negotiations that began after production averaged seven years. The federal government encouraged unitization of reservoirs on federal land at an early stage in the exploration process. Since leaseholders had little information about the quality of their holdings at that early stage of the development process, information asymmetries between parties were less severe. Oklahoma and Texas required fields to be fully developed prior to unitization, making unitization more difficult. Texas required 100 percent agreement on unitization, but once 66 percent of a field in Oklahoma agreed to unitize, the rest of the field was forced to join the unit. This rule difference, combined with the greater dispersion of ownership in Texas, led to much higher unitization rates in Oklahoma.

The rules governing the extraction of oil and natural gas continue to shape the transaction and production costs in these industries. Secondary oil extraction, injecting a fluid or a gas into the reservoir to enhance underground pressure, requires coordination across an oil field. Fracking techniques for natural gas, which send horizontal wells thousands of feet from a central well pad, are limited when property rights near the well pad are not unified. In most countries, subsurface mineral rights are owned by the government, making oil field unification moot. Fields split by a border can cause serious international disputes. Iraq's stated rationale for its 1990 invasion of Kuwait was that Kuwait had used "slant drilling" to extract oil from Iraq's side of the Rumaila oil field, which straddles the border between Iraq and Kuwait, but is primarily located in Iraq (Hayes, 1990). Kuwaiti drillers denied Iraq's accusations of slant drilling, arguing that it was

---

[7] When reservoirs partially unitize, considerable investments can be made to protect oil from flowing to the non-unitized areas of the reservoir. On the Slaughter field in West Texas, 427 water injection wells were sunk at a cost of $156 million in order to "prevent migration of oil across subunit boundaries" (Libecap, 1989: 107).

unnecessary to slant drill when oil flowed so easily under the border. The subsequent invasion of Kuwait can be seen, at least in part, as an attempt to merge control of the oil field by force after repeated attempts by negotiation had failed.

The oil field unitization example can be analyzed through the lens of four theories of the firm that we examine in this chapter: neoclassical theory, agency theory, governance theory, and new property-rights theory.[8] This is by no means a comprehensive exposition of the many theories of the firm, but describes a few of the most important contributions to the field. A neoclassical explanation for unitization would focus on the economies of scale from expanding the production of a single firm. Do average costs fall as the size of the firm increases? Agency theory focuses on the alignment of incentives between a principal and an agent. Under unitization, the unit operator is the agent, the property owners are the principals, and the central question is how to structure the unitization contract in order to maximize the principals' profits. Governance theory focuses on matching transactions with the most appropriate governance structure. If the property owners can overcome the holdout problem and unitize a reservoir, they can eliminate the costs of market-based transactions. Finally, the "new" property-rights theory focuses on who should control productive assets. The party with the most to gain from bundling together the ownership of assets should retain ownership of those assets. We discuss these theories in more detail below, along with additional examples of their application.[9]

Firms in Classical and Neoclassical Economics

The precursor to modern economics is the work of the classical economists, the most important of whom was Adam Smith. While Smith did not have a fully developed theory of the firm, he did have important insights into specialization and the organization of production that remain powerful explanations for the organization

---

[8] See Kim and Mahoney (2005) for the application of various theories of the firm to the oil field unitization story.

[9] See Foss, Lando, and Thomsen (2000) for an overview of the modern theory of the firm, and Klein (2005) and Bresnahan and Levin (2013) for empirical evidence on vertical integration. Gibbons and Roberts (2013) is a handbook with entries on many of the current topics in organizations and contracts.

of economic activity. Two famous examples, the production of pins and the production of a woolen coat, illustrate the division of labor in a single factory and across society. In his pin factory example, Smith compares the limited output of a single workman doing all stages of production with the increased output associated with specialization within the firm. Smith claims that a single workman could, "with his utmost industry, make one pin in a day, and certainly could not make twenty." In contrast, he describes a small factory, where "one man draws out the wire, another straights it, a third cuts it, a fourth points it, a fifth grinds it at the top for receiving the head; to make the head requires two or three distinct operations," and ten men could "make among them about ... forty-eight thousand pins in a day" (Smith [1776] 2007: 9).

Smith had a similar description of the division of labor in the production of a wool coat. "The woollen coat ... is the produce of the joint labour of a great multitude of workmen. The shepherd, the sorter of the wool, the wool-comber or carder, the dyer, the scribbler, the spinner, the weaver, the fuller, the dresser, with many others, must all join their different arts in order to complete even this homely production" (13). The production of a coat requires "the assistance and co-operation of many thousands" (14) who are geographically and organizationally dispersed. What Smith does not explain is whether this division of labor should happen in a single or in separate firms. Who owns and controls the inputs used in the production process? Who is an employee and who is a boss? What brings the ten workers together within the pin factory while the thousands of workers producing the coat are organized by the price mechanism? The implicit answer is that the production of pins is done at a lower cost within a single manufactory, while the stages of production of a woolen coat are done at a lower cost when performed within separate organizational units.

Smith provides explanations for the limits to the division of labor, the most important of which is the "extent of the market":

As it is the power of exchanging that gives occasion to the division of labour, so the extent of this division must always be limited by the extent of that power, or, in other words, by the extent of the market. ([1776] 2007: 19)

Smith points out an additional limiting factor that anticipates agency theory in the modern IOA, the behavior of managers versus the desires of owners. After describing how managers of joint stock companies have the incentive to act in their own self-interest rather than in the interest of owners, Smith concludes:

Negligence and profusion, therefore, must always prevail, more or less, in the management of the affairs of such a company ... They have, accordingly, very seldom succeeded without an exclusive privilege, and frequently have not succeeded with one. ([1776] 2007: 575)

To summarize, Smith provided foundational insights into the existence and limits of manufacturing firms. The growth of firms is due to the division of labor, and the limit to that growth is due to the extent of the market. A particular form of firm, the joint stock company, is limited in its usefulness due to the agency problem between owners and managers. This implies that the extent of the market is limited by the extent of transaction costs.

A simple neoclassical theory models firms as profit-maximizing entities. Firms use inputs (in a production function) to create output. The production function is all that we know about the firm. In the competitive model, the wages of the inputs and the price of the output are fixed, making the firm a price taker. The firm continues to grow until it maximizes the difference between revenues and costs, that is, when the value of the marginal product (the extra revenue gained from hiring an additional unit of input) is equal to the wage. Williamson (1985) summarizes the neoclassical theory of the firm circa 1970 in the following manner: "The allocation of economic activity as between firms and markets was taken as a datum; firms were characterized as production functions; markets served as signaling devices; contracting was accomplished through an auctioneer; and disputes were disregarded because of the presumed efficacy of court adjudication" (7). The firm was a piece of the larger theoretical framework for understanding the operation of markets, but its internal characteristics went largely unexamined.

Neoclassical price theory can have a variety of assumptions and predictions. Given the assumptions of perfect competition (many buyers and sellers, a homogeneous product, easy entry and exit, and zero transaction costs), firms are price takers and make zero economic profits in the long run. Given the assumptions of a single-price monopoly (a single seller with high barriers to entry selling a single product at a single price to many buyers), a monopolist can make positive economic profits in the long run. These market structures are the end points of the competitive spectrum. Firms in the neoclassical model are monopolists either because of economies of scale or because barriers to entry keep competition at bay.[10] Non-standard contracting, such as resale price maintenance or exclusive dealing, "was presumed to have monopoly purpose and effect" (Williamson, 1985: 26). Transaction cost analysis muddies these relatively clear waters (Klein, 1980). Are deviations away from the perfectly competitive outcome solely due to monopoly power, or are there efficiency explanations for firm behavior? Answering this question requires expertise and judgment on the part of the analyst and means that there are fewer clear generalizations that can be made from simple assumptions.

Monitoring and Agency Theory

One strand of the theory of the firm literature focuses on costs of measuring actions and outputs and asks how contracts can be structured to best incentivize agents to act in the interests of their principals.[11] This literature assumes that there is an information asymmetry between principals and agents. As described in Chapter 2, either there is a "hidden action" that the agent can take or there is "hidden information" that only one party to the transaction knows (Arrow, 1985). Hidden action can lead to moral hazard, where one party to a transaction may undertake actions that are difficult to monitor and affect the other party's valuation (Arrow, 1968; Pauly, 1968). Hidden information can lead to adverse selection, where one party to a transaction has information relevant to the transaction that is costly to transmit and that affects the other party's valuation (Akerlof, 1970). In the health insurance market, an example of moral hazard is an increase in risk-taking after individuals purchase insurance. An example of adverse selection is when actors with preexisting conditions hide that information when initially signing up for insurance. The problems disappear if insurance companies could costlessly measure the actions or the quality of applicants, or if customers could costlessly signal their actions or quality.

---

[10] See Goldberg and Erickson (1987) and Masten and Snyder (1993) for a reevaluation of antitrust cases in petroleum coke and shoe manufacturing.

[11] All modern theories of the firm have their roots in Coase (1937). Coase posed the fundamental question: why do firms exist given that they must absorb monitoring costs? His answer: there must be costs of using the market.

Alchian and Demsetz (1972) offer one view of the firm based on the transaction cost of ensuring worker output. They note that "the classic relationship in economics that runs from marginal productivity to the distribution of income implicitly assumes the existence of an organization, be it the market or the firm, that allocates rewards to resources in accord with their productivity" (778). But when there is information asymmetry, linking productivity and rewards is costly. These costs consist of "(1) the monitoring expenditures of the principal, (2) the bonding expenditures of the agent, and (3) the residual loss" (Jensen and Meckling, 1976: 308). Some mechanism must be in place to incentivize work. Alchian and Demsetz's question is why that mechanism is sometimes located in the marketplace and sometimes inside a firm.

For some types of production, work effort and output are directly correlated, and measured output can therefore be used as the basis for a compensation scheme. However, some types of production are done using a team production process, which requires multiple resources whose output is not a good measure of individual effort.[12] One option for compensating a team would be for the firm to offer a contract that pays a wage based on the productivity of the team as a whole. However, this contract encourages shirking on the part of individual workers. Additional effort by a team member will increase overall productivity, but the team member only receives a fraction of that additional productivity. Workers will therefore shirk. A centralized monitor who observes effort rather than output would be able to reduce shirking (Alchian and Demsetz, 1972). Rather than measuring how many boxes have been stacked or sales have been made, the monitor measures how hard each member works at contributing to the joint output of the team. In Alchian and Demsetz's theory, the firm has no greater or lesser ability to order the actions of the employee. It merely has an improved ability to monitor work effort and mete out rewards for that effort. The question becomes, "Who will monitor the monitor?" That is, how does one ensure that the boss is working hard? Their answer is that by making the monitor the residual claimant of the

---

[12] An example of a job in which work effort and observed output are closely correlated is a fieldworker tasked with picking crops. An example of a team production process is a group assignment for class for which the professor sees the output of the entire group but cannot measure how hard each group member worked, nor their human capital or knowledge into the output.

firm's net revenues, the monitor has the incentive to monitor the work effort of the employees.[13]

Alchian and Demsetz (1972) define the firm in terms of property rights. The owner of their "capitalist, free enterprise" firm has the rights: "(1) to be a residual claimant, (2) to observe input behavior, (3) to be the central party common to all contracts with inputs, (4) to alter the membership of the team, and (5) to sell these rights" (783). When team production makes market contracting with individual owners costly, parties choose the organizational structure of the firm. If the output of the worker were a perfect measure of productivity, or if work effort could be monitored perfectly within a market setting, then work could be organized either through a market transaction, a firm, or any other organizational form.

An important advance in a measurement theory of the firm came in a series of papers by Holmström and Milgrom (1991, 1994), who analyze a multitask principal-agent model. Again, there is a measurement problem. Some metrics of employee performance may be either costly to measure or do not capture the totality of the agent's contribution to profitability. Incentivizing one measurable aspect of a job while not incentivizing another unmeasurable aspect will cause workers to spend too much effort on the measurable aspect. An example of this phenomenon is whether to base teacher pay on the performance of their students on a standardized exam. Holmström and Milgrom (1991) model two types of activities that teachers engage in: teaching basic skills and teaching higher-order skills. They assume that the standardized exam can test basic, but not higher-order, skills. If teaching the two skills are complementary in the teacher's private cost function, then incentivizing the teaching of basic skills will also incentivize teaching higher-order skills. But if the two inputs are substitutes, then incentivizing basic skills will reduce the incentive to teach higher-order skills. Teachers will "teach to the test," or, even worse, engage in cheating to raise their students' scores (Jacob and Levitt, 2003).[14] In general, when inputs are substitutes, more of an input will be supplied

---

[13] The residual claimant receives the firm's profits or bears the firm's losses. For example, in a sole proprietorship, the owner is the residual claimant.

[14] Similarly, college students are often graded based on their performance on several tests. They therefore have the incentive to study material relevant to performing well on the test rather than material that may be more central to understanding the content of a course.

by either raising the incentive to supply it or lowering the incentive to supply substitutes.

The "incentive instruments" available to the principal in a principal-agent relationship are complementary (Holmström and Milgrom, 1991). Suppose the agent performs three tasks: produce a high level of quality output, follow the principal's directions, and maintain the capital stock. If the principal-agent relationship is within a firm, the agents are likely to have weak output-based incentives, be subject to the firm's authority, and not own the assets with which they work. Firms are more likely to hire employees when some important dimensions of a job are unmeasurable. Giving employees high-powered incentives on a measurable metric, like output, may cause the employee to fail to perform an unmeasurable task, like maintaining the firm's assets. If the principal-agent relationship is structured within the market, independent contractors are likely to have strong output-based incentives, not be subject to the firm's authority, and own the assets with which they work. If all of the important dimensions of a job are measurable, that job is more likely to be done by an independent contractor. Evidence from the structure of employment of the sales force in the electronic components industry, provided by Anderson and Schmittlein (1984), supports the hypothesis that the "perceived difficulty of measuring sales of individual salespeople (due to team selling or costly record keeping) was the best empirical predictor of the use of an in-house sales force" (Holmström and Milgrom, 1991: 37).

Case Study: Postbellum Southern Agriculture

What happens when de jure property rights to an important input into the production process are suddenly taken from one group and given to another? This happened in the United States (and elsewhere) with the abolition of slavery. The abolition of slavery transferred the de jure rights to labor from slave owners to former slaves. The disruption of labor relations was enormous. The Emancipation Proclamation and the Thirteenth Amendment were formal changes in the rules. The interpretation of institutions and the extant norms surrounding race relations continue to have ramifications through today, including questions surrounding the Voting and Civil Rights Acts, reparations, racial profiling, and racial preferences in college admissions. And yet, with all the turmoil in the US South after the Civil War, some things stayed the same. While their legal status changed, many African American laborers stayed on the farm, under the supervision of plantation owners who were previously their owners. Labor relations needed to be organized around the newly acquired de jure rights of freed slaves.

A great deal of experimentation followed emancipation, with regularities in organizational choice occurring over time. The three "grand classes" of contractual forms included: "wage labor, crop sharing, and fixed-payment land rental" (Alston and Higgs, 1982: 329). These contracts formed a rough agricultural ladder, with wage laborers at the bottom and renters at the top. Rental contracts are most similar to a market transaction, while wage labor is most similar to a firm, but there was great variety within each grand class. For instance, sharecropping contracts could vary in the share ratio, the assets supplied by each party, and the amount of supervision by the landowner. Other examples of hybrids include "croppers who worked some of the time for wages, or tenants who paid a share rent on their cotton crop and a fixed rent for their corn land" (Alston and Higgs, 1982: 329). The wide diversity of contractual arrangements continued through at least the middle of the twentieth century.[15]

Many factors affected the contracts between the suppliers of labor and land. Landowners wanted workers who stayed on the farm, worked hard, and maintained the capital stock. Cotton is a seasonal crop, and demand for labor is highest during harvest. Wage laborers had an incentive to leave the farm during harvest in search of higher-paying work, while sharecroppers and tenants, due to their residual ownership of their output, were incentivized to stay on the farm. This residual ownership also gave sharecroppers and tenants a greater incentive than wage workers to work hard, all else equal. Why then were wage contracts used at all?

One explanation for the contractual mix rests on the varied human and physical capital of farm workers. If a laborer did not own any physical capital, landowners could supply mules and other equipment needed to farm. Landlords would supervise the use of mules in order to protect themselves against capital loss. This supervision often involved the housing of mules in a central barn and control over their daily use.

---

[15]   See Allen and Lueck (2003) for a well-developed model of crop share versus cash rent tenancy contracts.

If the landlord was already supervising the use of capital, the marginal cost of monitoring work effort was low, leading to more wage and fewer share or rental contracts. A lower-powered wage contract would also reduce the incentive to overwork the mule. The use of wage contracts was particularly likely for younger workers who neither owned sufficient levels of physical capital nor possessed the requisite knowledge to farm on their own. Older laborers were more likely to have higher levels of human and physical capital, requiring less monitoring, and were therefore more likely to see rental contracts. While there was great variability of contracts, the complementarity of monitoring costs along with other factors help explain "the spatial and temporal variance of the contractual mix" (Alston and Higgs, 1982: 341).

Asset Specificity and Governance Theory

Governance theory develops a framework to explain why "different kinds of transactions are more efficiently governed by different modes of governance" (Tadelis and Williamson, 2013: 163). An important question within this literature is whether to make or buy: when should firms produce intermediate parts internally and when should they contract for them in the marketplace? The central determinant of whether to make or buy lies in the type of assets used to make the intermediate part. If the assets used to make the part are specialized, then the firm is more likely to internalize production. If the assets are general and can be used for many purposes, then the firm is more likely to purchase the part in the market.

The decision to make or buy partially rests on the different de jure rights granted to market vs. internal firm transactions, which shape the transaction costs of using alternative organizational forms. Masten (1988) finds a series of differences in how agency law views employment versus commercial transactions, particularly the power that employment gives employers to monitor workers and the greater incentives employees have to follow their employer's instructions. These include the duty of an employee to obey the rules and instructions of the employer, to reveal greater levels of information than required in a commercial transaction, and to maintain "friendly relations" with the employer. The doctrine of *respondeat superior* makes employers liable for employees' actions that are performed within the context of the employment relationship. This doctrine shelters employees from liability for harm that they cause while following the instructions of the employer and gives the employer the incentive to monitor the actions of the employee. Masten (1988: 195) concludes that the "differences in legal defaults, sanctions, and procedures governing commercial and employment transactions provide a constructive, as opposed to merely descriptive, connotation to the notion of the firm."

Different rules (norms and institutions) govern relationships within firms than relationships within markets: "Whereas courts routinely grant standing to firms should there be disputes over prices, the damages to be ascribed to delays, failures of quality, and the like, courts will refuse to hear disputes between one internal division and another over identical technical issues ... Accordingly, hierarchy is its own court of ultimate appeal" (Williamson, 1996: 98). The examples provided by Masten and Williamson indicate that there are differences in the allocation of property rights between standard form employment and commercial contracts. While parties to an employment contract have the ability to "contract out of or away from" the governance structures of the state by devising private orderings" (Williamson, 1996: 121), doing so incurs additional costs. We therefore observe a great deal of economic activity organized around a group of standard forms, like corporations and partnerships, the production and transaction costs of which must be evaluated in a comparative perspective.

Specific assets play a central role in explaining the limits of the firm in governance theory.[16] Assets are specific when their productivity is higher in one specialized use than in alternative uses. Specific investments can be made in human capital, like learning how to navigate a unique operating system; in physical capital, like a die used only to stamp a specific auto body part; or in capacity, like a mine built to service only one customer. A pipeline that transfers oil from a well to a refinery is more specific than a truck used for that same purpose. If the owners of the well and the truck come to a disagreement, the truck can be put to many alternative uses. The pipeline can be disassembled and moved only at great cost. The use of specific

[16] Foundational work in this literature includes Williamson (1971, 1975, 1985) and Klein, Crawford, and Alchian (1978).

assets leads to quasi-rents, the difference in the value of an asset in its current use and its next best use.

Investments in specific assets lead to lock-in between two trading partners, allowing one or both of the parties to act opportunistically towards the other. This is possible because contracts are incomplete. No contract can cover all of the contingencies that might occur, and the costs of enforcing contractual stipulations are positive. When assets are specific, the "wider variety and greater sensitivity of control instruments that are available to enforcing intrafirm in comparison with interfirm activities" makes fiat "frequently a more efficient way to settle minor conflicts (say differences of interpretation) than is haggling or litigation" (Williamson, 1971: 114). Identifying and formalizing the source of the differences in inter vs. intrafirm transaction costs is a continuing source of inquiry in this literature (Gibbons, 2005; Tadelis and Williamson, 2013).

Suppose that a manufacturer needs component parts in order to produce a new product. Which of these parts will it produce in-house and which will it acquire from outside suppliers? For any one part, the manufacturer may initially be able to choose between many possible suppliers. Once the manufacturer decides on a supplier, that supplier may need to invest in assets specific to producing the parts. Once that specific investment is made, the trading partners are no longer operating in a competitive market, but have entered into a bilateral relationship. Williamson calls this switch from a competitive market to a bilateral relationship the "fundamental transformation." Once this shift occurs, several contracting costs arise, including: "(1) the maladaptation costs incurred when transactions drift out of alignment ... (2) the haggling costs incurred if bilateral efforts are made to correct *ex post* misalignments, (3) the setup and running costs associated with the governance structures (often not the courts) to which disputes are referred, and (4) the bonding costs of effecting secure commitments" (Williamson, 1985: 21; emphasis in original).

Williamson uses two characteristics of transactions – their frequency and the specificity of assets used to support them – to predict the governance of transactions. Transactions that use non-specific assets are most likely to be organized through market governance, thereby taking advantage of economies of scale and specialization. Transactions that use idiosyncratic assets and are recurrent are most likely to be organized using unified governance, reducing the ability of either party to act opportunistically. Transactions with intermediate levels of specificity will be governed through either trilateral or bilateral governance. Trilateral governance is used when transactions occur occasionally, and rely on third parties, such as the courts or an arbitrator, to settle any disputes. Bilateral governance is used when transactions occur frequently, and rely on the continuing relationship between the contracting parties. Bilateral and unified governance are relational contracts, in which the parties are in a long-term relationship and which occur when actions "cannot be specified *ex ante* or verified *ex post*" (Gibbons and Henderson, 2012: 697; emphasis in original). Because these relationships are hard to describe, they can be slow to diffuse between firms.[17]

If the costs of using the marketplace are positive, Williamson asks why all transactions are not incorporated into a single firm. Cost-reducing integration could be achieved by judiciously using fiat for the market transactions that are most troublesome while retaining market-like governance for all remaining transactions. His answer is that there are transaction costs of organizing economic activity within a firm. These include the costs of maintaining high-powered incentives within a firm, such as asset utilization losses and accounting contrivances. Asset utilization losses occur when managers with high-powered incentives allow assets to depreciate in order to pump up short-term profits. Accounting contrivances occur when owners and managers with high-powered incentives try to alter the internal transfer price, the price at which intermediate products are transferred between divisions of a firm and an important metric used to measure a manager's performance. Additional costs are those associated with switching from market to bureaucratic control, such as forgiveness and logrolling. Forgiveness refers to the greater likelihood that a firm will forgive an unexpected cost increase from an employee than a supplier. Logrolling is related to a norm of reciprocity, where managers in a firm engage in reciprocal back-scratching.[18]

---

[17] An example of this slow diffusion is provided by Helper and Henderson (2014) and Gibbons and Henderson (2012), who describe the difficulty that American auto manufacturers had in understanding the operation and benefits of the Toyota Production System. This example was covered in more detail in the Introduction to Part I.

[18] Milgrom and Roberts (1990) argue that the transaction costs of operating within the firm are the costs associated with influencing the actions of people within the firm who have the ability to make decisions over assets.

Case Study: Coal Mines and Power Plants

The contracts that govern the transfer of coal between mines and power plants exhibit tremendous regional variability in the United States, with contracts lasting between one and fifty years. Joskow (1985, 1987) gathered data on approximately 300 contracts between mines and power plants to test for the effects of three types of asset specificity on contract duration. Coal varies in its Btu, sulfur, moisture, and chemical content, and power plants are specialized to burn one type of coal. The coal market exhibits strong regional variation in characteristics related to asset specificity. The market is generally thicker in the East than the West, with the East having denser rail and water transportation networks, more power plants, and more coal mines. The coal mines in the East are more often underground, while surface mines in the West are generally much larger. Contracts are therefore typically for larger quantities in the West than in the East. Mines in the West are also often located "cheek by jowl" with the plant, supplying most or all of the plant's needs.

Because of these regional differences, mines and power plants in the West are more likely to make specific investments that can be appropriated by their trading partners. Investments are site specific, co-located to reduce transportation costs; physical asset specific, requiring plants and mines to make investments specific to the other party's needs; and dedicated, made to satisfy the trading partner's needs. Mines in the West sign contracts that are approximately five years longer than those in the East, and mine-mouth plants sign contracts between fourteen and sixteen years longer than other plants (Joskow, 1985: 47).

Contracts involving mine-mouth plants are often complex. The typical length of a contract is thirty-five years, and contracts include requirements for quality and methods for determining price. Both parties benefit from quality requirements. Power plants want coal that has been cleaned properly and has a higher Btu content. Quality requirements can reduce a mine operator's incentive to save costs by delivering low-quality coal. But mines also can benefit from quality requirements, as those requirements can protect them from claims by the power plant that the mine is not providing good coal. A clearly written contract can protect both parties from opportunistic behavior. A second transaction cost is associated with the process of determining the transfer price of coal over the length of the contract. Since there is no good spot-market reference price for mine-mouth coal, firms determine prices by cost-plus or base price escalation rules, and contracts sometimes have clauses for price renegotiation. A final set of transaction costs arise out of dispute resolution. In order to settle disputes in a low-cost manner, the contracts often contain provisions for arbitration. This takes the contract dispute out of the legal system and places it into what is often a lower-cost arbitration system.

Ownership and the "New" Property-Rights Theory

A "new" property-rights theory of the firm has developed around the work of Grossman and Hart (1986), Hart and Moore (1990), and Hart (1995), often referred to as the GHM theory. This theory shares the assumptions of incomplete contracts and specific investments with Williamson's governance theory, but focuses on how to optimize investment incentives when some investments are non-contractible. An investment is non-contractible when it cannot be verified by third parties, such as courts. For example, a nursing home might make verifiable investments in amenities in room quality but unverifiable investments in patient care. Because the room can be entered and checked, room quality is easily verified. But the quality of patient care can be strategically altered and difficult to document, making it costly to monitor and convey to a third party. In the GHM framework, the firm is a collection of physical assets, and incentives to make non-contractible investments increase for the party who owns the asset. When two firms merge, the acquiring firm has stronger incentives to invest, while the target firm has lower incentives. This theory not only provides a rationale for market transactions versus unified control, but also provides an explanation for which direction control rights will go when two firms integrate.

An example can illustrate the basic logic of the model. Suppose there are two stages to a production process. The upstream supplier makes an intermediate part that it sells to the final producer, who sells it to the consumer. The model assumes both firms incur some costs of production that are verifiable and some that are not. The verifiable investment might be in a piece of machinery, while the unverifiable investment is an update to the operating system that runs the machinery. Making the unverifiable investments reduces the overall cost of production. The model assumes that the firms cannot contract on the unverifiable costs, the price of the intermediate good, or on a cost-sharing rule. They can costlessly contract to a 50/50 split of the verifiable profits, which are the final sale price minus verifiable costs. Because of these assumptions, the benefit of a non-verifiable investment is shared equally between the two parties, but its cost is paid entirely by the party who makes it. Situations can occur in which both parties would be better off if they both made the non-verifiable investment, but neither party has the individual incentive to do so.

This is a classic prisoner's dilemma game. Given the assumptions of the model, it is not possible to get either party to make the unverifiable investments. Integration can partially solve the problem. If the upstream supplier buys the final producer, then the upstream supplier will be the residual claimant of the integrated firms' profits instead of splitting profits 50/50 with the final producer. Even after the merger, the non-verifiable investments remain non-verifiable, so the final producer cannot be forced to make the non-verifiable investment. All the benefits from the merger come from the acquiring firm's greater incentive to invest. This example not only provides the rationale for integration, but the rationale for who should own the productive assets. The party whose ownership will result in investments that lead to the largest marginal gain in profits should own the assets.

While the governance and GHM theories of the firm share many of the same assumptions, their empirical implications differ. Williamson's governance theory posits that transactions are matched to a wide array of organizational choices, with greater levels of uncertainty, complexity, and asset specificity moving a transaction away from market and towards unified governance. In the GHM model, productive assets should be owned by the party that generates the highest marginal return from making the non-verifiable investments. Identifying the non-verifiable investments and measuring their marginal returns are both difficult, making the GHM model hard to test empirically (Whinston, 2003). However, it is an important building block for other theories, including the ownership structure of the firm.

Ownership of the Firm

Extensions to the GHM framework provide insights into who should own a firm. Hansmann (1996, 2013a, 2016) thinks of a firm as a "nexus for contracting" with the firms' patrons, including customers and suppliers of labor, capital, and intermediate products.[19] A firm can be owned by any group of these patrons. Consumer cooperatives are owned by the firm's customers, worker cooperatives are owned by the suppliers of labor, and business corporations are owned by the suppliers of capital. Ownership grants the right to the firm's profits and control the firm's actions.

One reason to make a set of patrons the owners of the firm is to reduce the costs of contracting between the patrons and the firm due to "market power, asymmetric information, or the need for the patrons to make transaction-specific investments" (Hansmann, 2013b: 898). An example is the exploitation of customers by firms that have monopoly power. Historical examples include grain elevators, local telephone service providers, and grocery stores. Having these firms owned by their customers gave the customers the right to reduce those firms' profits by lowering prices closer to marginal costs. While retail cooperatives are rare today, consumer cooperatives are still common in the wholesale markets of many industries, supplying independent grocery, hardware, and drug stores (Hansmann, 1996).

Corporations are cooperatives that are collectively owned by the suppliers of capital and provide protection for those owners. Were firms to raise capital only in the debt market, then the creditors would be subject to agency problems discussed in Jensen and Meckling (1976). Suppose a firm is run by its managers, who are also the residual claimants, while capital is raised as long-term debt. Since creditors receive a fixed rate of return, the managers have an incentive to pursue risky profit opportunities. If the bet pays off, the managers receive a large payoff. If the bet does not pay off, then the lenders bear the cost. Knowing this, lenders will charge a higher interest rate, driving up the cost of capital. Making the providers of capital the owners of the firm reduces the incentive for excessive risk-taking.[20]

---

[19] Hansmann (1988: 270) defines the firm's patrons as "all persons who transact with a firm, either as purchasers of the firm's products or as suppliers to the firm of some factor of production, including capital."

[20] The agency cost of debt is balanced against the agency cost of non-manager owned equity, which is that managers have an incentive to manage companies for their own benefit rather than the benefit of shareholders.

While suppliers of any input into the production process can cooperatively own the firm, in practice, only three types of supplier-owned
enterprises are common: "investor-owned firms, worker-owned firms,
and farmer-owned firms" (Hansmann, 1996: 142). The reason why
ownership is usually held by a group with homogeneous interests is that
the costs of collective decision making increase with the heterogeneity of
the owners' interests. Stockholders in a corporation all have their own
interests, but their interests in the firm are "typically homogenized by
giving them all shares of a single class of common stock with uniform
rights" (Hansmann, 2013b: 904). Stockholders want to earn returns by
the appreciation in the price of the stock or by receiving dividends. An
example of a worker-owned firm is a law firm, where partners are
residual claimants and exercise residual control rights. Partners at leading
law firms are often compensated by age, sacrificing productivity incentives to homogenize their interests in the firm and reduce conflicts over
compensation schemes. Firms in which ownership is split between different classes of patrons with heterogeneous interests often end with failure.
Such was the case of United Airlines, whose reorganization in 1994 split
ownership between investors, pilots, and mechanics. The divergent interests of those three groups contributed to conflicts that resulted in United
Airlines' reorganization as an investor-owned corporation.

Even local governments can be modeled as consumer-owned cooperatives (Hansmann, 2013a). Residents demand services, such as roads,
schools, sewage, and police, that could be provided by either private
enterprises or local governments. Because relocation costs are high,
residents are locked into a locality, giving the providers of services some
monopoly power. Residents can counteract this monopoly power
either through regulation of a private enterprise or through the provision of the service by the government. Services that are more subject to
competition, like trash collection, are more likely to be organized as
private enterprises than services that are likely to be monopolies, like
sewage or water. Residents have residual control over their governments that they can exercise in the voting booth or through other forms
of political participation.

Hybrids

The governance of production can be structured in many different
ways, with hierarchies and the price mechanism at two ends of the

spectrum (Hennart, 1993). But the "swollen middle" between those two endpoints accounts for much productive activity. The great variability in how production can be organized led Cheung (1983: 10) to conclude that "it is futile to press the issue of what is or is not a firm ... The important questions are why contracts take the forms observed and what are the economic implications of different contractual and pricing arrangements." Franchises are an important example of an organizational form in the swollen middle and account for a large portion of economic activity within certain sectors. Traditional franchisees, like automobile and gas dealers, are retailers that sell the franchisor's product. Business format franchisees, like chain restaurants and hotels, adopt the franchisor's business plan and are trained, supported, and monitored by the franchisor. Combined sales of these two forms totaled 9.2 percent of US GDP in 2007 (Kosová and Lafontaine, 2012).

Hybrids differ from the price system and hierarchies because there are some rights to decisions or to payoffs that are shared by the two partners. In the case of franchising, the franchisee gives up some decision rights while pooling payoffs with the franchisor "to benefit from brand names and joint actions" (Ménard, 2013: 1072). For example, about 80 percent of McDonald's restaurants are owned and operated by franchisees, who "maintain control over staffing, purchasing, marketing and pricing decisions, while also benefiting from the strength of McDonald's global brand, operating system and financial resources."[21] For most of the restaurants, McDonald's owns or leases the land and building, and the franchisee "pays for equipment, signs, seating and décor." Franchisees pay rent, a royalty on sales, and an up-front fee to open a new location. This arrangement is more complicated than a simple arm's-length market transaction, but only scratches the surface of the intermediate forms available between the price system and hierarchies.

Ménard (2013) and Baker, Gibbons, and Murphy (2008) provide frameworks for classifying and identifying hybrids, parts of which we will use here to illustrate some of the benefits and costs of "going hybrid." Two firms (1 and 2) have assets (A and B) that are private to each, and assets (a and b) that are only valuable if used together. The rights to these

---

[21] See www.sec.gov/Archives/edgar/data/63908/000006390816000103/mcd-123 12015x10k.htm.

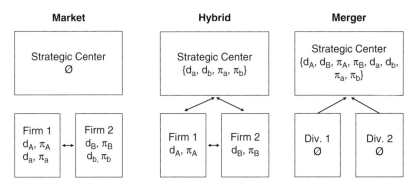

Figure 3.1 Modes of organization
Source: Modified from Ménard (2013: 1074).

assets can be classified as either decision rights or rights to payoffs. The decision rights are d_a and d_b for the joint assets and d_A and d_B for the private assets.[22] The rights to the payoffs for the joint assets are π_a and π_b. These are assumed to be zero if used separately, and positive if they are used jointly. The payoffs of concern for the private assets are those that involve spillovers from the joint assets. These could be either positive or negative. *Ex post*, coordinating with Firm 2 could make Firm 1 better off when there are positive spillovers or worse off if there are negative spillovers. Neither party knows *ex ante* whether the outcome will be positive or negative. This is indicated by a state variable s that is revealed after the governance structure is chosen. The values of the spillovers on the private assets are therefore $\pi_A(s)$ and $\pi_B(s)$. Three allocations of these rights are illustrated in Figure 3.1.

In a pure market transaction, each firm controls the decision and payoff rights to both the private and joint assets. If the firms merge, the unified firm controls all of the rights and the two firms become divisions of the merged firm. But in a hybrid, the joint rights (or a subset of them) are placed in the strategic center, outside of the control of the two firms. In the center figure of Figure 3.1, both firms divest themselves of their joint assets, which is a total divestiture. In a strategic divestiture, the rights of only one firm are placed in the strategic center. In a licensing agreement, the decision rights to the joint asset from one firm, say Firm 2, are

---

[22] There could be multiple decision rights associated with each asset, so there is a vector of rights. This harkens back to the view of property rights as a "bundle of sticks."

transferred to Firm 1, while Firm 2 retains the return on its asset (Baker, Gibbons, and Murphy, 2008).

Why might firms decide to "go hybrid" and cooperate with their competitors? There are many potential explanations, but we focus on the spillover effects of the joint investments on the private investments of each firm.[23] When Firm 1 and Firm 2 decide to give up some decision rights to the strategic center, they are losing control over the use of assets, but may receive payments from those assets and spillovers from those joint assets on their private assets. Two subcategories under spillover effects are the complementarities between the joint and private assets and the learning that occurs from the joint investments (Ménard, 2013: 1080). Giving up some control may help secure access to new markets or resources that are unavailable to the individual firms. It may also allow firms to learn from their investment in the strategic center in ways that allow them to use their core assets more productively.

Many McDonald's restaurants outside of the United States use a developmental licensing agreement, in which the licensees provide all the capital and McDonald's receives an upfront licensing fee and royalties based on sales. Using the terms from Figure 3.1, assume McDonald's is Firm 1 and a local entrepreneur is Firm 2. Both firms transfer some of their assets to the strategic center, which is the new McDonald's restaurant. This investment will yield direct returns that each party can capture and also has spillover effects on their other assets. Using such an agreement allows McDonald's to enter markets in which it may be costly for it to own real estate and negotiate with local regulators. A local partner can negotiate the uncertainty involved in opening a new restaurant better than McDonald's can. Opening the restaurant may either increase or decrease the return on McDonald's core assets. If it is a success and McDonald's can add another country to its list of locations, the value of the brand goes up. If the restaurant reflects poorly on the brand, the brand's value goes down. McDonald's may also learn how to enter new markets through the experience. Similarly, the local entrepreneur's reputation may rise or fall with the

---

[23] Ménard (2013) also discusses the role of uncertainty as a possible explanation for hybrids. Makadok and Coff (2009) model a hybrid's ability to motivate cooperation in the spirit of Holmström and Milgrom (1994). Williamson (1996) explains hybrids as an intermediate form of contracting with moderate uncertainty and asset specificity.

success of the restaurant and the entrepreneur may learn from the experience in ways that allow her to be successful in other non-McDonald's ventures.

Sports leagues are another example in which competitors cooperate and in which the spillover effects can be enormous. While the New England Patriots and New York Giants are competitors on the field, they cooperate through the National Football League (NFL). Without a league to structure their interaction, their individual game would be much less valuable. Both teams give up certain rights (the league makes and enforces rules about how the game is played and how players must act both on and off the field) in exchange for a much higher return on their private assets.[24] The NFL is organized as a trade association, with the commissioner and conference presidents elected by the team owners and revenues from broadcasting deals split evenly between the teams.[25] In 2016, NFL teams shared more than $7 billion in league revenues.[26]

Hybrids vary in their degree of formality. Some, like McDonald's franchises, can be seen as quasi-integrated, with significant decision rights being held by the franchisor. Others, like biotech alliances or trade associations, can be more informal, with fewer decision and payoff rights moved to the strategic center.[27] Firms engaged in hybrid relationships can act opportunistically towards one another either by transferring assets to the strategic center that are below the agreed-upon quality or capturing output above the agreed-upon sharing rule. For example, a McDonald's franchisee could shirk and provide level of service below that specified by the franchisor, free-riding on the brand name. Biotechnology firms involved in a joint R&D venture could transfer resources to the joint venture that maximize their own returns rather than the collective returns of the joint venture. Uncertainty and information asymmetry are inherent in R&D projects, making it

---

[24] The rules give the commissioner broad powers to investigate and punish "conduct detrimental to the integrity" of the NFL.

[25] Prior to 2015, the NFL was organized as a non-profit.

[26] See www.bloomberg.com/news/articles/2016–06–24/nfl-revenue-reaches-7–1-billion-based-on-green-bay-report.

[27] The degree of formality can be correlated with the strength of the network. Robinson and Stuart (2006: 243) find that "better networked firms rely less on explicit control mechanisms such as equity ownership and more on implicit, network-based control, all else equal."

difficult to specify output-sharing rules ex ante and giving both parties the ability to capture rents.

Firms use a variety of instruments to protect their property rights in a hybrid organization. One method is to find trading partners who are more likely to act faithfully. Signals of reputation include dealings in other hybrid arrangements and information from shared social ties.[28] Firms also build trust from repeated dealings. Baker, Gibbons, and Murphy (2008) find that firms in the pharma-biotech industry engage in alliances that "are often long-lived and involve continuing interactions between the parties," and "engage in repeat alliances with the same partner" (161). Firms can also use screening procedures to find partners more likely to act faithfully. Kaufmann and Lafontaine (1994) analyze McDonald's methods for screening for franchisees who have "ketchup in their veins." These include 2,000 hours of training, policies forbidding passive investors and absentee owners, and structuring the franchise fee so that promising, but wealth-constrained, franchisees can afford to buy a franchise.

Because the actions of the actors are costly to specify ex ante and verify ex post, firms in a particular network may choose not to formalize every aspect of their relationship into contract and rely instead on a mix of contractual and relational mechanisms. These agreements can be enforced in many ways, including the use of private arbitration systems, the threat of expulsion, the private use of violence, reputational networks, and the use of the legal system (Ménard, 2013). Courts have at times upheld aspects of unwritten arrangements simply because participants had established a long-standing way of doing business with one another, but such enforcement is unusual. Private arbitration systems can be used to replace the legal system, as shown by Bernstein (1992) for diamond dealers in New York City and Ménard and Raynaud (2010) for millers in France. Since defecting from these arrangements without notifying the other party can create significant costs for the remaining party, multiple enforcement margins are often used. Bernstein (2015) finds that reputation within a complicated supply chain can tightly bind formally separate firms. Significant aspects of the relationship, while enshrined in contract, come to resemble private entities in their own right that outstrip traditional notions of

---

[28] Greif (1993) documents the importance of social ties in enforcing agreements among the eleventh-century Maghribis traders.

contractual arrangements. Of course, this type of organizational form carries its own set of costs. Large-scale machine manufacturers relying on numerous parts suppliers often require their suppliers to go through a costly and invasive vetting process before engaging their services in what is likely to be a profitable and highly repetitive relationship (Bernstein, 2015). The larger manufacturer needs a certainty of supply chain stability that exceeds simple contracting, and the smaller parts suppliers want the guarantee of business that will result if they prove their reliability and quality ex ante. Ultimately, the multiple forms of hybrid arrangements and enforcement mechanisms are choices on a menu of contractual and organizational options that is much richer than a simple make-or-buy decision.

Conclusion

In a world in which all transaction costs are zero, the boundaries, internal organization, and ownership structure of the firm would be indeterminate. Any good or service could be acquired by a contract that clearly specified the rights and responsibilities of each party. These would include the quality of the part, the timing of delivery, and the expected response to any and all contingencies. While zero enforcement costs implies that an outside judge or arbitrator is able to observe each party's behavior, disputes would never get to the judge, as the trading partners would know exactly how the judge would rule. Similarly, the establishment and maintenance of property rights could be done entirely using the structure of a firm. Property rights would be effortlessly established and maintained within the hierarchy, efficiently organizing economic activity.

The IOA maintains that transaction costs are positive and that property rights can be established and sustained at different costs within different organizational forms. The analysis of the cost of organizing property rights begins with the social order of a society. Beneath this, the institutions and norms of society shape individuals' abilities to make decisions over productive resources. Individuals expend additional private resources to establish and protect property rights. Some of those costs are fixed and some are variable. There are fixed costs to organizing economic activity within a firm that include the establishment of the firm's institutions. Norms develop on their own over time. Adopting a standard legal form, like that of a corporation or a partnership, brings with it a host of default rules that govern the behavior of individuals within the firm. Variable costs rise with the level of production, including additional monitoring and enforcement activities along with the recognition, and at times formalization, of norms that might work within a small organization but are unwieldly in a larger one.

Transaction costs are complementary; establishing property rights over one aspect of an asset will alter the costs of maintaining other rights. The agency, governance, and new property-rights theories presented above focus on different costs of organizing economic activity. Integrative frameworks, such as Alston and Gillespie (1989), show how these theories focus on different stages in the production process. Analyzing one transaction cost in isolation without understanding the legal rules, the norms, and the complementary institutions and their enforcement, can lead to faulty analysis, including the classification of efficiency-enhancing practices as being in violation of antitrust law. By incorporating transaction costs into the analysis of markets, we deepen our understanding of how market participants choose to organize economic activity.

PART II

From Economic Outcomes to Political Performance

Introduction to Part Topics

In Part I, we introduced and defined many of the central concepts of Institutional and Organizational Analysis (IOA), in particular, institutions, norms, property rights, and transaction costs. In Figure I.1 in the Introduction, we presented a framework that tied these concepts together, describing how institutions and norms determine property rights and transaction costs, which in turn affect economic performance through their effect on technology and contractual choice. In Chapter 2 on property rights and transaction costs, and Chapter 3 on organizations and contracts, we provided several examples that illustrated the many channels and mechanisms through which these core concepts and other related ideas affect behavior and ultimately economic performance.

Whereas Part I started from a given set of institutions and norms taking economic performance as the dependent variable, Part II inverts the cycle and explains the typical determinants of institutions taking as fixed the basic constitutional rules and the current realization of economic performance. In this part of the book, we analyze the process through which groups and individuals lobby and government supplies laws and regulations. The distinction between constitutional rules and collective-choice institutions is not always clear-cut, but it is a useful distinction for analytical purposes. The collective-choice institutions are rules in the form of laws, regulations, and policies that enable and constrain the behavior of groups and individuals in their economic and social relations. The constitutional rules are those that determine who gets to set and change the collective-choice institutions and through which procedures (Ostrom, 2005). In Part III, we relax the assumption of fixed constitutional rules and analyze how these higher-order institutions emerge and change over time. In Part II, however, we take the rules on making rules as given.

In Part I, we discussed the concepts of property rights and transaction costs mostly in economic contexts and related to economic organizations. Here, we use the same tools and concepts primarily in political contexts and related to political organizations and relations. Part II consists of four chapters. In Chapter 4, we address the demand for institutions by individuals and organizations and focus primarily on the role and impact of interest groups on government policy. Every policy is potentially redistributive, so firms and individuals organize themselves to try to influence redistribution in their favor. The supply of institutions is the result of the interactions of a series of other actors that form the government and other organizations that participate in the process of policy making. Though this structure varies across countries, some basic units are present with variations in most countries.

In Chapter 5, we cover the role of the legislature and the executive, which are usually the main actors in charge of creating and implementing legislation. Most countries – whether democratic, authoritarian, presidential, parliamentary, imperial, or other – have some variation of an executive and a legislative branch that concentrate most of the action in producing laws and policies. In this chapter, we cover research on the nature, functioning, and impact of executive and legislative institutions seen in different countries.

In Chapter 6, we address the role of the bureaucracy. Although the bureaucracy is not typically in the front line of the policy-making process and can appear to simply implement the decisions made by other actors, there is a large literature showing that a country's bureaucracy can have significant impacts on the content, quality, and effectiveness of the outcomes of laws. There is great variation in bureaucratic organization across the world, which can distort legislative intent and, in turn, is a measure of political effectiveness. The bureaucracy's structure and process determine, for example, how large, effective, and accountable it is, as well as to whom it responds and to what extent it acts as a check on the three main powers.

In Chapter 7, we conclude Part II with an analysis of the role of the judiciary. Although judiciaries also vary greatly across countries and serve a wide array of functions, the focus in this chapter is twofold: we first consider the ways in which institutions can influence the structure and output of the judiciary, and then examine the impact that judiciaries have on institutions themselves. For example, is the judiciary independent? Or, are the judges elected or appointed, and if appointed, by whom? Different structures of the judiciary affect the nature and impact of the laws that ultimately prevail. A central interest here, especially as related to the rest of Part II, is the judiciary's role in providing judicial review of legislation passed by the other powers, as well as an important check on the use of power by these other actors.

These categories – special interests, executives, legislatures, judiciaries, and bureaucracies – cover most of the process through which government produces political institutions that shape political performance, but several additional organizations to which we do not dedicate an entire chapter also can play a substantial role. The press, for example, is the key player in disseminating or obstructing information and can act as an important watchdog. Similarly, district attorneys, audit offices, and even police forces play active political roles in many countries. In many societies, the military is a key player. Wherever appropriate, we will reference additional actors in Part II.

Tools and Concepts for Analyzing Institutions and Government

In describing the policy-making process above, we made use of the metaphor of demand and supply for policies, with individuals and groups as demanders and governmental agents as suppliers. Although this is a useful metaphor for some purposes, it is not always adequate. In particular, it gives the notion that actors/organizations transact/ negotiate policies in a "market" in the same way as regular economic goods with a focus on price and quantity. If taken in this manner, institutions remain in the background. It also may give the impression that there is a unique outcome when there are clearly multiple outcomes possible, ex ante. Moreover, the central premise of our book is that institutions are essential parts of the analysis, and we cannot neglect them without compromising our understanding. So, although the metaphor of a market for policy may still be used where appropriate, the basic tools and concepts used in this part of the book to understand governments and policy making are grounded in the fundamental concepts that were the focus of Part I, namely, institutions, property rights, and transaction costs.

The chapters in Part II make use of five related models or concepts that have institutions, property rights, and transaction costs as their basic building blocks:

1. Principal-agent models;
2. The "Coase Theorem" and credible commitment;
3. Institutions, commitment, and performance;
4. Impossibility, chaos, and structure-induced equilibria; and
5. The Riker Objection.

We briefly describe each of these analytical tools, with more detailed explanations in the chapters where we use them to examine specific issues. In order to set the stage, it is useful to think of the policy-making process as a web of relations among the agents/organizations that take place in the process. Figure PII.1 portrays the web of relations by showing the variety of actors involved with arrows indicating interactions. The figure is only an illustration, as different countries at different times may have different actors with different interactions. The figure includes the objects of the four chapters (interest groups, consumers, firms – Chapter 4; legislature and executive – Chapter 5; bureaucracies – Chapter 6; judiciary – Chapter 7), along with other potential participants (e.g., the press). The interest is on what the figure does not show, that is, how the institutions that determine the structure of the web and the details of the interrelationships affect

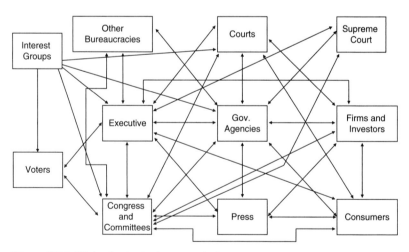

Figure PII.1 Web of principal-agent relations

the outcomes of the interrelationships, which are policies and their impact on society.

Principal-Agent Models

A crucial characteristic of the web of relations that underlies the policy-making process is that it is a network of interlinked principal-agent relations, where the key element is the asymmetry of information between/among the agents. The asymmetry gives rise to transaction costs that affect the ability of the players to establish contracts to structure the relationship efficiently in a first-order sense. We first describe a single principal-agent relation and then consider what happens when you have multiple simultaneous relations.

Principal-agent theories (and information theory more generally) have been the major way to incorporate real-world informational constraints into the analysis. A principal-agent relation involves a principal, who delegates a task to an agent, who in turn receives some form of compensation – such as a payment, votes, praise, campaign contributions – to perform that task. The agent has her own preferences regarding how she should pursue the task, and information asymmetries make it costly for the principal to monitor fully the effort by the agent in pursuing the task. The incentives offered by the principal cannot be made contingent on effort, which is not completely observable, but must rather be made contingent on outcomes, which are affected by effort but also by many other elements not under the agent's control, including chance and serendipity. The upshot is that problems of moral hazard and adverse selection between the principal and the agent plague the contract in ways that might cause the relationship to break down, foregoing the gains from trade due to delegation.[1] When confronted with the problems posed by information asymmetries, rather than simply giving up on the potentially mutually beneficial exchange, agents/organizations have an incentive to structure the relationship in ways that align the interests of the

---

[1] Moral hazard refers to behavior where the agent exploits his informational advantage by performing the task differently than what was contracted, for example, by shirking. Adverse selection happens when the agent misrepresents her type/ability when establishing the contract with the principal, for example, when a utility inflates the cost it declares to a regulator. Moral hazard thus takes place ex post to the contract and adverse selection ex ante.

principal with incentives of the agent to act opportunistically. This has the effect that when pursuing her own interest, the agent will, even without monitoring, be simultaneously also forwarding the interest of the principal.

Theoretically, principals can design an incentive mechanism in the contract, as illustrated in the mechanism design literature (see, e.g., Myerson, 2008). Theorists describe such solutions as high-powered (second-best) optimal solutions to the principal-agent problem. But, though highly elegant, in the real world we do not observe a high incidence of such incentive schemes. Instead, low-powered contracts tend to prevail (Dixit, 1996). Particularly in political relationships, as opposed to more economic relations such as labor contracts and relations among firms, the norm is low-powered incentives. The design of incentives does not control agents by getting their marginal incentives precisely right to induce the desired behavior, but rather relies on blunter methods that simply prohibit some actions, relies on costly and imperfect monitoring, or simply tolerates many obvious supposed inefficiencies. These are situations where the dictum in Coase (1960) applies, that "it would cost too much to put the matter right." In general, the specific institutions that are the rules of the game played by politicians, voters, interest groups, courts, and others, determine the incentives that permeate the many principal-agent relations in the political realm. The institutions are built into the electoral rules, the legislative rules, partisan rules, judicial rules, the Constitution, and many others, including both the codified institutions and their de facto manifestations. The solutions to the principal-agent problem imposed by these institutions are usually far from the second-best optimum that a high-powered mechanism could achieve, but they are robust and give the relationship stability and predictability.[2]

One often comes across relationships between economic or political agents structured in ways that may seem odd or unusual because the relationship appears to generate wasteful behavior or leave profitable opportunities unrealized. Typically, one would expect parties in

[2] "Second-best" is the most efficient outcome possible given that there is an information asymmetry (or other social cost). The first-best is the absolute most efficient outcome, but it requires completely removing the source of the social cost, for example, the information asymmetry, which is generally not possible. In real applications, the second-best is usually the best one can hope for. Political actors rarely achieve even the second-best.

a principal-agent relationship to structure delegation and compensation through a standard contract that establishes a payment by the principal for the agent to complete a prespecified task, possibly contingent on many states of the world. When instead of a simple payment, one encounters an apparently unusual arrangement structuring the relationship, it is tempting to conclude that this is inefficient or irrational behavior. However, often the unusual arrangement may have a hidden purpose, to solve or ameliorate the principal-agent problems imposed by information asymmetries. Especially if the apparently senseless arrangement has existed for a long time, it bears considering whether it is fulfilling some non-obvious function of aligning incentives or inducing cooperation.[3] For example, in some circumstances, employment relations can include, in addition to the contractually determined wage, an element of paternalism where the employer provides non-market goods in exchange for faithful service. At first blush, paternalism might seem as unusual or provincial behavior, but in some circumstances, it serves the purpose of aligning the interest of employer and employee, reducing monitoring costs and turnover, and making the relationship viable despite the hazards that originate from the information asymmetry (Alston and Ferrie, 1993).

Having more than one principal, agent, or task often exacerbates the tendency of a principal-agent relation to yield low-powered incentives and inefficiencies.[4] With two principals pushing an agent to exert effort in two different tasks, you have the information asymmetry due to the unobservability of effort leading to a second-best outcome. In addition, each principal will realize that any incentive they provide for the agent to perform their preferred task will be partially neutralized by incentives given by the other principal. Thus, each principal will choose to provide fewer incentives than would be the case in a single principal

---

[3] Non-standard contracting in political interactions can be a sign of rent-seeking instead of an efficiency-enhancing response. In a competitive market, it is more likely that an unusual arrangement has an efficiency rationale, but the political interactions that we examine in this part of the book are less likely to face competitive pressure.

[4] A large literature explores extensions to simple principal-agent relations, among them, common agency models (Bernheim and Whinston, 1986), multiple-principal models (Martimort, 1996), multiple task models (Holmström and Milgrom, 1991), and multiple-principal-multiple-task models (Dixit, 1996).

situation, resulting in even less agent effort. This multiple-principal distortion adds to the moral hazard from the informational asymmetry leading to third-best outcomes. As Figure PII.1 shows, the policy-making process is composed of numerous multiple-principal-multiple-task relations. The general ubiquity of "inefficiencies," waste, and distortions in the policy-making process is compatible with what one would expect from theory. In addition, we expect that institutions arise to mitigate these problems and allow the parties to realize benefits from their relationships. In Chapters 4–7, we explore these insights in specific contexts, focusing on how specific institutions relate to the nature of the relations among the players portrayed in the policy-making network in Figure PII.1.

The "Coase Theorem" and Credible Commitment

We described the "Coase Theorem" in Part I. Here, we invoke its main insights to focus on the key determinants of the policy-making process in government. In the absence of transaction costs, property rights are perfectly defined and enforced, so the principal-agent problem would not exist and the parties could easily remedy the inefficiencies that permeate the policy-making process. In this transaction-cost-free world, parties to a relationship that is yielding third-best outcomes costlessly get together and rework the contract to enable the first-best outcome. Under the assumptions of zero transaction costs, there are no impediments to discovering a better way to organize the relationship or in making the necessary promises to convince each party to accept and comply with the new contract. This means that the specific laws and regulations are not that important because a society can contract around them to reach optimal outcomes. In this world, the distribution of property rights in the policy-making process, say giving agenda powers to one committee instead of another, or to the executive instead of Congress, affects the distribution of payoffs, with those parties that hold the rights capturing most of the gain. However, the design of the final policy is independent of who holds the rights. Parties will always choose the most efficient or surplus-maximizing policy, with compensatory side-payments established to ensure that no one is harmed.

Of course, Coase's (1960) whole point is that in the real world, transaction costs do exist, making property rights incomplete and insecure, so that the specific details of laws are consequential.

The difficulty of making credible commitments makes it hard to realize the compensating side-payments that ensure the changes do not make anyone worse off. The types of transactions that are involved in making such promises are even more subject to opportunism and moral hazard than purely economic transactions in goods. In the political realm, transaction costs involve the exchange of votes and pledges that are hard to quantify. In addition, the quid pro quos generally occur in different periods of time between actors that may have different time horizons, for example, you vote for my project today and I will support you in some future endeavor if you are still in office (Acemoglu, 2003; Alston and Mueller, 2006; Weingast and Marshall, 1988). In these circumstances, the specific details of the laws have direct consequences for the policies that ensue. Even if waste and inefficiencies riddle the current situation, those holding the property rights to change may choose to block surplus-enhancing reforms due to the inability of the other participants in the transaction to credibly commit to compensating reformers for losses. This means that the property-rights structure inherited from the past, concentrating power in some players as opposed to others, is crucial to understand the nature of the policy-making process. Similarly, the nature of the transactions and the associated transaction costs in different countries and in different types of governments, that is, democracies versus autocracies, parliamentary versus presidential, are also crucial determinants of outcomes.

Institutions, Commitment, and Performance

The two concepts/results analyzed state that (1) government and the policy-making process is composed of a network of multiple principal-agent problems where low-powered incentives and distortions abound and (2) transaction costs and incomplete property rights limit the ability to reform the system. From this, it follows that the specific institutions of countries crucially determine their economic and political performance because institutions determine property rights and transaction costs. This is simply the basic tenet of new institutional economics: institutions matter. Much of the research in this area involves mapping of institutions to outcomes in specific contexts.

In Figure PII.2, we illustrate a mapping from institutions to policy to performance in a decision tree. This is based on the seminal book by

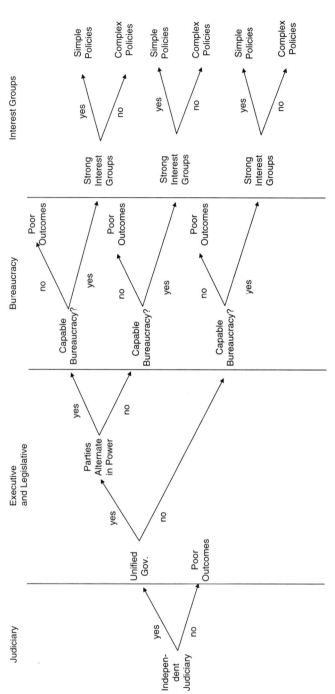

Figure PII.2 A decision tree mapping from institutions to outcomes
Source: Based on Levy and Spiller (1996: 8).

Levy and Spiller (1996), who proposed a framework for understanding how institutions affect a nation's capacity to attract investment and innovation in the telecommunication sector by enabling or preventing the government from committing not to break the rules and expropriating investments. The authors applied the framework to five country case studies with very different institutions. They found two cases where institutions promoted successful performance (United Kingdom and Chile), two cases of institutional failure (Argentina and Philippines), and one case of mixed outcomes (Jamaica).

We adapted Figure PII.2 to include institutions related to the themes of Chapters 4–7, covering interest groups, executive/legislature, judiciary, and bureaucracy. The idea is to display the different combinations of institutions that a country can have and map the combinations to the characteristics of the policies that we expect to emerge as a result. Clearly, the variety of possible institutions is very large and the total number of combinations is unwieldy. Thus, in Figure PII.2, we consider only two alternatives for each actor. For example, in the figure, the judiciary is either independent or not independent from the undue influence of other powers. Independence provides incentives that have consequences on policies and therefore on performance. The figure is a simplification because it treats independence as an all-or-nothing category, and we do not display other characteristics, such as corruption, ease of access, and speed.

The endpoints of the decision tree are outcomes. They are a function of the combination of institutions that led to that point. Here, too, it is necessary to simplify the figure for tractability. The only outcomes considered are "poor outcomes," "simple policies," and "complex policies." "Poor outcomes" arise from situations where the institutions do not provide conditions for the actors to make intertemporal political transactions to escape various forms of inefficiency or waste that permeate their relationship.[5] That is, the institutions do not enable cooperation, coordination, collective action, contracts, or reduction of transaction costs. In such situations, policies emerge, but they dissipate many of the potential gains. In the case of regulatory policy

---

[5] In the graph, different endpoints may display similar labels, for example, "poor policies," that represent different outcomes. That is, the policies will be "poor" for different reasons.

studied in Levy and Spiller (1996), the outcomes involved, for example, government ownership of utilities, which has historically proven to be a suboptimal way to arrange the sector.

"Simple policies" are policies that require institutions that give better incentives but still contain many weaknesses, so that only limited levels of commitment are possible. These institutions allow for policies that can ameliorate some of the hazards inherent in the policy-making process. But simple policies are not sufficiently sophisticated to achieve the second-best solutions that eliminate most of the remediable market failures. Simple policies often have to be very rigid to be credible, so they may work well in some situations but then cease to be effective when conditions have changed.

"Complex policies" are those that seek to get incentives right even at the margin, often using sophisticated mechanism design principles to align incentives, reveal information, and maximize social welfare in ways that adapt to shocks and changing conditions. Complex policy requires giving a considerable amount of discretion and power to the agent in charge, so it ultimately only works well if there are other institutions that can check the abuse of power by the agent without stifling the implementation of the policy. Levy and Spiller (1996: 7) highlight that the key lesson for a country with a given set of institutions is to achieve a good fit between their institutions and their policies, as the worst outcomes arise when policy making "proceeds without attention to institutional realities."

Consider a given country and let us use Figure PII.2 to see how its institutions map into performance. The first step is to ask whether the judiciary is independent. If the answer is no, then poor performance is likely, irrespective of the other institutions.[6] Without an independent judiciary, an important check of executive and legislative power is missing, as is an incentive for private contracting. The policies that emerge either will fail or will have to have other costly and constraining safeguards, such as government ownership.

The second level, if there is an independent judiciary, considers whether there is a unified or divided government. A unified government could be a parliamentary government where the executive and the

---

[6] The specific mapping presented in the figure is only an illustration. It is still debatable whether judicial independence is a necessary condition for good policies. As we will discuss in the following chapters, much depends on the context within each country.

legislative powers are always controlled by the same party or coalition. A divided government, by contrast, allows different groups to have majority control over the executive and legislature, as is often the case in the United States. The key distinction here is that a unified government does not have important checks and balances between the powers. Though a unified government may be more decisive and provide more governability, it lacks a check on executive discretion that can compromise policy effectiveness and infringe on minority rights. In the figure, we take the unified government as a weakness (perhaps this is a developing country with a history of authoritarian rule and presidential overstep). Yet, this weakness can be moderated or exacerbated if parties alternate in power. With alternating parties in a context of unified government, there is not only excessive discretion but also frequent reversals leading to policy volatility and balkanization. If there is no or little alternation in power, then though there might be some abuse due to lack of checks, there can be greater policy coherence.

The next step is to determine whether the country's civil service is closer to a high-capability bureaucracy that is stable, trained, motivated, and well paid, or whether it is closer to a low-capability bureaucracy that is incompetent, uninterested, corrupt, myopic, and subject to nepotism and favoritism. A high-capability bureaucracy can play an important role as a check on the other powers as well as an important repository of information and best practices. In the top-most branch in Figure PII.2, an independent judiciary would not be enough to compensate for a unified government with alternating parties if there is not a strong bureaucracy – the outcome would be poor policies. But, if there is a high-capability bureaucracy to counterbalance the other powers, it becomes possible to move up to the next level.

The final step for the analyst is to distinguish between situations where interest groups are oligarchic, that is, few, well organized, and powerful, from situations where interest groups are competitive, that is, that are fragmented and dispersed. Oligarchic interest groups could form iron triangles with bureaucracies and politicians, hijacking policy in favor of a small minority. As portrayed in the figure, with oligarchic interest groups, simple policies may be the best that a country can do. These might be rigid and unresponsive to changes in contextual conditions. The inflexibility has an efficiency cost, but may be necessary to avoid greater costs due to capture.

Once again, the figure is a simple illustration of mapping institutions into policies and outcomes. In specific contexts, the analysis can add considerable detail selecting the relevant institutions and more fully spelling out the outcomes. The analyst can take a positive perspective, investigating which combinations of institutions lead to good performance, or a normative point of view, suggesting which kinds of policies will be credible and more suited for a country with a given institutional endowment. In Chapters 4–7, we cover the literature in IOA to analyze interest groups, the executive/legislature, the judiciary, and bureaucracies.

Impossibility, Chaos, and Structure-Induced Equilibria

The notion that institutions affect outcomes may seem uncontroversial, yet many approaches often disregard or neglect them.[7] Though getting much better, many scholars in neoclassical economics still oversimplify, ignore, or push institutions to the background. Weingast (2016) called it the "neoclassical fallacy." In much of social choice theory, institutions are also often left out of the picture. Early social choice theory entailed the aggregation of preferences from various individuals with cycling and instability as the outcomes (Arrow, 1951; McKelvey, 1979). In Part II, we focus on similar relations and interactions between political actors as in social choice theory but made in different fora, such as committees, plenaries, assemblies, courts, and bureaucracies. Applying simple social choice without understanding the institutions would yield predictions of policies churning. The losers from the previous round attract a subset of the winning coalition by making a new proposal in which the subset would be even better off than in the status quo.[8]

In Figure PII.3, we illustrate the problem in a two-dimensional policy space.[9] Panel A shows the preferences of five different actors (A, B, C, D, and E) and the status-quo point at x. The circles mark the set of points where each player is indifferent to the status quo. A player will

---

[7] For readers not familiar with spatial models, you may wish to read the appendix before this section.

[8] The instability of voting rules is known as the Arrow Impossibility Theorem.

[9] With only one dimension and standard preferences, the problem of cycling does not arise and the median voter theorem can be used to determine which choice will arise in equilibrium.

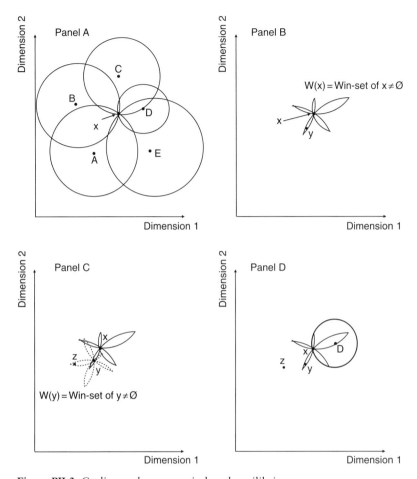

Figure PII.3 Cycling and structure-induced equilibrium

vote for any proposal within or on his indifference circle, and vote against those outside.[10] We can take any reasonable preference aggregation rule, such as pure majority rule (PMR), and determine which proposal would beat another in a direct vote.

Panel B shows only the set of points that will beat x through PMR, that is, with at least three votes in favor. The figure shows only the relevant portion of the indifference circles to avoid clutter. Together,

---

[10] The assumption is that points closer to one's preferred point are preferable to points further away in any direction.

the five petals that stem from x are known as the win-set of x, that is, the set of points that will beat x in a head-to-head vote. A key result from social choice theory is that the win-set of any point is non-empty, so that there always exists at least one, and possibly many other points, that will beat any given point.[11] Put differently, no point is invulnerable. Proposal y, for example, is inside the win-set of x, so it would win a vote between the two. However, Panel C shows that this just pushes the problem one step further, for y also has a non-empty win-set (dashed lines). If y defeated x, those that were harmed by this change could attract one or more members of the winning coalition who preferred a different point in the win-set of y, for example point z, and defeat y. But, z also has a non-empty win-set as does any other point and the proposals would cycle continuously. Furthermore, there is no predicting or controlling the path that the cycling would take, thus the notion of "chaos."

If social choice actually leads to endless and unpredictable cycling and anything can happen, then institutions do not seem to be that important. Yet, simple observation of real-world instances of social choice, from Congress to courts to PTA meetings, suggests that we are surrounded by considerable stability and predictability. Although surprises do happen occasionally, in general we can easily anticipate changes and, once realized, they tend to persist.

The explanation for the mismatch between observation and theory is that real-world social choice is not made in the pure conditions of social choice theory, where any player can bring forward a new proposal at any time. Real-world practice of social choice is always constrained by a series of rules that limit who can participate and how actions proceed. Congress, for example, has a very complicated set of rules that regiments: Who can initiate a new proposal under what circumstances? Who has voice? Who can veto? What path does the proposal take? What other proposals must it beat? And, what determines approval? The same is true of a dissertation committee, a central bank committee, or a family deciding on a restaurant for lunch. The specific rules that establish the choice procedure effectively constrain the full set of proposals that each player can bring up against the status quo. By doing so,

---

[11] There is a perfectly symmetrical configuration of preferences such that a given point cannot be beaten, but this situation is of little relevance for real-world applications.

they limit the tendency of cycling and ensure greater stability. In Panel D, for example, suppose there is a rule that individual D can veto the choice made by the group after it has reached a decision. This has the effect of reducing the win-set to only those points that D prefers to x. Under these rules, points y and z, along with many others, would not beat x. There is, thus, much more predictability over what can happen. Shepsle and Weingast (1981) call the restricted set of outcomes that emerges after all the institutions have constrained the win-set a "structure-induced equilibrium." Far from being the unrestricted free-for-all from social choice theory, institutions and norms facing interest groups, legislatures, executive, judiciary, and bureaucracy constrain choices. The message, once again, is that institutions matter. They establish property rights and shape transaction costs, inducing outcomes and economic performance.

The Riker Objection

If institutions have a first-order impact on outcomes, then self-interested agents would find it in their interest to try to change the higher-order rules as a means to induce their preferred outcomes. The distinction between rules as exogenous and rules subject to manipulation mirrors the distinction we made in Chapter 2 between institutions-as-rules and institutions-as-equilibrium. Similarly, in political science, the distinction has led to what has become known as the Riker Objection, having been originally formulated by William Riker (1980). The issue is whether the choice of a choice rule should be treated as a special type of decision, or just as one more instance of many issues that a society faces (Barbera and Jackson, 2004). Shepsle (2008) explains the Riker Objection as follows:

The rules of the game are not fixed and inflexible. The constraints are not etched in stone. Even if no unforeseen contingencies are experienced, even if there are no ex ante uncertainties that come to be realized ex post in unexpected ways, there still is a role for amendment procedures to play. The *positivist* fact of the matter is that they provide strategic opportunities, quite apart from any welfare-enhancing justification for their utility in a constitution. The Riker Objection is both a recognition of the endogeneity of rules and procedures – they cannot be taken as preset and unvarying – and an acknowledgement of their strategic potential. (Shepsle, 2008: 1041; emphasis in original)

In the chapters in Part II, we take economic outcomes as given and focus on the play of the game within a given set of political institutions that in turn determine the new institutions that loop back and affect the actors and actions in Part I in subsequent periods. We will take the higher-ordered rules as exogenous. The simplification allows us to focus on the concepts of property rights and transaction costs in the political/governmental arenas. Because the distinction is not realistic, however, the issue of changing the higher-order rules will occasionally appear even in Chapters 4–7. In Part III, we fully relax the assumption and endogenize higher-order institutions, allowing for the full-blown process through which institutions emerge and change over time.

Appendix: Primer on Spatial Models

In Part II, we use spatial models to present and illustrate some concepts and guide the discussion. For those readers who are not familiar with these types of models, this appendix provides a short introduction on how to understand and interpret them. For a rigorous mathematical treatment of spatial models, see Schofield (2008). Here, we present instead a brief graphical introduction compatible with the examples used in our book.

In general, spatial models consist of (1) a policy space consisting of one or more dimensions, (2) a set of players, (3) players' preferences, (4) rules of the game (institutions and norms), (5) information of players, and (6) initial conditions. Given these elements, the analyst can then deduce the sequence of moves and the equilibrium outcome of the game. Consider each of these in turn. The policy space is commonly one dimensional (a straight line where a policy sits, for example, on the left-right continuum), or two dimensional, as in Figure PII.A1 where, as an example, the horizontal dimension measures the extent to which a policy favors consumers or businesses, and the vertical dimension measures whether a policy is conducive or adverse to environment. Three-dimensional models can also be drawn, but are harder to visualize. Higher levels of dimensionality must be treated analytically rather than graphically.

In Panel I of Figure PII.A1, we place the players A, B, and C according to their most preferred point in the policy space. In this example, A and B are politicians that represent, respectively, consumers and businesses,

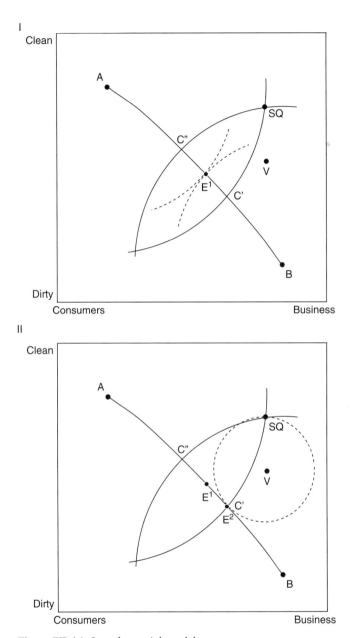

Figure PII.A1 Sample spatial model

and V is a regulator that oversees the policy area. As drawn, A prefers a clean policy that favors consumers, and B a dirty policy that favors business, though note that neither wants the most extreme policies possible, which would be at the respective corners. The initial policy condition is given at SQ (status quo), which is biased towards clean environment and business. The preferences of the regulator are close to the status quo policy on the horizontal dimension, but not on the environmental (vertical) dimension.

The players' most preferred policies are shown at A and B, but to fully portray their preferences, it is useful to draw indifference curves at different distances from their bliss point (their most preferred policy). It is common to assume that preferences are such that the players prefer points closer to their bliss point than points further away. In this case, the indifference curves are circles concentric on the bliss point, where further circles represent points that are less preferred to points on closer circles. And by definition, the player is indifferent to points on the same circle. It is possible to allow a player to care more about one dimension than another, in which case the curves would be ellipses (though this is often an unnecessary complication). Also, in order to keep the figures free of clutter, only the relevant parts of the indifference curves are usually drawn. In Figure PII.A1, for example, we only show the relevant points on the curves where A and B are indifferent to the status quo. The curves make a lens that represents an important concept in spatial models, the win-set. This is the set of points that beat a given policy point given the specific rules of the game. In the example, the win-set of the status quo (which can be written as W(SQ)) are all the points inside the lens that stem from SQ. It can be shown by inspection that any point within the lens but not on line-segment C'-C", also has a non-empty win-set. This means that any such point also has a lens emanating from it, and thus commands its own non-empty win-set. The implication is that none of these points are invulnerable to at least one other potential policy. Some points, however, are immune to change, as they have the Pareto property that any change will necessarily make one or more of the players worse off. In the figure, the locus of Pareto-optimal points, known as the contract curve, is shown as the line from A to B. On this line, the indifference curves of the players are tangent to each other, so that no lens is created. One pair of such indifference curves (dashed) is drawn as an example. If A and B negotiate to change the policy from SQ to E^1, we should not expect any negotiated change thereafter as there are no further gains to trade, unless compensating payments are made outside of this game.

In order to deduce the equilibrium of the game, we need to know the rules that restrict and enable the moves and strategies of players. The rules are not shown in the figure and must be explained in the accompanying text. They determine who can do what at each point in the game and under which circumstances. Once we know the rules as well as the preferences, it becomes possible to determine which point or set of points we expect to be reached. In panel I of Figure PII.A1, for example, if A and B are free to choose a new status quo (suppose each has proposal power and veto power over the new policy), we cannot determine precisely what that will be, but can narrow it down to those points on the C'-C" line segment. Point E^1, which is more or less midway between both players, would be a good prediction. If, in addition, it is the case that the regulator V has a final veto over any negotiated change of the status quo, then we can narrow down the win-set of SQ still further. The dashed indifference curve in panel II of Figure PII.A1 shows the set of points that the regulator will not veto. These intersect with the contract points C'-C" that would beat SQ for A and B, only in point E^2. Under these expanded rules, therefore, the model would predict E^2 to be the final equilibrium.

Spatial models provide a powerful means to analyze and to describe strategic situations where different players interact to shape policy. The example given here illustrates the basic moving parts of a simple spatial model. Often these can become much more involved, including many more players, more complex rules, and different levels of information across players over the preferences and information sets of others. The examples in our book, however, are straightforward and can be understood with the information given here.

4 | *Special Interests and Citizens*

Institutions are not necessarily or even usually created to be socially efficient; rather they, or at least the formal rules, are created to serve the
interests of those with the bargaining power to create new rules. In a zero
transaction cost world, bargaining strength does not affect the efficiency of
outcomes, but in a world of positive transaction costs it does – and it thus
shapes the direction of long run economic change.

— *North (1992: 5)*

Introduction and Opening Case: Interest Groups and the Legalization of Marijuana

Benjamin Franklin famously declared that in this world nothing can be
said to be certain, except death and taxes. But interest groups seem
similarly inexorable. Wherever there is government, there is redistribution and, consequently, groups trying to capture the potential benefits
and avoid the potential costs that intentionally or unwittingly result
from government policy.[1] Whether government action corrects a social
cost or creates a deadweight loss in the form of inefficiencies, it will
generate benefits to some groups in society and costs to others.[2]
Knowing this, groups and individuals don't passively wait for their
draw in the redistributive lottery, simply hoping for the best. Rather,
groups actively and often preemptively engage in actions to influence
outcomes.

But though death and taxes are certain, the actual form that they take
is not predictable. The same is true of interest groups. They can take
many different forms and pursue their objectives through a wide array

---

[1] In Part III, we treat interest groups as part of government, but in Part II, we
   disaggregate the demand side of government from the supply side of government.
[2] We use the Coasean term "social cost" instead of "market failure" to highlight
   the notion that it is not that the market fails, but rather that it "would cost too
   much to put the matter right" (Coase, 1960: 39). We address this distinction in
   more detail below.

131

of strategies and channels. The statement that interest groups heavily influence government policies and outcomes is not controversial. It is a perception widely held across experts and the lay public alike. But, what is the extent of influence and what are the channels through which it operates? More importantly, what is the impact of interest group influence on society's welfare and that of different groups in society? Interest groups are so pervasive across countries and time, and the efficiency and distributive issues that they give rise to are so important, that the specialized literature is huge and spans the social sciences. Guilds, professional organizations, and trading companies were early manifestations of interest groups. In a famous passage in *The Wealth of Nations*, Adam Smith ([1776] 2007: 105) notes that "(p)eople of the same trade seldom meet together, even for merriment and diversion, but the conversation ends in a conspiracy against the public, or in some contrivance to raise prices." Whereas this might seem as a reference to the dangers of collusion among firms, and not directly related to interest groups, in the less-remembered continuation to this passage, Smith recommends that "(i)t is impossible to prevent such meetings ... but though the law cannot hinder people of the same trade from sometimes assembling together, it ought to do nothing to render them necessary" (106). Smith recognizes that the propensity of interest groups (factions) to form and to seek private benefit at public expense will naturally gravitate towards the most effective means to do so, which is through the law and government policy.

Given the myriad ways that interest groups seek to influence policy, many of them covert and hard to measure, there are no good estimates of the size of the efforts relative to GDP to ascertain whether the general suspicion about their pervasiveness and magnitude is accurate (Del Rosal, 2011). Nevertheless, data on some of the more well-documented channels of influence – lobbying expenditures and campaign contributions – can give us a notion of the magnitudes involved. According to the non-partisan research group, Center for Responsive Politics (CRP), which "tracks money in US politics and its effect on elections and public policy," lobbying expenditures in the United States exceeded $3 billion every year since 2008.[3] The mid-term elections of 2014 witnessed the lowest voter turnout since World War II and the

---

[3] Extensive data and reports on lobbying and interest groups in the United States are made available by the CRP on their website (www.opensecrets.org).

highest level of lobbying expenditures ($3.8 billion), suggesting a possible shift over time in the relative influence of voters versus organized interest.[4] The number of registered lobbyists fluctuated from approximately 10,000 in 1998 to nearly 15,000 in 2007, with the global depression bringing the number back down to 11,000 in 2014. Table 4.1 gives a notion of the diversity and identity of interest groups in the United States by listing the top 20 interest groups giving to members of Congress in the 2016 cycle. Overall, the rankings have not changed much from 2000 to 2016.

The data capture only a fraction of the actual pressure that interest groups apply on governments and policymakers. Not only are there other levels and powers of government, but there are also non-registered transfers as well as non-pecuniary support, such as providing information or obfuscation and swaying public opinion, to name a few of other creative channels of influence. There is no reason to suspect that pervasiveness of interest groups in countries outside of the United States is much different, though the forms of organization and channels of influence are highly country-specific.

We illustrate the notion that interest groups are simultaneously inevitable and unpredictable by the recent move in some American states to legalize marijuana. The traditional approach of treating cannabis as an illegal drug has long proved ineffective to prevent its production, distribution, and consumption. The "War on Drugs" failed miserably to achieve its objectives on regulating marijuana and generated huge costs of enforcement and a host of side-effects and unintended consequences, such as violence, gangs, overcrowded prisons, consumption of poor-quality product, and overdoses, inter alia. Despite this dismal policy performance, which probably fails any cost-benefit analysis, few people predicted that the United States would be one of the first countries to move towards legalization as an alternative strategy. In November 2012, voters in Colorado and Washington approved initiatives that legalized the recreational use of marijuana, setting a precedent that may be followed by most other states and the federal government. Although a few other countries have already implemented the legalization of marijuana, such as Uruguay since 2014, the American experiment will probably be the bellwether that will guide many other countries.

---

[4] www.opensecrets.org/about/donor_report.php.

Table 4.1 *Top 20 interest groups giving to members of the*
US Congress (2016 cycle)

Rank 2016 (2000)	Interest group	Total	Democrats %	Republicans %
1 (2)	Retired	$ 21,672,190	30	70
2 (1)	Lawyers / Law Firms	$ 15,651,757	55	45
3 (5)	Securities / Invest	$ 15,094,273	34	64
4 (4)	Real Estate	$ 12,351,051	38	62
5 (3)	Health Professionals	$ 11,113,548	34	66
6 (6)	Insurance	$ 11,017,939	31	69
7 (12)	Leadership PACs	$ 9,805,546	31	69
8 (10)	Oil and Gas	$ 7,023,845	9	91
9 (8)	Lobbyists	$ 6,611,021	38	62
10 (20)	Pharma / Health Products	$ 6,603,900	34	64
11 (7)	Commercial Banks	$ 5,588,606	25	75
12 (14)	Electric Utilities	$ 4,961,890	28	72
13 (24)	Misc. Finance	$ 4,779,340	32	68
14 (13)	Misc. Manufacturing and Distribution	$ 4,435,029	26	74
15 (15)	Business Services	$ 4,125,653	44	56
16 (29)	Retail Sales	$ 4,085,087	26	74
17 (37)	Defense Aerospace	$ 3,966,653	36	63
18 (27)	Crop Production	$ 3,307,940	29	71
19 (21)	Accountants	$ 3,600,076	37	63
20 (23)	Electronic Manufacturing / Equipment	$ 3,425,250	46	54

Source: Center for Responsive Politics (www.opensecrets.org/). For the methodology of how the data were classified, see www.opensecrets.org/industries/methodology.php.

As with any other policy, the legalization of marijuana is redistributive, creating winners and losers. Some of the winners and losers will form groups that will try to influence policy, depending largely on their cost of organization and ability to overcome within-group free-riding. The standard approach to identify which groups lose and which groups win from a given policy change is known as an incidence analysis. It tries to work out all the consequences of a given policy, tracing out who benefits and who is harmed. The groups are potential interest groups in the sense that they have a motive to try to influence policy, promoting or blocking its passage or changing its content. Which groups actually form and which are more successful depends on many different characteristics of the groups, such as size, homogeneity, and level of organization, as well as the type of policy and the current political institutions. It is often the case that the final winning and losing coalitions are quite unexpected. Although most policies typically have some obvious direct beneficiaries and losers, there are often many unexpected indirect ramifications of policies that impact apparently unrelated groups. It is often the case that groups that otherwise have very little in common with each other may suddenly find themselves on the same side of an issue, giving rise to the "Bootleggers and Baptists" phenomena. This term refers to the unusual alliance of some religious groups with illegal producers of alcohol in favor of prohibition in the United States (Yandle, 1983).[5]

We observe both of these hard-to-predict characteristics of interest group emergence in the case of marijuana legalization. A report by the CRP (2015) on this issue describes the groups that have already mobilized. The National Organization for the Reform of Marijuana Laws (NORML) has existed since 2002, having since contributed more than $109,000, mostly for candidates supporting legislation that increases access to medical marijuana and to protect state marijuana laws. Another organization, the Marijuana Policy Project (MPP), has been in activity since 1998 and organizes state ballots to liberalize marijuana laws, backing candidates who support the cause. A third organization, the Drug Policy Alliance (DPA), has spent more than $4.2 million in lobbying in opposition to the War on Drugs. Then there is the National Cannabis Industry Association (NCIA), created in 2010 to represent the interest of state-sanctioned marijuana producers. One of their interests is to protect banks that have marijuana-related businesses as clients from being prosecuted at the federal level. Finally, there are the cash-strapped state governments for whom the prospect of new tax revenues from legalized pot is

---

[5] A current example is nuclear energy and natural gas companies siding with environmentalists on restrictions for carbon emissions.

a strong temptation; in 2014, Colorado collected $44 million in sales and excise taxes.

On the other side of the issue are some perhaps more surprising interest groups. The first are police unions that have come to depend on the financial resources that come from the War on Drugs, both in the form of direct funding as well as from seizures in the course of enforcing the laws. These unions include the National Fraternal Order of Police, the National Association of Police Organizations, the International Union of Police Associations, and the International Association of Chiefs of Police. Private prison companies are another group that has opposed drug legalization. These companies benefited significantly from the high incarceration rates that result from the War on Drugs and stand to lose from any change that might reduce arrests and imprisonment. According to the CRP report, one of the largest private prison companies, the Corrections Corporation of America, has spent almost one million dollars annually since 2008 in lobbying efforts. For similar reasons, prison guard unions have also opposed the trend towards legalization. The CRP report registers that the American Federation of State, County and Municipal Employees (AFSCME), which represents many prison guards, has lobbied actively against the cause.

Pharmaceutical corporations and producers of alcoholic beverages, Big Pharma and Big Booze, have also fallen on the same side of the issue as police, prisons, and guards in a manifestation of the Bootleggers and Baptists theory.[6] The first is concerned with the competition that marijuana poses for some important blockbuster drugs, and the second with the competition for wine, beer, and other alcoholic drinks.[7] Both are major lobbyers responsible for massive spending in contributions and influence, though not focused solely on marijuana.

The data and the examples above show that interest groups are pervasive and can have important impacts on the economy and society. The examples also show that which interest groups form, how they operate, and their impact is not at all obvious ex ante.

---

[6] Oddly, the CRP report does not cite Big Tobacco as having lobbied this issue.

[7] In Colorado, the legalization of marijuana consumption in bars and restaurants (in addition to residential consumption) is currently being considered, though it is not obvious what will be the position taken by the industry's groups and associations.

In this chapter, we focus on two basic questions about interest groups. First, what form does the competition between interest groups take and what determines who wins and who loses from that competition? Second, to what extent do interest groups affect economic performance and social welfare through their impact on policy? The large amounts of resources that groups expend to pursue their interest suggests that they must have great impacts on outcomes, yet there is not even consensus in the literature whether that impact is positive, enhancing social welfare by allowing for voice and plurality, or negative, by biasing political representation and generating distortions, deadweight losses, and inefficiencies. The point in this chapter is that a proper analysis of both of these issues necessarily incorporates the institutional detail that surrounds the case. Interest groups act in real-world situations where organizations (e.g., legislatures, committees, courts, agencies, voters, the press) interact in specific arenas (i.e., Congress, the media, the streets, and smoke-filled back rooms) under very specific extant political norms and institutions.

The chapter starts with self-interest theories of interest group competition, and shows how they improve on public interest theories by adding politics. We then show how the explicit attention to information asymmetries and institutional detail can add further value. A simple spatial model is used to underscore three important results from the interest group literature. First, interest group competition takes place in a web of multiple principal-agent relations with the upshot that low-powered incentives often predominate. Second, although interest group competition is subject to cycles and instability inherent in social choice, structure-induced equilibria tend to narrow down the possibilities and promote stability and predictability. Given this important role played by political institutions, interest groups do not limit themselves to compete for influence under the extant institutions, but also to change the rules of the game.

Public Interest and Simple Capture Theories

What determines government policies and the pattern of interventions it chooses to regulate the economy and society? A review of different theories provides a good guide for understanding the many different ways that interest groups have been conceptualized in the literature.[8] Early theories focused on whether government policy favored primarily the public interest or private interest, but shortcomings in these approaches eventually led subsequent theories to incorporate the interest of other groups such as politicians, bureaucrats, and voters.

An early way of understanding government policy was through the lens of Pigou, who argued that markets are fragile and inefficient. The view that government action is basically a response by government to public demands for the remediation of social costs is known as the Public Interest Theory.[9] The Pigouvian school made the positive statement that what governments do is to correct market failures. Joskow and Noll (1981) referred to this view as the Normative Analysis as a Positive Theory. The pervasiveness of interest groups in practically every area of government policy, noted in the Introduction, already suggests that this theory is wrong. It just seems too simplistic that interest groups are unrelated to many of the policy inefficiencies we routinely observe. More sophisticated theories – such as Becker's (1983) model of interest group competition – partially rehabilitate some of the expectations of the Public Interest Theory.[10]

A reformulation of this theory to account for its obvious incongruence with observed reality posits that government policy does seek the public interest, but its endeavors are often not successful because of the complexity and intractability of many of the necessary tasks, together with lack of experience and expertise. While this reformulation is a bit

---

[8] For a more detailed review of this literature, see Viscusi, Harrington, and Vernon (2005).

[9] Pigou was perhaps the most influential, along with Samuelson's exposition in his textbook. Coase argued strongly against the "externality" view of markets. Coase maintained that all costs are reciprocal and it was a matter of assigning property rights such that the least social harm occurs whether or not the transfers are made to the harmed party.

[10] Perhaps the most extreme statement compatible with the Public Interest Theory is Wittman's (1989) *Journal of Political Economy* article, "Why Democracies Produce Efficient Results." He argues that: "Behind every model of government failure is an assumption of extreme voter stupidity, serious lack of competition, or excessively high negotiation/transfer costs. Economists are very suspicious of similar assumptions regarding economic markets. This skepticism should be carried over to models of government behavior" (1989: 1421).

less naïve than the pure Public Interest Theory, it still seems an unsatisfactory explanation of the pattern of government intervention in the economy and society.[11]

On the other side of the spectrum, there are a series of theories that presuppose that government policy is not guided by the public interest at all but rather by private groups that capture the policy-making process in order to promote the interests of their members. Posner (1974: 335) notes that these "capture" theories have been "espoused by an odd mixture of welfare state liberals, muckrakers, Marxists, and free-market economists," in what might be considered an academic example of the Bootleggers and Baptists phenomena. The motivation for the theories is clear. Many businesses are big and influential and have much to gain and lose from government policy, so it is not surprising that they use power systematically to assure the policies they want. Whereas this view of the world seems at first blush to accord well with the evidence around us, of patently biased and inefficient policy, it is nevertheless just as naïve as the Public Interest Theory, for it gives no reason why it would be that some groups are able to capture the government rather than others. Consumers are greatly affected by government regulation and they have the power to vote, so why is it that business interest should always prevail? Furthermore, a closer look at the evidence shows that in many cases the interests of customers and other apparently weaker groups are in fact often promoted by government policy, so that a view that postulates that only one set of groups has influence does not explain all observed outcomes.

The timing of the creation of state commissions to regulate electric utilities in the United States in the late nineteenth and early twentieth centuries provides a thoughtful test of whether public or private interest is the main determinant of government intervention. Jarrell (1978) shows that the first states to create state commissions were those where the utilities faced more competitive markets and where prices and profits were consequently lower. This evidence suggests that the motivation for regulatory reforms was not monopoly power, but rather demand by the utilities to deter entry and protect higher

---

[11] Posner (1974) provides a highly detailed critique of the Public Interest Theory. Stigler and Friedland (1962) is an early paper showing evidence that even the regulation of natural monopolies often does not lead to lower prices.

prices. He cites J. Allen Smith, former dean of the University of Washington, who in 1914 wrote:

No other proposed reform in recent years has had so much influential support, or encountered so little opposition from sources which usually offer more or less determined and effective resistance to every legislative proposal designed to increase popular control over corporations of this sort ... It is also significant that this movement, though ostensibly designed to give cities more effective protection against public utility abuses, has not had its origin in any popular demand from urban communities. The initiative in this matter seems to have come very largely from the public utility interests. (cited in Jarrell, 1978: 293–94)

Yet though the evidence seems to suggest the ubiquity of interest group influence, Capture theories, like Public Interest theories, are not really proper theories but rather coarse hypotheses that seek to explain some stylized facts. The first approach to interest groups based on more solid theoretical foundations is associated with George Stigler and the Chicago School.[12]

Demand for Government Intervention

Stigler's important insight was to treat the redistribution that is inherent in any government policy not as something that happened as a mere side effect of the government's actions, but rather as an economic good that was purposefully demanded by interest groups and supplied by the government.[13] If these transfers are economic goods, standard microeconomic theory can be used to generate hypotheses regarding transfers. In particular, the approach yields a negatively sloped demand curve for redistribution that shows how much the different groups are willing to "pay" for the policies they want through the provision of direct and indirect contributions to politicians as well as other forms of support. Faced with the bids from each of the interest groups, the

---

[12] By starting with the Chicago School, we do not mean to imply that there were no other important self-interest theories of government intervention. The literature on interest groups is just so large that our account cannot be comprehensive and we have to focus on some contributions to the detriment of others. An influential early reference was Bentley's (1908) *The Process of Government*. Also, the Public Choice approach predates many of the references highlighted in this section, but we will discuss this approach later in the chapter.

[13] Stigler's insights were extended and formalized by Peltzman (1976).

government can then choose the specific form of the policy that yields the set of transfers from some groups to others that "clears the market" and maximizes the government's net political support.

In this view, politicians determine taxes, subsidies, tariffs, rates, entry, prohibitions, and all other sorts of policies and regulations, not based on their inherent merit to the economy and society but based on the levels of political support they will elicit from those that benefit from the opposition of those harmed. The politician has no inherent preference for any kind of policy, no ideology, and no preference towards any particular group or class in society. All that matters is to maximize political survival. It may seem a cynical and simplistic portrayal of the motivation of political organizations, but it yields powerful hypotheses.

Which groups benefit and which groups are harmed? As in standard economic markets, those with more wealth and stronger preferences for the transfers are able to bid more for the redistribution, but there is also another important consideration that strongly advantages some groups over others. Groups that are more readily able to overcome problems of collective action and avoid the free-riding of its members will be better placed to generate the support for the politicians and assure favorable redistribution (Buchanan and Tullock, 1962; Olson, 1965). The ability of groups to organize and generate contributions, support, votes, and information is a key characteristic in determining which interest groups prevail. It means that often size is a disadvantage and that organization and unity are decisive.

Although simplified, the model is built on more solid theoretical foundations than its predecessors, making the objectives of actors explicit and incorporating the cost and benefits of different choices. This buys us four hypotheses about which interest groups will tend to benefit from government policies and the form the transfers will take. The first of these hypotheses is similar to the simple Capture Theory and is intuitive. But the other three hypotheses that emerge from the model are more subtle and unforeseen, and provide important insights into the nature of interest group competition that can then be tested.

The first hypothesis is that government policy will tend to redistribute to small, homogeneous, and well-organized groups that are better able to provide support to politicians. Or, in Stigler's words: "as a rule, regulation is acquired by the industry and is designed and operated primarily for its benefit" (1971: 3). Large, heterogeneous, and dispersed groups like consumers may have the numbers to potentially offer votes and contributions, but the high costs of collective action make it extremely hard for them to actually overcome the free-rider problem to deliver that support. Although their stake in the final form taken by the policy is collectively large, it is individually small (e.g., a reduction of $20 in your utility bill), so it is often not even worthwhile to become informed, much less to actually join the fight. Yet for the producers – Adam Smith's "people of the same trade who seldom meet together even for merriment or diversion" – the costs of organization are lower and the stakes worth investing to try to influence policy.

The second hypothesis is that the policies that result from the interest group competition will not produce corner solutions, providing all the benefits it could to the winning groups and taxing the losers as much as possible, but rather only to the point where the marginal support elicited from the winners by an additional unit of transfer is greater than the marginal opposition elicited from the losers. Because the level of support from the winners grows at lower rates, the greater the level of transfers, and the level of opposition from the losers grows at increasing rates, the final policy will settle on an intermediate level of redistribution from losers to winners. Once stated, this seems very intuitive: interest group competition does not result in all-or-nothing transfers. But previous theories essentially predicted that either public or private interests would take the whole bounty, that is, the Public Interest Theory or Capture Theory. Furthermore, the model allows for interesting comparative static results. When an interest group acquires greater capacity to become organized and to offer support or opposition, this will lead *ceteris paribus* to a realignment of policy to reflect those changes, resulting in greater transfers if the group was in the winning coalition, smaller taxes if it was in the losing coalition, or even a switch from being a net loser to a net gainer.

The third hypothesis states that politicians in search of support will tend to focus their efforts reforming sectors or industries where big consequential changes can be made, like breaking up a monopolized or highly concentrated industry, or conversely, creating a monopoly in a previously competitive sector. This is because such changes hold the potential for achieving much greater net gains in political support for politicians than changing sectors or industries that are already in an intermediate situation where the opposing interests are well balanced so that any gain in support is quickly offset by increased opposition. This prediction seems to be well borne out by evidence, with government intervention often concentrated on competitive sectors, such as agriculture and taxicabs, and on concentrated sectors such as utilities, and not so much on intermediate sectors where there is some, but not perfect, competition.

Finally, the fourth hypothesis is that rather than leading to coarse separation of groups affected by the policy, such as consumers versus producers, or employers versus workers, policy will be calibrated in order to separate within each group which subgroups are better able to provide support and opposition. Instead of catering only to the interest of industry at the expense of consumers, policy distinguishes a vector of attributes, for example, firms in the industry according to size, location, technology, origin of capital, unionization, or level of population, and consumers according to income, preferences, corporate versus individuals, geographic location, and political views. The coalition that will be net benefitted by the final policy will contain both firms and consumers. The better politicians are able to make these distinctions and fine-tune policy to these configurations, the greater the net support they will be able to extract. The prediction is: government policy will tend to be complex and detailed and not favor a single homogeneous group.

Competition among Interest Groups

The view of interest groups and government policy based on the "demand" for redistribution came to be known as the "Economic Theory of Regulation." It was further refined when Gary Becker wrote "A Theory of Competition among Pressure Groups for Political Influence." Becker (1983) added to the Stigler/Peltzman model something that had been conspicuously missing. In the standard model to political behavior, politicians were assumed to design policies with an eye only to the marginal support and opposition that different configurations of transfers elicited from the different affected groups. But any redistribution through taxes and subsidies also necessarily entails deadweight losses that reduce efficiency. Like a leaky bucket to take water from one group to give to another, deadweight losses mean that one dollar that is taxed will allow less than a dollar to be given as subsidy. The more inefficient the design of the policy, the greater will be the hole. Because politicians want to maximize their net support, they have an incentive to choose methods of taxing and subsidizing that avoid high deadweight losses. With this additional consideration, Becker's model added four additional testable hypotheses to the economic theory of politics.

The first is that what matters in determining which groups will be taxed and which will be benefited, and by how much, is the *relative* ability of each group to produce pressure, not the absolute ability. The competition between interest groups is zero-sum in influence and negative-sum in taxes and subsidies, due to deadweight costs. Thus if both groups, taxed and subsidized, increase their level of pressure, this might not lead to much change in net influence and consequently little change in the equilibrium amount of transfer. It also implies that when we observe a group that seems to be ineffective at producing political pressure being benefited by governmental policy, it probably means that the taxed groups are even worse.

The second hypothesis is that if marginal deadweight losses increase, the taxed group will apply more pressure against the policy and the subsidized group will reduce their pressure, leading to less of the transfers. It's as if the higher deadweight losses have made the transfer more expensive, so less of them are realized in equilibrium. Increases in deadweight losses reduce the amount of redistribution resulting from the competition among interest groups. Becker (1983: 381) interprets this to imply that when we see wasteful programs in real life, it means that these "politically successful programs are 'cheap' relative to the millions of programs that are too costly to muster enough political support."

The third hypothesis states that the politically successful groups will tend to be small relative to the groups that are taxed to pay for those transfers. This comes about because deadweight costs increase at increasing rates, so that it is better to fund a given transfer by taxing a large group with a small less-distorting tax than to get the same amount through a larger, highly distorting tax on a smaller group. For example, when agriculture is a large portion of GDP, as in many developing countries, it is common for agriculture to be taxed through price controls or exchange rates, to benefit industry, which is a smaller part of the economy. In countries where agriculture is a small part of

GDP, like the United States and France, it is subsidized by taxes on other sectors.

Finally, the concern over inefficiencies in the transfer of resources means that the competition among interest groups has the effect of leading the most efficient method of taxation to be used, as both groups can be made better off with more efficient forms of transfers. This leads Becker (1983: 396) to conclude that "this analysis unifies the view that governments correct market failures with the view that they favor the politically powerful by showing that both are produced by competition among pressure groups for political favors." Strangely enough, the Chicago approach to interest groups ends up partially rehabilitating some of the conclusions of the Public Interest Theory, even though its premises and outlook are completely different.

Public Choice and Rent-Seeking

While the Chicago approach tended to ignore the "supply" side of government, the Public Choice approach embraced it, though both approaches are founded on the very similar premise that people and groups naturally try to seek rents for themselves through the political arena.[14] The point of departure for Public Choice is the assumption that people who act in their own self-interest in usual market situations do not stop doing so once they step into office or administrative positions, so that politicians and bureaucrats must be similarly modelled as self-interested rather than public-spirited servants of society. But, although this is very close to the Chicago School premise that politicians set policies so as to maximize their net support, the conclusions about the policy-making process differ. For the Chicago School, political competition assures that arrangements that arise and persist are as efficient as can be expected, so that any reform to try to eliminate existing forms of redistribution and transfers among interest groups will probably make matters worse. Faced with proposals to reform current policies to eliminate perceived inefficiencies, a typical Chicago response would be that probably some important cost is being ignored

---

[14] For more details on the Public Choice literature, see Mueller (2003) and Rowley and Schneider (2004).

in the proposal.[15] The Public Choice approach, on the other hand, sees no efficiency-enhancing properties of political competition, but rather that due to imperfect information that makes voters and citizens poorly informed, politicians will often opt for inefficient "sneaky" methods of redistribution over more transparent efficient methods (Coate and Morris, 1995: 1212). As a remedy for these pathologies, the approach believes that constitutional rules and better methods for aggregating preferences (e.g., voting mechanisms, legislative rules, or bureaucratic structures) could be designed so as to curb rent-seeking behavior. James Buchanan (1985), for example, famously argued in favor of balanced budget amendments.

The difference boils down to the sensitivity of demand for the transfer to the increase in deadweight loss. The next best transfer method will entail a larger deadweight loss, but it may still lead to approximately the same level of transfers, if the demand for redistribution is insensitive (inelastic), or to a great reduction if it is sensitive (Lott, 1997). For example, Alston and Mueller (2006) studied the use of pork by the Brazilian executive to gain support for its projects in Congress. The executive has great discretion whether to implement or ignore small amendments to the budget made by individual congressmen that involve resources for minor public works or geographical distribution in their districts. The transfers are of great local electoral value to the congressmen, and many are willing to vote in favor of the executive's programs so as to have their transfers approved. There is great criticism of this exchange of pork for support under the argument that legislators should vote the public interest and not their own personal or constituents' interests: the executive should use the budget for the greater social good and not for buying political support. Several reforms of the system have been suggested, in particular, removing the executive's discretion whether to implement budget amendments and thus its ability to use them strategically as a political currency. Doing so would only lead to the same political negotiation of support to be realized through more costly and distorting methods (Alston and

---

[15] Lott (1997: 224) puts it this way: "If an economist had a model of how to design a perpetual motion machine, the normal response would be that he has left out some important frictions (costs) out of his analysis. A Chicago School response to an economist who produces a new optimal tax is 'if it is so optimal, why don't we see it?' In other words, what important costs have you left out of your model?"

Mueller, 2006). In Brazil, pork is a relatively "cheap" means of attaining the support that the executive uses to approve important reforms that the country direly needs. From a societal view, it is better to put pork (the political currency) in the hands of the executive who ought to have voters at large in mind versus members of Congress who cater to the demands of their constituents, that is, geographic redistribution. Moreover, the total value of the individual amendments is a very small fraction of the total budget, and the pork that is given generally goes into local projects that generate social value, even if not the optimal social use of those resources. Alston and Mueller's position is compatible with the Chicago School view that the demand for redistribution is inelastic and will persist even if the existing method of effecting transfers is prohibited. Those who propose reforms that eliminate the current method of redistribution expect that the level of rent-seeking will be reduced once it becomes more expensive, in terms of deadweight losses, to make the exchanges of pork for support. Which view is right turns out to be an empirical issue and highly contextual (Lott, 1997).

For the Public Choice perspective, the form chosen by politicians to redistribute resources is often not determined by efficiency considerations, but rather to conceal what is going on from voters. Thus, rather than using direct cash transfers or other transparent methods, politicians often use large public projects, such as building an airport or developing a new military technology, which indirectly benefit selected interest groups, but may or may not also benefit the rest of society (Coate and Morris, 1995).[16] Citizens usually have less information about whether the project will benefit them than the politicians do, and even after the fact they cannot perfectly observe whether the project was in their interest. Military technology, for example, benefits the defense industry for sure, but benefits to citizens depend on future events such as war or peace, which may be endogenous to expenditures. Because these types of public projects could be undertaken by public-spirited politicians, self-interested politicians can take advantage of the incomplete information to redistribute resources in a concealed manner without harming their

---

[16] Coate and Morris's (1995) article is a critique of Public Choice approaches for not being more explicit about the sources or the imperfect information that allows inefficient redistribution to take place.

reputations, something that would not be possible with transparent methods such as cash transfers.

 Empirical evidence of the ubiquity and increase in size of megaprojects throughout the world in the past one hundred years seems consistent with this view of transfer choice. Flyvbjerg (2014: 6) defines megaprojects as "large-scale, complex ventures that typically cost US\$1 billion or more, take many years to develop and build, involve multiple public and private stakeholders, are transformational, and impact millions of people." The Joint Strike Fighter aircraft program, China's high-speed rail project, the Burj Khalifa building in Dubai, or the Rio Olympic Games are examples of megaprojects. Flyvbjerg (2014) shows that total global spending in megaprojects is currently of the order of 8 percent of total global GDP and with strong growth in size and frequency over time, so that we may soon be entering an era of trillion-dollar projects. Driving the megaproject boom are the "four sublimes" – technological, political, economic, and aesthetic – that make them appealing to a broad coalition that stands to gain and support the projects: engineers and technologists, politicians, business people and trade unions, and designers and people who love good design. The "Iron Law of Megaprojects" – *over budget, over time, over and over again* – makes megaprojects convincing evidence of the notion that they may be a form of concealed inefficient transfers to interest groups (Flyvberg, 2014: 11). Cost overruns, for example, are frequently large, and happen in all countries irrespective of income, geography, political system: for example, overruns amounted to: 1,900 percent, the Suez Canal; 1,600 percent, the Scottish Parliament Building; 1,400 percent, the Sydney Opera House; 560 percent, the Medicare system in the United States; and 440 percent, the Bank of Norway building, just to name a few. By analyzing the seventy years of available data, Flyvbjerg (2014: 11) comes to the following dismal assessment:

Success in megaproject management is typically defined as projects being delivered on budget, on time, and with the promised benefits. If, as the evidence indicates, approximately one out of ten megaprojects is on budget, one out of ten is on schedule, and one out of ten delivers the promised benefits, then approximately one in one thousand projects is a success, defined as "on target" for all three. Even if the numbers were wrong by a factor of two – so that two, instead of one out of ten projects were on target for cost, schedule, and benefits, respectively – the success rate would still be dismal, now eight in one thousand.

Empirical Tests of Interest Group Theories

Interest group theories yield many testable implications of rent creation, the distribution of rents and the impact on economic efficiency.
Crude tests of the importance of political rents try to detect changes
in prices, profits, entry, exit, and other variables after policies change
and then associate the changes with the interest groups. But this kind
of test tells us very little about the mechanism and channels through
which interest group pressure operates. More rigorous tests focus on
specific events surrounding policies, such as a roll-call vote in
Congress or a reform imposed by a bureaucracy. We can use the
proposed policies to perform an incidence analysis of which groups
stand to win and to lose from each of the competing propositions.
This allows a test of whether the final form taken by the policy, after
interest groups have competed to influence the outcome, conforms
to initial expectations from the theory, for example, does the new
policy favor small, homogeneous, and well-organized groups?
A standard empirical strategy regresses the votes by congressmen
on a given bill that has clear redistributive consequences against
measures of the size, strength, and cohesion of affected interest
groups in each legislator's constituency, controlling for other factors
that might also influence their votes. Although the empirical strategy
is relatively straightforward, in practice it has been plagued by many
problems.

The first is that it is hard to measure the strength and level of
organization of different interest groups, which is the crucial explanatory variable. Typically, researchers rely on crude proxies and broad
socioeconomic measures to correlate with the characteristics of the
relevant constituency. Examples include: the value of an industry's
production as a measure of its capacity to produce pressure, or the
number of members of special issue groups, such as environmental
organizations. Typical proxies for the constituency of a legislator are
party affiliation or ratings produced by political organizations (such as
ADA scores, a measure of political liberalism).[17] These broad measures
may capture some of the more obvious pressures on legislators, but

---

[17] ADA scores are calculated by the Americans for Democratic Action (www
.adaction.org/) based on key past roll-calls, with a zero indicating conservatism
and a 100 indicating liberalism. These scores are widely used in academic work
to measure legislator's ideology, record, and constituencies.

individual legislators also face a myriad of other idiosyncratic constituencies that are hard to detect and control for in a regression.

The second problem in most of the tests of interest group theories relates to identifying the effect of the treatment (interest group pressure) on the shape of the final policies. Most of the tests in the literature preceded advances in empirical methods that tightened the standards for claiming causality rather than simple correlation. As such, they show little concern for establishing an empirical strategy that can rigorously capture the causal impact of interest groups on outcomes. Many studies simply assume that the causation runs from interest groups to policy outcomes. But in many cases, it may be that the causality also stems from previous redistributive policies making some interest groups stronger and more influential. In the same vein, there are frequently omitted variables that haven't been measured or can't be measured, that may be the actual underlying determinant of both the distribution of interest groups and of the policy (e.g., beliefs or ideology).

A third problem is what Roger Noll (1989b: 1277) has called the "lurking danger of tautology, i.e., of attributing causality to an inevitable consequence of any public policy action." Because every policy leads to some redistribution, there are always winners and losers, so it is very tempting to ascribe to those interests that win the key role in having pursued and approved the change. Such functionalist accounts appeal to intuition, but are often misleading due to the complex nature of policy change, which is not fully controlled by any of the parties and is commonly full of surprises and unintended consequences.

A final concern with the empirical literature is publication bias that rewards positive results, that is, editors select primarily studies where interest groups have been shown to have been key determinants of policy change, while underrepresenting or ignoring cases where interest groups were not found to matter. An illustration of the concern comes from *Chicago Studies in Political Economy* (1988) edited by George Stigler. Part III of the book contains eight articles that display empirical tests of the Stigler/Peltzman/Becker approach. These tests cover the 1962 Drug Amendments,[18] automobile safety,[19] public ownership of

---

[18] Originally published as Peltzman (1973).
[19] Originally published as Peltzman (1975).

urban transit facilities,[20] discrimination in the Department of Health, Education, and Welfare,[21] the 1973 Mattress Flammability Act,[22] no-fault automobile insurance laws,[23] redistribution through commodity markets,[24] and environmental regulation.[25] All of these studies are well done and are, to a greater or lesser extent, convincing that interest groups played crucial roles in shaping policy changes. One may wonder, however, in how many instances were interest groups not determinant, and therefore the case was not subject to academic inquiry or publication. There are possibly at least as many cases where no impact from interest groups could be found. When is it that interest groups play a role, and when is it that they will not? It is likely that there are situations and circumstances related to a country's political institutions and norms that affect when interest groups will have a greater or lesser impact.

Clearly, all the critiques of empirical tests of interest group impact presented above can be ameliorated by effort and hard work to, for example, get better data, use better statistical methods and empirical strategies, and avoid functionalist explanations. Much of the literature on interest groups purposefully seeks to be general and not tied to institutional detail. Yet, even many authors were aware that generality comes at a cost. Gary Becker states in the conclusion of his seminal 1983 paper: "I recognize that progress has been obtained at the expense of various simplifying assumptions that should be modified. These include a neglect of voting, bureaucrats, politicians, and political parties" (396). Similarly, Peltzman (1989: 7) notes that Chicago School models purposefully suppress the "details of the machinery of politics." Even later influential models, such as Grossman and Helpman (2001), strive to minimize the institutional details insofar as such a thing is possible when trying to model lobbies and government in a representative democracy (Baron, 2002: 1227). In the next subsection, we show some of the costs of abstracting from the underlying institutional context. Then, in subsequent sections, we give

---

[20] Originally published as Pashigian (1976).
[21] Originally published as Borjas (1978).
[22] Originally published as Linneman (1980).
[23] Originally published as Landes (1982).
[24] Originally published as Gardner (1983).
[25] Originally published as Pashigian (1985).

examples of research on interest group impact that takes care to measure the role of political institutions.

When Predictions Fail: Deregulation and Interest Group Theories

In the early 1970s, a strong movement towards deregulation of various sectors gained momentum in the United States and subsequently spread across many other countries in the world. In the United States, this started with deregulation of rail and truck transportation, and was followed by airline, energy (especially gas and electricity), telecommunications, and finance, generally reducing barriers to entry and increasing competition. At the same time, there was an increase in other types of regulation, particularly environmental, product and workplace safety, and labor contracts. The trend was not simply ideological or partisan as it was pursued by presidents as diverse as Nixon, Carter, and Reagan.

The strong move towards deregulation presented many problems for both interest group theories and for public interest theories, as the natural prediction that emanates from both these theories is high levels of regulation and not deregulation. Public interest theories expect high levels of regulation because governments are modelled as seeking to correct market failures. Unless market failures had suddenly fallen, there should be no reason for deregulation to increase at such a rapid pace. Curiously, the increase in deregulation in economic markets was accompanied by an increase in social regulation.

Self-interest theories also do not sit well with deregulation, but for different reasons. One of the main predictions of these theories is that regulation will tend to favor small, homogeneous, well-organized groups, such as firms in concentrated sectors, at the expense of large, diffuse, and unorganized groups like consumers. Yet, deregulation seems to do exactly the opposite. Of course, here, too, one could argue that changes in technologies, demand, information available to voters, organizational technologies (facilitating collective action), and so on, could explain the changes as a shift in the equilibrium that arises from the competition among interest groups. But although many of these changes were real, they don't seem to salvage the theory. The shape and scope of deregulation were so antithetical to what self-interest theories would expect, that in 1989, Sam Peltzman, one of the main proponents of the Chicago School approach, was compelled to publish an article called "The Economic Theory of Regulation after a Decade of Deregulation," where he takes stock of the performance of the Chicago School approach in light of the evidence. Peltzman is extremely candid about the theory's shortcomings and limitations when confronted with the facts,[26] though he maintains that in many ways the theory remained useful and at least had fared better than public interest theories.[27]

Interest Groups in a Web of Principal-Agent Relations

The inability of the early self-interest theories to adequately account for events such as the trend towards deregulation and the strengthening of social regulation in the 1970s in the United States hints at crucial missing elements: information asymmetries and institutions.[28] The Chicago School theories place incredible informational demands on politicians. They are expected to know all the interest groups; the degree of organization of interest groups; and the reaction of interest groups to policies. After calculating the optimal policy that maximizes net political support, the policy is communicated to a perfectly subservient bureaucracy for implementation. Even understanding that models necessarily simplify reality, the complexity of real-world politics suggests that information asymmetries are simply too central to interest group competition to be assumed away.

Information asymmetries are an inescapable element of the interaction of interest groups with other organizations.[29] The real-world

[26] For example, when reviewing the changes in trucking regulation, he admits that "here then is an industry in which substantial and sustainable rents received the fullest measure of organized support from the beneficiaries. There is simply no way I know of to square the wholesale elimination of these rents by political action with any current version of the ET" (economic theory) (1989: 26).

[27] The same issue of the journal brings comments by Roger Noll and by Michael Levine, as well as by assorted other participants in the meetings where the paper was presented, assessing Peltzman's defense. The general tone is highly critical.

[28] Two other important elements for this research are beliefs and leadership. Both played crucial roles in the United States' move towards deregulation. Both of these elements will be examined in detail in Part III of the book.

[29] We use the term "organization" rather than actor or player to be consistent with our definitions in Part I. Organizations are the unit of action for a unified response to the incentives created by institutions and norms. We recognize that it is individuals within organizations who take action.

process of social choice is much more complex than abstract models that have politicians on one side and interest groups on the other. The process involves a wide variety of different organizations, each with different preferences and different capacities to influence outcomes, as determined by the norms and institutions. Politicians are not a uniform group; there are presidents, representatives, senators, committees, parties, among others. Agencies, departments, regulators, ministries, secretariats, among others, each with different preferences and powers, implement policies. Courts at different jurisdictional levels can be invoked by other parties or may proactively intrude. In addition, there are voters with widely varying preferences and different levels of information and willingness to participate in the process. The media can play an important role by giving certain issues more salience and affecting the quantity and quality of information of other parties, often in non-disinterested ways. A further complication is that many of these organizations are aggregates of different individuals, even though we may refer to them as a single entity, such as "the court," the "committee," and "the median voter." Although it is sometimes a useful simplification to treat an aggregate group as a single actor, it is important to keep in mind, and sometimes to explicitly consider, that each group must have an underlying process of social choice that determines the aggregate's preferences and action.[30]

How do interest groups fit into this complex web of relations? Because there are so many different organizations involved in any specific policy-making event means that an interest group has many different points of entry into the process. An interest group can, for example, focus on lobbying the president using campaign finance. Alternatively, it may opt to use the courts and judicial review to change a piece of legislation. It can also do both simultaneously and even explore other channels of influence. Public sector unions, for example, are well-placed to lobby directly with members of Congress who sit on committees that deal with budgets and agencies. Instead of simply

---

[30] Institutional and Organizational Analysis (IOA) generally presupposes methodological individualism, which is the view that all explanations of economic and social phenomena must be in terms of individuals and the relations between them (see Hodgson, 2007, for a discussion on different definitions of the term). Most other approaches, such as Public Choice, Law and Economics, and even neoclassical economics, are also generally founded in methodological individualism, though the focus on organizations such as firms and households means that often the basic element is not the individual.

listing the main strands of the literature, we provide structure to the discussion by couching our exposition in a simple spatial model that highlights the role of information asymmetries as well as the network of relationships. In the model, we stress the importance of political institutions in determining the relative power of the organizations as well as the sequence and locus of play for each organization.

One of the most influential early applications of the principal-agent model to political relations argued that apparently inefficient designs of the structure and process of government agencies serve as a means for political principals to control the agencies without having to incur in constant costly monitoring (McCubbins, Noll, and Weingast, 1989). Here, we extend their analysis to include committees, courts, voters, and other organizations to illustrate the web of principal-agent relations in which interest groups take part. In Figure 4.1, Panel I, we show the preferred position of the President (P), House (H), and Senate (S) on a two-dimensional policy space. Here, we assume that each legislative body is homogeneous and can be treated as a single agent (we relax this unrealistic assumption below). The two policy dimensions could be, for example, in the case of marijuana legalization lobbying, the price of the drug to consumers on the horizontal axis, and how hard it is to access the drug on the vertical axis. The initial legislation is at point Q_0. We draw the relevant portions of indifference contours (I_j, for $j=P, S, H$) for each of the political organizations showing which points they prefer to the status quo.[31] The lines between each pair of actor's preferred points, forming a triangle, are the contract curves that show for each pair the locus of points where there can be no Pareto improvements through negotiation. Any point outside of the triangle has at least one point on or in the triangle that all three parties prefer. We assume that P, H, and S have a veto over any proposition, so that once policy has been moved into the triangle or its border, it cannot be subsequently moved, as at least one of the three players would veto the change.

Given the preferences in Panel I, we can predict that the status quo has a good chance of being moved to some point in the lens that

[31] The indifference contours are circles centered at each player's preferred point that show all policies that have the same utility for that player. Standard assumptions assure that the curves are well behaved and have only one global maximum at the preferred point. As with indifference curves, there is an infinite number of contours, but we only show those of interest in the diagram.

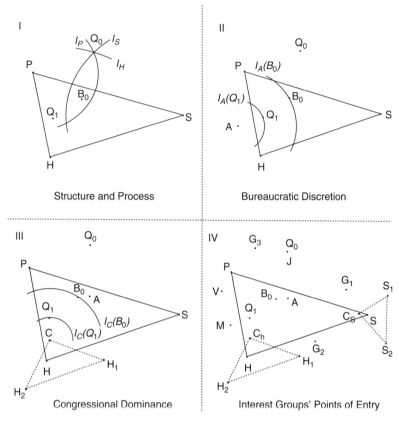

Figure 4.1 Interest groups in a web of principal-agent relations
Source: Panel I adapted from McCubbins, Noll, and Weingast (1989: 438).

emanates from Q_0. Further, we can predict that if it is moved, it will end up in the portion of the lens that is in the triangle. The exact point depends on negotiations during the process of passing a new law and also on contextual features. But once the policy has been moved into the triangle, any further proposed change should be vetoed by at least one of the three players.

  McCubbins, Noll, and Weingast (1989) highlighted the principal-agent problem between the coalition formed by *P*, *H*, and *S* (the principals) and the bureaucracy charged with implementing the legislation at B_0. The problem arises because once the delegation occurred, it is very difficult for the politicians, who have neither the expertise nor the time, to monitor the bureaucracy and assure that it faithfully implements B_0.[32] The bureaucracy can take advantage of the information asymmetry and instead implement a different policy, say Q_1. This bureaucratic drift can go unnoticed by the coalition for a considerable amount of time as policymakers' attention is a scarce resource (Jones and Baumgartner, 2005). Once the coalition does notice the deviation, however, it can be too late to set things straight. It is not simply a case of the coalition reiterating to the agency that it must implement B_0 instead of something else by threatening some form of punishment or by making the legislation more explicit. The drift away from B_0 will necessarily make at least one of the three principals better off (in the example, P is slightly better off and H is much better off, while S is harmed).

When the organizations made the delegation to the bureaucracy, they would be aware of the danger of drift. Because it is too difficult to predict in which direction the agency will deviate, the principals were, in a sense, subject to a lottery where each could win or lose from the bureaucracy's actions. Politicians are risk-averse, so this is a lottery they would rather not play. Therefore, they have incentives to seek ways to prevent the bureaucracy from deviating in the first place, and thus avoid putting the coalition under stress. This is done by setting the bureaucracy's structure and process in such a way to tie the bureaucracy's hand ex ante so that it is unable to deviate in the first place (McCubbins, Noll, and Weingast, 1989). "Process" refers to the rules and standards that constrain a bureaucracy's policy decisions and that guide judicial review. "Structure" establishes who has the authority to make decisions in the bureaucracy and resource allocation. For example, legislation might prohibit a bureaucracy from considering regulatory impact analyses when making a decision. Or, it might require a bureaucracy to hold hearings where stakeholders can voice their support or opposition to the proposed policy change. In the United States, Congress does not try to closely monitor what agencies do, but rather sets up a system of formal and informal institutions that empower individual citizens and interest groups to examine and participate in administrative decisions (McCubbins and Schwartz, 1984). The institutions are akin to fire alarms that interested parties can use to warn Congress about bureaucracy deviations even before they take

---

[32] In Chapter 6, we discuss the role of the bureaucracies in more detail.

place. Together, structure and process can have a profound impact on what the bureaucracy does and crucially determine its performance.

Given its impact on performance and outcomes, one would expect that structure and process would be carefully set based on established principles of public administration and best practices. Instead, structure and process are primarily set by the enabling coalition to strategically reduce the risk inherent in the principal-agent problem (McCubbins, Noll, and Weingast, 1989). Organizations build into the bureaucracy's design safeguards and constraints that impede the bureaucracy from deviating from the contracted policy. These restrictions might reduce the bureaucracy's performance, making it less nimble and less able to respond to the exigencies of the moment, but this cost purchases the assurance that the bureaucracy will not be able to take advantage of its informational cover to surprise the coalition with a fait accompli that they would be unable to revert. When confronted with a bureaucracy that seems woefully slow and ineffective, consider that this may not be due primarily to incompetence and laziness, but rather a case of "inefficiency" by design, that helps mitigate a principal-agent situation.

Our framework can now be used to analyze the variety of ways through which interest groups have been found to participate in policy-making processes populated by multiple other organizations. In the other three panels of Figure 4.1, we add additional organizations to the model. In each case, it is necessary to discuss the preferences of the new organizations and their powers. We bring in interest groups only after all other organizations are in place. We are then in a position to highlight the multiple options faced by interest groups to influence policy.

In Panel I of Figure 4.1, it was not explicit why the bureaucracy shifted the policy from B_0 to Q_1. In Panel II, we consider one possibility that could have led to this outcome: bureaucratic discretion. In this scenario, the bureaucracy in charge of implementing B_0, the policy accorded with the coalition of P, H, and S, has preferences centered at point A.[33] What determines the bureaucracy's preferred point? It is often assumed that the bureaucracy's preferences are ideological, with bureaucrats self-selecting into jobs where they can

---

[33] Contours are not drawn for all organizations simultaneously in order not to clutter the figure, but they can be easily inferred.

pursue their worldviews (Prendergast, 2007; Rourke, 1984; Wilson, 1989). Alternatively, bureaucrats can be modeled as maximizing their own utility by maximizing the bureaucracy's budget, as this translates into wages, perks, and prestige (Niskanen, 1975). The story in Panel II is that the bureaucracy is able to take advantage of the information asymmetries that make its actions opaque to its political principals to deviate from the principal-agent contract by pulling the policy closer to its own preferences. As long as the new policy remains in the triangle, the coalition would not be able to send it back to B_0 even when they realize what is happening, as P and H would veto such a reversal. In this scenario, the bureaucracy is largely insulated from its political principals and it is thus the bureaucracy's preferences and actions that are the key determinant of policy implementation. Note that this analysis assumes the organization as a single actor and abstracts from what may have been the method of aggregating individual preferences within the bureaucracy. Wilson (1989), one of the seminal defenders of the Bureaucratic Discretion view, gives armies, prisons, schools, and regulatory agencies as examples of organizations that are often insulated from their political principals.

In Panel III, we assume that the bureaucracy has preferences very close to the legislated policy at B_0, but is forced to implement policy at Q_1 by its oversight committee in Congress. This is the scenario known as Congressional Dominance, which posits that Congress (and, in particular, committees and subcommittees) often has a series of very effective and subtle mechanisms related to the budgetary process, appointments and reappointments, and subtle fire alarm oversight, among others, that allow close control of bureaucracy behavior even without constant direct oversight and monitoring. Weingast and Moran's (1983) case study of the Federal Trade Commission (FTC) shows that the bureaucracy's sharp turn from highly interventionist in the 1970s to much more hands-off regulation in the 1980s cannot be traced to a preference shift of the bureaucrats, but rather to the electoral shakeup of the members of their direct oversight committees in the House and Senate; laissez-faire proponents replaced interventionists.[34]

---

[34] For a critique of the Congressional Dominance view and of the FTC case study, see Moe (1987).

We portray Congressional Dominance in Panel III by explicitly considering the process through which preferences aggregate in the House to reach preference H. We assume a three-member legislature composed of H_1, H_2, and a committee C that has agenda-setting power, *ex-post* veto, and other prerogatives that allow it to disproportionately determine outcomes in the House (Shepsle and Weingast, 1987). To reach the aggregate preference of the House at H, a prior process of deliberation and voting had taken place in the House where the committee was able to pull the policy close to its preferred point C.[35] The outcome at Q_0 in Panel III is achieved by the House and particularly by the relevant committee through use of its instruments of political control over the bureaucracy.[36]

For an interest group intent on affecting policy, it makes a lot of difference when deciding on a strategy, whether it is in the Bureaucratic Discretion or the Congressional Dominance scenario. In the first case, it would do best to focus its effort to establish a direct relationship with the bureaucracy, for example, providing it with information (possibly biased or distorted) and/or offering post-bureaucracy revolving-door employment to the commissioners. In the second scenario, a completely different strategy focused on committee members would be warranted, perhaps also involving information as well as campaign contributions. Which scenario is apt depends on the contextual political norms and institutions. Political institutions and norms determine whether it is committees that matter or some other organization. It is the norms and institutions that dictate who has voice, who can veto, who must be heard, and the sequence and locus of each step in the policy choice process. This is why an institutionally rich approach to understanding interest group competition is so important.

In Panel IV, we add three additional organizations to the picture: the median voter (V), a court (J), and the media (M).[37] Each is arbitrarily given a policy preference and each is treated as a single actor for exposition. It is technically incorrect, for example, to invoke the

---

[35] The final outcome of this process at H was determined by a previous status quo, a reversion point, and a series of regimental rules that are not discussed here, as they are not directly related to the argument. See McCubbins, Noll, and Weingast (1989: 435–37) and Shepsle and Weingast (1987) for spatial models of the predominance of committees in the US legislative process.

[36] In this example, there is an assumption that it is the House and not the Senate or the executive that exert predominant agency oversight.

[37] In Chapter 7, we discuss the role of the judiciary.

median voter theorem for a two-dimensional case such as this. Any actual analysis would have to consider the whole distribution of voters, the information of voters and their ability to mobilize. The contextual details of the case would also indicate whether the Supreme Court and/ or other courts are the relevant organizations. Even within a court, there may be a preference aggregation rule that might be relevant, placing more influence on some members over others (i.e., the chief justice or the median justice). Similarly, with the media, there is often great competition to influence public opinion and voters. Also, it is relevant whether the media primarily portrays the facts, whether it can be influenced by powerful patrons, or whether it has its own agenda.

As drawn in Panel IV, the court (J) prefers policy to be at the old status quo at Q_0, indicating a possibility of judicial review of the legislation that moved it to B_0. The median voter or public opinion has preferences close to the president, consistent with a presidential election. The media is close to the median voter (perhaps it influenced the presidential election), but lower on the vertical dimension. Note also that the legislative process within the Senate has been made more explicit. There, too, a committee is able to dominate the policy choice.

Faced with the specific context portrayed in Panel IV, what should an interest group do? An interest group G_1 is shown in the figure, as are two competing groups, G_2 and G_3. G_1 was not particularly pleased with the legislation that moved the policy from Q_0 to B_0, and was positively displeased with the bureaucratic drift to Q_1. Is it more effective for the interest group to try to lobby the bureaucracy, the president, the House committee, the Senate committee, or the judiciary? Should it focus its pressure on one organization or adopt a multipronged approach? Would it be more productive instead to try to co-opt voters to embrace a cause that would favor the interest groups' position, possibly using the media to sway public opinion? Given that the other interest group also lies in the same general position on the horizontal axis relative to the current status quo, would it make sense to join forces on this issue? To answer these questions and choose a strategy to influence policy, an interest group would need four important sets of information. Not by coincidence, this is also the information that a researcher analyzing interest group behavior and impact would need to have. The first and easiest is a list of all the organizations directly and indirectly involved. Panel IV gives an idea of the variety of different organizations that might have a stake or an influence over the policy and more could be added, for example, competing agencies and other bureaucratic organizations, district attorneys, advocacy groups, and even foreign governments. The whole federal and state divide has also been left out of the figure, abstracting from many possible subnational and local issues.

Interest groups also need to know the preference of each of the other organizations. This involves not only the location on the policy space but also the intensity of the preferences. Also, the trade-offs between dimensions can be important. How much is a given organization willing to give up on one dimension to gain along another? By assuming circular indifference contours, we are implicitly assuming equally weighted dimensions, but in practice the contours could very well be elliptical. To complicate further, in Figure 4.1 we subsumed the policy into two dimensions, but actual policies may involve many additional dimensions. Identifying the preferences of some organizations may be easy, but for others it will be much harder. A further complication lies in the fact that most of the organizations are actually collectives composed of more than one individual, so there is often an underlying instance of preference aggregation as well as a need to solve collective-action problems (Olson, 1965).

In addition, interest groups need to know the relative power of each organization. This requires understanding how norms and institutions function. Norms and institutions are rules that specify who participates at each point of the process; the prerogatives of the organizations; what constraints they face; which instruments they can use; and in which arenas the interactions take place. Whereas the graphs in Figure 4.1 provide data about the first two sets of information – organizations and preferences – they say little about the rules of the game. This information has to be filled in when explaining the game represented by the figure. Knowledge of the actual workings of the norms and institutions is a critical input for an interest group's success in influencing policy.

The fourth type of information that an interest group needs is knowledge of how much information each of the other organizations has about the first three types of information, that is, players, preferences, and powers. Knowing what and how much each other player knows turns out to be critical given the strategic nature of the interactions, including the knowledge of how much other organizations know about what the interest group knows, and so on in game-theoretic fashion.

Interest groups use four channels to affect outcomes: organizations involved, preferences, power, or information. Any real-world case typically involves all four channels, but often most of the action is focused on one of the four areas, making it useful to think of the cases in these terms. In what follows, we give some examples of interest group research in each of the channels.

Influencing Policy by Affecting the Organizations Involved

The set of organizations that take part in the policy-making process of any given issue is not under the control of an interest group and must be taken as given. In some cases, however, the interest group can try to influence the venue where the issue is considered, bringing some organizations into play that might not otherwise participate in the process. One example is when an interest group initiates a lawsuit against a bureaucracy's implementation of a policy, thus bringing the courts into the policy-making process (Shipan, 1997). In Panel IV, for example, interest group G_3 was made worse off when P, S, and H moved the policy from Q_0 to B_0, and even worse off after the bureaucratic drift to Q_1. It would probably be expensive and ineffective to try to lobby the coalition of P, S, and H to bring the policy back closer to where it originally had been. However, G_3 can take advantage of the fact that the court's (J) preferences are centered on the old status quo Q_0 to bring the court into the game by litigating B_0. In the United States, the court can be overturned by Congress, so it may not be willing to take the risk of reverting B_0 all the way back to Q_0. It can be shown that, under assumptions of rational-choice behavior, if the president has veto power then the final equilibrium would be on the P-S contract curve.[38] This would be an improvement for G_3, especially over the de facto status quo at Q_1. Furthermore, in real-world situations,

---

[38] If the court reviews agency implementation of B_0, the House and Senate can revert the court's decision and effectively choose a new status quo. If the president does not have veto power over the decisions in Congress, this new status quo would likely be on the H and S contract curve. Aware of this, the court would not intervene in the first place, as this would be worse for it than leaving the policy at B_0. If the president does have veto power, the court could put the new status quo on the P-S contract curve. The Senate would not collude with the House to revert the court (as that could lead to a veto). See Gely and Spiller (1990) for this and other models of the strategic interaction between the president, Congress, and Supreme Court.

transaction costs and uncertainty obstruct Congress's ability to revert the court, making litigation an attractive strategy.

Interest groups can bring additional organizations into the game by publicizing and giving salience to an issue so as to recruit voters, who otherwise might be quite aloof, into active participants in the policy-making process. Of course, this will only be a good strategy if the preferences of the voters are such that they will help to promote an outcome preferred by the interest group. Many successful advocacy groups, such as Greenpeace and other environmental groups, put in a lot of effort to make voters aware of the issues they defend. This indirect way of lobbying by spurring voters to pressure policymakers is often more effective than direct pressure. If voters would otherwise simply not participate in the process, the approach of strategically getting them involved is different than that of changing preferences of other organizations.

Changing Preferences of Other Organizations

Advocacy for a given cause and proselytizing to change other people's minds can work for some more ideological issues, but where the policy has direct impacts on peoples' pocketbooks or on politicians' political survival, their preferences tend to be set and cannot be easily changed. The standard approach in mainstream political science as well as in political economy is the Downsian assumption that political organizations are self-interested and their preferences are motivated by political survival (Downs, 1957). If voters are absolutely well informed and engaged, this means that the preferences of politicians reflect that of their relevant constituency (which is different for P, S, and H). If voters are rationally ignorant, the preference would reflect the preference of interest groups, although there may also be space for politicians to pursue their own views of the world, that is, ideological consumption (see Kalt and Zupan, 1984, 1990).

Interest groups can influence other organizations by paying them to act in favor of a project or policy that they would not otherwise support. This is the most direct way for interest groups to get what they want; simply buy the support you need to make it happen. When interest groups buy votes from legislators, bribe judges, give campaign contributions to the president, offer post-employment jobs to bureaucrats, purchase coverage in the media, or use any of a plethora of other legal and illegal means to change the actions of other players in the policy-making game, they are not really changing these players' preferences, but are getting them to act as if their preference coincided with the interest group. In Panel IV, for example, the implementing bureaucracy A has very different preferences from that of interest group G_2, so persuasion and advocacy would probably be ineffective. But if the policy is sufficiently important to G_2, it could try to get A to implement the policy closer to point G_2 by offering bribes or revolving-door employment that covered the bureaucracy's opportunity costs.

This purchase of support, however, is not as straightforward as it may seem on the surface. Complications arise because there are typically several organizations interested in any given policy so that attempts by an interest group to get another organization to move a policy in one direction can be met with reactions from other organizations who would lose, exhorting the policymaker in another direction. There are typically multiple principals pressuring for multiple tasks, so that the final policy position will be the net result of several groups with different strengths pulling in different directions. The multiple tasks refer to the fact that each interest group would like to have the organization pursue different, often conflicting, outcomes. With multiple principals and multiple tasks, the optimal incentives provided by the principals and the optimal amount of effort incurred by the organization turn out to be even more low-powered than in the simple principal-agent case. The organization's incentives are now not only dampened by the non-observability of effort leading to a second-best level of effort, but in addition the incentives by one interest group can largely cancel out with the opposite incentives by other interest groups, leading to a third-best outcome that is even further from the optimal first-best situation. In addition, there is a bias where the organization focuses on the tasks that are more easily observable to the detriment of those that are harder to perceive and quantify (Bernheim and Whinston, 1986; Holmström and Milgrom, 1991). The upshot is that what emerges from interest group competition under common bureaucracy and asymmetric information turns out to be much different than what would be expected from the Chicago School models where outcomes closely reflected relative interest group wealth and cohesion, and where forces worked to minimize the inefficiencies needed to effect the redistribution. Once the full transaction costs inherent in these relationships are added to the analysis, a much messier picture emerges of low-powered incentives brought on by seemingly inefficient norms and institutions. For example, Spiller (1990) shows that under some circumstances, legislators who are competing with an interest group to influence a bureaucracy might find it in their interest to simply allow the bureaucracy to be captured by the private interest, as they can then extract the rents from the bureaucracy through their powers of appointment and budgetary control.

An important implication is that even citizens, an unorganized interest group, which does not mobilize and consciously try to influence the policymaker's choices, end up being represented in the process. Voters are typically too dispersed and heterogeneous to overcome the costs of collective action, but because they vote, legislators will take into consideration how they would perceive any support given to an organized interest group. Denzau and Munger (1986) provide a model of the interaction of organized interest and legislators under the shadow of voters. They derive a "supply price" for public policy demanded by the interest group from the legislator. This price, which is paid in campaign contributions and other forms of political support, depends on both the legislator's productivity of effort – how well he is placed to affect the outcome (e.g., committee membership) – and also by the preferences of the constituency of the legislator. If the interest group seeks a policy that is egregious to the legislator's constituency, he may still be willing to supply effort towards that outcome, but it will be more costly for the interest group. Thus, interest groups have an incentive to shop carefully for support, seeking out those legislators who are better able to affect the policy and whose constituency is less unsympathetic to the issue or less informed of what the legislator does because of rational ignorance. The upshot is a more nuanced view of the policy-making process than the simple vote-buying story:

Interest groups do not control this process, but neither are special interests powerless. Contributions can have some influence on policies about which voters are divided, ignorant, or indifferent. The geographic constituency is not represented to the exclusion of all other groups, but departures by legislators from their voters' interests are constrained by the strong preferences voters have on some issues, and by the threat of informing and mobilizing public opinion that the news media and potential competitors always represent. (Denzau and Munger, 1986: 102–103)

Changing the Powers of Other Organizations

An interest group may try to change the rules that determine the powers of other organizations in the policy-making process. Institutions and norms determine structure and process and social choice. In most situations, interest groups take the rules of the game as fixed and try to do the best they can under the rules. But given that interest groups are in the business of influencing policy outcomes, there is no reason why they would not also try to influence the rules.[39]

Nearly all the literature on constitutions assumes that there is a fundamental difference between constitutional politics and ordinary politics that makes choices about the rules more insulated than choices within the rules (Ginsburg, 2010: 263). Choices made in these "constitutional moments" are supposedly more stable, enduring, and consequential than regular policy choices. But Ginsburg goes on to note:

Even if one believes in theory that veil of ignorance rules can solve the problem of self-interest at the constitutional level, true veils of ignorance are unlikely in the formation of real world constitutions. Political actors in the real world are embedded into constitutional orders to which they sometimes invest strategic energy. And they seem willing and able to move across levels when need be. (2010: 264)

The Congress in Brazil drafted the Brazilian Constitution of 1988 and was as far as possible from the conditions of a veil of ignorance. Interest groups jockeyed to influence the rules that would subsequently determine lower-level laws. Mueller (1998) used roll-call votes to show that legislators representing the interest of large landowners in the constitution-drafting process managed to secure rules for land reform that drastically reduced their risk of land expropriation. Similarly, Libecap (1992) showed that legislators in the United States passed the Sherman Act of 1890, which would become a landmark statute in US antitrust, partly at the behest of small slaughterhouses and farmers that were being harmed by large Chicago meat-packers using new refrigeration technology.

---

[39] For examples of rule breaking, see Shepsle (2017).

Affecting Policy by Manipulating Information of Other Organizations

Although direct pressure, such as vote buying, is the most obvious means for an interest group to pursue its interest, indirect strategies to change what other organizations do by changing information flows is another strategy. Policy making takes place in a network of principal-agent relations that are fundamentally defined by information asymmetries. The distribution of information is a crucial determinant of the structures and arrangements that emerge as well as the actions taken by organizations. Interest groups, by their very nature, often know more about their issue area than politicians, bureaucrats, and voters. When legislators produce, bureaucrats implement, and courts review legislation, they need information on how the world really works related to the issues involved. Interest groups have a comparative advantage in providing that information. Although the interest groups clearly have incentives to misrepresent the information, it can be preferable for policymakers to have biased information than nothing at all, as they can always try to discount the bias.

More nuanced than the use by interest groups of the information about the parameters and working of the issue area is the strategic use of information related to the three items discussed above: organizations, preferences, and powers. In terms of Figure 4.1, Panel IV, we can conceptualize the issue by modeling each organization in a separate figure, each with different levels and accuracy of information about who are the organizations, what are their preferences, and what they can do. Because each of the organizations makes their choices in the policy-making game using their own set of information, organizations can affect the choices of others by changing their information.

Alston, Libecap, and Mueller (2010) provide an example of an interest group that strategically targets the information of voters in order to subtly affect the level of pressure that voters put on policymakers. With one of the most concentrated landownership structures in the world, Brazil has tried to carry out land reform at least since 1946. Congress and the president passed and implemented legislation and policies, but very little redistribution took place until the mid-1990s. In the 1990s, the Landless Peasant Movement (known as MST for Movimento Sem-Terra) devised a strategy of invading unproductive land as a means to attract government authorities to expropriate the land in their favor. The strategy worked remarkably well and massive areas have since been redistributed to landless peasants, equivalent to the area of France, Austria, Ireland, and Portugal combined. At first sight, this is a very crude interest group strategy, based simply on violence and potential violence. Why did it work for the MST when it did not work for other interest groups, such as the urban homeless and the people displaced by dam constructions, both of which have similar organizations and have tried similar strategies?

When the MST invades a property, its intention is not a straightforward land grab. Instead, they are trying to change the nature of the multiple-principal multiple-task relation between landowners and voters – the principals – and the federal government, which is charged with land reform – the agent (Alston, Libecap, and Mueller, 2010). The crucial factor to understand is that in Brazil, land reform has extremely high salience and valence as a political issue. Over time, land reform has come to be a symbol and banner of disapproval with historically derived inequality and oppression. After the end of military rule in 1985, land reform was one of the first programs announced by the new democratic government and has since been a major part of the political debate. Even urban voters (Brazil is 85 percent urban), who are not directly affected by land reform, have been highly in favor of far-reaching land redistribution to correct the injustices of the past. The MST invades land to get the voters' attention on land reform (Alston, Libecap, and Mueller, 2010). This has the effect of informing voters that they should question the claims of government that it is doing the best it can to fulfill its electoral land reform promises. The strategy of the MST is to reduce the information asymmetry between voters and the government, so that voters apply more pressure and more land gets redistributed. It is an indirect but highly effective strategy. It is not reproducible by other groups in Brazil because they lack the same level of voter sympathy to their cause.[40]

---

[40] For other examples of indirect pressure by interest groups through lobbying the voter, see Sobbrio (2011) and Yu (2005). For more on landless peasants and land reform in Brazil, see Alston, Libecap, and Mueller (1999a, 1999b, 2000). For studies that focus on the role of the media in interest group competition, see Baron (1989, 1994, 2005), Besley and Burgess (2001), Besley, Burgess, and Prat (2002), and Stromberg (2004).

Conclusion

Inherent in interest group competition is the notion of winners and losers. In all of the models and examples given in this chapter, there was always a set of organizations that benefited from the policy outcomes and another set that was harmed. But why don't the losers get together and propose another policy that makes themselves and a subset of the winners better off than the current status quo? In general, such an alternative policy always exists. And if this could be pulled off by the current losers, it could also be pulled off by the subsequent losers of the new status quo. A major result from Social Choice Theory is that when societies make choices, there is no method of aggregating the preferences of many individuals that always leads to a "good" choice, given some very reasonable desiderata for socially acceptable outcomes (Arrow, 1963; McKelvey, 1976). Simple majority rule, the most common method for making social choices across time and space, for example, does not guarantee that outcomes will be stable or optimal in any sense. According to the earlier theory, social choice is inherently unstable and subject to endless cycles, where what is decided today gets changed tomorrow as the losing parties introduce new propositions that break the current winning coalition by offering some of the winners more than they currently get.

Interest group competition is a means of making social choices about the allocation and distribution of resources. As such, it should be subject to the problem of cycles, instability, and chaos. Yet, even though interest group politics might seem at first glance as being inherently chaotic, on closer inspection most outcomes are quite stable and predictable. Once legislation has passed and been implemented, the policies tend to persist for long periods of time. It is uncommon for those harmed by a decision to quickly bring in a new proposal that breaks the winning coalition and upsets the status quo. Instead, decisions are usually persistent and foreseeable.

So why is interest group politics apparently not subject to the stark results of Social Choice Theory? Both Chicago School models reviewed in the second section and the more institutionally rich models reviewed in the third and fourth sections implied stable unique equilibria and an absence of cycling. But each of these did so in very different ways. The Chicago School models essentially assumed the social choice paradox away by positing an interest group influence function measured in dollars that essentially collapses the policy choice onto a single dimension in which a standard median voter equilibrium always exists (Noll, 1989a: 54). The cost to this approach is the loss in realism given the extreme simplification of a complex policy area into an easily manageable one-dimensional choice.

The institutional models, on the other hand, took a different path of increasing the realism of the analysis. In real-world politics, social choice is not made in an unconstrained way in which anybody unsatisfied with the status quo can simply introduce a new proposal at any time. Rather, social choice takes place under very specific rules that specify who can do what and when. The rules are the contextually specific political norms and institutions. They vary tremendously from one country and context to another. By determining which proposals can be brought to consideration and the process that the choice must follow, the institutions and norms strongly reduce the set of viable policies that can beat the status quo. For example, if the rules establish that Congress can revert a decision by the Supreme Court, then any ruling by the court that makes Congress worse off than the status quo will not be an equilibrium (Gely and Spiller, 1990). As another example, if specific committees in the House and Senate are allowed to change the proposal approved on the floor of each chamber, the committees in effect hold an ex-post veto and the floor will tend to defer to the preference of the committees, removing from the set of possible equilibria proposals not preferred by the committees to the status quo (Shepsle and Weingast, 1987). In this way, the entire set of rules in any given context drastically reduces the set of policies that can overturn the status quo, thus greatly increasing the chances of a predictable and stable outcome. The outcome is in a sense induced by the norms and institutions, and is thus known as a Structure-Induced Equilibrium (Shepsle and Weingast, 1981). It does not mean that the outcome cannot be beaten by several other proposals where losers and some winners form a new coalition. Rather, it means that the proposals where this is possible are ruled out by the extant institutions and norms and cannot upset the current outcome. Because the political institutions and norms reflect the distribution of power in society, they are in essence means through which the dominant groups seek to assure the outcomes they prefer, even if this often comes, as we have seen, at a high price in terms of distortions and inefficiencies.[41]

To say that political institutions and norms are crucial determinants of the outcome of interest group competition does not mean that everything is preordained and perfectly foreseeable. A major theme of this book is the dual perspective of play under a given set of institutions and norms; as well as strategies to determine the institutions.[42] Much interest group competition plays out with all parties taking the rules of the game as given, but in other instances the competition is instead to change the rules themselves. This means that especially over longer periods of time, there is a dynamic process of change that can alter institutions and consequently the outcomes of interest group competition. This process of dynamic change is both endogenous and due to exogenous shocks, and can happen incrementally or in punctuated shifts. The changes are linked to beliefs, and often there is a role for leadership to induce and shepherd the process. We take up these themes in greater detail in Part III.

---

[41] Several authors have stressed the intimate relationship between institutions and form taken by interest group competition (see Cox and McCubbins, 2000; Levy and Spiller, 1996; Lijphart, 1977; North, Wallis, and Weingast, 2009; Spiller and Liao, 2008).

[42] As noted in Chapter 1, norms are more stable than institutions, which can be changed by those with power.

5 | The Legislature and Executive

Our intellect does not draw its laws from nature, but it tries – with varying success – to impose upon nature laws which it freely invents.

— Popper (1963: 259)

In the previous chapter, we addressed what we called the demand side of government policy, where citizens and interest groups seek to pressure and compete for the benefits that government can bestow in the form of redistribution and policies. In this and the next two chapters, we cover the supply side, through which government responds to that demand. As we noted earlier, the metaphor of a market for policy where supply meets demand is imprecise, as the process of policy making is much different than a simple exchange of goods for money; there are multiple equilibria. Yet, it is a useful way to structure and present the chapters in this part of the book. In this chapter, we grouped the executive and the legislative powers, rather than having a separate chapter for each. The interactions with the other organizations are critical, and we address those with the bureaucracy in Chapter 6 and with the judiciary in Chapter 7.

The literature on the executive power, the legislative power, and the relation between them is perhaps the literature that most explicitly incorporates the central tenet of Institutional and Organizational Analysis (IOA), that is, "institutions matter." Much of the literature focuses on a given institution and seeks to work out the consequences of that institution in terms of outcomes. The rules are things like presidentialism versus parliamentarism, open versus closed lists in parliamentary elections, majoritarian versus proportional electoral rules, and partial versus total veto power of the president. The list of different rules is very large and so is the corresponding literature. For each choice of rule, an expected outcome is typically theorized. It has been suggested, for example, that presidential systems are more prone to gridlock than parliamentary systems (Linz, 1990); open-list proportional systems lead to individualistic relations between voters and politicians and weaker parties (Ames, 1995); and proportional systems lead to multiple parties, to balkanization of Congress, and to less governability as coalitions have to be formed and maintained (Lijphart, 1999). The rules are not only expected to have political consequences but also economic consequences, for example, the suggestion that majoritarian electoral systems lead to greater fiscal discipline than proportional systems (Hallerberg and Marier, 2001; Roubini and Sachs, 1989).

We make no attempt to cover the entire literature on executive and legislative institutions in this chapter or to fully cover any of the many specific themes. Instead, we give a series of examples that illustrate two important characteristics about executive and legislative institutions. The first is that political institutions matter and are amenable to analysis, which is the central justification for the research covered in this book. But the second characteristic is a qualification on this broad statement. Although political institutions are consequential, it is often foolhardy to try to establish law-like statements linking a given class of institutions to a specific type of outcome. Political institutions are rules that incentivize executive and legislative behavior. They determine who has voice, who participates, who has a vote, who has veto and gate-keeping power, who originates a new initiative, and what are the fora it must traverse, in what sequence and with what timing. Although the rules are clearly central determinants of the types of outcomes that emerge in countries that adopt them, coarse-grained mappings from institutions to outcomes have often failed to explain the rich diversity of experience across countries. There is no unique outcome. The system is too complex with too many interactions.

Any political system is necessarily characterized by a very large set of rights, rules, structures, and processes, such as (1) separation of powers, (2) decree power, (3) exclusive rights to introduce some types of legislation, (4) veto power, (5) urgency requests, (6) electoral rules (e.g., majoritarian versus proportional), (7) partisan legislation, (8) term limits, (9) types of electoral districts, (10) one or two rounds in elections, (11) open list versus closed list, and many, many more. With so many different parameters to consider when analyzing or designing a political system, it is no surprise that in the end no two countries' political institutions will be identical. Importantly, the impact of each of the rules is not linear and is not additive, as there are important interactions between them, as well as with other non-institutional characteristics such as a country's level of development, culture, history, religion, and geography.[1]

The general law-like statements that research often tries to establish, such as "majoritarian systems are more decisive" or "fiscal federalism leads to more efficient public good provision," often fail. Specific institutions that have a given effect in one context can have different effects in other situations. And the interactions, non-linearities, and samples with low variability make it so that it is not simply a case of adding more control variables. It is not that the institutions do not matter – they do crucially. But the effects are more highly contextual, fine-grained, and subtle than is evident from much of the literature.

In this chapter, we substantiate these claims through three examples that illustrate established debates in the literature about the effects of specific executive and legislative institutions. Each debate is about the effect of specific institutions on specific sets of outcomes, and usually center on a claim of the kind "institutions x lead to outcomes y." The common pattern in each of the examples is for a seminal paper or author to be associated with the initial claim, followed by considerable supporting evidence. Eventually, there is a challenge to the conventional wisdom, which suggests new theoretical ways to analyze the claim, also followed by supporting evidence. In some cases, the process of thesis and antithesis leads to a synthesis that maintains some of the validity of the initial observation, but reduces it from a broad overarching law to a much more context-specific conditional statement.

The three examples we cover are:

1. Presidentialism versus parliamentarism;
2. Distributive versus informational versus party cartel theories of Congress; and
3. Duverger's Law, and multiparty versus two-party systems.

Presidentialism versus Parliamentarism

The relative merits of presidentialism versus parliamentarism is one of the most enduring debates in political science. Academics and politicians have endlessly disputed the virtues and vices of each of the forms

---

[1] In Part III, we will discuss modes of analysis that deal explicitly with some of these issues.

of government as regards the political and economic outcomes that each is more likely to induce. There are two central assumptions behind the debate. The first is that presidential and parliamentary systems are sufficiently different across categories and sufficiently similar within, that they can be grouped into just two distinct categories. The second is that each system, presidentialism and parliamentarism, will tend to induce distinct and well-defined outcomes. This is therefore a prototypical example of the kind of issue that IOA is well placed to analyze. If institutions matter, then certainly adopting a presidential versus a parliamentary form of government will have important consequences for outcomes. The point that we highlight in this section is that, indeed, the institutions do matter tremendously, but they do so in more nuanced and sometimes counterintuitive ways than has often been portrayed in the literature.

The key distinction between presidential and parliamentary systems lies in the ways through which the executive is chosen and dismissed. In parliamentary systems, the executive is chosen by the legislature and can be dismissed by it through a vote of no-confidence before its term is over. In presidential systems, in contrast, the executive is directly elected by voters and faces a fixed term in which it cannot be removed (except through exceptional measures). Parliamentary systems are expected to yield governments that are unified and cohesive and have more governability and resoluteness. Presidential systems, on the other hand, are frequently divided and fragmented, which is assumed to make them prone to gridlock and crises of governability. Scholars generally assume that parliamentary systems are more institutionalized and party-based and presidential systems are more centered on individual politicians. There is also the expectation that presidential systems generate a fragmented interest group structure while parliamentarism produces more corporatism. Another difference is in the greater level of checks and balances that is produced by a divided system, which also generates more information for voters and society and more transparency. Other outcomes that have been suggested to be affected by the choice of governmental system are "survival of democracy, economic policy, budget deficits, economic performance, social cleavage management, ethnic conflict, international peace, international co-operation, the quality of democracy, party systems, human development and accountability" (Cheibub, Elkins, and Ginsburg, 2013: 516).

Because of the nature of the postulated effects, there has often been a predilection among academics and other analysts for parliamentary over presidential systems. Linz's (1990) article, "The Perils of Presidentialism," was highly influential in making the case for the superiority of parliamentary systems, perhaps because events around the world seemed to be demonstrating worse results in countries that had opted for presidential systems, especially regarding the breakdown of democracy. Latin America, in particular, had wholly opted for presidentialism and had been the stage for frequent reversals from democracy to dictatorships. But at the same time, Linz's argument also gave rise to a series of other papers questioning whether it even made sense to assume that all the various different democracies can be neatly classified into a presidential/parliamentary dichotomy, given that there are so many different arrangements and details in the specific institutions (Mainwaring and Shugart, 1997; Shugart and Carey, 1992).

Cheibub (2006) forcefully examines the hypothesis that presidential systems are more prone to democratic breakdown. The expectation arises because of the separation between the executive and the legislature. There are fewer incentives for cooperation, higher propensity for conflicts, and greater danger of coups or revolution. The data do show that historically, presidential systems have on average lasted for shorter periods of time than parliamentary democracies; 24 versus 58 years from 1946 to 2002. Cheibub questions the presumption that the difference is due to the different systems of government. Other authors have suggested other variables that may be responsible for the difference in democratic survival across systems, such as wealth, rates of economic growth, or location (Mainwaring and Shugart, 1997; Przeworski et al., 2000). Parliamentarism is more common in (1) richer countries, which in turn are more likely to remain democratic; (2) countries with faster economic growth; (3) countries with smaller populations; and (4) in Europe versus Latin America and Africa. However, Cheibub (2006: 139) shows that even after controlling for these variables in regressions that explain transitions to dictatorship, there is still a greater propensity for presidential democracies to fall into dictatorship.

So, if it is not the institutional differences between the systems of executive-legislative relations, and it is not any of the other variables, what explains the empirical fact that countries with parliamentary systems tend to have greater democratic survival than presidential countries? Cheibub suggests a surprising explanation: it was a historical coincidence. Countries that had been military dictatorships in the middle of the twentieth century chose overwhelmingly a presidential system when they democratized due to an institutional inertia that favored presidentialism even after a radical change in the nature of government. When democracies did break down, they did so, more often than not, through military interventions (more than 80 percent of cases). Therefore, a military legacy indicates a higher probability of breakdown, and because military legacies also tended to produce presidential systems, there is a correlation but not causation between presidential systems and the collapse of democracy. When military legacy is added to the regressions explaining transitions to dictatorship, it is highly significant and the presidential system variable loses its explanatory power.

The discussion suggests that it is ill-advised to try to categorize institutions into very broad definitions and then derive general claims about the effect of the different classes of institutions. Parliamentary and presidential systems seem like very distinct and self-contained categories, where general rules might apply, but the literature has shown that even here this is not the case. Cheibub, Elkins, and Ginsburg (2013) created an index of similarity of constitutions within and across parliamentary and presidential systems using 401 constitutions from 1789 to 2006.[2] They categorize each constitution as parliamentary or presidential according to the defining issues of who elects the head of the state and whether the executive is subject to the assembly's confidence. They examine six elective attributes of the systems: executive decrees, emergency powers, initiation of legislation, legislative oversight, executive veto, and cabinet appointments. The classic approach to presidentialism versus parliamentarism has clear expectations for the existence or the strength of each of the attributes under each system. Parliamentary systems are expected to have stronger decree power, weak emergency power, initiation of legislation by the executive, weak legislative oversight, no executive veto, and cabinet appointed by the legislature, while presidential systems have the opposite expectation. The authors find, however, that there

---

[2] They included a third category of semi-presidential systems, which we will not discuss here.

is a surprising variety of combinations of the elective attributes under each system, and it appears that they are orthogonal to the type of system. The similarity index is created by counting the percent of defining and elective attributes that each pair of constitutions have in common. This yielded 80,200 pairs of constitutions. Of these, 14 percent matched all attributes, yet 56 percent of the perfectly matched pairs were composed of different government types. A comparison of all the pairs showed that the classic definitions had very modest power to predict the package of legislative and executive powers.[3] Cheibub, Elkins, and Ginsburg conclude:

Knowing the century or the region in which the constitutions were written allows one to predict the similarity of their institutional attributes better than one could by knowing only that they are of the same system type. This is our principal and, we believe, somewhat unsettling finding for those of us who have come to rely upon – and teach – the classical conceptualization of regime types. (2013: 537; emphasis in original)

Our review of the parliamentary-presidential debate shows that institutions matter and are the fundamental determinant of performance, but context and details matter, and the mechanisms can often be complex and nuanced.

Distributive/Informational/Partisan Theories of Congressional Committees

In a foreword to a book on positive theories of congressional institutions (Shepsle and Weingast, 1995a), John Ferejohn opens with a statement that summarizes the main message of our chapter:

An important contribution of positive political theory as applied to legislatures (or anything else) is just how elusive the empirical world can be. Very different theories of legislatures can have quite similar observational consequences in a wide range of settings. (1995: ix)

---

[3] The index was also used as the dependent variable in a regression, with explanatory variables being dummies for whether each pair of constitutions were both presidential or both parliamentary, with the cross-system pairs being the left-out category. In addition, they controlled for region, century, and whether the constitutions belong to the same country. The results show that while pairs where both constitutions are presidential have some similarity above the cross-system pairs, parliamentary pairs actually exhibit less similarity.

Positive political theory using rational-choice models and non-cooperative game theory is currently a dominant force in the literature on executive and legislative institutions. The literature started in the 1950s and 1960s with authors such as Arrow (1951), Black (1958), Plott (1967), and Buchanan and Tullock (1962), who pioneered abstract rational-choice models of politics, leading to important insights about majority cycling, vote trading, and coalition formation (see Shepsle and Weingast, 1995a: 6 for a brief review of the literature). This led to a subsequent literature that sought to apply the insights to real-world legislatures. The authors in the first-generation literature in rational-choice legislative politics showed that congressional institutions were subject to cycling, impossibility, and chaos results; rational individual behavior leading to irrational collective outcomes; and other pathologies.[4]

But although some of the results did seem to fit observed behavior and outcomes in legislatures, others did not. In particular, there was a conspicuous absence of majority rule cycling.

If we look at the real world, however, we observe not only is there no endless cycling, but acts are passed with reasonable dispatch and then remain unchanged for very long periods of time. Thus, theory and reality seem to be not only out of contact, but actually in sharp conflict. (Tullock and Brennan, 1981: 189)

For the sake of generality, the original models were poor in institutional detail. By abstracting from most of the details of legislative structure and process, the first-generation literature left out the very elements that were instrumental in assuring stability and predictability. This prompted a second generation of rational-choice legislative scholars to propose models and theories that explicitly sought to incorporate real-world institutional structure and processes that had the effect of inducing specific equilibria by eliminating through rules many of the alternative proposals that would otherwise cause instability. Shepsle and Weingast's (1981) notion of a structure-induced equilibrium substituted a no-holds-barred world, where an infinite sequence of new

---

[4] Cycling, impossibility, and chaos are findings from social choice theory that in situations characterized by simple majority rule (i.e., in democracies), there is no predictable equilibrium. This approach expects policies to either change (cycle) indefinitely and unpredictably, or to settle in inefficient outcomes where alternative outcomes could make more participants better off.

proposals under majority rule was replaced by real congressional institutions that constrained who could propose what and when, greatly reducing the win-sets. The new approach highlighted that there was heterogeneity of preferences among legislators so that although they competed for scarce resources, such as pork and policies, there was scope for cooperation and gains from trade. This led to a view of legislative institutions as primarily driven by the intention to facilitate the political exchanges made possible by existence of the gains. In particular, the committee system was interpreted as a structure and process that helped to provide the credible commitment and cooperation to overcome the barriers to trade (Shepsle and Weingast, 1987; Weingast and Marshall, 1988).

The models, based on a distributive rationale for political institutions, brought theory and empirical results much closer than was the case in the first generation of models. Policy and redistribution emerged in the legislative process, taking the institutions, such as the committee system, the seniority rule, gatekeeping powers, and so forth, as exogenous, and showing existing institutions facilitated the distributive intent of the players. Yet despite the great advance made by the models, in the late 1980s some new perspectives within the rational-choice positive political theory emerged to challenge the centrality of distribution and gains to trade. The third-generation models brought in additional institutional details ignored by the second-generation distributive models by taking a supply-side perspective. In addition, the third-generation models were concerned in heeding to the Riker Objection (see the introduction to Part II and Riker, 1980), that higher-order institutions are not fixed, but rather can be changed, reformed, amended, or eliminated by a suitable majority.

The first challenge was based on the notion that the act of legislating and producing laws is often subject to great uncertainty as to the effect of different ways of setting up policies. Given the uncertainty, different actors in the policy-making process risked seeing their interest harmed by a policy that did not turn out to have the intended effect. The risk provides incentives for institutions that foster the acquisition of information by specialized actors in the policy-making process so as to mitigate the chance of unintended consequences. Scholars proposed a series of informational theories, suggesting that institutions, such as the committee system, should be understood as means to facilitate the acquisition and revelation of such information (Austen-Smith and Riker, 1987; Banks, 1991; Gilligan and Krehbiel, 1987; Krehbiel, 1992).

A second challenge emerged from considering the powers of the majority party in each chamber of Congress that makes the party akin to a legislative cartel (Cox and McCubbins, 2005, 2007). The majority party uses the power to control committees and the legislative agenda to pursue its own interest. In this view, legislative institutions can only be understood as a purposeful choice of the majority party that has the power to control the institutions and associated practices.[5]

In the remainder of the section, we briefly describe the three main positive political theories of congressional institutions and discuss the predictions that each makes for how we should expect committees' structure, process, and practice to materialize if that theory were the right way to understand those institutions. We then present some empirical results from the literature that highlight that even though each theory makes different testable hypotheses, and even though there is plenty of data available to test those hypotheses, in the end there is no clear consensus on which view does better.

Distributive Theory of Congressional Institutions

The distributive theory is the basis of the second-generation models of legislative organization. It sees committees as agents of distribution and allocation by exploring the gains from trade that arise from different demands from legislators who care about different issues. They pursue different policies, and respond to constituencies with different preferences and characteristics. The problem is not a zero-sum game of dividing the pie, but rather that of dividing a pie that contains slices

---

[5] The three theories mentioned here – distributive, informational, and majority party – are not the only rational-choice theories to have been proposed. Kiewiet and McCubbins (1994), McCubbins, Noll, and Weingast (1987), and others have proposed an approach that focuses on the logic of delegation to the committees within a principal-agent framework. Epstein and O'Halloran (2001) seek to explain legislative organization in general and the committee system in particular as crucially determined by the separation of powers. Committees that supervise executive agencies are organized to act as a counterweight to executive branch policy making. We focus on the three main theories, as these have received the most attention.

of many different flavors, so that there are potential Pareto-improving deals to be made (Groseclose and King, 2001: 4).

When a legislator's interest involves benefits that accrue to only his own constituents, and costs that are spread out among all other legislators' districts, there is little chance of approval unless some kind of cooperation can be achieved. The first-generation literature recognized the scope for gains to making deals, but reached the conclusion that such deals would necessarily be prone to cycling. The exchange of support among legislators is not a straightforward proposition, as there are other hazards besides cycling that can undermine the deals and unravel the requisite cooperation among the parties. Given the large number of legislators and the heterogeneity of interests involved in a dynamic setting that extends through time, the transaction costs to identifying, realizing, and enforcing the trades are very large. One problem is the intertemporal sequence of different policies and projects. Political deals extend through time so that some legislators will have to hold their part of the bargain today without guarantees that others will reciprocate in the future. Another problem is that many times the goods being exchanged can be revoked in the future by a subsequent proposal. If, for example, a bargain involves support for a bridge in one legislator's district in exchange for support for a subsidy stream to constituents in another legislator's district, then the first legislator can renege on the support for the other legislator's subsidies once the bridge has been built (Weingast and Marshall, 1988).

Scholars of distributive theory see the committee system as an institutional solution to the intertemporal problems, enabling the gains from trade to be realized. Rather than making the trades one deal at a time, the committee system concentrates influence over all policies in a specific area. This allows legislators to self-select into committees that monopolize power over specific jurisdictions, such as finance or agriculture. Because the legislator cannot be removed from the committee, she has an effective property right to disproportionately influence outcomes in that class of legislation. A series of powers ensures that decisions by committees will not be undone by the floor once a proposal is put to vote. Gatekeeping power and proposal power provide the means to veto and initiate legislation. Additionally, control over the conference committee, which can revise the proposal approved by the floor, gives the senior members of committees an *ex-post* veto that has the effect of strategically discouraging the floor from changing the committee's proposal (Shepsle and Weingast, 1987). Furthermore, the system allows for adaptation to changes in preferences and circumstances over time, although occasionally the structure needs adaptation, perhaps by creating new committees, for example, the Committee on Homeland Security in the House, which became a permanent committee in 2005.

Several testable hypotheses emerge from the distributive theory. If committees serve the purpose of enabling the realization of gains from trade, then it should be possible to show that they have and occasionally use gatekeeping power to kill proposals contrary to the committee's median preference. Similarly, there should be evidence that the floor accedes to the committee by not blocking or changing the committee's proposals, not out of deference, but due to strategic constraints imposed by the conference committee procedures. The most common tests of legislative and committee organization have been of the type that analyzes the preference composition of the committees, as the different theories have very different expectations as to what should be the median preference of the committee relative to the chamber as a whole. We focus only on this class of testable hypotheses here. In the case of the distributive theory, the prediction is that the committees should be composed of preference outliers, that is, members whose interests in that jurisdiction are distinctively unrepresentative of the parent chamber. The data for this kind of test require some measure of legislator preference, such as NOMINATE scores, ADA scores (Americans for Democratic Action ratings), or other measures based on roll-call data or interest group ratings (see Groseclose, 1994, for a critique of some tests and data, and suggestions for more appropriate tests). The preference data then allow a direct test of whether the committee (usually the median preference) compares to the preference of the chamber in the manner predicted by the theory. Weingast and Marshall (1988) and Weingast and Moran (1983) find very strong evidence that committees in the US Congress are composed of preference outliers.

Informational Theory of Congressional Institutions

The third-generation theories of congressional institutions focused not on the demand for legislation and redistribution, but on supply-side issues related to their production. The theories also made important advances by incorporating the majoritarian postulate that institutions themselves are the result of aggregate choices and therefore cannot systematically make the majority of Congress worse off. The informational theory relies on policies selected by a legislature involving a great deal of uncertainty as to the outcomes it will engender once implemented. More specifically, they assume that a policy has a systematic component that is common knowledge, but that there is also a random component that can significantly alter the final outcome. The effect of the random component can be discovered by investing time and effort into learning about its impacts, but the costs and public good nature of the information collection means that the effort will not automatically emerge. The main argument of the theory is that the floor of the chamber may choose to establish incentives for some of its members to specialize in specific areas in order to collect and reveal the information about the random component of policy proposals. In particular, the committee system can be interpreted as an institution primarily designed to give such incentives to specific legislators. In this view, specific committees are repositories of expertise in their narrow jurisdiction, which makes the entire chamber better off by helping to shape policy so as to avoid disastrous unintended consequences and capture potential, possibly hidden, opportunities. The members of the committee have their own preferences regarding the policy and have to be given power to induce them to incur the costs of learning. They will not necessarily reveal the information truthfully, but might choose to act strategically to pursue their own ends. For this reason, the theory predicts that the floor will allocate members to the committees with preferences that mirror those of the chamber. Whereas the distributive theorists predict preference outliers, the informational theorists predict the opposite. Under informational theories, committees will never fully reveal the information they obtain, but the closer the preference of the committee median and that of the floor, the better informed will be the legislative process with greater potential gains relative to a situation under greater uncertainty. Gilligan and Krehbiel (1987) and Krehbiel (1992) provide several tests for the US Congress that support the informational theory.

Majority-Party Theory

The majority-party theory (or procedural cartel theory) is also a supply-side third-generation model. Like the informational theory, it adheres to the majoritarian postulate, but assumes that what matters are the preferences of the majority party, as congressional institutions (at least in the United States) assure a central role in legislative proceedings to the majority party and its leadership. The power is used by the majority party to redesign legislative institutions, control the agenda, and essentially assure most of its interests. In this view, a central problem faced by the majority party is to coordinate the efforts of its members so as to mitigate the externalities, collective dilemmas, and other inefficiencies that arise as each pursues the interest of their individual district. The party leadership acts as a central coordination device restraining destructive individualistic behavior, maintaining the party's reputation (a public good), and resolving disputes, so that members' collective gains and reelection prospects can be maximized.

Under the theory, the composition of the committees is not expected to be made up of preference outliers, as in the distributive theory, but neither is it expected to reflect the composition of the parent chamber as in the informational theory. Instead, committees are expected to mirror the preference of the majority party and in particular its leadership, which has the power to control the process. The testable hypotheses that emerge from the majority-party theory are somewhat more nuanced. For those committees that involve overwhelmingly local and circumscribed issues that have few externalities and other impact on other party members, the composition is allowed to be that of preference outliers. But for committees that involve overarching policies that interact with many other jurisdictions, the theory predicts that the majority party will be careful to assure a composition with preferences close to its own. Cox and McCubbins (2007) provide much evidence and several tests that support the theory.

Choosing among Theories

Each of the three theories presented above are rational expectations theories that pay close attention to institutional detail. Each one has a solid theoretical foundation based on observed facts from real-world legislatures, and each focuses on a different key aspect – distribution, information, or majority-party power. The common goal is to explain legislative organization and outcomes, and special emphasis is placed on explaining why committee systems are organized the way they are and what is the impact of the institutional design. Each theory yields distinct testable hypotheses, and there is ample data to perform those tests. One would therefore expect that the data would eventually refute two of the theories and the third would be recognized as the best explanation for why the specific congressional institutions that we observe have emerged and what is their impact (at least until a new better theory shows up). But it turns out that choosing among theories is not that simple, even with plenty of good data.

Groseclose (1994) tested the three theories using a Monte Carlo method that created a distribution of thousands of randomly assigned committees against which he could compare the median preference of committees. Comparing the median preference to the distribution of random committee preferences, he could determine how well each theory explained outcomes. For the distributive theory, the result obtained was that only two of the twenty-one committees tested rejected the null hypothesis of random allocation, that is, were composed of preference outliers. And because the null hypothesis had a 5 percent chance of being rejected even when it was true, the final result is that it is likely that even one or both of those two rejections might not be due to a truly preference outlier committee. Similar tests for the information theory and for the majority-party theory also failed to reject the null hypothesis of random committee assignment. The first involved a test of whether the committee is representative of the floor, and the second a test of whether the median preference of the committee is similar to the median preference of the majority party. He concludes that "this essay provides little, if any, evidence to reject the assertion that committee selection is random" (Groseclose, 1994: 455).

In a subsequent paper, Groseclose and King (2001) take a different approach to testing the theories. Rather than focusing solely on the preferences of the committee members, they take sixteen different institutions, procedures, and rules related to congressional committees and investigate whether the existence of those rules and their specific details are compatible or not with each of the theories. The institutions are things like the fact that committees are separate and not joint across the chambers or that seniority is counted as time in the committee and not in the chamber. The fact that the minority party also receives committee seats, for example, is compatible with the informational theory (to assure the committee is representative of the floor), and is also compatible with the distributive theory (so that preference outliers from the minority party can self-select into the committee), but is not compatible with the majority-party theory (why not monopolize all seats?). The authors make a table in which the rows are the different institutions and the columns are the theories. Each cell receives a plus sign, minus sign, or interrogation mark when the institution is compatible, incompatible, or indifferent with the theory. The result is that

the first thing that stands out is that no theory consistently gets all plus marks for "explaining" the way things really work in Congress. This would be troubling to some political scientists who believe that any "minus" mark would constitute falsification of the theory. No single existing theory captures the complexity of today's congressional committees, and we doubt that any single theory really ever has captured the reasons for the existence and persistence of committees. (Groseclose and King, 2001: 24)

The lack of definition and inability to tell an unambiguous story about the causes and impacts of the legislative institutions is frustrating to those who would like a science composed of law-like statements that have great generality and overarching applicability. But with institutions, as with many other objects of study, details and circumstance matter, and it is just the case that simple cause-and-effect relationships are rare. Robinson and Torvik (2011) make a similar case for how some well-known results in the literature, which are often taken as definitive, are conditional on institutions. And should the institutions be different, very different outcomes could materialize. New economic shocks, such as new available land, new technology, discoveries of natural resources, and so forth, create new opportunities whose utilization depends on the strength of institutions. They note, for example, the Black Death in the fourteenth century, by killing up to 200 million people and reducing the supply of labor, led to the decline of serfdom in Western Europe, where institutions were "stronger," but to its intensification in Eastern Europe, where they were "weaker." Similarly, the discovery of natural resources turns out to be a curse in some countries but a boon in others. Also, the discovery of the New World and opening up of trade opportunities in the Early Modern period led to economic growth in Britain and Holland but to decline in Spain and Portugal. They argue that in the many other well-studied cases, "it is the nature of institutions which determines the comparative statics of an equilibrium" (Robinson and Torvik, 2011: 37).

In this chapter, we also stress the conditionality of cause-and-effect relations, but focus not on how institutions condition the impact of shocks on outcomes, but rather on how the impacts of institutions depend on circumstances and detail. All three theories surveyed above try to explain the existence and working of legislative institutions as fulfilling certain functions related to enabling different forms of cooperation among different groups of legislators. The inability to come to a conclusion about which are those functions does not mean that the institutions don't matter, only that they arise and operate in complex ways that usually cannot be reduced to simple categorical statements. This should not be interpreted as a statement that theory and empirical validation are not important and cannot be done properly. Theory is crucial for providing potentially valuable explanations of observed outcomes. And it is only through empirical testing that we can choose among those explanations and further our knowledge. The point we make is that the process of selecting among competing theories often requires a more granular understanding of the specific context within which a specific political system is functioning, so that typically a theory will not hold in a law-like manner across nations. Similarly, the point about context and institutions does not vitiate empirical testing, but rather makes it much more challenging. In raising the bar for explanatory sufficiency for empiricism, institutional analysis also makes good empiricism more valuable.

Given the lack of consensus on which theory best explains congressional institutions, there has often been a temptation to argue that perhaps the three theories are complementary and can all be valid at the same time, perhaps each focusing on different aspects of congressional life and organization. Shepsle and Weingast (1995b: 22–23), for example, have argued that:

Nothing inherent in the logic of these approaches makes them antithetical. Accepting one of the principles described above as important for the understanding of congressional organization does not require that we reject the others. From an a priori theoretical standpoint, they are not mutually exclusive and may instead represent different and important parts of the same very complex puzzle. Congress is a multifaceted organization, one that is unlikely to be understood in terms of a single principle.

However, the idea that all the theories could somehow simultaneously be part of a greater unifying theory has never really prospered. Groseclose and King (2001: 25), for example, have classified the notion that there could be a weighted average of the theories as "wrong and unimaginative." And even though the different camps sometimes make conciliating statements about the other theories, more often than not the exchange has been intense and even bitter.

It has also been suggested that the existence of the different theories can best be understood as a consequence of the fact that Congress itself has changed significantly over the years and perhaps different theories were motivated and are best applied to each of the different epochs. The distributive model would be more apt to understand the textbook Congress that arose after World War II, for example, and the majority-party theory a better fit to the post-1970 reforms in Congress when parties acquired more power.

Be that as it may, institutional analysis should be leery of grand monolithic theories. Even physics, the purest of all sciences, cannot point to single explanations as Newtonian physics, relativity, and quantum mechanics offer often-incompatible accounts of reality. This does not diminish the value of institutional analysis, but reminds us about the nature of the enterprise and the importance of having an eye for details and context.

Two-Party Systems versus Multiple-Party Systems

Duverger's Law: The Causes and Impacts of Plurality Rule versus Proportional Representation

Most countries in the world can be divided into two-party systems or multiple-party systems (the exceptions being a few one-party systems). Examples of countries with two party-systems are the United States, Britain, Australia, Canada (in some provinces), Malta, Jamaica, Guyana, Trinidad and Tobago, Belize, Bahamas, Barbados, Zimbabwe, and Brazil during its military dictatorship (1964–1985). Examples of multiple-party systems are: Brazil, Canada, Denmark,

Finland, France, Germany, India, Pakistan, Indonesia, Ireland, Israel, Italy, Mexico, Nepal, the Netherlands, New Zealand, Norway, Portugal, Russia, Spain, Sweden, and Taiwan.[6] The distinction is important. Scholars debate the impact of multiple-party versus majority-party systems on representativeness, governability, democratic stability, public account solvency, among other characteristics. So why are some countries' politics organized in two-party systems and others in multiple parties? Is it a question of culture, or historical contingency? At first sight, there might seem to be some pattern in the lists above, with English-speaking countries tending towards two parties and others towards multiple parties, but there appears to be no easy answer.

In this section, we describe Duverger's Law, a highly influential explanation of institutional determinants of the choice of two-party rule versus multiple parties. In the subsequent subsection, we provide a case study of the early determinants of the two-party system in the United States, the prototypical application of Duverger's Law. The case study shows that it took a long time to solidify a two-party system.

A protracted debate over the determinants of two-party versus multiple-party systems generated controversy at least since 1850. The most prominent explanation states that countries that use a plurality rule, or first-past-the-post, where the candidate with the most votes wins, will end up with two-party systems, whereas countries with proportional representation, where seats are distributed in some proportion to the votes received, will become multiple-party systems. Even as many countries were adopting electoral systems for the first time, it was noted by many commentators that electoral rules could have important systematic impacts on the political system and in particular in the number of parties that emerged and persisted (Riker, 1982: 755). Henry Droop, an English barrister, in 1881 gave the earliest explicit

---

[6] The classification of a country as a two-party or multiple-party system is not always clear. Even two-party-system countries sometimes see other parties gain some representation, and often there are complex intraparty dynamics such that more than two groups are in contention even in a two-party system. Siaroff (2009: 201) argues that there are six types of party system: (1) competitive two-party system, (2) imbalanced two-party system, (3) a moderately multiparty system, (4) a two-and-a-half party system, (5) a highly multiparty system, and (6) one-party predominant system. We stick to the two-party multiparty classification in this chapter, as this dominates most of the literature.

statement that there is a link between plurality rule and two-party systems:

> These phenomena [i.e., two-party systems] I cannot explain by any other theory of a natural division between opposing tendencies of thought, and the only explanation which seems to me to account for them is that the two opposing parties into which we find politicians divided in each of the countries [United States, United Kingdom, etc.] have been formed and are kept together by majority voting. (cited in Riker, 1982: 756)

By the turn of the century, the issue had become a common topic of debate and thereafter gained broad acceptance in scholarly work, prompting Maurice Duverger (1963: 217), a French sociologist, to call it a "law." Since then, it has been known as Duverger's Law and, according to Dunleavy (2012), "it is no exaggeration to say that this proposition still underpins whole fields of research."

So what exactly is Duverger's Law? Duverger (1963) made two distinct claims. The first, and the one on which we focus here, states that "the simple-majority single-ballot system favors the two-party system."[7] Duverger himself stated that "of all the hypotheses ... in this book, this approaches most nearly perhaps to a true sociological law" (1963: 217). The second claim is that "the simple-majority system with second ballot and proportional representation favors multiple parties." Riker called it the Duverger hypothesis, as it does less well against the data than the impact of simple majority systems, suggesting a strong probabilistic association instead of a "law."[8] Overall, Riker concludes "the revised law is entirely consistent with our knowledge of the empirical world, accounting for both the long history of two-party competition in Anglo-American countries with plurality voting and the apparent exceptions ..." (1982: 761). Many other authors have agreed

---

[7] There is some confusion in the use of the term "majority," which requires that one candidate receive more than half of the votes, and "plurality," where a candidate can win with less than half of the votes as long as she receives more votes than the other candidates. The correct formulation of Duverger's Law is that plurality rule is always associated with two-party competition.

[8] Regarding Duverger's Law, however, Riker went to some length to argue that it did hold, despite a couple of counterexamples. His purpose was not so much to defend the law itself, but rather to argue that political science was a true science in the sense that knowledge accumulates over time through the formulation of new hypotheses and the reformulation of empirically falsified or theoretically discredited old hypotheses, as opposed to political science as *belle lettres* (Riker, 1982: 753).

with Riker, though subsequent analysis has qualified many conditions in which the relationship is expected to hold (see, in particular, Cox, 1997; Dunleavy and Diwakar, 2013).

If we accept that Duverger's Law has some explanatory power, what are the mechanisms through which it operates? Duverger identified two effects that map from electoral rules to the number of parties. The first he called the "mechanical effect," and it consists in the disincentive to form new small parties due to the fact that the winner-takes-all system makes it very hard for the parties to get any seats or representation at all, whereas in proportional systems, even a small share of the votes can lead to some participation in power. The second effect is the "psychological effect" in which voters are loath to throw away a vote on a party that has little chance of winning even if they prefer that party's platform. Riker downplays the channel through voters, noting that from a rational-choice perspective, it is already uncertain why voters would vote at all, independent from electoral rules, but he sees a much stronger rationale through potential party leaders and donors, who would be reluctant to invest any time or resources in parties that can promise little chance of yielding any returns (1982: 765).[9]

Much of the controversy has been between political sociologists and institutional determinists. Political sociologists repudiate that the nature of political competition could arise from simple electoral rules. Instead, they see the features as fundamentally determined by the social structures and cleavages in society, with parties arising to represent the varied social interest, such as workers, occupation, races, religions, and geographic location (Lijphart, 1977, 1999). The institutional argument, taken to the limit, is that electoral rules are all that matters, and social cleavages are mere window dressing.

Institutions are fundamental, but their effect depends in complex ways on several intervening factors. In the context of the dispute between those who favor social cleavages and institutional determinism, our position is well captured by Ordeshook and Shvetsova (1994: 100): "in learning the influence of institutions on outcomes, we should

---

[9] For a more in-depth analysis of these effects, sorting out when they operate in the electoral process and whom they affect, see Cox (1997), Dunleavy and Diwakar (2013), and Riker (1982).

consider the possibility that similar institutions in different social contexts yield different outcomes." Ordeshook and Shvetsova find a strong interaction between the proportionality of electoral rules and the diversity of social structures in determining the number of parties. In homogeneous societies, they find that increasing the proportionality of the electoral system does not lead to an increase in the number of parties, but does so in heterogeneous societies. In the same manner, they find that increasing the diversity of social structures in more majoritarian countries does not lead to more parties, but does so in proportional electoral systems (Cox, 1997: 25).

The determinants of the number of parties is not the only issue related to legislative and electoral institutions where the impact of institutions is conditioned by other contextual factors. Once a country has become a multiparty system, what is the effect on other political and social outcomes? Scott Mainwaring (1993) attributes the democratic stability of Britain and the United States after World War II versus the instability of Germany and Italy to the strong two-party systems in Britain and the United States. Lijphart (1977) countered the hypothesis that multiple parties caused instability. Multiple parties give diverse social groups voice, and could be more stable, especially in very plural societies. The issue remains controversial in political science.

Multiple-party systems provide legitimacy and voice for minority interests, but this could come at a cost. In particular, the literature in Latin American politics has been highly critical of multiparty systems, no doubt due to the high levels of democratic instability and economic crises in the region since the 1970s. Hypotheses critical of multiple-party systems include: (1) countries subject to coalition governments are more prone to larger and more persistent budget deficits (Poterba, 1994; Roubini and Sachs, 1989); (2) due to the norm of universalism, the greater the number of parties, the larger will be public expenditures and consequently the potential for deficits (Inman and Fitts, 1990; Shepsle and Weingast, 1981; Weingast, 1979); (3) political fragmentation, as measured by the number of effective political parties, has a positive relationship with the size of the government and with subsidies and transfers (Scartascini and Crain, 2002); and (4) multiple parties cause more difficult bargaining situations that might lead to lesser governability (Schofield, 1993).

Looking at the specific case of Brazil, a highly fragmented party system with thirty-two parties represented in Congress in 2016,[10] Ames (2001), in a book called *The Deadlock of Democracy in Brazil*, linked many of the country's problems to the lack of governability. As no president's party will likely have a majority in Congress under such a fragmented system, he expected that presidents would always remain hostage to coalition partners, having to pay a steep price in terms of patronage to get anything done. Similarly, Mainwaring (1999) argues that the weakly institutionalized party system in Brazil leads to volatility, weak parties, and lack of legitimacy, with nefarious economic and social consequences.

Both of the authors discussing Brazil, as well as most of the literature cited in the previous paragraphs, was written during the 1980s and 1990s when much of the world, and Brazil in particular, was going through an extended series of crises. Brazil, in particular, transitioned from an economically declining military dictatorship to a hyperinflationary democracy. It seemed natural to associate the country's extreme party fragmentation to the perverse economic and political outcomes it was experiencing. However, by the 2000s, even though the hyper-fragmentation was still in place, a new strand of the literature started pointing out that other institutional rules and structures associated with high levels of executive power counteracted many of the perverse effects and enabled not only governability but even expedient policy making (Alston et al., 2006, 2016; Alston and Mueller, 2006; Figueiredo and Limongi, 1996, 2000; Pereira and Mueller, 2000, 2004). The compensating institutions emanated from the constitutional powers of the president, which enabled strong decree power, line-item veto, monopoly to initiate legislation in some areas, control over most budgetary procedures, and several political currencies in the form of pork and jobs with which to purchase support.

This is another example showing that some institutions (multiple-party system) can have one effect in one context but a different effect in another. Whereas multiple parties do often induce deadlock and over-spending, when combined with strong presidential powers subject to

---

[10] There were thirty-two parties in Congress in 2016 and another forty parties seeking to get in. Nevertheless, the effective number of parties (a concept used by political scientists to consider only those that have a greater impact) is six or seven.

checks and balances, the elements might be subdued. The historical experience of Latin America with strong executives has not been positive, so the notion of strong presidential powers often raises concern. However, because of the different nature of the electoral connections held by the president versus those held by Congress, there are advantages to giving the president more power, as she should care more about national issues, such as economic growth and inequality, than legislators who are more concerned with local interest and geographic redistribution (Alston and Mueller, 2006). One way to reconcile the two opposing forces is to have strong checks and balances to push strong executives to act in the public interest. In Brazil, an independent judiciary, independent district attorneys and court of accounts, a free press, and a highly participative civil society provide a check on the strong powers of the president (Alston et al., 2006, 2016). Whereas the recent corruption scandals and misguided policies of the Dilma Rousseff administration (2010–2016) show that strong presidential powers can be abused, the subsequent impeachment is a testimony to the functioning of Brazilian checks and balances.

Another alleged consequence of the multiple party is the tendency to generate clientelism, patronage, cronyism, and party politics. Alston and Mueller (2006) examine the exchange of pork for policy in Brazil's hyper-fragmented strong presidential system. At first glance, the exchange of votes by legislators for pork and jobs in the vast federal administration is reminiscent of the image often associated with multiple-party countries in general and that often characterize Latin American presidential systems. The Brazilian president has extreme discretion to dole out pork and jobs and uses the political currencies openly and systematically. Scholars (e.g., Ames, 1995, 2001; Shugart and Carey, 1992), as well as journalists and public opinion, have often lamented this form of governing and ascribed to it many of the problems faced by the country. Alston and Mueller (2006), however, present a model that shows that the strategic use of the dispensation of pork and jobs by the president allows gains to cooperation between the executive and Congress to be realized at low budgetary cost and in such a way that provides greater governability and ability to implement reforms. Although this form of executive-legislative relation is inferior to one where altruistic politicians pursue the common good, the counterfactual is one where the president is unable to accomplish his policy agenda and where policies would be highly unstable or in gridlock.

The Origins of the Two-Party System in the United States

Duverger's Law predicts that plurality voting, when applied to single-member geographic districts, generates a two-party system. Interestingly enough, the scholarly acceptance of this phenomenon preceded the evolution of electoral laws, lending themselves to a two-party system in the United States; the theory was widely accepted by contemporary political theorists in 1881, although it was not formalized as a law until Duverger's seminal work in 1950. Riker surveys refinements to Duverger's Law, as well as apparent exceptions to the law, Canada and India, reconciling the exceptions by noting that the existence of a significant third party on the national level is driven by the persistence of third parties in local and state politics in both of the countries. This incomplete convergence to a two-party system emphasizes the broader point of our chapter: the "laws" (or, more accurately, probabilistic institutional patterns) operate gradually and imperfectly, even where they are arguably present.

In the nineteenth-century United States, a two-party system emerged twice at the national level and subsequently returned to a multiparty system both times. The return to party plurality occurred when a member from neither of the two dominant parties either seriously contended, or won, a presidential election. Given the theoretical and historical background, one sees the final coalescence of US politics into the two-party system known today occurring near the end of the nineteenth century as a result of changes in state and local political systems.

In the decades surrounding the turn of the twentieth century, two major institutional changes in the structure of voting appeared that led to the stable two-party system that has persisted over the course of the twentieth century and beyond. The first was the adoption of the Australian ballot. The name stems from its historical origins in the Australian electoral process, but its important features lie in its legal definition of a single, state-printed ballot, and the secret nature of voting. Prior to its inception, the onus of printing ballots lay on the various political parties themselves, whose effects for small parties were theoretically ambiguous. On the one hand, small parties had no entry costs beyond the printing of ballots, and in polemic elections, could garner a significant share of votes. Also, there were no restrictions on a candidate appearing on the ballot of multiple parties; a given "minority" candidate could win an election based upon support from numerous marginal parties.

Minority and majority parties used the technique, known as "fusion," throughout the nineteenth century. Most of the historically notable victories of minority parties such as Grangers, Independents, and Greenbackers in the 1870s and 1880s relied on a fusion between the groups and the Democrats. Fusion also allowed Democrats to "secure the votes of independents or disaffected Republicans who never considered voting directly for the Democracy they hated; it permitted such voters to register their discontent effectively without directly supporting a party that represented negative reference groups and rarely offered acceptable policy alternatives" (Argersinger, 1980: 290). Importantly, each party's contribution to the winning candidate could often be readily calculated, an aspect clearly lending itself to the preservation of party autonomy (Scarrow, 1986: 637).

Of course, the non-fusion candidates adopted a line encouraging opposing voters to support only those candidates who were willing to be labeled as strictly representing one political party, accusing the others of ideological inconstancy. In a time where "rigid party allegiance was standard, and straight-ticket voting was the norm" (Argersinger, 1980: 289), the arguments met with a degree of success. Republicans even went so far as to underwrite separate campaigns by non-fusion minority parties with the aim of splitting the opposition vote, in the hopes of countering the very real threat fusion parties presented (Argersinger, 1980: 290).

However, not all aspects of the party-printed ballot system were directly conducive to the success of minority parties. A voter seen to take the ballot of a given party from its representatives was a clear signal of one's electoral decision, and in this respect, a given voter might not choose to vote against the majority party for fear of social reprisal or ostracization. Finally, this form of balloting gave an advantage to all parties when a voter only weakly preferred their party, for it was quite difficult to vote for different candidates across parties. This involved collecting the different party ballots, tearing them apart, and reconstituting a custom ballot from the pieces of each ballot.

While in principle the party-printed ballots did not render a clear advantage to majority or minority parties, the adoption of the

Australian ballot, and the legislation governing its creation, yielded a clear advantage to the majority parties. It came from the requirement that in order for a party to be listed on the official ballot, they had to have either received a large number of votes in a previous election (given the proportion required, the requirement was typically only satisfied by the two major parties), or obtain a sufficient number of signatures via petition. The last restriction can be seen as the entry requirement for small parties, and is clearly more costly than simply appearing on election day with a stack of ballots. A single example from Kentucky (one of the first two states to pass such laws) is typical: "*Official*; prepared and distributed at public expense by the county clerks of the several counties; obtainable by the voters only from the election officers, at the polls, on election day" (Ludington, 1911: 121; emphasis in original).

The electoral reform advantaged the Republican Party, the dominant party in the country, by restricting the entry of minor parties. In the face of eroding popular support nationwide, and a political arena in which minority parties increasingly played a decisive role (holding "the balance of power at least once in every state but Vermont between 1878 and 1892" [Argersinger, 1980: 290]), the Republicans clearly wished to reconsolidate their grip on national and local politics. A ballot with a reduced number of party options meant the Republicans could expect to capture a portion of these, while commensurately decreasing the number of votes for their opposition. The advantages to this in a plurality system are unquestionable.

In the United States, the Australian ballot took two forms: Office Bloc (OB), a ballot in which each office was listed with the candidates (and the party or parties they represented) competing underneath; and Party Column (PC), in which the ballot listed the candidates based on the party to which they belonged, and the office for which they were running. While the precise wording of each law differed, it suffices to give a single example of each type: the OB type, first adopted by Massachusetts: "*Office group*; the names of the candidates are arranged in alphabetical order, according to surnames, under the title of each office ... Each candidate's name is followed by his party designation" (Ludington, 1911: 131; emphasis in original); and the PC type, from Kansas: "*Party Column*; emblems; columns arranged in such order as the secretary of state may direct, precedence, however, being given to the party which polled the highest number of votes for the head of its ticket at the last preceding general election" (120; emphasis in original).

The restriction on the order in which parties appeared on the Party Column ballot differed from state to state, but it roundly favored one of the two majority parties, or left such a decision at the hands of the secretary of state (who was with high probability a member of one of the two majority parties). The states that passed Australian ballot laws in the first years did not include restrictions on whether a candidate could be listed as representing more than one party (in the case of Office Bloc ballots) or listed underneath the heading of more than one party (in the case of Party Column ballots).

A list of the years in which each given state adopted the Australian ballot system follows (Engstrom and Kernell, 2005: 546–47):

1888: Kentucky (OB), Massachusetts (OB)
1889: Indiana (PC), Minnesota (OB), Missouri (PC), Montana (OB), Rhode Island (OB), Wisconsin (OB)
1890: Maryland (PC), Oklahoma (PC), Vermont (OB), Washington (OB), Wyoming (OB)
1891: Arizona (OB), Arkansas (OB) (Ludington, 1911: 94), California (PC), Colorado (PC), Delaware (PC), Idaho (PC), Illinois (PC), Maine (PC), Michigan (PC), Nebraska (OB), Nevada (OB), New Hampshire (OB), North Dakota (OB), Ohio (PC), Oregon (OB), Pennsylvania (PC), South Dakota (OB), West Virginia (PC)
1892: Iowa (PC)
1893: Kansas (PC)
1895: New York (PC)
1896: Utah (PC)
1905: New Mexico (PC)
1909: Connecticut (PC)
1911: New Jersey (OB)

While political theorists have touted the adoption of the Australian ballot as the demise of the multiparty system on a state and national level (Scarrow, 1986: 638), the explanation suffices neither theoretically nor empirically. OB and PC laws still allowed for some of the advantages of fusion, noted in the party-printed ballot setting, in which a candidate could garner the support of multiple parties. Granted, the number of parties that a non-majority candidate could rely upon was necessarily diminished, but local and national politics at the time nonetheless support this interpretation, as the Boston mayoral election of 1899 (the first using an Australian ballot) was contested between a Citizen/Democratic candidate, and a Citizen/Independent/Democratic/Republican candidate while at the national level, William Jennings Bryan was a Democratic/Populist candidate in the 1896 presidential election (Scarrow, 1986: 635). In both the cases, the fusion candidates could claim that voters were staying true to their ideologies while at the same time voting for a candidate who had a chance against the majority opposition candidate.

The fusion between Democrats and Populists that Bryan represented was a significant threat to Republican hegemony in many local election outcomes as well, and it was the local contests that prompted the final institutional changes rendering a single-party opposition to the majority as the only viable means of competition. Argersinger's 1980 survey of fusion politics and subsequent anti-fusion legislation provides two telling examples of the first local stages from which this legislation began to later sweep the nation. Republicans controlled the local legislature in Oregon, although the party only represented a minority of voters in the state. In the hopes of ousting the minority incumbents, the Democrats withdrew a number of candidates in the state, exhorting their voters to support several fusion candidates instead. However, the legislation in Oregon delineating the adoption of the office-bloc form of the Australian ballot in the previous year contained an important clause: "No candidate's name is to appear more than once on the ballot, but each candidate's name is to be followed by the party or political designation, expressed in not over three words, of each party or group which nominated him and whose nomination he accepted" (Ludington, 1911: 169).

Once this clause became publicly known, the Democrats demanded that the ballot form be changed to party column format, in which they claimed their preferred candidate, Pierce, could appear with both the Democrats and the Populists. The clause came to light sufficiently late in the campaign to where there was not time to render a legal decision, and so the election in Oregon consisted of a mixture of ballots, with Democratic county clerks placing Pierce's name under both parties on a party column ballot, and the more legal-minded clerks and Republican county clerks listing Pierce only under the Populist heading, although designating him an affiliate of both.

The statistical differences in support for Pierce between counties with different ballot types show the ideological dissension the office-bloc system generated.

In those counties in which his name was listed under both Democratic and Populist groupings virtually all Populists voted for their fellow partisan, while 92 percent of the Democrats also supported Pierce, an indication of some hostility to fusion but also of a general willingness to vote the Democratic ticket and all who were designated on it. (Argersinger, 1991: 155)

However, in the counties where Pierce only appeared under the Populist Party group, but with a Democratic designation next to his name, he only received support from 91 percent of the Populist voters, and only 71 percent of the Democratic voters (Argersinger, 1980: 293). Clearly, for a large portion of the voters at the time, voting underneath the heading of another party, or voting for someone designated with the name of another party, even under one's own party heading, proved to be too much to swallow. Although Pierce narrowly won the election, his margin of victory would have been significantly larger had he been allowed to appear twice under two different party headings on every ballot.

From the same year, Argersinger provides a similar example. The Minnesota legislature was similarly controlled by Republicans representing a minority of voters in the state, and Democrats once again chose to withdraw four of their nine candidates, choosing nominally Populist candidates instead, anticipating that the given candidates would appear twice underneath each office, given that Minnesota's Australian ballot law had specified the office-bloc format. The Republican secretary of state proceeded to only list the fusion candidates once, even though no such provision had been included in the original ballot legislation. The Democrats understandably raised an outcry, but the lateness of the situation prompted the courts to rule that they had no jurisdiction in the matter, allowing the Republican-printed ballots to serve their official role. The results are entirely in line with those seen in Oregon, except in this case the widespread "anti-fusion" ballots achieved their aim, with the Republicans sweeping the elections, although only representing a minority of voters in the state.

While local elections, by definition, do not directly impact national electoral results, the outcomes in Oregon and Minnesota were sufficiently salient that Republicans in other states began to understand the advantages anti-fusion legislation could provide them. The anti-fusion laws differed slightly depending on whether the state had adopted an Office Bloc or Party Column type of ballot. While the wording of each type of law differed in a given state, we cite one of each type to give the general idea of the legislation passed: for PC ballots (from South Dakota), "No candidate's name is to be printed in more than one column on the ballot but a candidate nominated by two or more parties may choose in which column his name shall be placed" (Ludington, 1911: 178); and for OB ballots (from Minnesota), "Nor shall any person be named on the official ballot as the candidate of more than one party, or of any party other than that whose certificate of his nomination was first properly filed" (Ludington, 1911: 136).

Similar to the case of Australian ballot laws, with each passing year, the list of states passing anti-fusion legislation grew (Argersinger, 1980: 298–302):

1892: South Dakota (Ludington, 1911: 178)
1895: Michigan, Oregon, Washington
1896: Ohio
1897: Illinois, Indiana, Iowa, North Dakota, Pennsylvania, Wisconsin, Wyoming
1899: California, Nebraska
1901: Kansas, Minnesota
1903: Idaho
1907: Montana
1913: Missouri (Scarrow, 1986: 639)
1919: Idaho (Scarrow, 1986: 639)

The widespread adoption of the anti-fusion legislation is an account for the demise of minority parties, the last obstacle to the two-party system in use today. Local politics ultimately proved to be the driving force behind "antifusion legislation in those states where, at the aggregate level, it did not seem necessary or important"

(Argersinger, 1980: 296). By driving a wedge between Democrats and the third-party groups (usually Populists), the Republicans succeeded in capturing a significant degree of the vote, forcing the Populists to choose between the less disliked of two non-ideal candidates: "if forced to vote for fusion as Democrats, many Populists declared, they would prefer to return to the GOP or simply not vote at all" (Argersinger, 1980: 303). We note that the above list is not as exhaustive as the preceding chronology of Australian ballot legislation. The reason for this is simple; in states where the two major parties enjoyed a great degree of organized support, the adoption of additional legislation was unnecessary in the face of the unquestionable supremacy the Australian ballot reforms had afforded them. Regardless, by 1920, twenty-five states had some form of anti-fusion legislation (Scarrow, 1986: 639).

Beliefs in political fairness or a desire for political stability did not drive anti-fusion laws. Rather, partisan politics mattered; Republicans pushed legislation through state legislatures. They first sought to ensure primacy over their two principal rivals, the Democrats and Populists, and later for the electoral advantages legislation obviously provided in more closely contested states. Regardless of the effects the changes had on the degree of true representation in the US political system, the stabilizing influence they brought to the system is clear. The two majority parties maintained their supremacy at the national level since the 1896 election. The decline of fusion candidacies on the local and state level occurred more slowly, as evidenced by Scarrow's (1986: 636) comprehensive tabulation of fusion candidacies. The decline can be seen as a feedback effect; once local electoral laws had changed in those states where fusion candidates had a significant chance at the national level, the national system converged to a two-party system, and as the years passed with the only national contenders coming from the two majority parties, the ideological allure third parties still held at the local level naturally declined as their voter base had to choose between the majority parties at the national level.

The slow feedback between state and local-level candidacies and national-level electoral contests provides a rich backdrop with which to consider the way in which probabilistic institutional patterns operate. The slow and imperfect convergence to a two-party system in the United States indicates that the effects of the probabilistic institutional causal mechanisms are both gradual, and governed by factors that the theories at best predict. Whether a particular institutional theory is deemed a "law," the regularity with which laws operate in the natural sciences weakens when it comes to their application to complex social systems consisting of nested layers of political, economic, and legal relationships. The United States is widely recognized as a nation displaying the institutional outcomes predicted by Duverger's Law. But the means by which the law emerged was gradual and iterative, and very much subject to the contextual complexities of the United States in the latter half of the nineteenth century and first decades of the twentieth.

Conclusion

Executives, legislatures, and their interaction are one of the main topics of study of the impact of institutions on outcomes, as this is where much of the supply of policy takes place. In this area of study, it is critical to use IOA because of the insights that it yields about the rules of the game that determine laws, their implementation, and enforcement. We covered three examples from the literature: presidentialism versus parliamentarism; theories of committee organization; and the causes and impacts of multiple-party systems. Rather than simply describing the role of institutions in each case, however, we also highlighted a methodological issue that affects all institutional analysis. While institutions are central determinants of economic and political performance, there is the temptation of looking for grand statements that are universally valid. Although it might seem obvious that this is not the case, and that everything is conditional and subject to interactions, the three examples in our chapter show that it is common for the literature to swerve in that direction in the competition of ideas and the quest for generality. Bird (1992) recognized the pervasiveness of this type of excess:

Much fiscal analysis of developing countries is on the following pattern: the academic literature is drawn on to construct a model fiscal system; the existing situation in a particular country is examined to determine how it diverges from the model; and a fiscal reform is then proposed to transform what *is* into what *ought to be*. This approach is deficient because it does not require sufficient detailed examination of existing reality to ensure that the assumptions postulated in the model are congruent with reality, that the recommended changes can in fact be implemented, or that, if implemented, they will in fact produce the desired results. In contrast, my approach is first to study in detail exactly *how* the existing system works, and *why* it works that way, in order to have a firm basis for understanding what changes may be both desirable and feasible. (x; emphasis in original)

6 | *Bureaucracies*

Introduction and Opening Case: "Let Them Be Bribed"

In the two previous chapters, we analyzed how interest groups, executives, and legislatures interact to change the laws of society and their enforcement. We examined several specific cases where rational political actors strategically interact under a given constitutional background to further their own ends. Interest groups lobbied for transfers or policies. The executive and Congress vied with each other to design laws as close as possible to their ideal points. In all of these cases, we were careful to show how the institutions and the resulting property rights and transaction costs, subject to information asymmetries and other imperfections, led to a specific outcome or set of outcomes. Throughout that analysis, there was an implicit assumption that once the interaction between these players had taken place and a specific decision had been reached, it would be faithfully and immediately implemented by the relevant bureaucratic agency. We assumed that bureaucrats did not have their own preferences or did not deviate from the orders received from above. Clearly, this simplification is not realistic. The earlier neglect of the bureaucracy as a separate player was to reduce a complex subject into more manageable pieces. In political science, the study of bureaucracy was traditionally a backwater (Moe, 2013: 1148). Though understood that bureaucratic behavior was important to understand outcomes, scholars did not sufficiently recognize that the way bureaucracies are organized determines how they behave and that consequently their organization is endogenously determined. Instead, studies in the field of public administration focused on good management and the efficacy of policy implementation.

Spiller's (1990) analysis of congressional delegation of regulatory authority illustrates well many of the issues that can arise when we explicitly consider a self-interested bureaucracy in charge of implementing policy that might impose gains and losses to interest groups.

He considers a situation in which members of Congress have interests that are related to various different groups including voters, so that a given interest group might choose to try to influence policy directly through the bureaucracy as a complement or substitute for influencing the legislature.[1] There is thus competition for the bureaucrats' favors. Members of Congress take into account the fact that there is asymmetric information in their relationship with the bureaucracy and that interest groups might lobby the bureaucrats directly. They, therefore, adjust the form of delegation accordingly, in extreme cases even choosing not to delegate. An interesting implication arises from the career path of bureaucrats. The competition between Congress and interest groups to affect bureaucrats' actions means that bureaucrats are able to extract rents from both sides. From interest groups, the rents might come in the form of direct transfers of cash or goods (e.g., trips), but can also take less transparent forms such as revolving-door post-governmental employment. From Congress, the rents are typically not in the form of higher salaries, which usually follow rigid rules, but rather through larger budgets, extended jurisdiction, perks of the job, and higher jobs in government. But because members of Congress appoint the bureaucrats, they might be able to extract the rents in the form of staff work or direct monetary contributions.[2]

Under certain circumstances, Congress could refrain from the inglorious task of trying to reduce interest groups' influence on bureaucrats through oversight and restrictions and instead, as the title of Spiller's (1990) paper puts it, "let them be bribed." Because Congress can appropriate the rents received by the bureaucracy through the power to appoint those positions, in effect the interest group's transfers to the bureaucrats are indirect transfers to the politicians. There is no suggestion here that this situation is prevalent in the United States or elsewhere. It requires several conditions to be plausible, for example,

---

[1] Spiller (1990) considers the relationship between Congress, a regulatory agency, and interest groups. The analysis can, nevertheless, be broadened to consider presidents or other principals, and other bureaucratic organizations.

[2] Whether the president, Congress, or other players actually appoint and approve the heads of bureaucratic organizations depends on the specific institutions of the country in question. In Spiller (1990), the focus is on Congress's relation with regulatory agencies in the United States. In that case, presidents appoint the candidate and the Senate oversight committees have to approve the appointment, which allows the Senate to effectively limit the set of candidates from which the president can choose.

that members of Congress care sufficiently more about the transfers than they do about the policy outcomes and their electoral consequences. We are unaware of any study that has systematically measured this effect, and Spiller (1990) provides only a limited preliminary test. Nevertheless, the example illustrates how the relationship between interest groups and politicians becomes more complex when we consider the nature of the delegation to bureaucracies and the specific institutions that structure those relationships.

Who Controls the Bureaucracy?

In the 1970s, political scientists and economists began to analyze political organizations, including bureaucracies, with new theories and tools. We have already discussed many examples of these approaches in the two previous chapters, where scholars used transaction costs, principal-agent models, and game-theoretic approaches to analyze the interaction of interest groups, executives, and legislatures. In this chapter, we use the same types of models to understand how the delegation of policies to bureaucratic agents impacts the production of laws of societies and their enforcement. As before, we take the Constitution and higher-level rules as fixed and analyze the impact from institutions, such as a meritocratic versus a patronage-based selection of civil servants, on which laws are chosen and how they are enforced. Here, once again, the Riker Objection is relevant. Because the organization of the bureaucracy can affect outcomes, the rules that determine that organization will naturally be the object of strategic manipulation by political actors. Yet, in this part of our book, we focus primarily on the play of the game under fixed constitutional rules, although at times we consider changes in the constitutional rules.

To structure the chapter, we focus on the central issue of delegation. Every time a political decision is made and the implementation delegated to a bureaucratic agent, the issue arises of whether what gets done is what had been intended in the original decision. Bureaucratic agents are extremely varied. James Q. Wilson's (1989) classic book covered police departments, school systems, the CIA, the military, the State Department, regulatory commissions, the Postal Service, the Social Security Administration, the Army Corps of Engineers, and the Forest Service, among others.

It is common for individuals to have strong feelings against bureaucrats and bureaucracies. Johnson and Libecap (1994) refer to this as "the problem of bureaucracy."

Cynicism about the federal bureaucracy is widespread. The general public views federal employees as aloof, uncaring bureaucrats who are unresponsive to their requests. Throughout the country there is a prevailing sense that government is synonymous with inefficiency and waste and that the federal bureaucracy is essentially out of control. (Johnson and Libecap, 1994: 1)

Similarly, Wilson (1989: x) states that citizens and taxpayers view bureaucracies as "lethargic, incompetent hacks who spend their days spinning out reels of red tape and reams of paperwork, all the while going great lengths to avoid doing the job they were hired to do."

In addition to the population, other governmental powers also systematically disapprove of what bureaucracies do and how they do it. The recurring attempts at reform of the bureaucracy in many countries are testimony to this fact. Reforms in the United States include: in 1905, President Theodore Roosevelt instituted the Keep Committee; in 1912, President Taft created the Commission on Economy and Efficiency; in 1936, President Franklin Roosevelt put together the Brownlow Committee, followed by President Truman's Hoover Commission in 1949, which was renewed in 1953 under President Eisenhower; in 1977, President Carter established the Reorganization Project; in 1982, President Reagan came up with the Private Sector Survey on Cost Control; and in 1993, Clinton enacted the National Performance Review (Johnson and Libecap, 1994: 1). Since then, several other attempts at reforming the bureaucracy have followed. The most recent being the passage in the House in July 7, 2016 of the Government Reform and Improvement Act of 2016, which has the following highlights:

This bill establishes or revises government operations and personnel laws concerning the security of federal information systems, restrictions on access to websites, probationary periods, the senior executive service, employee use of official time, and the maintenance of Internal Revenue Service records. It also prohibits agencies from proposing or adopting certain rules during a moratorium period after a presidential election before a new President is sworn in. (www.congress.gov/bill/114th-congress/house-bill/4361)

The recurring attempts at reforming bureaucracies to change behavior in alignment with principals suggest that reform efforts have not been fully successful, as the efforts have had to be renewed continually. Unsuccessful reforms indicate an intrinsic and inevitable characteristic of the relation of bureaucracies with other political actors.

In this chapter, we cover the institutional literature on bureaucracies, which explains bureaucratic behavior and the typical shortcomings in performance relative to general expectations not as a failure in public administration, which could be remedied through the use of more effective management techniques, but as the result of the logic of delegation. The problem is what Kiewiet and McCubbins (1994: 26) call "Madison's dilemma": resources and authority granted to an agent for the purpose of advancing the principal's interest can be turned against the principal, as the agent exploits the favorable strategic situation in which it has been placed. The delegation often gives rise to a multiple principal-agent problem between the bureaucracy and a series of other actors (executive, legislators, courts, interest groups, and agencies' own members). In this context, the lack of agency effectiveness is an expected outcome and can at times be a purposeful goal. There are situations in which agency ineffectiveness is there by design, for example, as a means for one principal to stifle the agency's capacity to attend to another principal's interest. Or, bureaucracies could be subject to "fire alarms" that interest groups may activate to warn the agency's unaware principal that the bureaucracy is about to make a move that will harm the principal's interest (McCubbins and Schwartz, 1984). With multiple principals, it is not even clear what it means to say that a bureaucracy is ineffective, as different principals prefer different actions from the agent.

We organize the sections that represent the five different answers that have been proposed in the literature to the question of "Who controls the bureaucracy?" This was the title of a seminal paper by Hammond and Knott (1996), whose subtitle offered the options: "Presidential Power, Congressional Dominance, Legal Constraints, and Bureaucratic Autonomy in a Model of Multi-Institutional Policy-Making." The first section describes the theory of "congressional dominance," which was the first to make use of the instruments of rational actors strategically pursuing their interest subject to institutional constraints. The theory, based almost entirely on the US case, proposed that political institutions gave Congress instruments of *ex-ante* and *ex-post* control of the bureaucracy, so that in essence, the principal-agent problem between Congress and government agencies was easily resolved and bureaucratic action could be understood as following the interest of their relevant congressional principal (i.e., the overseeing committee or subcommittee). In the second section, we present the argument that the principal-agent problem is so severe that the bureaucratic agencies are essentially able to evade control by any principal. Protected by information asymmetries, the bureaucracies are able to generally pursue their own interests, be they ideological or in the form of shirking, except for those rare occasions, possibly triggered by some shock or scandal, which prompt one or more of the principals to make a concerted effort to bring the agency back in line.

In the third section, we examine a critique of the previous two arguments. The critique maintains that the president holds several key powers that actually give her the upper hand in controlling most bureaucratic agencies. In particular, the power to appoint the heads of the agencies and the power to set the agenda in the budgetary appropriations provide the president with extraordinary leverage over the bureaucracies.

In the fourth section, we assess the influence of the courts. The power of the courts to render judgment on the procedures of agencies, as well as over substantive issues, implies that bureaucracies will strategically take into consideration the preferences of the courts when implementing or setting policy. Finally, in the last section, we consider the argument that all of the above hypotheses capture some aspects of bureaucratic organization. In essence, there is a multiple principal-agent problem, and even when the data indicate that the bureaucracy responds to one of the principals, it is probably the case that that response is being constrained and conditioned by the influence of the others. The view that no single line of control is universal and overarching, but rather many different relations can be determinant in different contexts and circumstances, fits with the main argument in our last chapter. Here, once again, the literature has evolved through a debate over which single principal controls the bureaucracy. Even though the focus was almost exclusively on American politics, there is much variation in institutions across agencies, sectors, and over time, so that it is not surprising that different theories have been able to present supporting evidence.[3]

We do not strive to present a complete picture of the literature on bureaucracies in this chapter as a whole or in any of the sections for that subset of theories. We skip, for example, the early rational-choice theories of public bureaucracies, such as Tullock (1965), Downs (1967), and Niskanen (1971). For excellent surveys, see Moe (2013), Miller (2005), and Hammond and Knott (1996). Instead, each section presents the general argument for that class of explanation for who controls the bureaucracy and then focuses on one or two selected papers that helped advance that view.

Congressional Dominance

In the United States, Congress plays a very visible role in the oversight of bureaucratic agencies. Early work on political institutions was predominantly interested in the puzzling absence of voting cycles in real-world situations as opposed to the chaos predicted by theory, so attention naturally turned to legislatures, where most voting took place (Moe, 2013). It was only natural that this literature, which has traditionally concentrated on the US case, would focus initially on the capacity of Congress to control the bureaucracy. The seminal paper in this area, and the one that coined the term "congressional dominance," is the analysis by Weingast and Moran (1983) of the regulatory policy making by the Federal Trade Commission (FTC). It is difficult to distinguish if agencies are independent from the legislature (and other principals) or controlled by it, because the evidence that one would expect to encounter in either case is observationally equivalent, that is, both theories would yield the same expected outcomes in terms of the relationship between principal and agent. Both theories are compatible with

---

[3] Much of the literature that we discuss in this chapter deals specifically with the bureaucracy in the United States. The American system, however, is not very representative (Moe, 2013: 1158), and bureaucracies embedded in different institutions will naturally have different structures and outcomes. There has been some work done for bureaucracies in parliamentary systems, but less work done for the context of developing economies with weaker institutions. The major issues in the bureaucracy literature in developing countries address two questions: is the bureaucracy corrupt and is it competent? A lot of the discussion surrounds compensation to address these questions.

(1) the lack of oversight hearings; (2) the infrequency of congressional investigations and policy resolutions; (3) the perfunctory nature of confirmation hearings of agency heads; (4) the lack of ostensible congressional attention to or knowledge about the ongoing operation and policy consequences of agency choice; and (5) the superficiality of annual appropriations hearings. (Weingast and Moran, 1983: 767)

Under agency autonomy, we expect these outcomes because the principals realize the futility of trying to direct the agencies. Under congressional dominance, the legislature's controls over budget, appointments, and oversight are so effective that the agency behaves in accordance with the interest of the relevant committee or subcommittee without the need of close monitoring and enforcement. That is, the more effective the control, the less visible it becomes.

To distinguish between the two theories, Weingast and Moran suggest that it is necessary to look closely at legislative institutions to understand how they create a system through which the diverse interests of legislators can be simultaneously met, by giving to different members extraordinary power over the agencies that can directly affect their interests. This is the "gains to trade" approach to legislative institutions that we discussed earlier in Chapter 5. In the United States, the committee system promotes legislators self-selecting to the committee that oversees the agencies that are important for the policies that their constituents care about the most. This creates a credible exchange mechanism whereby each committee's members refrain from interfering in each other's area and in exchange gain extraordinary control over the area they most value. Specifying this model of congressional oversight is useful because it provides testable hypotheses that make it possible to overcome the problem of observational equivalence. In particular, we expect that if it is the case that the committee controls the agency, then sharp changes in the preferences of committee members should lead to changes in the behavior of the agency. If changes in committee preferences do not match compatible changes in what the agency does, then congressional dominance becomes less likely.

Weingast and Moran test the hypothesis by analyzing the behavior of the FTC in the United States in the late 1970s. After a long period of extreme activism in pursuing consumer interests through direct interference in a variety of different markets (from insurance, to advertising, to breakfast cereals), the FTC was finally reproached by

Congress, which shut down many of its investigations and antitrust suits and even threatened to close the agency. The traditional interpretation for these events was that only after many years of the FTC running free and pursuing its own agenda did Congress finally manage to catch up to the agency and bring it back in line. Had it not gone too far, it would have been able to continue its indulgence indefinitely.

Weingast and Moran (1983) refute this interpretation by showing data on the composition of the FTC's oversight committee in the Senate, the subcommittee of Consumer Affairs (Committee on Commerce). They use ADA scores (produced by Americans for Democratic Action), which they show to be a good measure of senators' preferences on FTC issues (higher scores indicate greater preference for FTC activism), to measure the median preference of the committee at different times. The exercise reveals that during the period from 1966 to 1979, in which the FTC exhibited highly intrusive behavior, the Senate subcommittee had significantly higher ADA scores than the Senate as a whole. And the subcommittee's chairman (who wields the most power within the subcommittee) was even higher. In 1979, however, there was significant electoral turnover in the subcommittee reversing the situation. The subcommittee median preference switched to a position statistically lower than the Senate as a whole, and the new chairman was even more pro-market. These data suggest that, all along, the FTC was not a loose cannon doing whatever it pleased. On the contrary, at all times it was acting in accordance with the interest of the majority of the subcommittee members. Before 1979, the subcommittee was dominated by interventionists and the agency intervened accordingly. After 1979, the subcommittee became overwhelmingly market-oriented and the agency obliged. The commotion in 1979, when the agency came under scrutiny of the media, was not a result of a runaway agency being finally disciplined by a helpless Congress, but rather the rumblings due to the change of the guards in the subcommittee, which was dutifully followed by a turnaround of agency behavior.

McCubbins, Noll, and Weingast (1987, 1989) elaborate on the theory of congressional dominance by highlighting the design by Congress of the structure and process of the agency to avoid the bureaucratic drift that can occur due to information asymmetries.

Because the political principals are risk-averse and cannot predict ex ante which way an agency will drift, they establish strategically chosen procedures by which the agency must abide, which have the effect of revealing private information, enfranchising favored constituencies, stacking the deck on policies, setting up early warning systems on agency intentions, and generally giving Congress higher levels of control. The design of bureaucratic agencies' structure and process is not so much a function of the quest for administrative effectiveness and the pursuit to fulfill the agencies' declared mandates, as it is to assure political control by the overseeing principals (McCubbins, Noll, and Weingast, 1987, 1989).[4]

Bureaucratic Discretion and Autonomous Agencies

The theory of congressional dominance came to achieve some dominance of its own. But it did not go unchallenged.[5] Scholars critiqued that the theory has overlooked or misinterpreted the role played by other actors, such as the president, courts, and the agency itself. We examine the critiques and alternative theories in this and the next three sections.

Wilson's (1989) *Bureaucracy* is one of the seminal books on bureaucracy in America. It is packed with details and descriptions of how bureaucratic agencies work and how they relate to other political actors, from interest groups to the president, Congress, and the courts. Wilson does not deny that Congress has a large arsenal of weapons – legislation, appropriations, hearings, investigations, personal interventions, and "friendly advice" – to use against rogue agencies, but he stresses that what matters is to understand "under what circumstances are the resources available to Congress likely to be most effective in shaping agency behavior?" (236–37). There are at least four major reasons why actual control of bureaucracies by Congress may be

---

[4] We explore other aspects of the McCubbins, Noll, and Weingast set of papers in the introduction to Part II and in Chapter 5.

[5] Weingast and Moran (1983) cited James Q. Wilson's (1980) *The Politics of Regulation* as one of the main adherents of the agency autonomy hypothesis. Wilson's (1989: chap. 13) subsequent book, *Bureaucracy: What Government Agencies Do and Why They Do It*, responds with a strong critique of the congressional dominance idea and the empirical tests in Weingast and Moran (1983). Other explicit critiques are Moe (1987), Muris (1986), and Hammond and Knott (1996).

much rarer than congressional dominance proponents would have one believe.

The first reason is that, in many cases, Congress has neither the interest nor the inclination to intervene, or even to be informed about, what an agency is doing. Politicians face time constraints and focus on those few issues that are most important for their political survival. Therefore, many agencies are free to pursue their own agendas away from political oversight, as long as they do not push too far in the wrong direction and bring upon them the wrath of aggrieved legislators who may then seek to reform the agency's mandate, personnel, and powers. Displays of entrepreneurial politics by reformers tend to occur in brief impassioned outbursts, but these are usually short-lived, and "as they subside they leave a new constellation of interest that may or may not have a stake in pursuing the original legislative visions" (Wilson, 1989: 250). The result is that most bureaucracies live in a state of stability and incrementalism in which they have considerable autonomy to follow their own interest, but are subject to unpredictable punctuated shifts that might drastically change or even extinguish the agency (Baumgartner, Jones, and Mortensen, 2014). Whereas congressional dominance scholars rely on fire alarms as a means for politicians to overcome the cost of policing the agencies, scholars subscribing to bureaucratic discretion dismiss fire alarms as insufficient to allow close control.

A second reason for the insulation of bureaucracies is because they often possess information and expertise about their specific policy area that other political actors lack and cannot access at low cost. When this is the case, the principal-agent problem between these actors and the agency is so severe that it becomes impossible to establish rules that align incentives. Under such circumstances, direct monitoring is too costly and ineffective, so the principal may simply not bother trying to steer the agency.

The notion that specialized bureaucracies have information about the outcomes of policies that their political principals do not has become the central element of an important part of the literature on bureaucracies (Epstein and O'Halloran, 2001; Gilligan and Krehbiel, 1987; Huber and Shipan, 2002). Scholars in this literature formally model uncertainty by assuming a unidimensional policy space on which the agency implements a policy. But the actual outcome of the policy can be somewhere else in the policy space as a result of policy uncertainty. The key aspect of the models is that the agency has information about the distribution of the error term between the policy intention and the actual outcome. This expertise presents politicians with a trade-off when appointing bureaucrats or when trying to control their actions. A close ally may be more responsive, but may also have less information about the policy uncertainty and be less capable of achieving a desired outcome. An expert might be better placed to deal with the uncertainty, but may choose to exploit that informational advantage for her own purposes. Under these circumstances, the optimal decision for the principal involves achieving an optimal combination of control and discretion. In those cases, where the level of policy uncertainty is high, the optimal amount of discretion can be correspondingly high.

A different approach to understanding the origins of bureaucratic discretion explores the historical process through which the political masters who often decry their own lack of control purposefully put into place the system that ties their own hands. Johnson and Libecap (1994) describe how the US civil service system was designed to reduce the cost of competition between Congress and the president for control over the bureaucracy. As the economy grew and modernized in the nineteenth and early twentieth centuries, the patronage system that then prevailed not only became too costly and wasteful in terms of inefficiencies and low productivity but also became too difficult for federal politicians to manage and supervise. The reforms implemented by both Congress and the president to institute tenure, indexed spending increases, and many forms of insulation weakened their own powers to exercise control of the bureaucracy and at the same time created a new and influential organized interest group of federal employees who would be very successful in pursuing further reforms of the civil service system. One of the results of the reforms is greater bureaucratic discretion.

A third reason for agency autonomy arises when local citizens who have different preferences from national majorities are in charge of bureaucracies that implement national policies (Gerken, 2013). Because residential patterns are lumpy, it is very common for the citizens that serve as local agents of national bureaucracies to have different views and preferences from the median. Their position within the bureaucracy allows them to wield considerable power to adjust the implementation of the national policy to local preferences.

In some cases, the central bureau voluntarily cedes the discretion, and in others it is just too difficult to control. In either case, the result is that this federalism "gives minorities the chance to be the majority ... it gives them more than influence at the local level; it gives them control" (Gerken, 2013: 1365). Examples include that of a school board implementing the policy set by the Department of Education, or state officials taking environmental regulation in a deregulatory direction.

The fourth major determinant of agency autonomy is the multiple-principal nature of bureaucracies. Even the relation between Congress and an agency involves multiple principals, as the agency has to relate to several different committees and subcommittees in both the House and the Senate, and even with individuals. A key finding of the multiple-principal literature is that it dampens considerably the influence of any one given principal, as opposing incentives cancel out (Dixit, 1996; Holmstrom and Milgrom, 1991). Wilson (1989: 237) suggests this result applies to the US bureaucracy and Congress:

No agency is free to ignore the views of *Congress*. An agency may, however, defer to the views of one part of Congress (say one committee) instead of another, or balance competing demands of the White House with those of some parts of Congress in ways that other parts may not like. The bureaucracy cannot evade political control nor sustain for long the view that there is a realm of "administration" that is immune from "politics." But it can maneuver among its many political masters in ways that displease some of them and can define its tasks for internal reasons and not simply in response to external demands. (Emphasis in original.)

Presidential Control of Bureaucratic Agencies

Legislators and bureaucrats were the central focus in much of the early bureaucracy literature. Other actors, such as the president and courts, have either not garnered much attention or have entered the analysis playing a marginal role, such as being mere constraints on the legislatures and agencies. Terry Moe, in particular, has been a vocal critic of the sidelining of presidents in the literature (we turn to courts in the next section) (Moe, 1985, 1987; Moe and Wilson, 1994). Although there have been some attempts to include presidents "as the pivotal actors they are, not as a planet orbiting the legislative sun," "the legislature is still the center of its political universe, and other institutional actors – the president, the courts, even the bureaucracy – are given far less serious attention than they deserve" (Moe, 2013: 1173–74).[6]

What are the powers and characteristics of the president (in the United States) that justify treating him as a central player in the control of the bureaucracy? One widely held view associated with Neustadt (1990) was that though the president has very little power, the president relies on personal attributes such as prestige, persuasion, and character for strong leadership. In the Institutional and Organizational Analysis (IOA) literature, the view of the personal presidency has given way to that of the institutional presidency; even though personality and charisma are important, it is ultimately the institutions that are the foundation of presidential power (Moe and Howell, 1999b: 850). Here, we are interested in those powers that help the president control the bureaucracy.

The first is the power to veto legislation, which gives the president great leverage to affect Congress's attempts to influence agencies. The threat of a presidential veto can affect the behavior of legislators. The second is the power to appoint the public officials that will head a large number of different bureaucratic agencies. In 2012, there were 1,212 senior-level positions appointed by the president, subject to Senate confirmation. In addition, there were 353 positions that did not require Senate confirmation, as well as 680 non-career members of the Senior Executive Service and 1,403 other appointments who serve in a confidential policy role (Plum Book, 2012).[7] Although these appointments also include some non-bureaucratic roles such as ambassadors, these numbers suggest a formidable power for a president to imprint his preferences on the federal bureaucracy. The need for Senate confirmation of many of the top positions can mitigate the power to appoint, especially if government is divided, but even then there is a tradition for Congress to defer to presidential choice on all except the most controversial appointments (Moe, 1987).

The third power held by the president is that of unilateral action, that is, the power of making law on his own, through executive orders,

---

[6] Studies of the bureaucracy with a more central role for the president include: Moe (2013); McCarty (2004); Volden (2002); and Huber and Shipan (2002).

[7] http://presidentialtransition.org/blog/posts/160316_help-wanted-4000-appointees.php.

memoranda, proclamations, executive agreements, or national security directives.[8] Although the Constitution grants the power to make laws to Congress, the president in the United States has always been able to make law unilaterally. Examples of important legislation passed through executive orders include: Louisiana Purchase in 1803 (Jefferson); Emancipation Proclamation in 1863 (Lincoln); prohibition of discrimination in employment in 1965 (Johnson); outlawing the use of political assassination in 1976 (Ford); intergovernmental review of federal programs in 1982 (Reagan); establishment of the Office of Homeland Security in 2001 (G. W. Bush); "protecting the nation from foreign terrorists' entry into the United States 2017" [sic] (Trump). The last example shows that unilateral presidential action can be blocked or overturned by other political actors – President Trump's executive order was quickly blocked by a federal judge and is under consideration by the Supreme Court. Nevertheless, many laws born from unilateral action survive and the power has become central to the modern presidency (Moe and Howell, 1999a). Kennedy (2015) tested whether agencies respond to executive orders. He used data on all executive orders in the United States from 1989 to 2011 and found that the probability they are implemented increases significantly if the agency is named in the order and promulgation is clearly requested. It is not necessarily the case that the president will say: "Do this! Do that! And nothing will happen," as President Truman predicted of incoming President Eisenhower.[9]

The discussion above has referred to the US presidency and system of government. Obviously, in other systems, different institutions lead to different politics of structure and control of the bureaucracy. In the US system, laws are difficult to pass given the separation of power, so it is possible to enact bureaucratic structures protected from future reversal. Whatever gets enacted tends to endure. In parliamentary systems, on the other hand, it is easy for the majority coalition to pass new laws. As a result, bureaucracies receive much greater discretion and insulation, though, as we noted in the previous

---

[8] On unilateral action by presidents, see Howell (2003), Kennedy (2015), Moe and Howell (1999a), and Rudalevige (2012).

[9] The proper quote is "He'll sit here, and he'll say, "Do this! Do that!" And nothing will happen. Poor Ike – it won't be a bit like the Army. He'll find it very frustrating" (www.bartleby.com/73/1514.html).

chapter, the actual form taken depends on the specific details of the entire set of political institutions.

In Brazil, for example, the system of government is formally presidential, but due to the nature of coalition government, Brazil has some characteristics of a parliamentary system. The president possesses a suite of proactive and reactive powers that allow her to greatly set the agenda in Congress and to assure the passage of most of that agenda (Alston and Mueller, 2006). These include a line-item veto (stronger than the simple veto), ample use of executive decrees, monopoly of proposal over many policy areas, and power to discharge committees, among other powers. Importantly, the president has access to several political currencies that are used to assure a large majority in Congress, overcoming the fragmented party structure that implies that the president's own party will almost never hold a majority of seats. These political currencies include more than forty thousand positions to appoint federal bureaucrats (at all levels) and the power to execute or not to execute legislators' individual budget amendments, which is the main way legislators have to take pork-barrel projects back to their districts. Those legislators who do not support the executive's proposals risk their amendments not being executed. The result is that the president not only has the ability to directly and indirectly make law, but also to imprint her preferences on the bureaucracy and to assure that Congress goes along with both. In Brazil, Congress has practically no role in controlling the bureaucracy, whereas the president is well equipped to do so.

In much of the literature on the bureaucracy, the president is included only by assuming that the agency's preference is the same as the president's, or by having the president as a veto point that Congress considers when making legislation. The discussion in this section suggests that the president has powers that imply a much more central role.

Legal Constraints on Bureaucratic Action

Courts do not have the ability to proactively interfere in the bureaucracy, as do Congress and the president, but they nevertheless can have an important role in shaping what bureaucracies can and cannot do. Judges, just like any other political actor, have preferences and ideologies (Epstein, Landes, and Posner, 2013; Segal and Spaeth, 2002;

Spiller and Gely, 2009). It is therefore reasonable to expect that in many circumstances courts may act strategically and exhibit judicial activism. The main mechanisms used by courts to influence the actions of agencies are through procedural and substantive constraints. In the process of fulfilling their mandates, agencies must follow a prespecified set of procedures determined in administrative law and in the statutes of agencies. If agencies do not adhere to those procedures, interested parties may appeal to the courts to restrict or overturn the actions of agencies. A prominent view in the literature goes so far as to hold that administrative procedures are instruments of control of the bureaucracy, purposefully designed to restrict agency policy to certain desired outcomes (McCubbins, Noll, and Weingast, 1987). Alternatively, the courts can rule directly on the substance of an agency's decision, striking it down if it is deemed unconstitutional or against the agency's statutes.

Is there evidence that ideological judges with a sophisticated understanding of the legislative process and of other actors' preferences use these powers to, in a sense, control the bureaucracy? Spiller and Gely (1992), Eskridge (1991), and others have shown that when reviewing an agency's interpretation of a statute, courts are careful to select policy decisions that will not be reversed by Congress. The power of the court depends on how its preferences compare with those of the House and the Senate. If the court has extreme views relative to both chambers of Congress, then its power to influence the agency is constrained. But, if the court's median preference is within the contract curve of the House and Senate, it will be well placed to impose its preferences on the agency.

If bureaucracies are also strategic, then they will be aware that courts have preferences and can have the power to overturn their interpretation of statutes on procedural or substantive grounds. Forward-looking agencies would take the court's preferences into account and suitably adjust their interpretation to avoid reversal. What is the evidence that bureaucracies are in fact constrained in such a manner by potential court reactions? Howard and Nixon (2003) tested whether the Internal Revenue Service (IRS) in the United States, an agency often accused of being out of control, changes its behavior in light of the ideological composition of the local appeals court. They focus on the decision of the IRS to perform more audits of businesses or of individuals. Using a measure of judicial ideology based on NOMINATE scores, they show that when the federal court of appeals becomes more liberal, the audit rate of individuals decreases relative to that of businesses, and the opposite occurs when the court is more conservative. While they also find that executive and legislative preferences also mattered, the impact of the courts was larger. In a related study, they show that the IRS exhibited a similar behavior when choosing whether to focus audits on wealthy versus less-affluent individuals (Howard and Nixon, 2002). The main result is that when the local federal court of appeals is more liberal, the IRS focuses more on equity by reducing audits on the poor and increasing them on the rich. Similarly, Canes-Wrone (2003) analyzed more than 18,000 decisions by the Army Corps of Engineers whether to grant permits to develop wetlands, from 1988 to 1996, and found that a permit was less likely to be granted the more liberal the relevant lower court.

Bureaucracies and Delegation in a Multiple-Principal Context

In the previous sections, we presented arguments and evidence for five different answers to the question, "Who controls the bureaucracy?" But, of course, there is no reason why this question must have a single answer. A careful reading of any of the answers reviewed above makes it clear that other principals are always also involved. When making the case for congressional dominance, the president and the courts were there in the background, and when making the case for the courts, it was necessary to account for legislative and presidential preferences. In all cases, multiple principals were involved. It is perhaps the academic predilection for grand theories, which we discussed in Chapter 4, that has led the literature to segment itself in such a way. In a seminal paper about the organization of the bureaucracy, Hammond and Knott (1996: 126) assessed these characteristics of the literature as follows:

Taken collectively, these bodies of literature highlight several factors of undoubted significance for efforts at understanding who, if anyone, controls the bureaucracy. They also suggest that relationships among the president, Congress, courts, and the bureaucracy are quite complex. In fact, it may be this complexity, with the resulting ambiguities of understanding, that has given rise to such divergent arguments about who controls the bureaucracy. And of course, this complexity has made it difficult to develop a general theory of how the president, Congress, and courts interact to influence bureaucratic policy-making.

But if no single principal controls the bureaucracy on its own, how can we understand all the evidence that has been presented over the years by each school of thought? Hammond and Knott (1996) note that many of the empirical tests used in the literature have been based on a syllogism that expects that if one principal changed its preferences and the others did not, and then the agency changed its policies, then it is that principal that controls the agency. They recognize that this power to bring about a change in what the agency does is important, but they also argue that it is only part of what is necessary to really have control. Another important part is the issue of which principal is most responsible for forcing the agency to change? And a third issue is which principal benefits the most from the change in agency policy?

In Figure 6.1, we illustrate three aspects of control in a spatial model similar to our presentation in the introduction to Part II. The figure assumes two policy dimensions and shows the preferred points of a bureaucratic agency (A_1), the president (P), the Senate (S), and the House of Representatives (H). This is a simplified situation in which we are leaving out other principals, such as the courts, as well as abstracting from issues of preference aggregation in Congress. The agency would like to implement the policy at its preferred point A_1 (upper panel), but that point would be vulnerable to defeat by some other point that P, S, and H unanimously prefer to it. Any point outside of the triangle formed by the contract curves between the three political players always has some points on, or within, the triangle that defeat that original point. The agency therefore strategically chooses a point on the triangle, such as SQ_1, that is the best it can do and that cannot be defeated by any other point within the triangle. Any change from SQ_1 would make at least one of the principals worse off. Since each of them has veto power, as long as nothing else changes, SQ_1 is an equilibrium.

Now, suppose that the president's preferences change from to P to P' (due to elections or change of views). The contract triangle has now shrunk and point SQ_1 is no longer invulnerable. The shaded-in lens is

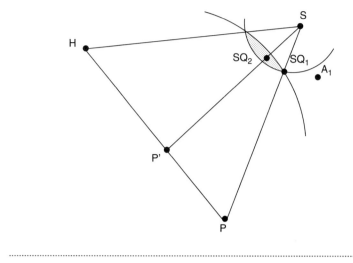

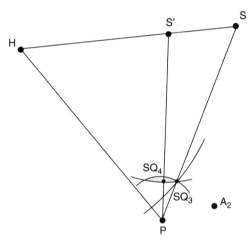

Figure 6.1 Multiple principals and bureaucratic control
Source: Based on Hammond and Knott (1996: 154–55).

the set of points that P, S, and H prefer to SQ_1. It is reasonable to expect that they would pass new legislation establishing a new policy at SQ_2. In this example, the president changed preferences and this led to a change of policy by the agency, even though there was no change in the preferences of the Senate and the House. This is the first manifestation of power that Hammond and Knott (1996) singled out. It is the simple syllogism that scholars have often used as the basis for empirical tests. The authors emphasize that this evidence is not enough to establish who controls the agency. A second issue requires the determination of which of the principals is responsible for actually forcing a change in policy. Because each principal has the power to veto any change, it turns out that "it is the threat of joint legislative action by all three institutions, not just one, that forces a change in agency policy" (Hammond and Knott, 1996: 156). That is, even though S and H did not change their preferred points, they were still instrumental in determining the change in policy from SQ_1 to SQ_2. Attributing control only to P would be misleading.[10]

A third issue in determining control involves establishing which principal gets most of what they want. In the upper panel, it was the president's change in preference that created the opportunity for change in policy, but in the end, the change from SQ_1 to SQ_2 favored all three principals. Furthermore, the new policy was very close to the Senate's preferred point, even though the Senate was not responsible for creating the opportunity for change. In the lower panel, it is the Senate that creates the opportunity for change by moving from S to S'. Nevertheless, the new policy at SQ_4 is closer to the president's preferred point than it is to that of the Senate. The president exerts control by not allowing the new policy to stray away from close to his preferred point. These examples show that the initial policy allocation determines which principal will be most advantaged by a change in equilibrium, and it will not necessarily be the same principal that initiated the change.

When there are multiple principals involved, the determination of who controls the agency becomes much more complex than simply establishing a link between a change by one principal and a corresponding change by the agency. Making the examples more realistic, for example by including other principals and by allowing for asymmetric information (which would allow for bureaucratic drift), would make the analysis even more complex. It is the interactions among the principals, and not only with the agency, which make this such a rich topic for analysis. Inevitably, one has to pay close

---

[10] It is not the case that all principals will always be able to influence a change in policy. Which players have power depends on institutions that determine political property rights. With three principals, at least two will be involved in any change in policy, as it is the boundary between the two that determines the location of the new status quo.

attention to the detailed political institutions that assign property rights and determine transaction costs in each specific situation if we are to understand who controls the bureaucracy and why it does what it does. It is not enough to analyze the implementation of policy by the bureaucracy as a separate stage from the formulation of policy. Even though it can be the last stage of the game, it is taken into consideration by players at earlier stages, and crucially affects which laws and policies get chosen in the first place.

Conclusion

This chapter has focused on the ways in which institutions determine the answer to the question, "Who controls the bureaucracy?" As noted by Moe (2013: 1149), "a theory of political control and delegation is ultimately a political theory of bureaucratic organization: one that shows how the structural details of bureaucracy arise out of the political process and how they are connected to the strategies and motivations of those who exercise (or influence) public authority." This mirrors the main message stressed throughout Part II of our book: institutions are fundamental determinants of performance and outcomes. Delegation and control has been one of the major issues of interest in the IOA of bureaucracies, but it is not the only theme to be investigated. A less explored but growing area of interest is the application of the same set of tools and questions to other systems besides the United States, such as parliamentary systems and bureaucracies in non-democratic countries. Another theme that we have not addressed is the dynamics of interaction within a bureaucracy, as different individuals or subsets of the organization compete and cooperate to achieve their goals. A final example of an alternative avenue to explore is the ability of some bureaucracies to affect the electoral prospects of their political superiors, inverting the direction of control in the relationship (Moe, 2013: 1177).

7 | The Judicial System

The judicial branch of government is unique in that its influence on institutions typically comes after another branch of government has acted. The judiciary is responsible for the ultimate application of the laws of society. It acts after the legislature has drafted or passed a law, or after the executive has enforced that law through regulatory or police action.[1] The judiciary is forward-looking, for the decisions of the courts guide actors in future interactions. A rule that has been applied or clarified today helps define which parties have actionable legal claims in potential interactions tomorrow, which in turn influences the behavior of individuals and organizations subject to that law. An overturned law, or one prevented from passage, informs the legislature and the executive as to the limits of their authority in the future. The judiciary is also unique in that it is the branch of government that treats the law most closely and has a daily incremental influence on the institutions of society. We can think of the core functions of the judiciary as including dispute resolution, coordination of future interactions in society, and rule interpretation (Shepsle 2010).

In this chapter, we focus on two questions: (1) How do specific institutional design choices affect the judiciary? (2) How does the judiciary influence institutions in society? In the first section, we deal with institutional design issues and discuss how judicial independence, accountability, reputation, and limits on authority all matter greatly for how a given judiciary functions. The incentives that judges face

---

[1] Some functions of the legislative and executive branches in the United States have proven to be fungible in practice. A trade-off exists between the extent of regulation of commercial activity, and the extent to which commercial actors resolve their disputes in the courts, whose precedent then "regulates" future commercial actors and their potential disputes. The United States has been characterized as transitioning from reliance on the courts to reliance on executive regulation during the late nineteenth and early twentieth centuries (Glaeser and Shleifer, 2003).

influence the independence, accountability, reputation, and limits on authority of the overall judicial system[2] (Garoupa and Ginsburg, 2015: 111). As a means of showing the iterative and uncertain process by which the institutions impacting the judiciary develop, the first section is followed by a case study analyzing one of the most famous US court cases in history, *Marbury* v. *Madison*, 5 US 137 (1803).

In the chapter's second section, we examine the specific ways in which the judiciary influences institutions and organizations in society. The judiciary typically provides constitutional oversight, administrative oversight, and facilitation of a range of ideal characteristics of a legal system.[3] We conclude the chapter with a case study examining the new institutions governing Kenya's judiciary. Kenya's modern experience highlights many of the key lessons from our chapter, including the critical role that the judiciary plays in legitimizing the law and how, absent a sufficient level of accountability and independence, the judiciary can do precisely the opposite and create a need for its own wholesale institutional overhaul.

One function of the judiciary is constitutional oversight, but in Part II (this part) of the book we largely take a nation's constitution as given, instead examining how the judiciary can affect institutions, without considering the ways that the judiciary influences constitutional moments that formalize changes in fundamental governance beliefs across society. In contrast, in Part III of our book we define the essential role constitutional moments play in altering the institutional trajectory

---

[2] Both institutions and norms influence the institutional features of the judiciary that we describe in the first section of this chapter. One lesson from the scholarship is that judges can only be imperfectly monitored, causing the norms of judicial behavior to play an important role in determining the way in which a judiciary influences the institutions of society. Judicial norms can lead judges to value independence, reputation, and accountability to those they govern, and their desire to achieve these outcomes operates as a complementary but conceptually distinct incentive mechanism from the specific institutions governing judicial behavior.

[3] Institutional analysis of the judiciary straddles a difficult divide between ideal principles of governance and the real-world contextual factors that influence the realization of these principles. Throughout this chapter, institutional principles are frequently described positively as if they are perfectly realized in practice. This is not our view. A theoretical analysis of the ideal functions of the judiciary is an important prerequisite to understanding how specific institutional contexts encourage or hinder these ideal outcomes. Qualifying every statement with ideally, comparatively, relatively, largely, inter alia, would greatly weaken the explanatory force that these ideal types do possess for institutional scholars.

of a given society. The subsection on constitutional oversight in this chapter draws this distinction in greater detail. Keeping this distinction in mind centers the discussion in this chapter on the functional role of the judiciary in determining institutions.

Institutional Analysis of the Judiciary

Independence

A number of scholars in the Institutional and Organizational Analysis (IOA) have emphasized the importance of judicial independence as an important precursor to the rule of law and modern democratic institutions more generally (North and Weingast, 1989; Kiser and Barzel, 1991; Ostrom, 1991). But the word "independence" carries an implicit qualifier: independent from whom? We will consider the answer to this question to be independence from the powerful organizations in society. Judicial independence means a given judge is not beholden to the powerful actors who are brought before the court to answer for crimes, injuries to others, or failure to abide by the terms of a contract into which they entered. At different times in history, the powerful who acted with impunity in society may have been either private or government actors (e.g., royalty).

"Independence from undue influence" is a more general definition of independence that excludes the possibility of judges being improperly influenced by any individual or organization.[4] If a judge systematically favors family members or the poor over the outcomes clearly dictated by the laws themselves, this also stands as a lack of judicial independence under this broader definition. However, the focus on freedom

---

[4] Perfect independence from undue influence is an example of an institutional ideal that is not fully realized in practice. Nonetheless, the concept is an essential one in theory and practice for understanding the outcomes associated with the judicial systems around the world. The prevalence of the concept of judicial independence can result in the problematic tendency "to present judicial independence as fact rather than as an ideal or set of normative values about courts" (Peretti, 2002: 103). A related question is to what extent influences other than the right laws and procedure applied to a well-developed factual record can ever be totally eradicated from an institution composed of individuals who are subject to all the imperfections and inconsistencies of human behavior. As examples: time since their last meal influences the rulings of judges (Danziger, Levav, and Avnaim-Pesso, 2011); and whether or not judges have daughters influences their rulings on cases that present women's issues (Glynn and Sen, 2015).

from the undue influence of the powerful shows how independence creates a desirable institutional outcome for the legal system: impartial adjudication of claims brought before the court.

Early institutional analysis of the importance of judicial independence draws on the historical context following the Norman Conquest of England, when the nature of elite relationships in society changed in a way that increased the value of stable contract enforcement (North and Weingast, 1989; Kiser and Barzel, 1991). The emergence of judicial independence ensured that contracts were enforced in a way that did not systematically favor the most powerful. Kiser and Barzel label judicial independence, as it occurred in England following the Norman Conquest, as a "proto-democratic" institution. The critical importance of reliable and impartial contract enforcement for economic outcomes has since been extended and developed by a number of other institutional scholars (Arruñada and Andonova, 2005). The early studies of England emphasize that while judicial independence is an important precursor to the rule of law, it was not wrought from liberalizing motives on the part of the elite.[5] This view of judicial independence benefiting the elite in their economic affairs corresponds to broader arguments as to the emergence of the rule of law as necessarily being consistent with the interests of the elite coalition governing a particular society (Wallis, 2018a).

The early studies presaged the realization that understanding modern economic outcomes involving large-scale firms and complex contractual commitments required a more granular understanding of the law and the judiciary's enforcement (Hadfield, 2005: 175). This focus on contracts is consistent with the historical emergence of judicial institutions: the elite had an interest in impartial contract enforcement that was distinct from the benefits ordinary individuals receive from judicial independence. The move to impersonal contract enforcement has also been explained as a shift away from enforcing contracts based upon the personal characteristics of the parties to enforcing contracts against the property of individuals (Arruñada, 2012). Other research has tied the extent of judicial independence to the degree to which

---

[5] It should be noted that this early form of judicial independence was a relative one, especially by modern standards. Kiser and Barzel note how post-Conquest judges still would tip the scales in favor of the king occasionally. This shows how judges are ultimately still reliant upon those who influence their appointment and retention, a point emphasized subsequently.

political parties have divergent policy preferences: the greater the degree to which major political parties' platforms differ, the greater the value judicial independence provides in ensuring against drastic policy change when the government changes hands between parties (Hanssen, 2004). This offers a similar reason for the emergence of judicial independence to that of contracts: even the most powerful in a given society had reasons to insulate themselves against the possibility of future regime change. This limiting effect on the magnitude of change any given regime turnover can imply for society is a fundamental determinant of the comparative economic and political success of developed nations (Weingast, 2015: 6).

From its early and limited origins, the importance of judicial independence has since become widely recognized, appearing in international human rights standards as a cornerstone of civil and political rights (Universal Declaration of Human Rights, International Covenant on Civil and Political Rights). Vicki Jackson (2012) highlights three necessary components for a legal system to achieve a greater degree of judicial independence in practice: judges must themselves (1) value independent decision making, (2) have the requisite level of competency to understand the ways in which undue influences might manifest themselves, and (3) be situated within a legal and political system that creates incentives for independent decision making. A judge's desire to be seen as independent from undue influence underscores the self-reflexive nature of institutional development. Only if the judicial profession is seen as honorable and virtuous will it attract individuals who value such institutional attributes. More generally, institutions that lend themselves to judicial independence have been characterized as channeling self-interested behaviors away from their most destructive ends (Epstein, 1990). Because of self-enforcement, norms of judicial independence are necessarily more fragile than those of the other branches of government. In underscoring the fact that the judiciary does not wield government authority in a way that can reinforce its own power as easily as the other branches of government, Alexander Hamilton noted how the judiciary has neither the power of the sword nor the purse, nor is it capable of direct legislative or administrative action (Peabody, 2011: 13).

Nonetheless, there are a number of specific institutional characteristics of a given system that lend themselves to judicial independence. These institutional remedies can be divided into preventive and corrective methods. In order to prevent undue influence on judicial proceedings, judges can be subject to a variety of restraints intended to reduce conflicts of interest. Judges are often required to recuse themselves from proceedings in which they have a prior interest, and are discouraged, if not outright prohibited, from associating with lawyers likely to appear before their court. Similarly, judges are typically not allowed to engage in outside business activities, lobby the legislature, or otherwise be remunerated for their time in a way that could pervert their incentives when deciding cases. Judges also tend to be insulated from the political process, either by being appointed (or elected) for a lengthy period, up to and including life tenure in some instances, or by preventing the legislature from altering their tenure or compensation.

Just as a number of institutions have emerged intended to prevent undue influence, there are a number of corrective measures intended to identify problematic judicial outcomes, and ideally, deter them from occurring in the first place. First, the larger the group that has access to judicial decisions, the more effective a check on arbitrary or corrupt judicial decisions (Cross, 1953). The groups with an interest in judicial independence, as well as the groups whose interests were disregarded in a given problematic judicial decision, are able to protest the decision, and ideally, reduce the likelihood that similar outcomes will occur in the future.

Second, including the deciding judge as information helps observers determine whether a judge systematically favors one group over another, or one set of rights over another (Leflar, 1961). Finally, a robust legal academy composed of former and practicing jurists and judges among other scholars creates an environment in which unrestricted, and often public, commentary regarding controversial decisions is the norm (Hadfield, 2005: 186). This creates an additional deterrent effect upon judges who may otherwise wish to decide a case based upon factors other than those demanded by law.

Ultimately, judicial independence allows the judiciary to secure its legitimacy, and hence, power, more effectively. In a society where other modern liberal institutions are in place, or are developing concurrently, the incentive for empowerment through legitimization encourages judicial enforcement of the law to ensure it effectively governs social interaction according to the institutional principles we detail in this chapter. The very role of the judiciary in legitimizing the law, and in doing so, signaling this legitimacy to cement its reputation, can create an incentive-compatible equilibrium. If the judiciary's ability to credibly enforce the law relies on broad perceptions of the judiciary's legitimacy, this can operate as a self-reflexive constraint in conjunction with the independence of the judiciary. This is an important outcome for a branch of government whose legitimacy depends in part upon its operating free from the constraining influences of other branches of government, and as importantly, signaling this independence to the people over whom it has the authority to impose final legal judgments. Successfully signaling independence, among other desirable outcomes including accountability, results in improved judicial reputation.

The relationship between independence and reputation is one way in which these institutional outcomes interact with one another. Another such relationship surrounds independence and accountability. Judicial independence is affected by ways in which judges are selected, compensated, and retained. If the executive branch appoints and removes judges, then the judiciary is less independent than the case where the executive can appoint but not remove judges. Both these scenarios create less independence than the case where judges' selection is removed from other branches of government, or the case where judges are granted lifetime tenure. North (1989: 1323) notes how lifetime tenure of judges in the United States was a specific design choice intended to insulate the judiciary from special interest pressures. The scholarship surrounding judicial selection, punishment, and retention emphasizes the importance of these institutional design choices for how judges enforce, interpret, and apply the law, on a range of outcomes including their level of independence, as well as their accountability.

Accountability

Judicial accountability is the extent to which a given judge can formally be held accountable by the constituents of the legal system. Essential throughout the literature on judicial selection is the notion of accountability, for specific selection processes are seen as trading off judicial independence and judicial accountability. Accountability is the extent to which judges are subject to formal processes that influence outcomes they care about, such as tenure, compensation, and public reputation. Notably, the ways in which selection processes vary indicate differing views as to the groups to whom judges should be accountable. In some jurisdictions, including a large number across the United States, constituents elect judges. This method creates direct accountability to the individuals most likely to be affected by a given judge's decisions: if a judge's constituents don't like the judge's performance, they can vote the judge out in the subsequent election.[6] In other jurisdictions, a group of experts in legal matters appoints judges. Another selection method is for the executive to appoint judges. Executive appointment promotes accountability to the representatives that elected the executive, at least in theory. This diffuses direct popular pressures on the judiciary, for a given executive is evaluated on many other factors than their choices regarding judicial appointments. To give an idea of how much selection processes vary, of the fifty highest state courts in the United States, twenty-three are elected, eight are appointed, and nineteen are selected based upon merit (Garoupa and Ginsburg, 2015: 100–101).

Executive appointment with legislative consent has been characterized as less subject to democratic pressures than direct judicial elections (Handelsman Shugerman, 2012). Nonetheless, there is a body of research suggesting that popular pressures still influence these forms of selection processes. United States senators engaged in confirmation hearings arguably consider their constituents' preferences, as well as those of special interest groups (Kastellec, Lax, and Phillips, 2010; see also Segal, Cameron, and Cover, 1992; Caldeira and Wright, 1998; Owens et al., 2014). This corresponds to the fact that senators can be punished in reelection contests if they deviate significantly from these preferences as well (Overby et al., 1992). Similarly, an analysis of

---

[6] A recent empirical finding (Lim, 2013) suggests that elected judges display significantly more variance in their decisions than appointed judges, and that elected judges tend to reflect the preferences of the locality from which they were elected as opposed to appointed judges who tend to reflect the preferences of the median voter in the state. Other scholarship suggests that judicial accountability plays an important role in checking other branches of government, especially when the separation between the legislature and the executive is weak or absent (Alt and Lassen, 2008). However, the relationship between selection and judicial output is more complex in practice than the simple distinction that elected judges care more about the public's reaction to their decisions. One study provides evidence that in the United States, elected judges are not less independent than their appointed counterparts; the main distinction between the two selection methods results in a greater quantity of opinions from elected judges, although these opinions were slightly less likely to provide clear legal reasoning as compared to those of appointed judges (Choi, Gulati, and Posner, 2010).

congressional legislation that weakened judicial independence has been characterized as resultant from legislators responding to popular dissatisfaction with the judiciary (Clark, 2011).

Despite the persistent variance in judicial selection across the United States, countries are converging towards merit selection methods, usually in the form of judicial councils. The specific powers of a judicial council can vary from country to country, but the councils are typically tasked with oversight of judicial selection, discipline, management, and promotion. The view of these councils as promoting better judicial outcomes has not been well-supported empirically, but nonetheless has emerged as a "best practice" for countries engaged in judicial reform (Garoupa and Ginsburg, 2015). Whether or not the institution of merit selection results in outcomes that better balance the trade-off between judicial accountability and independence, or if such outcomes are instead more defined by other institutional or contextual factors, is an important empirical question for future research. One such study suggests that striking the right balance between accountability and independence makes them complements, and that a sufficient level of accountability is linked to higher levels of per capita income in nations around the world (Voigt, 2008).

The set of potential benefits institutional scholars have identified associated with merit selection is clear: a means of selection that chooses judges more on the basis of merit than politics better resolves principal-agent problems associated with the judiciary. For judges to perform their functions free from undue influence, they need to be independent. But this very independence creates its own difficulty: how should a given regime of governance best ensure independent judges while also making them accountable for their performance? A classic way to frame the issue is with the question, who watches the watchmen? Despite the variance in selection methods across the world, they all represent different institutional solutions intended to resolve this fundamental trade-off between accountability and independence.

Punishment and removal of judges is another institution whose variance worldwide emphasizes the trade-off between independence and accountability. Despite the variance in punishment and removal processes, the grounds for discipline and removal and the procedure and authority for determining culpability are typically clearly specified. In Australia, for example, a judge can be removed by Parliament if both houses decide by majority vote that a particular judge is incapable of serving in the office, or if the judge's behavior makes them unfit for the office (King, 2002–2003: 175–76). These grounds for removal are quite general, but removal of judges is still rare in Australia (Parliament of Australia, 2012). In contrast, other countries have developed highly specific judicial codes of conduct that govern most or all judges in the system.[7] In addition to outright removal for more serious offences and incapability, many judicial systems also allow the highest court or the judicial council to publicly sanction judges for misconduct.[8] Notably, removal and sanctions are rare, such that when they do occur, the punishing authority often emphasizes the disrepute a given judge's actions have brought upon the judiciary as a whole.

Reputation

Judicial reputation is the third institution that influences individual and collective outcomes. Reputation is closely tied to the concept of judicial independence, but highlights the distinct point that perceptions matter. If citizens perceive the judiciary as corrupt, lacking independence, or exhibiting some other undesirable characteristic, then this perception can matter as much for formal and informal institutional outcomes as the underlying truth of independence or corruption.[9] If the judiciary has a reputation for independence and accountability constraining its power, then this reputation increases the likelihood that individuals in

[7] In the United States, justices of the Supreme Court are not bound by the Code of Judicial Conduct that binds other federal judges. Nonetheless, the code is typically heeded by Supreme Court justices to the point where it approaches a norm of behavior. For example, Justice Bader-Ginsburg's public statements about a presidential candidate were met with widespread disapproval, even from editorial sources that very much agreed with the substance of the justice's remarks. The disapproval reached the point that Justice Bader-Ginsburg nearly apologized outright, admitting the remarks were a "mistake" (see, e.g., Shear, 2016).

[8] In Florida, the highest court of the state declared that a public reprimand of a lower court judge from the agency tasked with judicial oversight was insufficient, and ordered the judge to take anger management classes as an additional sanction for the way she treated a domestic abuse witness who failed to appear in court to testify against her alleged abuser (see, e.g., Guerra, 2016).

[9] The broad perception of the judiciary relates to the extent that individuals' perceptions of the judiciary are tied to their perceptions of the legitimacy of the law overall. This type of broad perception surrounding governance institutions is one aspect of the fundamental belief structure that we discuss in Part III.

society, whether powerful or atomistic, will perceive the judiciary's enforcement of the laws as a meaningful and predictable constraint upon their actions. Absent sufficient judicial reputation for impersonal enforcement of the law, the powerful are able to act with more impunity. Similarly, ordinary individuals are less likely to view the law as legitimate, and are more likely to calculate the benefits and costs of breaking the law, as opposed to respecting the law in its own right.

The importance of preserving a judiciary's reputation has led to the development of a specialized legal doctrine in the United States. In instances such as fund-raising surrounding judicial elections, preserving the integrity of the judicial institution from the appearance of corruption has been identified as more important than freedom of political speech for campaigning judges. See, for example, *Williams-Yulee* v. *Florida*, 575 US 1–2 (2015), citing *Caperton* v. *A. T. Massey Coal Co.*, 556 US 868, 889 (2009), identifying the public interest at stake in restricting direct judicial campaign fund-raising as "public confidence in the fairness and integrity of the nation's elected judges." Given how much protection political speech receives in the jurisprudence of the United States, this is a testament to the extent to which the United States' highest court values the appearance of independence, and considers it a legitimate public purpose animating government policy that otherwise would be considered an infringement of fundamental rights. Because the Supreme Court's decision focused on the appearance of corruption, as opposed to corruption itself, it provides a ready introduction to the distinction between reputation and freedom from undue influences.

Garoupa and Ginsburg (2015) characterize reputation as addressing two problems the judiciary faces more than other branches of government. First, because the judiciary's work is highly specialized, technical, and resultant from group effort, monitoring behavior is more difficult than other public actors whose expected actions are more easily verifiable. Second, the difficulty in monitoring creates an incentive for some judges to act in ways that vary from the desires of those they govern, be it the dominant network or the population at large. The relevant group that needs to perceive the judiciary as legitimate can vary significantly across nations. In modern liberal societies, selection and punishment tend to operate as popular checks on the behavior of the judiciary. In less democratic societies, the judiciary may be more concerned with job security.[10] In this sense, reputation matters everywhere, but the larger institutional structure can greatly determine the set of individuals or groups with whom the judiciary is interested in generating reputational capital.

One of the essential trade-offs in judicial reputation is the extent to which institutions encourage the development of individual reputation, versus the collective reputation of the judiciary as a whole. Both aspects of judicial reputation are important, and linked in a number of ways. The actions of individual judges can significantly impact the legitimacy of the judiciary as a whole, a point emphasized when discussing sanctions and removal in the previous subsection. Similarly, the reputation of the judiciary as a collective can define the extent to which society heeds the decisions of a given judge. Different systems have led to significantly different methods of judicial output: in some systems, the author of a judicial opinion is publicly known, whereas in others, the entire judiciary is seen as the author of any given opinion.[11] One system encourages judges to develop their individual reputations for career success, while another rewards seniority and collaboration. The distinction is traditionally associated with the structural differences in common law versus civil law systems.[12] Common law systems derive from the colonial influence of the United Kingdom, for all countries with a common law system, the United States included, inherited it from their former colonial authority.

---

[10] Myanmar's Constitutional Tribunal resigned in September 2012 after a conflict with the ruling party (see Crouch and Lindsey, 2014). A more comprehensive example of judicial purges at the hands of a dictator can be seen in Turkey, where Recep Tayyip Erdogan's regime has detained or dismissed thousands of judges in the 2014–2016 period, including two members of the Constitutional Court, following the failed coup attempt on July 15, 2016 ("Turkey: Protect Rights, Law after Coup Attempt," *Human Rights Watch*, July 18, 2016).

[11] A related means of creating individual reputation is allowing judges who decide a case in a group to dissent from the majority opinion, articulating their reasons for disagreeing with the outcome. Although dissents may reduce the appearance of the judiciary as a collective whole in reaching their decisions, their effect on overall reputation is theoretically unclear. By providing a different, non-binding rationale in cases treating controversial issues, a dissenting judge can placate parties in those cases where a contrary ruling may damage the parties' perception of the judicial system writ large.

[12] The distinction between civil and common law systems has also been identified as influencing broad patterns of economic development, beyond the impact on the incentives of judges themselves (La Porta, Lopez-de-Silanes, and Shleifer, 2008).

Civil law systems originated in France and Germany, with important distinctions between the systems that originated in each country. Nonetheless, as compared to the common law, the French and German civil law systems are functionally quite similar (Cooter and Ulen, 2011: 56–59).

Judicial systems that reward individual reputation tend to reward ideological signaling more than systems that encourage collective reputation. In the United States, for example, studies suggest that ideology matters more than qualifications to the public as well as to legislators when evaluating nominees for federal judgeships (Hoekstra and LaRowe, 2013; Owens et al., 2014). The experiment on the general public's relative weighting of ideology versus qualifications also emphasizes the trade-off between collective reputation and individual reputation: those individuals who viewed the federal court system favorably were more likely to care about judicial qualifications than those who held an unfavorable view of the courts. The ability of judges to perform their duties is related to the way an individual perceives the system overall. This shows that even in judicial systems that place greater weight on individual reputation, the reputation of the institution as a whole still matters in complex ways.

Limits on Judicial Power: Diffusion and Separation of Authority

The distinction between civil and common law systems influences the judiciary in more ways than the distinction we discussed previously between individual and collective judicial reputation. For instance, civil law systems typically split the jurisdiction of the highest court into distinct areas governed by distinct courts. This is the model developed in France, where one court reviews the constitutionality of proposed legislation, one court reviews claims against the government, and another reviews appeals from the lower courts. In contrast, the highest courts in countries with common law systems typically review all these claims.

Ultimately, each system limits the concentration of judicial authority, but in significantly different ways. In the French system, for example, the Constitutional Council is empowered with exclusive jurisdiction to hear claims of a constitutional nature, but this concentrated review power over constitutional claims is limited by the inability to hear claims of other kinds. In contrast, the US Supreme Court is the final authority on all legal questions emanating from the lower courts, but this authority is effectively limited to cases that have already been treated by other courts, as well as to questions that do not fall exclusively under the purview of the laws of a particular state (Amar, 1989).

While each system limits the ways in which the final judicial authority can exercise its power, the United States system concentrates more power in a single set of justices than do systems of divided authority such as France. This makes the appointment of a new US Supreme Court justice an event of greater political and social significance than the replacement of a justice of a specialized high court. This is not to say a judicial replacement in a system of divided authority is not a significant event, but simply that the replacement of one among seven individuals with final authority over a nation's laws is more significant than the replacement of one among a much larger number of individuals with authority over only a subset of legal and constitutional questions.

Another trade-off associated with the distinction between civil and common law systems is the nature of legal precedent. In common law systems, cases previously decided in the same jurisdiction are binding in future cases dealing with the same underlying law, a legal doctrine known as *stare decisis*. A common law court can overrule precedent, but such a decision from a lower court is much more likely to receive scrutiny from the courts above (Costello, 2005). The trade-off balances the greater lawmaking authority judges in common law jurisdictions possess: while a decision today will effectively create law for parties governed by the same jurisdiction and subject in the future, today's decision is highly constrained by the bulk of legal precedent that came before it.

In contrast, civil law systems treat the precedent of prior cases as persuasive. In civil law systems, a judge is free to consider the legal reasoning applied in previous similar cases, but can depart from this reasoning if desired. However, the more uniform prior precedent is from previous cases, the more likely a given civil law judge will treat the precedent as soft law for the purposes of the case (Fon and Parisi, 2006). In one sense, judges in civil law systems are less constrained by the weight of prior precedent, but this carries its own limitation in that their decision is accordingly less dispositive in future cases.

The distinction between the two systems is another example of how each judicial system creates institutions that simultaneously empower and limit the decisions of particular judges, similar to the trade-off between independence and accountability explored in the first subsections.

The emphasis on the lawmaking nature of judicial rules in common law systems has led to another institutional distinction in terms of the fact-finding activities that occur during a given case. In common law systems, where judges are more salient figures and fewer in number, the opposing sides engage in the costly process of discovery. In civil law systems, the process is largely guided by the judge who decides which witnesses lawyers can call and what evidence they can present. In common law systems, the power of judges to independently muster evidence in the case before them is sharply curtailed as compared to judges under civil law systems.

The institution of federalism, more generally deemed decentralization, has its own implications for judicial outcomes. If legislative authority is separated between national and subnational units, this diffuses authority over different sets of law to different judges. This separation results in the emergence of distinct areas of jurisdiction over which a given judge has authority. This type of separate jurisdiction is an additional limitation on the power of any given judge. Even the Supreme Court of the United States has to defer to state judges' interpretations of certain state laws and constitutions. For example, states have strong powers over voting procedures in their own elections.[13]

However, despite the importance of civil versus common law systems for a given society, not all systemic variance is attributable to the difference between the systems. Another institutional design choice that influences judicial incentives is that of trying cases in groups. The US Supreme Court may be the most famous example of this, where appeals courts at the federal and state level hear cases in panels. The most controversial or important cases in appeals courts can also be retried "en banc," which means that instead of a selection of judges from the particular appeals court hearing the case, the entire body of judges decide the case. Some courts, such as the Supreme Court and

---

[13] This was prominently pointed out in *Bush* v. *Gore*, 531 US 98 (2000). The court ruled that the state of Florida's court-ordered manual recount of vote ballots was unconstitutional.

state supreme courts, always hear cases en banc. The benefits to hearing a case in groups directly flow from the heterogeneity of judges. Each judge has a unique background that lends itself to expertise in trying certain types of cases, as well as experience with some aspects of life and segments of society more so than others. However, "specialization" also has a downside, in all of those areas that a particular judge is less familiar, as well as any specific individual biases their background gives them. Selecting a number of judges, as opposed to just one, operates as an institutional choice to mitigate individual biases while benefiting from a greater breadth of judicial experience and background knowledge. The increase comes at a cost, however, for it necessarily reduces the number of cases a given court can hear in any period. Also, reaching a majority, let alone a unanimous decision, becomes more difficult as the size of the court increases. This is not entirely negative, for each judge's individual reputation being on the line, as well as the reputation of the body as a whole, creates the positive outcomes described in our subsection on judicial reputation. Ultimately, despite the benefits that come from hearing cases in groups, this is a design option typically reserved to the higher courts, be they dedicated to appeals or the court of last resort, largely due to the high costs of hearing every case in society with more than one judge.

Another major constraint on judicial outcomes is the source of governing law itself. While in both common and civil law systems the law emanates from the other branches of government, another important distinction is that of secular versus religious legal systems. Some nations formally separate their governance institutions from religious beliefs, while others identify religious law as the ultimate source of legal authority in the nation, in some cases exceeding the supremacy of the Constitution itself (Ahmed and Ginsburg, 2014). In Islamic law, for example, all judicial decisions must be in accordance with the Qur'an and the traditions of the prophet, but may also draw upon secondary sources of law known as *fiqh*, which are based upon a variety of factors, some related directly to Mohammad and his teachings, and others based more upon the application of the primary sources of law over time (Abdal-Haqq, 2002). Even in nations where ordinary law is secular, individuals and communities of a specific religious tradition can opt in to some aspects of religious law, most commonly those governing marriage and the family.[14] Nonetheless, whether a given judge is bound by secular or religious law in determining a case can significantly influence outcomes from one nation to another.

Other structural design choices can influence judicial outcomes. One clear example is the requirements to become a judge. Qualifications typically include a minimum age, legal or other advanced academic training, licensure to practice law, and a set number of years of relevant legal experience. The functional benefit of the requirements is largely self-evident: deciding legal matters necessitates a high degree of specialization in the procedures and law that define the legal system of a given country. Training and actual experience are clearly related requisites to specialization, and age implies a certain level of experience with the day-to-day interactions in society that result in disputes likely to be brought before a court of law.

Furthermore, different societies have created additional compositional requirements such as proportional representation in the judiciary for women or different minority groups.[15] The institution requiring that previously less represented groups occupy the judiciary is a recent phenomenon, and so there is relatively little research identifying how these requirements affect outcomes for the judiciary. Nonetheless, it is clear that requiring the presence of certain groups among the judiciary will change the output in important functional senses. At a minimum, these types of requirements have arisen in societies where the judiciary's reputation was lacking, in part because of the perceived non-representativeness of the judiciary with respect to certain groups. Thus, proportional representation is another institutional means of constraining judicial outcomes according to the preferences of constitutional drafters or legislators.

---

[14] Catholic, Hindu, Islamic, and Jewish law are all available to some extent in nations where each given religious tradition enjoys sufficient support and acceptance.

[15] In some societies, such as the United States, there appears to be a social norm on having diversity on the court. So, de facto, there now are compositional requirements. In others, the requisite stands as a constitutional mandate. Kenya's 2010 Constitution has been interpreted to require most branches of government, including the Supreme Court, to have no more than two-thirds of any gender among its members.

Theories of Judicial Behavior and Incentives

Each of the institutional choices discussed involves an implicit hypothesis as to what motivates judges when they decide cases. Because of this, there is also a robust academic literature treating how judges respond to incentives.[16] If judges have more independence, how are they likely to behave? If judges are elected, as opposed to appointed by an executive or a specialized authority, how will their behavior be affected? A primary assumption emerging from the literature is that judges are self-interested in that they value their tenure, and so will respond to the incentives created by those with authority over their selection and reappointment (Posner, 2005). If elected, they will be more responsive to the preferences of their constituents, and will increasingly rule in ways likely to satisfy these preferences as their reelection window approaches. One study looked at published versus unpublished judicial opinions in a subset of cases from the United States Court of Appeals. In published opinions, a given judge's ideology was a good predictor of the nature of their ruling, whereas it was not a significant predictor in unpublished opinions (Keele et al., 2009). Judges also value career advancement. In civil law systems, the length of tenure of a particular judge within the system overall determines advancement, whereas in common law systems, a judge's individual reputation is much more determinative of advancement, especially in terms of ideological signaling.

Derivative of the considerations of security of tenure and career advancement, judges want to achieve their intended functions.

---

[16] Many of the predominant theories of judicial motives and incentives are summarized in an approachable fashion in Shepsle (2010). Ultimately, although a given judge's motivations for action or inaction are not an institutional constraint, they are an important element to consider when seeking to better understand the institutional environment in which a given judge performs her functions. The extent to which a judiciary is ensured independence and held accountable will greatly determine their behavior under that set of institutional constraints. To make reliable predictions as to how institutional change will influence a given judge's behavior requires a theory of this behavior. This is a specific case of the more general focus in law and economics on the incentives created by any given law, and how any given law interacts with the larger legal system of which it is a part (Posner and Parisi, 1997). Relatedly, the role of judges in creating law is one among a number of means by which law is created. The incentives of judges are essential to understanding how law that emanates from judicial decisions is created and changes over time (Parisi and Fon, 2009).

The financial independence of the court is valuable to judges themselves, for absent significant financial discretion, a court must depend on the branch of government that most closely controls financial disbursement. This is often the executive branch, and the Kenya case study treated at the end of the chapter provides a ready example of the negative consequences associated with a lack of financial independence. The desire to achieve intended judicial functions depends greatly on the institutional constraints and structures within which the judiciary operates. In an environment lacking judicial independence, the intended functions of the court may be to provide order and not upset the status quo in the event influential individuals bring claims to or are brought before the court. In a context that better achieves the right balance between independence and accountability, judges are more likely to value their reputation for facilitating justice and promoting the rule of law.

Finally, judges may care about having a positive reputation with salient audiences, which depend on the structure of government and institutions where judges perform their duties. In the United States, the relevant audience includes the public as a whole, individuals with authority to appoint judges to a higher court, the legal academy, and practicing lawyers who contribute to public discourse surrounding the appropriateness of a given judge's decisions and conduct. However, care for reputation extends beyond career self-interest in terms of appointment, reelection, and advancement. Judges have also been characterized as subject to the almost universal human desire to be well-liked, or viewed in a positive light (Baum, 2009). Again, institutional constraints will greatly determine the set of individuals whose opinions regarding a particular judge can influence outcomes for the judge. Relatedly, scholars have examined the extent to which a given judge's ideology influences their rulings. In one sense, a judge's ideology matters from rational self-interested reasons because the extent to which their rulings correspond to their ideology as understood by their constituents influences their likelihood of reappointment, and often, reelection. However, a judge's ideology is also likely to influence how they interpret facts and legal requirements, such that even absent concerns of appointment, reelection, and career advancement, a given judge's ideology is likely to influence outcomes (Spiller and Gely, 2009). In sum, this subsection highlights how the incentives created by the institutional constraints that the judiciary faces are a necessary component to understanding the outcomes a judiciary creates for the society whose transactions and disputes it oversees.

Institutional Role of the Judiciary

Introductory Case: Marbury v. Madison

What does the application of the IOA teach us about the influence the judiciary has on the institutions of society? Just as institutions influence the judiciary, so too can the judiciary influence the institutions in society. These influences can often be closely related; in order for a judiciary to fully perform one of its critical functions, judicial review, it must be independent from the government branches whose legislation and actions the judiciary reviews for constitutionality.

The development of the power of the judiciary to review legislation is best associated with the famous case of *Marbury* v. *Madison*, 5 US 137 (1803), decided by the Supreme Court of the United States. The circumstances that gave rise to the case are essential to understanding how a judiciary that has come to enjoy a reputation for independence and legitimacy took its first steps towards securing that independence and cementing its reputation. In 1801, the outgoing President Adams signed a number of changes to the 1789 Judiciary Act into law, altering the structure of the judiciary in important ways, including the creation of new courts and the appointment of numerous new judges. Congress passed the act just before Thomas Jefferson assumed the presidency after the presidential elections of 1800. On the day before Jefferson assumed office, President Adams, acting under the provisions of the act, appointed sixteen circuit judges and forty-two justices of the peace.

Importantly, Adams was a Federalist, while Jefferson was from an opposing party, the Democratic-Republicans. The move by Adams, along with a Federalist-dominated Congress, was intended to retain a measure of Federalist influence when the incoming presidential administration and Congress had flipped to the opposing Democratic-Republican party. However, the slew of judicial appointments in the final hours of the Adams administration created a problem: the Judiciary Act required the judicial commissions be delivered in person to the appointees by the secretary of state. When President Jefferson took office, he told his newly appointed Secretary of State, James Madison, not to deliver the commissions to the judges and justices who had not yet received them from the former secretary of state. One of the Federalist judicial appointees, William Marbury, brought a suit challenging Madison's failure to deliver the commissions.

At the time Marbury brought his case, the Supreme Court was a modest institution compared to what it has become over the past two hundred years. The court lacked its own building, and up until the passage of the Judiciary Act, Supreme Court justices rode circuit, deciding circuit court cases in addition to those brought before the Supreme Court. Put more simply, the Supreme Court that decided *Marbury* had much less power than the contemporary court. The Marshall Court's analysis proceeded by answering three questions: (1) Did Marbury have a right to the commission? (2) Did the laws of the country give Marbury a legal remedy? and (3) Was asking the Supreme Court for a writ of mandamus the correct legal remedy?[17]

The court answered the first two questions in the affirmative in an opinion authored by Chief Justice Marshall: Marbury did have a right to the commission, and the laws of the United States, given the violation of this vested right, should afford Marbury a remedy. The third question is where the court treated the question of judicial review for constitutionality. After concluding that a writ of mandamus was the appropriate remedy to request of a court, Marshall's opinion proceeded to address whether the Supreme Court had original jurisdiction to issue a writ of mandamus in such a case (as opposed to reviewing a lower court's decision to issue a writ of mandamus). Marbury argued that the Judiciary Act granted the court this power, and that the jurisdiction granted to the Supreme Court in the Constitution was accordingly a floor to which Congress could add jurisdictional powers, as the changes to the Judiciary Act had done. The Marshall Court disagreed, deciding that the jurisdiction granted to the Supreme Court by the Constitution could not be altered by congressional legislation. Through this decision, the court held that Section 13 of the Judiciary Act of 1789 was invalid because it was at odds with Article III of the Constitution, which establishes the original jurisdiction of the

---

[17] A writ of mandamus is a court-enforced order compelling action by a government official.

Supreme Court. In the now-famous words of John Marshall, which were later engraved in marble in the Supreme Court itself: "It is emphatically the province and duty of the Judicial Department to say what the law is" (*Marbury* v. *Madison*, 1803: 177).

The case has come to stand for the principle of judicial review, because it was the first case under the United States Constitution where the Supreme Court overruled legislation that it deemed unconstitutional.[18] The ability to exercise judicial review depends on the ability to overturn duly-enacted statutes, and *Marbury* is widely considered the first instance of the exercise of this power. Given the uncertain nature of the court's power at the time, Chief Justice Marshall's opinion presented President Jefferson, and hence, the executive branch, with a choice between two undesirable alternatives. If Jefferson obeyed the ruling, the Democratic-Republicans would realize short-term political gains by thwarting a number of former President Adams' outgoing judicial appointments. This would come at a cost, though, for allowing the ruling to stand would signal the acquiescence of the other branches of government to the power of judicial review. The alternative, defying the *Marbury* ruling in some way because of the power with which it vested the Supreme Court, carried its own costs, for doing so would have involved appointment of, or redress for some or all, of the Federalist judges whose appointments were stymied by President Jefferson's administration. Despite President Jefferson later making explicit statements that he disagreed with how *Marbury* made the judiciary "the ultimate arbiters of all constitutional questions" (Jefferson, 1904–1905), his administration did not challenge or thwart the ruling.[19] Over time, *Marbury* has come to stand

---

18   The case is often erroneously identified as the origin of judicial review itself. However, the concept of judicial review predates the United States, arguably seen in English jurisprudence from the early seventeenth century. Richard Helmholz (2009) provides an extensive accounting of the legal scholarship treating the relevance of Dr. Bonham's Case to the development of judicial review, but also questions the true extent to which the case stood for the principle at the time it was decided. Regardless, the review by the Supreme Court of the United States of legislation for constitutionality appears in an earlier ruling, where the court reviewed a tax statute for constitutionality and upheld it (*Hylton* v. *United States*, 3 US 171 (1796)).

19   The extent to which Jefferson's views as to judicial review remained fixed over time has been the source of considerable scholarly exploration, but Jefferson is recognized by December 1801 as considering *Marbury* an overextension of judicial review power (Engdahl, 1992: 280).

for the supremacy of judicial review of legislation for constitutional conformity.

The case demonstrates that the institutions of judicial independence and reputation did not appear suddenly, and emerged through a highly political process, full of conflicts and trade-offs. An additional detail that emphasizes the contextual nature of institutional change: Chief Justice John Marshall, who decided *Marbury*, was the secretary of state under the Adams presidency, and Marshall had simply failed to be able to deliver all the judicial commissions in time, given the last-minute nature of the appointments. By modern standards of independence and judicial conflicts of interest, as well as scholarly debates as to the validity of the legal reasoning of the decision itself, the outcome of *Marbury* was by no means a certainty. This example emphasizes the gradual development of institutions such as judicial independence and reputation, and the effect of governance institutions on the balance of powers between the branches.

Constitutional Oversight

Judicial review, the institutional output of the judiciary for which *Marbury* has come to stand, is among the most important functions of the judiciary, and accordingly it is where we begin our discussion of these institutional outputs in this section. This function is also labeled constitutional review, and is one of the most important means by which the judiciary influences institutions around the world. This power allows the judiciary to be the ultimate arbiter of whether a law passed by the legislature and the executive is within the bounds of constitutional requirements and restrictions. The power of judicial review has emerged alongside the institution of constitutionalism, famously appearing in the case *Marbury* v. *Madison* discussed previously. Plainly put, judicial review grants the judiciary the power to review laws for their constitutionality.

However, the institution of judicial review varies in important ways around the world. Typically, the judicial review power is centralized with a single body, either a nation's highest court, or a specialized constitutional court. However, the review of constitutionality in the United States is diffused among the various levels of judicial authority, although such rulings are appealable until the Supreme Court has ruled on the issue, or declined to take the case, which leaves the lower court's ruling on the issue as dispositive. This is in contrast to the concentrated power of review for constitutionality seen in nearly every other legal system. Another distinction treats the scope of constitutional oversight. Some nations, the United States included, permit the courts oversight of all legislation for constitutionality. Other nations limit this oversight to laws that bear on fundamental aspects of the Constitution, such as rights or government structures. Finally, it should be noted that not all nations' judiciaries are granted the power of judicial review as it has come to be associated with countries that adopted the US model.[20]

Despite the historical roots of judicial review, the adoption of the institution around the world is a relatively modern phenomenon. In the six decades from 1951 to 2011, the percentage of countries around the world that had adopted the institution increased from 35 percent to 86 percent (Ginsburg and Versteeg, 2014). Scholars have proposed a number of hypotheses for the emergence. One hypothesis ties the emergence to the increasing recognition of liberal principles of governance, especially those surrounding restraint of government and the importance of the rule of law as compared to the excesses of unchecked government such as those experienced during colonialism and leading up to World War II (Cappelletti, 1989; Garlicki, 2007: 45). Another explanation links the institution to problems resultant from federal systems specifically, as well as to similar coordination problems arising among branches of government (Gardbaum, 2014: 615). Creating different levels of government with separate and concurrent authority to make law results in the need for an impartial third actor to resolve disputes as to which level of government has the authority to act in a particular area of policy. Another theory lumps the widespread adoption of the institution to the process of institutional diffusion more generally, implying that a strict set of expected benefits may not have animated the change (Law and Versteeg, 2011). Finally, other scholars have identified electoral turnover as motivating the adoption of the institution, arguing that uncertainty as to holding power in

---

[20] The principle of Parliamentary supremacy in England prevents the courts from exercising this type of oversight, although some measure of judicial review still has emerged over time (Elliott, 2001; van der Schyff, 2010). In other nations, such as Vietnam, the concentration of all government authority within the Communist Party similarly prevents this form of independent check on government behavior (La Porta et al., 2004).

future periods gives constitutional drafters the incentive to impose a constraint in those future periods (Ginsburg, 2003).

The final hypothesis has been supported empirically, but it also corresponds to more general theories as to the emergence of the rule of law (Ginsburg and Versteeg, 2014). In addition to facilitating commitments across organizations in the dominant network that were previously not credible, the rule of law serves as a form of insurance against the uncertainty of a given organization's standing in future periods. The rule of law provides assurance that even if a given member of the dominant network is less powerful in the future, their outcomes in court and under government policies will not suffer as much as in a system where outcomes are closely tied to one's level of power. The argument as to why constitutional review provides insurance against future electoral uncertainty is a similar one. If the interests represented at the drafting table are uncertain that their influence will be similarly reflected in future periods, they have a direct incentive to prevent legislative outcomes at odds with the balance of power represented in the constitutional document. Both institutions, the rule of law generally, and constitutional review specifically, serve as a form of insurance against negative future outcomes created by electoral or regime uncertainty. Each of these insurance benefits corresponds to the judicial independence subsection discussing similar reasons for the emergence of the institution.

The adoption of judicial review has been linked to a variety of additional beneficial outcomes, including improvements in democratic representation (Almendares and Le Bihan, 2015), as well as a smaller government in terms of government spending and the associated tax burden carried by society (Tridimas, 2005). Other empirical work has identified the institution of judicial review as closely tied to higher levels of political freedoms and human rights outcomes as measured by different indices (La Porta et al., 2004).

The explicit function of constitutional oversight means the role of the judiciary in influencing major constitutional moments is distinct from other government branches, as well as other actors in society writ large. This is because the judiciary's role is (1) explicit, and (2) bounded substantively by the Constitution itself, as well as existing jurisprudence and procedure. In contrast, other actors in government or society can induce a broader set of constitutional moments (defined and discussed in Part III) ranging from substantive amendments to societal-level belief changes. Although not constrained to interpretation of government action for constitutionality, other actors in society are also not afforded an explicitly "constitutional" role, and are not actively policing the boundaries of the Constitution the way the judiciary does.

Rulings of a nation's highest court inherently change the nation's constitutional structure by clarifying areas of the law that were previously undefined, especially by defining the bounds of constitutionality for law passed by the legislature and executive, as well as rulings from lower courts (in common law systems). Despite such decisions being "constitutional" by nature, and in some cases, explicitly change or refine the current understanding of the Constitution, they do not change the text, and are by and large not constitutional moments. From the sense of influencing institutions, the judiciary is very much a "constitutional actor," but when it comes to influencing constitutional moments, the judiciary can be a constitutional actor, but is by no means guaranteed to be one. Ultimately, through the power of judicial review, the judiciary plays a critical role in determining the constitutionality of laws and government action.

Constraint of Government Agents

The role of constitutional oversight is one way that the judiciary directly influences institutions. Another direct influence is through the oversight of government agents. The oversight role constrains the government as a whole and can be coupled with the power of judicial review, but the relationship between judicial review and oversight of government actors is not necessary in order for the judiciary to exert a constraining influence. However, scholars who have worked on measuring the rule of law around the world note that the independence of the judiciary is a critical prerequisite to effectively constraining the government (Botero and Ponce, 2010: 9). Of main relevance here is the ability of the judiciary to determine whether actions of the executive branch overstep the constitutional authority allocated to that branch. The view that judicial authority should act as a check against the exercise of unbridled government power has clearly been influential within the judiciary itself, being championed by former US Supreme Court Justice John Paul Stevens (1986: 291–92). Legal theorists have since identified a variety of benefits associated with judicial review of administrative action, including increased legality on the part of the government, more efficient allocation of resources used for public purposes, and the improved achievement of a diversity of legislative aims including protection of disadvantaged classes against discrimination (Sunstein, 1989: 522–25). Sunstein ties the power of government oversight to the legitimacy of the judiciary, which stands as an example of how the desirable institutional outputs of the judiciary can affect the institutions that define the incentives of individual judges within the legal system. In addition, the extent that oversight is always possible deters actions by powerful organizations upstream in the legislative or enforcement process. In short, organizations take actions under the shadow of the courts.

Another means by which oversight of executive action, and especially police action (Daly, 2011: 199), can be seen is through the development of procedural doctrines that have clearly specified requirements for the steps the government must undertake: to secure a warrant to investigate an individual past a certain point; to charge someone with a crime; and to ultimately convict them. Compliance by government agents with required legal procedures is an important check on the ability of the executive branch to freely exercise its police and prosecutorial authority. The requirement to comply with required procedure is known as procedural due process, and falls under the Due Process Clauses of the Fifth and Fourteenth Amendments to the United States Constitution.[21] However, the focus on the required procedure is only a portion of the government restraint exercised in the United States.

The courts in the United States have developed an additional requirement associated with the Due Process Clause, also requiring that legal proceedings against an individual display substantive due process in addition to the procedural component. Substantive due process relies on broader concepts of fundamental fairness and equality before the law. By requiring that government-initiated actions against an individual satisfy a broader set of concepts associated with justice, equity, and the rights found in the Bill of Rights, the judiciary's oversight role of government action is significantly expanded. The extent to which

---

[21] The Fifth Amendment made this requirement binding on the federal government, but it was not until the adoption of the Fourteenth Amendment in the wake of the Civil War that a similar requirement was imposed upon the states.

other societies have similar procedural and substantive requirements plays an important role in determining the extent to which the government is restrained by the judiciary. Nonetheless, comparative constitutional scholarship identifies criminal due process decisions as being a major component of modern decisions emanating from the nations' highest courts around the world (Hirschl, 2009).

In many nations, including the United States, the judiciary cannot independently investigate claims against actions undertaken by the government. The authority to monitor government actions for constitutional compliance is a powerful one, and so the ability to bring claims against the government is limited in some instances to a special government office, and in others, to affected citizens. Either way, limiting the ability of the court to independently investigate other government branches is an important institutional check on the power to constrain government agents. The solution is similar to the trade-off explored surrounding independence and accountability. In order to check the other branches of government, the judiciary needs to be granted considerable power, but this power must be balanced with limitations on its exercise. Preventing the judiciary from independently investigating infractions by the government stands as a clear example.

A modern concern associated with effective government oversight is that of the numerous security agencies whose authority emanates from the executive branch. Because of the direct national security implications of many of the methods and subjects of investigations by authorities, this has created a need for courts of special jurisdiction to oversee them. Oversight of all executive branch activity is considered a sufficiently important institution that even highly sensitive proceedings require judicial approval. In the United States and the United Kingdom, this trade-off involved the creation of courts with special jurisdiction whose proceedings are typically secret.[22]

Facilitation of Ideal Characteristics of the Legal System

The role of the judiciary in facilitating other desirable functional characteristics of a system of law is larger than simply constitutional

---

[22] In the United States, this court is the Foreign Intelligence Surveillance Court (or "FISA Court"), while in the United Kingdom, a similar court is deemed an Investigatory Powers Tribunal.

monitoring of laws and government action. Nonetheless, the judiciary's role of constitutional oversight, as described in the preceding subsections, creates an important outcome where a single fundamental rule set governs a more fluid stock of rule sets treating ordinary political and economic outcomes. In interpreting laws for constitutionality, the judiciary is the mechanism by which movement towards ideal legal characteristics is facilitated. The functions of judicial review and government oversight can be seen as facilitating a more desirable legal characteristic: legal supremacy. Legal supremacy facilitates consistency and clarity in the law by providing a universal benchmark against which all other laws and government actions can be judged. This is a function of constitutions that is relevant to understanding their role in determining incremental institutional change across societies. The set of desirable normative characteristics of a system of law have been identified as more than just legal supremacy. These characteristics also include clarity, consistency, generality, stability, prospectivity, public promulgation, finality, qualified universality, and impartiality; all of which we discuss in this subsection. As noted previously, legal supremacy facilitates consistency and clarity in the law. The attributes of consistency and clarity are especially important in a system of multiple jurisdictional levels, where the power to legislate on different topics resides with a particular level of government or is shared between levels of government. The law needs to be clear so that individuals can understand it and can adjust their behavior to comply with it. Consistency in law has also been labeled congruency, which emphasizes the need for the legal system to treat similar behaviors similarly. Severe punishments for a comparatively minor crime violate this principle, because they may over-deter social actors from committing the minor crime at the cost of providing less deterrence for more serious crimes. A related characteristic is that of non-contradiction, the requirement that one law not proscribe behaviors that another law explicitly permits.

Institutional scholars have identified other important characteristics of the legal system in addition to clarity and consistency, including generality, stability, and prospectivity (Fuller, 1977; Hadfield and Weingast, 2013). The law should be general enough that it applies to more than just the proceedings before the court in a given case. The law should be stable such that parties governed by it can come to understand it and order their affairs so as not to run afoul of its proscriptions and requirements. The law should also be forward-looking, such that it covers instances that may not have been present in the minds of the legislators at the time the law was drafted. The development of common law in the United States governing searches and seizures displays the role of the judiciary in facilitating legal prospectivity. A modern case before the Supreme Court treated the question of whether a GPS tracker attached to a suspected drug dealer's vehicle ran afoul of the proscription against unreasonable searches and seizures found in the Fourth Amendment. The Supreme Court held that use of a GPS tracker was a search governed by the Fourth Amendment, which requires a judicially authorized search warrant in order to proceed (see *United States* v. *Jones*, 565 US 1 (2012); see also *Torrey Dale Grady* v. *North Carolina*, 575 US 1 (2015)). Clearly, GPS technology had not been invented at the time of the drafting of the Bill of Rights, yet the legal structure constrained by them was able to update the protections to better suit modern circumstances.

Additional functional characteristics identified as improving the legal system include the law's public nature, finality, qualified universality, and impartiality in reasoning used in its application. The public nature of the law results in the law becoming common knowledge, for without this outcome, individuals cannot update their behavior according to the requirements of law. Similarly, publicly known and promulgated laws have long been identified as a constraint upon the arbitrary exercise of government power (Hayek, 1978: 169–75). Finality in the law creates certainty for parties brought before the court and clarifies outcomes for downstream participants in a way that would be impossible if decisions could be reviewed more than once by the same court, let alone indefinitely (Hart, 2012: 141–47). Qualified universality requires the largely uniform application of the law to different parties brought before a court and is partially a result of the degree of judicial independence a society enjoys.[23] Without qualified universality, undue influences can result in an opposing

---

[23] Strict universality would result in a variety of difficulties in laws that have very good reasons for treating individuals differently. Children and the mentally ill are widely recognized as warranting specific treatment under the law, and so are excepted from many laws and punishments that apply universally to mentally sound adults. Similarly, agents of the government, such as police officers, are often exempted from certain laws such as using force against other members of society, and are also subject to different requirements as they go about enforcing the law.

outcome resulting from the application of the same law being applied to a powerful individual or member of a dominant social group. Impartial legal reasoning is impersonal, in that it does not depend on the identity of the person brought before the court; neutral, in that it is not influenced by any of the judge's own personal preferences; and independent, in that it is free from undue external influences that could tip the outcome in favor of one party or another. The association of these ideal characteristics of the legal system to judicial independence and accountability is clear. Absent meaningful independence, a judiciary cannot reliably enforce the law in a way that systematically reinforces these ideal characteristics. But absent some measure of accountability, judges who significantly depart from ideal norms cannot be disciplined or removed, to the detriment of the reputation and functionality of the judiciary overall.

Notably, the role for a given judge in facilitating ideal outcomes can vary significantly depending on the degree of actual lawmaking authority the system grants judges. In common law systems, judges appropriately incentivized by the norms of independence, accountability, and reputation (and the institutions designed to facilitate these outcomes) should be more likely to rule in a way that furthers ideal characteristics of the legal system. This tendency to rule in a way that strengthens the legal system results in part from the training and specialization in the law required of judges, but this also ties back again to considerations of independence and reputation, where judges need to independently value the stable functionality of their institution, and must earn a reputation for facilitating normatively preferable characteristics associated with legal systems generally. This paragraph should not be read to undervalue the role of judges in civil law systems for furthering the ideal characteristics of the legal system. As noted previously, civil law judges are influenced by precedent, and still play an important role in signaling to social actors how future disputes are likely to be resolved.

The legal system has also long been viewed through a broader institutional lens: the rule of law. A robust literature exists surrounding the exact definition of the rule of law, and how it can be measured within and across countries (Manne, 1997; Skaaning, 2010; Ginsburg, 2011; Botero and Ponce, 2010). The rule of law, at its heart, is the institutional principle that individuals, organizations, and the government are accountable to fairly applied and enforced rules that are publicly known and promulgated. Because of how broad of a concept the rule of law is, the literature exceeds the scope of our book. What is important to note, however, is that the institutions in the first section of this chapter – independence, accountability, reputation, and checks and balances that limit and shape judicial power – are all linked to the institution of the rule of law more broadly. The implication of this is that in the performance of their functions, judges can have a critical impact on the extent to which a given society enjoys a measure of the rule of law or not. Indeed, Vincent Ostrom (1991: 108) identifies the separation of the judiciary from the lawmaking and enforcement authorities of government as a fundamental component of the rule of law. The rule of law stands as an additional institution that the judiciary can affect, either positively or negatively, in the performance of its routine functions. Of course, the rule of law has consistently been identified as fundamental to the development of modern prosperous societies.[24]

Despite the variety of desirable institutional characteristics a legal system displays, the main point of this section is simple. The means by which judges treat cases matters greatly for the stable functionality of the system as a whole, beyond the impact a given case has for the parties directly before the court. Judges, appropriately incentivized and constrained by the institutions treated in the first section of this chapter, play a critical role in determining a range of desirable institutional characteristics of legal and political systems themselves, as well as societal outcomes writ large.

Conclusion

Despite the judiciary's broadly recognized authority over the application of the law, a closer examination indicates that the judiciary serves a variety of important functions within this overly broad rubric. The judiciary reviews legislation for constitutionality, adjudicates disputes and criminal charges, and, in a common law system, creates law via precedent. The institutions governing the judicial system determine whether judges are independent of the executive and legislative

---

[24] For a comprehensive summary of scholarship identifying the benefits the rule of law and legal systems provide for facilitating economic development, see Rubin (2005).

branches, the powers of judges to make and interpret the law, and the incentives to bring cases to the legal system. The judiciary's unique oversight over legislation and government actions creates a direct need for independence. The specific institutions designed to balance independence and accountability create comparatively beneficial or detrimental outcomes that themselves feed into the individual and collective reputation of judges in a particular system. Understanding how judicial institutions influence outcomes also requires an understanding of the motivations of individual judges themselves. The subsequent case study on Kenya emphasizes the fragile nature of the institutions governing the judiciary, and how closely tied judicial institutions are to those tied to governance more broadly.

The ideal role of the judiciary is through application of the law, to reduce the likelihood of future disputes and crimes because parties subject to the law have specific guidance as to acceptable and unacceptable conduct. In order to come closer to achieving this ideal, the judiciary has to signal both its independence and accountability to secure the requisite level of reputation that makes it more likely court rulings will be obeyed. The desirable institutional attributes themselves influence the ability of the court to review laws for constitutionality, monitor the actions of the government, and facilitate important structural characteristics of the legal system in general.

Concluding Case (Kenya, 2010–2017): Reforms to Improve Judicial Independence and Reputation

Kenya's 2010 Constitution emerged after a period of political crisis. After Mwai Kibaki was elected president in 2007, a wave of serious electoral violence broke out. International observers reported electoral fraud occurring from both major parties, and the losing candidate, Raila Odinga, encouraged mass protests from his supporters in population centers around the country. The tensions underlying the 2007–2008 protests ultimately led to outright violence against Kibaki's supporters, the Kikuyus. Moreover, police reprisals against violent protestors led to shootings and deaths among the opposition. The continued unrest generated violence between ethnic groups that led to the deaths of members of parliament, and an ultimate death toll of more than 1,300, with upwards of 600,000 Kenyans being displaced due to the conflict. In this charged context, the United Nations orchestrated a transition government to ease the tensions that had resulted in several months of violence and political uncertainty within the country.

The post-conflict formation of a unity government, with Odinga as prime minister and Kibaki as president, was of necessity an interim solution, designed to lead the country towards a more comprehensive overhaul of government. This culminated in the enactment of a new constitution on August 5, 2010. Among the major issues identified as requiring reform was the judiciary's lack of independence and reputation for corruption (Gathii, 2016). The institutional changes the 2010 Constitution made to the judiciary reflect a number of the points made in this chapter. The changes were designed to either directly increase the judiciary's independence or improve its negative reputation among Kenyans. In many ways, the fixes themselves highlight the close relationship between judicial independence and reputation.

Notably, the post-electoral crisis did not create the realization among Kenyans that the judiciary was in need of reform (Constitution of Kenya Review Commission, 2005). Formal investigation of the need for judicial reform can be traced to at least 1998, when Justice Kwach's committee found evidence supporting the perception that judges were corrupt, incompetent, or negligent. The committee recommended a constitutional amendment to allow for the removal of judges in the preceding instances (Report of the Committee of the Administration of Justice, 1998). The finding was further supported by the work of a subsequent committee headed by Judge Ringera, which found evidence of corruption on the part of nearly a third of the magistrates in the country, but more troublingly, similar evidence implicated half the High Court judges, and 56 percent of the judges on the Court of Appeals (Report of the Integrity and Anticorruption Committee, 2003). However, it may be that the wholesale reform of the judiciary required a massive shock such as the post-electoral violence and subsequent political upheaval, because calls for judicial reforms went largely unheeded (Ozielo, 2010). Furthermore, the judiciary was seen as subordinate to the legislature and the executive due to its failure to review the actions of either branch (Gathii, 2016).

The long simmering recognition of the need for change led to the Kibaki government prioritizing a reform strategy culminating in a task force whose recommendations for reform were influential in those enshrined in the 2010 Constitution (Nichols, 2015). Several measures from 2010 indicate reasons the judiciary's reputation was in tatters. Transparency International surveys indicated that 43 percent of Kenyans who sought judicial redress had paid bribes in the course of doing so. In part because of capacity, with fifty-three judges and 330 magistrates overseeing a population of 41.4 million, the courts had a backlog of nearly 1 million cases (Gainer, 2016). The capacity issue creates a natural opportunity for corruption, both to expedite a given powerful or wealthy individual's case, and in the case similarly influential individuals did not want the trial being held, to delay cases indefinitely.

The first major change was financial. Previously, the judiciary's finances were tightly controlled by the executive branch of government through its control of the Treasury, which had ultimate dispensation authority for the budget allocations of the judiciary. Under the 2010 Constitution, in contrast, the judiciary's salaries come from the Consolidated Fund, which the executive does not control as tightly as it did under the prior constitutional regime. Furthermore, the 2010 Constitution creates a specific Judiciary Fund, which the legislature approves and has no oversight from the executive at all. The fund operates to ensure the judiciary the funds needed to perform its functions without veto authority from the executive branch.

Similarly, the appointment process for Supreme Court judges under the 2010 Constitution significantly reduced the role of the executive branch. Under the 1963 Constitution, the president appointed the chief justice of the High Court without the input of any other branch or agency of government. The president also had the power of appointment for the remaining judges of the High Court, although at least in principle, this was done "in accordance with the advice of the Judicial Service Commission" (Constitution of the Republic of Kenya, 1963). As significantly, the president appointed the body overseeing removal processes for High Court judges under the 1963 Constitution.

The president still nominally appoints the chief justice and deputy chief justices under the 2010 Constitution, but the appointment must be "in accordance with the recommendation of the Judicial Service Commission" and is "subject to the approval of the National

Assembly" (Kenya 2010 Constitution, Art. 166). The president appoints other judges in accordance with the recommendation of the Judicial Service Commission, which again limits the discretion the president had under the prior constitution. An additional reform regards the disciplinary procedures for judges. Judges may only be removed for specific types of misconduct, and misconduct proceedings may only be initiated by the Judicial Service Commission, acting under its own authority, or in investigation of a petition from any person. The president oversees the removal process for judges, but is required to act upon the recommendation of the Judicial Service Commission. Furthermore, the 2010 Constitution contains considerably more detail and stringency regarding the qualifications of judges at any court level, as well as restrictions on their tenure, including a discretionary retirement age of sixty-five, and a mandatory retirement age of seventy.

Most of the reforms in the 2010 Constitution are forward-looking, either limiting the influence of the executive body on judicial appointments or increasing the required qualifications for incoming judges. All of the changes seen in the 2010 Constitution emphasize the various structural constraints institutional framers can place upon the judiciary to induce independence from undue influence (separation from the executive and more transparent appointment and compensation procedures), accountability (limits on tenure and well-specified disciplinary procedures), and constraints designed to ensure expertise in legal matters (qualifications and more rigorous appointment procedures). The institutional change allowing voluntary retirement at sixty-five, and requiring retirement at seventy, provided a fixed limit on the tenure of judges that ensures turnover of the judiciary more quickly than would have otherwise occurred under the prior constitution.[25] Other changes to the selection process involved a significant increase in the transparency and competitiveness of how future judges would be selected under the new constitution.

---

[25] One clear example of this type of constraint potentially providing a lower-cost means of removing judges comes from 2016, when Supreme Court Judge Philip Tunoi was recommended for investigation surrounding allegations that he received a two million US$ bribe to influence the outcome of an electoral petition. However, the investigation was dropped once Tunoi was deemed of mandatory retirement age in a separate court ruling (Gainer, 2016).

Given the extent to which judicial reform was a priority, the Chief Justice and President of the Supreme Court at the time, Willy Mutunga, crafted the Judiciary Transformation Framework, which contained four pillars: (1) improved delivery of service for any given applicant to the court; (2) significant improvements in leadership, culture, and professionalism; (3) adequate financial resources and infrastructure; and (4) technological improvements (Judiciary Transformation Framework, 2012). Each reform priority indicates underlying problems that led to their inclusion as a major plank in the judiciary's transformation in Kenya. Individuals did not feel as if they would receive reliable, impartial, or timely service if they appeared before the court. The judges themselves were seen as corrupt, and the courts had a culture of moving slowly on any given case, unless induced to do otherwise. The executive branch was seen as having undue control over the court's finances, which led to capacity constraints for handling cases, as well as inferior and insufficient court buildings. Finally, modernizing court processes by allowing many motions and judgments to occur electronically was seen as improving the timely functionality of the court.

The reforms to the judiciary seen in the Judiciary Transformation Framework were intended to improve the judiciary as a whole, as well as future judges selected under the new processes. However, the problems identified by the committees in 1998 and 2005 also directly implicated individual judges in the sense that levels of corruption were perceived to be so widespread that the integrity and impartiality of many judges and magistrates stood in question. In recognition of this, and spurred by the recommendations of the 2009 task force, the drafters of the 2010 Constitution included a stringent requirement for the legislature of the incoming government. Within one year of the constitution coming into effect, Parliament was required to "establish mechanisms and procedures for vetting ... the suitability of all judges and magistrates ... to continue to serve ... " The strength of this mandate was underscored by the fact that the chief justice in office when the constitution was enacted had six months after the constitution came into force to decide whether he would undergo the vetting process or retire from the judiciary (Kenya 2010 Constitution, Schedule 6, Articles 23 and 24).

Despite the clear mandate the 2010 Constitution created for the legislature to treat the issue of judicial vetting, the actual provisions in the Sixth Schedule do not provide much detail as to the process for reform. This could be because the issue was a controversial one, even within the drafting assembly, or because the drafters considered such an important question to be properly reserved to Parliament. Regardless, such a major question involving the entirety of a nation's sitting judges was not without controversy in the legislature. There was considerable legislative debate surrounding the act, which then faced several constitutional challenges after its passage. The act ultimately prevailed, and the Judges and Magistrates Vetting Board assumed its functions in January 2012. The Judges and Magistrates Vetting Board consisted of nine members drawn from notable figures with legal and political backgrounds in both Kenya and abroad, including eminent African judges from Zambia, Ghana, and South Africa, each with experience on supreme or constitutional courts within their own country.

The board had three phases of its work, which corresponded to the three levels of Kenya's judiciary. The first phase involved review of the judgments of judges on the Court of Appeal at the time the constitution was enacted on August 27, 2010. The Court of Appeal was the name of Kenya's highest court under the prior constitutional regime. The review process involved the case records of nine Court of Appeal judges, eight of which continued on the Court of Appeal after the enactment of the 2010 Constitution, and one of whom went on to a position on the Supreme Court. The standard for review of the judgments relied on singular extreme cases viewed within the larger context of a given judge's decisions. If the singular cases along with the larger case record appeared to be "legally strained" to the point where "public confidence in the judiciary" was undermined, then the judge would be declared unfit to continue to serve in office (Maliti, 2012). In the case of the nine judges of the Court of Appeal, four were declared unfit for office, two by unanimous vote, one by an 8-to-1 margin, and the final by a 7-to-2 margin. Indicative of the extent to which no judge was exempted from the review process is that three of the four judges ordered to step down were the three longest-serving judges in the country.

From the Court of Appeal, the Judges and Magistrates Vetting Board moved to consider judges on the High Court at the time of constitutional enactment. By the board's sixth round of determinations, seven more judges had been declared unfit to serve. One indication of the extent of difficulties this process posed is that some of the judges being investigated had issued judicial orders forbidding the investigation (Center for Constitutional Transitions, 2013). During this same series of determinations, the board reaffirmed two of its earlier determinations of unfitness that had been challenged, and announced that it would again vet two of the Court of Appeal judges whose findings of continued suitability had also been challenged. This displays the inherently contentious and difficult nature of reviewing a judiciary in its entirety, and the phase subsequent to the High Court review displayed similar challenges.

The third and final phase of the process, which concluded on March 31, 2016, extended review to all magistrates of the lower courts, satisfying the legislative mandate that the board conclude its review by this date. At this time, the board had concluded its reviews of earlier determinations as well, such that findings of unsuitability for judicial service had finality. All told, the board declared four Court of Appeal judges, seven High Court judges, and fourteen magistrates unfit for service in a period of just over four years (Judges and Magistrates Vetting Board, 2016). Despite this being an inherently controversial process, it emphasizes the magnitude of institutional change required to begin to restore a judiciary's reputation. The successful completion of the process involved the support of the courts under the new constitution, as well as Parliament, which indicates how essential the intended outputs of the judiciary are for the stable functioning of society.

A critical question for Kenyan citizens, and interested observers, is whether or not the reforms succeeded. Providing a clear answer to the question is beyond the scope of this analysis. However, there are a variety of outcomes since the constitution's enactment that suggest institutions within the country, especially the judiciary, strengthened. At the same time, however, there are other outcomes that indicate how far the country still has to go.

Among the positive signals was a significant increase in Kenyans' confidence in the judiciary between 2009 and 2013, from 27 percent to 61 percent, although more recent measures bring the persistence of this confidence into doubt (Gainer, 2016). The backlog of nearly a million cases has been reduced significantly thanks to the measures implemented by the Judiciary Transformation Framework.

Among the problematic signals is that more recent public polls surrounding faith in the judiciary, as well as perceptions of corruption more broadly, are at best mixed. Relatedly, the Supreme Court's cursory handling of challenges to the closely contested presidential election of Uhuru Kenyatta in 2013, the first major test of the court's role in electoral processes, was broadly criticized. The blow to the judiciary's credibility was confounded by several corruption scandals ranging from 3 million to 25 million US$, which implicated top administrators in the judiciary, including the chief registrar. Kenyan citizens' perception of the judiciary may have been influenced by both issues given more negative results in recent polls, as compared to those surveyed earlier in 2013 (Gainer, 2016).

The extent of criticism surrounding the Supreme Court's consideration of challenges to the 2013 presidential election may have influenced the court, for on September 1, 2017, the court overturned the electoral results of the 2017 presidential election. The ruling is an important testament to judicial independence within the country, for it was the first time an African court annulled a sitting leader's electoral victory. The election marked another episode in a battle among families and tribes. The incumbent president, Uhuru Kenyatta, is the son of Kenya's first president who took power following independence from Britain in 1964. Kenyatta represented one of Kenya's largest ethnic groups, the Kikuyu, and through his 2017 running mates, the nation's third largest tribe, the Kalenjin. The opposition candidate, Raila Odinga, was prime minister from 2008 to 2013, and is the son of the country's first vice president who fell out with Jomo Kenyatta. He represented the Luo tribe, with running mates representing two other major tribes within the country. The personal and family rivalries are microcosms of larger tensions among the tribal groups that shape Kenya, and many other countries in the region.

Odinga has been a perennial opposition candidate for the presidency, and at the center of the major events of the last two decades. Resolving the 2008 crisis required international intervention, resulting in a power-sharing agreement with Kibaki as president and Odinga as prime minister. The coalition government presided over the drafting and enactment of the 2010 Constitution, under which Kibaki served as president until the first elections held in 2013. The top two contenders in the 2013 presidential election? Uhuru Kenyatta and Raila Odinga. As noted previously, the court rejected Odinga's challenge to the 2013 electoral results. Although unrest across the country accompanied the 2013 election, it never approached the level of violence seen in 2007 and 2008. By accepting the result, Odinga helped cement the constitution into place and improved Kenya's judicial institutions by adhering to the rule of law.

Events since the Supreme Court overturned the electoral results in September 2017 emphasize the fragility of judicial independence within a fraught political context. Instead of peaceful acceptance of defeat, Odinga's challenge hinged on irregularities surrounding the electronic submission of detailed official vote tallies required under electoral law. The Supreme Court then annulled the electoral victory of the incumbent Kikuyu president. In the African context, the outcome of such a direct judicial challenge to presidential power is anything but certain. Indeed, President Kenyatta's initial response to the court's decision displayed the options a powerful executive possesses. Kenyatta urged a peaceful response from his supporters. But he also decried the undemocratic nature of the verdict, claiming that it represented a decision of six people choosing to go against the expressed will of millions, and vowed to "fix" the court.

Subsequently, Odinga claimed that he saw none of the guarantees of changes to the electoral process necessary to restore his faith in the elections, and so he proceeded to boycott the new election held on October 27, 2017. In the weeks preceding the election, Parliament passed a law restricting the power of the Supreme Court to overturn future elections and allowing for changes to the leadership of the independent electoral commission within the country to proceed more easily. The law also included a provision intended to disincentivize a candidate from boycotting an election, because it specified that in instances where an election date had already been set, the candidate boycotting the election would lose to the standing candidate by default. Given Odinga's position regarding the October 27 election, there is little doubt that the provision was targeting him personally. Additionally, on October 25, a petition from the opposition to postpone the election was not heard by the Supreme Court because an insufficient number of justices appeared to hear the petition, giving various excuses ranging from a fear for their safety, to illness, to flight delays. Ultimately, Kenyatta won the October 27 election with more than 98 percent of the vote, due to the boycott orchestrated by Odinga. Predictably, the second election was challenged before the Supreme Court, but the court ultimately upheld the electoral results.

The preceding events emphasize how judicial outcomes do not occur in a vacuum, and are instead greatly subject to the constraints determined by the larger political and social context of a given country.

The initial move by the court to annul the first electoral results was widely lauded as an important signal of judicial independence, but subsequent events have proven how delicate the development of judicial oversight of the political process can be. Regardless of the particular outcomes of the controversy regarding Kenya's next president, it is certain that the electoral controversy will prove influential, for better or worse, in determining the strength of Kenya's judicial institutions in the future.

Whatever the outcome of the 2017 electoral controversy, the underlying political economy that enabled the reforms to proceed should be of interest to any scholar and practitioner of institutional reform of the judiciary. The specific means that facilitated such extensive reforms are certainly deserving of additional research beyond the cursory treatment given here. Nonetheless, at a broad level, the post-electoral violence created a window of opportunity for reform in terms of the widespread recognition of the need for wholesale change to judicial institutions. In terms of the leadership required to see the reforms through, Willy Mutunga, the former chief justice and president of the Supreme Court, has been the public face behind the implementation of the judiciary transformation framework, and is personally quite active in criticizing government bodies not seen as sufficiently supportive, as well as defending the reputation of the judiciary when it has come under criticism during the period we survey here.

Ultimately, a binary assessment of the success or failure of Kenya's judicial reforms may not be a useful way to view the institutional changes within the country. The reforms were brought about by a fundamental transition in governance wrought by a violent crisis in the wake of the breakdown of existing political institutions. After a long period of recognition of Kenya's weak judicial institutions, from a lack of independence from the executive branch, to the widespread corruption among individual judges, to clear indicators of functional deficiencies like a massive backlog of cases, the new constitutional regime provided the impetus for policies designed to correct perceived deficiencies. The changes enhanced independence from the executive in terms of finances, selection, and accountability. The judiciary underwent significant structural changes, including expansion and modernization, in order to improve processes and a professional culture that lacked accountability. Finally, every sitting judge when the 2010 Constitution was enacted underwent a significant vetting process to ensure suitability for continued service. The creation of the Judges and Magistrates Vetting Board with the authority and legitimacy to review the past records of every judge within the country was controversial, especially given that Parliament was given little constitutional detail as to the process. The range of significant institutional reforms emphasizes the value that judicial institutions provide for society, and how closely tied the independence and reputation of the judiciary is to the legitimacy of the government as a whole.

PART III

The Dynamics of Economic and Political Development

Introduction to Part Topics

In Parts I and II of this book, we covered a core set of tools used in Institutional and Organizational Analysis (IOA) and provided a series of examples to illustrate the state of the literature. In Part I, we presented the main concepts and definitions. We took institutions as fixed, and showed how they impact economic performance. In Part II, we explored how societies create the formal institutions that condition economic and political performance, given a fixed set of higher-level "constitutional" rules-for-making-rules. This toolkit has been tremendously successful in helping researchers, policymakers, and others to better understand how economies and societies function and evolve. In just a few decades, the IOA has grown from a relatively obscure field, largely absent from the main journals and departments, to a field that is fully absorbed into mainstream economics, political science, law, and related disciplines. Concepts like institutions, property rights, and transaction costs are now used with familiarity as if they had always been part of the orthodoxy.

A reader of this book might therefore feel that the whole story has been told and be tempted to stop reading at this point. But additional puzzles remain. If institutions are the key for better economic performance and are also "humanly devised" so that they are a choice variable, then why do societies not simply choose institutions that assure optimal economic and political performance?[1] That they do not do so is most clearly seen by comparing economic performance across countries and over time. In 1800, the richest nations in the world were about four times richer than the poorest in terms of GDP per capita. Today, the richest is more than two hundred times better off than the poorest. This is a staggering difference that emerged in

---

[1] We focus on institutions rather than norms because norms are less of a choice variable for those in the dominant network of power.

a relatively short period of history. This great divergence has led to the formation of a small group of about forty rich and developed nations at the top and a large group of undeveloped or emerging economies at the bottom.

While the shape of this distribution might not seem unnatural, its enduring stability presents a puzzle. There are good reasons in economic theory for predicting convergence of the incomes of poor and rich countries over time. The scarcity of capital in the poor countries, together with the greater presence of unrealized investment opportunities, should make capital investment in less-developed countries more profitable. Capital should flow to poorer countries where it would finance investment, which in turn would foster greater economic growth, closing the gap with the richer countries. Alternatively, because wages are lower in poorer countries, labor should flow to rich countries, thereby equalizing the marginal productivity of labor across countries.

While these dynamics are predicted by theory, they have not played out in practice. Very few nations have managed to make the transition from the group of poor to the group of rich countries in the past century, and empirical tests fail to uncover evidence of convergence across countries. Most of today's developed nations reached that status back in the nineteenth century, and since then only a handful of countries have managed to break free and join them there. Of the non-oil exporting countries, South Korea and Chile stand out as stars in the last fifty years. The remaining great majority of countries trodded along with periods of booms and busts that brought some improvement over time, but not enough to make that transition. This pattern suggests that it is not simply a matter of time until technological progress and improvements in human knowledge will raise all boats.

This state of affairs has led to an intense debate in the last two to three decades to find the fundamental cause of long-term development and prosperity. Whereas proximate causes such as technology, capital accumulation, human capital, and social capital are clearly important parts of the development process, the debate focused on the fundamental causes that could explain why these proximate causes, and ultimately prosperity, failed to materialize in most cases. The top contenders for the Holy Grail of explanations included geography and institutions. For a period, it seemed as if the debate was settled by

"Institutions Rule."[2] While this development has greatly improved the literature and our understanding of the world relative to the previous ahistorical and institutionally poor approach, in many cases the incorporation of institutions has been done in too simplistic and naïve ways. McCloskey (2016: chap. 15) deprecatingly calls this the "add institutions and stir" view. That is, although the recognition that institutions are an essential part of the story has been an important improvement, it is not enough to simply take institutions as given or assume that they will emerge as "good" or "bad," "inclusive" or "extractive," "adaptively efficient" or "inefficient," and thereafter recommend how they must be changed or not.

The inability of most countries to achieve sustained economic growth, despite the examples provided by more prosperous role models, suggests that growth is not as simple as choosing the "right" institutions. The prevalence across the world of institutional choices that systematically fail to produce growth and development and yet persist over time is something that needs an explanation. This is an area where there has been much less work in IOA, and where much remains to be done.

One explanation for the persistence of institutions that do not lead to growth and prosperity is the standard political economy story of a group of elites that blocks reforms that would increase social welfare as a whole at the expense of their own share and permanence in power (Acemoglu and Robinson, 2012; Alston and Ferrie, 1999; Sokoloff and Engerman, 2000). This class of explanation is often an accurate description of much of the failure of countries to grow and improve the lives of their citizens. Nevertheless, there remain several unanswered questions. Not all cases of failed development can be accounted for by those in power blocking wealth or democratic-enhancing institutional changes. Some societies still choose arrangements that do not produce prosperity or more political inclusion. Even when there are distributive issues, why are intertemporal political exchanges or side-payments to enable change not more common? Even though political transaction costs are typically high, the potential gains of exchange are arguably so large that we would expect this type of bargaining to be more common than it appears to be.

---

[2] See the heavily cited article by Rodrik, Subramanian, and Trebbi (2009) with the title "Institutions Rule: The Primacy of Institutions over Geography and Integration in Economic Development."

Another institutional explanation argues that the pattern of persistent inequality across nations may result not from a lack of economic growth on the part of poorer countries, but from the inability of these countries to avoid periods of economic stagnation or decline (Broadberry and Wallis, 2016). This explanation for the divergence of countries' economic performance over time is consistent with the benefits of voluntary exchange; all countries can be expected to experience the economic growth that results from the tendency of people to engage in specialization and productive exchange. However, some countries' choice of institutions enables the dominant network to better coordinate in the face of exogenous shocks such as natural disasters, regional geopolitical conflicts, or price volatility of commodities. For many countries, their set of institutions does not provide a viable framework within which members of the dominant network can credibly commit to costly responses to the shocks. In such nations, responses sufficient to continue economic activity at increasing levels are less likely, which creates a higher likelihood of persistent periods of economic stagnation and decline. Broadberry and Wallis dub this explanation "shrink theory," and its focus on the benefits to the dominant network of coordination complements our focus on the role of leadership in coordinating the beliefs of the dominant network.

In Part III, we cover an approach to these issues that focuses on the underpinnings of the choice of institutions by social actors. Although formal institutions are a choice variable for those in power, the world is complex and uncertain, making this choice difficult. The uncertainty and non-ergodicity of the world means that past experiences and the examples of others provide an imperfect basis on which to make choices for the future. In the absence of clear guides on how to choose the institutions that will induce the desired types of outcomes, those in power must rely on *something else* that will provide a vision of what is possible and how it can be achieved.

The *something else* can be identified as core beliefs and how they shape institutional change.[3] When making choices under uncertainty

---

[3] Core beliefs differ from behavioral beliefs in a fundamentally important way. Behavioral beliefs are akin to what we described in Chapter 1 as norms of behavior. They are very stable because people act on their behavioral belief that others will act in the same way. Core beliefs are more fundamental beliefs about how the world works. We elaborate in Chapter 8.

and non-ergodicity, beliefs are a lens that fills in the blanks, indicates where to look, filters what does and does not matter, and provides guidance, heuristics, and rules of thumbs. The guidance is often very poor and does not necessarily lead to growth and prosperity. There is usually no force pushing for the prevalence of a single "superior" belief, as one might perhaps expect. Instead, beliefs are highly diversified and persistent across societies. Although beliefs change, the evidence is that there is no guaranteed improvement in developmental outcomes over time. On the contrary, the most common outcome across countries has been poor economic and political performance.[4]

In Chapter 8, we present a framework that tries to capture the complex process through which countries choose institutions and how institutions may deepen over time. In Chapter 9, we provide several historical examples utilizing the framework to explain fundamental changes in economic and political developmental trajectories. We argue that development and institutional change will always be highly contextual. A change in core beliefs is at the heart of deep institutional change, and our analysis focuses on how this institutional change depends greatly on the core beliefs of those in society with the power to change fundamental institutions. Our framework for deep institutional change consists of the following: (1) core beliefs and institutions begin in a state of equilibrium, consistent with each other as long as expectations are fulfilled; (2) core beliefs become malleable when expected or actual outcomes diverge sufficiently from expectations, creating a potential window of opportunity for leadership to change core beliefs; (3) the dominant network changes institutions based on their new core beliefs in a constitutional moment; and (4) core beliefs take root over time through subsequent institutional deepening to the extent outcomes sufficiently confirm expectations.

While it might seem obvious that core beliefs have an impact on institutions and economic performance, most of the literature, even in institutional and organizational analysis, has proceeded as if those impacts are relatively unimportant for most issues and can be dismissed through the logic of Occam's razor, that is, the simplest theory or explanation should prevail. The view is apparent in the reaction to

---

[4] The likely explanation for the relative stasis in developmental trajectories is the standard political economy explanation. We are interested in explaining the outliers: those countries that do change their developmental trajectories dramatically, either for the better or worse.

Douglass North's (2005) book, *Understanding the Process of Economic Change*, published fifteen years after his acclaimed and pathbreaking book, *Institutions, Institutional Change, and Economic Performance* (1990). While the expectation was that the new book would follow the previous one by reiterating and further developing the importance of institutions for economic performance, North produced a treatise on the importance of beliefs, mental models, non-ergodic worlds, adaptive efficiency, and an emphasis on cognition. The anticipation of confirmation of already-accepted ideas was met instead with unfamiliar statements such as: "the way we perceive the world and construct our explanations about the world requires that we delve into how the mind and brain work – the subject matter of cognitive science" (North, 2005: 5). Apparently, the profession was not prepared for such a sharp epistemological shift, and the book had very little impact relative to expectation. North's subsequent book, *Violence and Social Orders* (2009, with John Wallis and Barry Weingast), though excellent and pathbreaking in its own way, contained very little on beliefs, and had a much better reception and greater impact on the literature.

Evidence of the growing recognition of the importance of culture and beliefs to understand economic performance is a recent surge in papers that seek to explicitly model and test the coevolution of institutions and culture, that is, the two-way causal interaction of these variables. A recent survey by Alesina and Giuliano (2015) covers more than two hundred (mostly recent) academic papers that deal directly with the two-way interaction of culture and institutions. These studies indicate that institutions are conditional on cultural beliefs and have consequences for outcomes. Pareto-inferior outcomes often arise and persist. Those institutions and outcomes can then have feedback effects that influence culture and beliefs. These studies have an important corollary implication for studies of the relationship between institutions and economic development: institutions can be a function of culture just as culture and other society-level outcomes can be greatly influenced by institutions. This suggests that those with the power to shape culture can shape institutions, either directly or indirectly, and will do so to the extent that such institutional change is perceived to be in their interest.

Though we agree that culture is fundamentally important, we will stick to beliefs as the determining variable for institutional change for several reasons: (1) culture is more resistant to change and much more nuanced than beliefs, (2) culture is also less resistant to exogenous changes by those in power, and (3) culture is much broader, and it is the interaction across the factors that determines culture that may determine core beliefs. This is not to dismiss culture as unimportant. We see culture as clearly a determinant of social order and, in many ways, will likely shape the beliefs of the dominant network as well as the long-standing norms in a society. But for now, the transmission mechanism remains a bit of a black box.

A recent example of the important interaction of culture and beliefs (or ideas) for understanding the impact of institutions on outcomes is McCloskey's monumental trilogy on *Bourgeois Virtues* (2006), *Bourgeois Dignity* (2010), and *Bourgeois Equality* (2016). The objective of the trilogy is to explain the timing, location, and process of the great divergence through which a small group of countries managed to attain sustained economic growth and prosperity. For McCloskey, the key factor that unleashed the mass flourishing was the rise of an idea that commerce and economic activity were dignified pursuits. Previously, the upper classes viewed commercial activity with disdain or, at best, acceptance. Society imposed a dishonor tax on commercial pursuits (Boudreaux, 2014).[5] As all taxes, it discouraged those activities and investments in human capital and innovation. The basic argument of McCloskey's trilogy is that the repeal of this dishonor tax by the bourgeois allowed, for the first time, the common man to "have a go," thus unleashing the waves of discoveries and innovations that underpinned the Industrial Revolution and the great divergence. However, the importance of attitudes to the institutions that can reflect them also played a role. As the dishonor tax diminished, and innovative entrepreneurial activity filled the gap, this led to a corresponding demand for institutions that better facilitated economic exchange. Beliefs that facilitate economic and institutional change can have significant positive feedback effects: to the extent that the beneficial institutional changes bring greater societal prosperity, then these institutional changes reinforce the changing attitudes in society towards economic activity.

---

[5]　The metaphor of a dishonor tax was suggested by Boudreaux (2014) in a debate of McCloskey's theses.

Mokyr (2017) also stresses ideas and beliefs' interplay with institutions as an explanation of why the Industrial Revolution and the remarkable resulting take-off in human prosperity happened in Europe in the eighteenth and nineteenth centuries instead of other places that had been well ahead in the process at different times in history (such as Song dynasty in China: 960 to 1279).[6] The proximate driver of that growth and prosperity was technological and scientific innovation, but Mokyr's analysis focuses on the beliefs that underpinned the development of that knowledge and understanding along with the enabling institutions. In short, it was the increasing acceptance in the Enlightenment that man can change the world around him that led to innovation and prosperity.

Mokyr stresses the "market for ideas" in sixteenth- and seventeenth-century Europe. The first element of this market for ideas involves the rise of a belief that material progress is not only possible, but also desirable. What provided such an environment in Europe and had been missing in many of the other failed take-offs, was political fragmentation across nations and city-states, and a Republic of Letters linking a large network of thinkers, inventors, and practitioners. Together, these two elements created an environment of competition that fostered the production of useful knowledge, that is, not knowledge for the sake of knowledge, or to glorify God, but rather knowledge of how to understand and control nature so as to benefit mankind. Of course, some useful knowledge also redounded to the individual entrepreneur and inventors. The political fragmentation allowed the innovators and producers of new ideas to evade the repression from those in power that tried to suppress their creativity and diffusion. This period experienced an intense circulation of thinkers and innovators who were sometimes persecuted at home but well received abroad. The result of the market for ideas was the dominance of the belief in useful knowledge that laid the foundation for the institutions that ultimately underpinned the Industrial Revolution and the subsequent unprecedented economic growth. Mokyr's explanation also displays the importance of institutional choice on the part of the dominant network within a given country. The political fragmentation in

---

[6] Our view of beliefs is more positive than McCloskey and more akin to Mokyr, who ties beliefs with institutional change. For us, beliefs embody a subjective view of how the beliefs inspire the formation of institutions with an expectation of how these institutions in turn will influence outcomes.

Europe meant a comparative diversity of institutional sets within which particular inventors could experience greater or lower levels of reward or repression. A greater diversity of institutional sets, within which comparatively beneficial ones emerged, provides an important blueprint for dominant networks when considering institutional change.

Those with the power to influence core beliefs also have the power and incentive to change institutions, and these changes can have significant positive feedback effects when the changes lead to greater economic and political development for society. Moreover, the divergence of economic and political development across countries now provides a blueprint from which the dominant network in society can consider changes to their own institutional set. But if the blueprint for a set of wealth-enhancing institutions exists, why the divergence in development outcomes around the world? The persistence of institutions that do not improve economic or political performance has an additional implication for our analysis: institutional change is costly, and marginal change does not typically result in superior outcomes. Therefore, if beliefs, norms, and institutions are sticky, it may take a window of opportunity before the costs of institutional change are outweighed by the benefits.

We see these studies of beliefs as complementary to studies that unpack the role of the more common political economy explanations in determining institutional change, and hence, economic development. North, Wallis, and Weingast (2009) as well as Wallis (2018a) have an explicit focus on the incentives and beliefs of the dominant network in society. By definition, this dominant network, unlike the majority of society, has the power to influence or determine institutional change across society. This is the closest literature from which the explicit role of core beliefs or mental models takes off. In the next two chapters, we follow in the footsteps of Eggertsson (2005), Greif (2006), North (2005), and Schofield (2006).[7]

The role of a dominant network in orchestrating institutional change requires an interest-consistent explanation about why the new

---

[7] Many others are working in this academic vineyard, but these scholars specifically make the link between beliefs and institutional outcomes. Iyigun and Rubin (2017) use ideologies (beliefs) to explain the inability of the Ottoman Empire to adjust to technological change from the West, which in turn led to their decline.

institutions provide expected benefits over the status quo. Given the wealth, power, and impunity of many dominant networks around the world, this isn't a clearly warranted assumption. At a minimum, diminishing marginal returns would suggest that even if the dominant network captures a lion's share of the benefits from additional economic development, the benefit alone might not be sufficient to overcome the losses associated with an acquiescence to the rule of law and accountability before an independent and impartial judiciary, or the competitive losses associated with liberalizing access to private and public associational forms like political parties and corporations (North, Wallis, and Weingast, 2009).

We agree with Wallis (2018a) that the majority of fundamental institutional changes must be expected to benefit the dominant network. Wallis focuses on the benefits of commitment credibility secured through increases in the rule of law and coordination in the face of unanticipated shocks. In contrast, our analysis considers the effect of these shocks, among other cases where political or economic outcomes diverge from expectations, on the rent streams of the dominant network, and how these expected or actual disruptions in rent streams create a window of opportunity for change in the fundamental institutions of society. Our framework further adds to the literature by focusing on changes to constitutional-level rule sets and beliefs in society in particular, as opposed to the marginal institutional change that can be expected from ordinary operation of political systems around the world.[8] In many instances, the expected impact from institutional change is fuzzy and fraught with uncertainty. In these instances, leadership can be decisive in bringing about a change in beliefs that will promote change. Moreover, not all leaders are self-interested in the standard narrow economic definition. Some leaders are playing for the history books and want to do the right thing, or are motivated by concerns other than the material.

We break with the traditional characterization of the dominant network as the sole decision maker and develop an explanation for the role of leadership within this dominant network in coordinating a transition to a new core belief enabling institutional change. We develop this

---

[8] We are by no means the first to use the lens of institutional analysis to consider the emergence and evolution of constitutional-level rule sets in societies. Stefan Voigt (1997, 2011) provides several in-depth surveys of contributions in this area.

perspective on the role of a leader in the next chapter through a specific framework that describes how beliefs that affect the choice of institutions arise and change over time. Fundamental institutional change entails an iterative process of institutional deepening and is self-reinforcing in terms of core beliefs as long as outcomes match expectations. Our framework is useful to understand the process of development in the modern world and indeed is also useful for understanding development in the Ancient World (Ober, 2017; Carugati, 2018). We illustrate the usefulness of our framework in Chapter 9 to analyze the case of four specific countries. The four cases include: (1) United States, 1783–1789: Transitioning from "States Rule" to the United States of America; (2) Argentina, 1912–1955: Budding Belief in Checks and Balances to Redistributive Populism; (3) Brazil, 1985–2014: Belief in Social Inclusion to Fiscally Sound Social Inclusion; and (4) Ecuador, 1998–2017: From a Neoliberal Belief to a Belief in Inclusive Politics.

8 | Developmental Trajectories

Institutional Deepening and Critical Transitions

In 1950, the GDP per capita in the Philippines was 25 percent greater than in South Korea (Maddison Project, 2013). In 2010, the GDP per capita in South Korea was nearly seven times greater than in the Philippines. In 1950, both the Philippines and South Korea would be considered developing countries. In 2015, Korea had ascended to the ranks of the upper-income countries and the Philippines remained in the ranks of low-income countries. This is a remarkable ascension for Korea because, as shown in Figure 8.1, the ranking of countries that comprise the upper-, middle-, and lower-income categories, as per their GDP per capita in 2010, has stayed relatively stable over the past sixty years.[1] Roughly 17 percent of the countries are in the upper category; 13 percent in the middle; and the vast majority in the low-income category. If one goes back one hundred years, the majority of the countries in the upper tier has remained the same (Maddison Project, 2013).

Why have incomes not converged? It is not because growth rates are always lower in the developing or middle-income countries than in the upper-income countries. When developing countries grow, they can grow at double-digit rates, far exceeding growth rates in developed countries. But growth is sporadic and frequently followed by civil wars and other turmoil leading low-income countries to shrink, which accounts quantitatively for their failure to converge in prosperity with wealthier nations (Broadberry and Wallis, 2016). Growth rates in the lower- and middle-income countries are more volatile (as are their political regimes) with bigger booms and busts.[2] For countries in

---

[1] We use GDP per capita as a rough measure of both economic and political development. Indeed, the two go hand in glove (Acemoglu and Robinson, 2012; among others). We dropped oil-exporting countries because their high GDP results from an oil endowment.

[2] These periods of stagnation and decline have an important implication that links the incentives of politicians within a given country to the comparative analysis we engage in here. Politicians are more concerned about absolute change

285

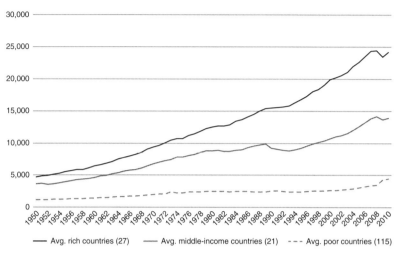

Figure 8.1 Divergence of economic growth across countries
Sources: When using the data: Maddison Project (www.ggdc.net/maddison/m addison-project/home.htm, 2013 version). When referring to underlying methodology and main results: Bolt and van Zanden (2014). When using individual country data: see country-source references in the appendix of Bolt and van Zanden (2014).

all three income categories, we use the term "autopilot" to describe the process of "normal" growth (or shrinking) in economic and political institutions. We captured these processes in Parts I and II.

All countries pass laws, and there has been development in general through the process of autopilot described in Parts I and II of our book. Global poverty rates are at all-time lows in the twenty-first century, as are many measures of global inequality (Lakner and Milanovic, 2016). Despite the daily news, the world is also becoming less violent (Pinker, 2011). And lower violence is a precondition for higher social order, which leads to economic and political development (North, Wallis, and

within their own political context, as opposed to growth levels around the world. However, if periods of stagnation and decline are precisely what domestic politicians wish to avoid, and the absence of these periods is also linked to the comparative prosperity of developed nations (Broadberry and Wallis, 2016), then understanding the institutional change that leads sustained periods of economic growth is of direct relevance to the incentives of politicians concerned more about growth within their own country. We return to the institutional dynamics that facilitate these sustained periods of growth later in the chapter.

Weingast, 2009). Yet, looking back over the past two hundred years does not give us confidence that convergence in developmental paths across the world just needs time (or more foreign aid). Countries tend to remain on their own trajectories of development. There has not been convergence. No universal playbook exists to guide deep development across the world, despite well-intentioned efforts by multilateral agencies such as the World Bank.

But there are countries, like South Korea, that break from their past and transition to a different developmental trajectory and to higher-income ranks. There are fewer countries that drop dramatically from the upper-income category. Argentina stands out as falling from grace, dropping from top ten in the first half of the twentieth century to a middle-income country in the twenty-first century.[3] Why is there so much stability in the trajectories of economic and political development? What is needed to break from a current developmental trajectory (autopilot) to a *critical transition* to a new trajectory of sustained economic and political development with less volatility? Conversely, what causes some countries to fall dramatically in a *critical transition* to a new trajectory of economic and political regression with greater volatility? Addressing these questions is the essence of Part III. In Chapter 8, we will discuss the dynamic frameworks of autopilot and critical transitions followed in Chapter 9 by applications of the framework.

Understanding Autopilot and Critical Transitions

A country in autopilot maintains a steady pattern of development. Autopilot is the norm for most countries during most periods. Institutions change, but generally only on the margin or at least not sufficiently to overcome the costs associated with a move to a different trajectory. Those in power tend to stay in power with little or no change in the dominant network – though there are always marginal entrants and exits. The difficulties in breaking out of autopilot explain why very few countries change their economic

---

[3] In Chapter 9, we have a case study of Argentina's change in its developmental trajectory. We do not address the case of South Korea because none of the authors has the contextual knowledge base to understand the how and why for South Korea, but we hope that other scholars will find our framework useful for pursuing South Korea as a remarkable case study.

and political trajectories and instead remain relatively fixed in the upper-, middle-, or lower-income category over time.[4] While there has been considerable economic development, the cohorts remain relatively closed. Within any country, those in power (typically) want to stay in power; institutions are a stabilizing force used to achieve that goal. In Part I, we explained how institutions and norms affect economic organizations, contracts, and economic performance in a world of autopilot. Similarly, in Part II, we explained how economic outcomes, special interests, and extant political, judicial, and bureaucratic institutions and norms affect new political outcomes and institutions under autopilot. In Part III, we show how a country can experience a *critical transition* when it breaks out of autopilot and makes a large and sustained change in its economic and political trajectory.

Critical transitions are periods of time when the *beliefs* about how institutions shape outcomes change. The *dominant network* (organizations and individuals) is the power behind the institutions in a society. Those in power establish the institutions under a *belief* about how institutions map into outcomes. Big enough deviations in outcomes relative to expectations make beliefs malleable. Belief change can also come about through the political entrepreneurship of leadership creating a window of opportunity out of extant conditions. *Windows of opportunity* surround the possibility of a move to new beliefs, new institutions, and a new trajectory of economic and political development.

The new belief that emerges during a window of opportunity is a reaction to the *ex-ante* status quo belief and its institutions or a proactive entrepreneurial effort to improve on the status quo. Changing the existing belief is a collective-action problem. For countries to change course requires collective action among the dominant network. Unless a sufficient number of organizations in the dominant network share the same belief, a country needs *leadership* to coordinate the transition to a new set of beliefs about the institutions needed to achieve desired outcomes. The leadership to a new belief results in *constitutional moments*, the institutional formalization of the new beliefs surrounding

---

[4] This also holds for positions in the rankings of the Human Development Index, for which we do not have a long time series.

governance. These *constitutional moments* generally entail a new constitution or significant amendments to a constitution. The transition to a new belief takes time and institutional deepening in a virtuous loop (or vicious loop). The concepts that we tie together to understand the dynamics in the economic and political system are: *critical transitions, beliefs, dominant network, institutions, outcomes, windows of opportunity, leadership*, and *constitutional moments*.

Understanding Why Developmental Trajectories Do Not Converge

Institutions and norms are the overarching concepts used in our book. Institutions and norms are the rules of the game that along with their enforcement provide the incentives for behavior. In Part I of our book, we took institutions and norms as exogenous, and they in turn shaped organizations, property rights, transaction costs, contracts, and ultimately economic performance. In Part II, we took institutions as endogenous to economic performance, special interests, executive/legislative behavior, the bureaucracy, and the judiciary. Institutions clearly change, but they change under the umbrella of a constitution.[5] In Parts I and II, we asserted that most of the time, institutions only change on the margin. There is a heavy hand of the status quo. We call this autopilot, but we did not discuss why. To do so, we need to introduce the concepts of a dominant network and beliefs. By a dominant network, we mean those organizations or individuals who possess the economic and political power to change institutions.[6] In complex societies of the modern world, the dominant network consists of many economic and political

---

[5] In Part II, we discussed the degree to which the Constitution was binding. To the extent that it is more akin to a law, then it would follow the same dynamics. To the extent that it is a shadow over behavior that constrains the different branches of government and other elite actors and is enforced by the courts, then it sets the bounds on institutional change.

[6] We draw on North, Wallis, and Weingast (2009) for the essence of a dominant network. It is similar to what Acemoglu and Robinson (2012) term "the economic and political elites" and Sokoloff and Engerman (2000) call the "elites." In practice, economic and political organizations are often outputs of the same interest group, given the extent to which powerful economic actors can often influence the political system, whether through a given company's public affairs office, or through a separate organization set up to achieve this purpose. However, for analytical purposes, distinguishing between these political and economic outputs is useful.

organizations.[7] Organizations in the dominant network are country-specific. Economic organizations in the dominant network vary positively with their economic clout in a society and are often by sector (e.g., financial, agricultural, mining, unions, exporters or importers, among others). Political organizations in society vary with their political muscle and include parties, committees, religious bodies, lobbies, numerous special interests, and, in many countries, the military.[8]

The support of sufficient numbers of non-elite individuals can itself influence the success of a particular political organization in achieving its intended outcome. Individuals can be supportive of the dominant network to the extent that they are beneficiaries. "Boss machine politics" would fit this scenario. In the late nineteenth century, US mayors of large cities who controlled infrastructure contracts received kickbacks from construction companies and the mayor would redistribute some of the rents to voters in return for votes. The same scenario still goes on in some cities. While the boundaries of the dominant network vary from society to society, the organizations created to engage in economic and political activity, and the extent of their popular support, are important determinants of the network in a particular society.

In a broad sense, beliefs are the subjective view of the way the world works (North, 2005). We focus our analysis on individuals' beliefs about how institutions affect expected economic and political outcomes through the incentives that they establish. Beliefs are positive views of the mapping between institutions and expected outcomes. There is not a direct mapping from institutions to outcomes. If this were the case, policy making would be very simple, except for rent-seeking. Organizations (and individuals within organizations) in the dominant network have preferences over economic and political outcomes, but they are constrained by beliefs of their own and others in the dominant network.[9] Organizations have differing beliefs. Beliefs about

---

[7] As societies become more complex, they become more resilient to shocks, but it also makes big changes more difficult because there are more veto players. We will discuss this in more depth when we discuss critical transitions.

[8] See Chapter 4 in Part II on special interests. Some would be considered in the dominant network and others outside of it, but it is a matter of degree. Even dictators need to sleep, that is, they need supporting organizations to stay in power.

[9] We use the phrase "organizations have beliefs" as shorthand for those individuals in power within organizations who have beliefs and express these beliefs through their decisions regarding the institutions/norms that they seek to create in the organization.

how institutions affect outcomes include the public interest to the extent that citizens constrain the dominant network.[10] Beliefs also take into account how laws filter through norms of societies. This is an additional reason for autopilot because laws need to be reasonably consistent with norms in a society or otherwise they will be prohibitively costly to implement.[11]

Dominant networks in different countries have different beliefs about the mapping from beliefs to institutions to outcomes.[12] Beliefs vary because of different contextual experiences, including culture and interpretation of events. A very poignant example is the belief over austerity or stimulus as the policy responses during an economic downturn. In Germany, decision makers typically opt more for austerity than stimulus as the response to negative macroeconomic shocks, whereas in the United States the response recently has been to engage in stimulus monetary policies, though even here the depth of the belief varies. Even within countries, different constituencies can hold different beliefs regarding the impact of institutions on outcomes.[13] If economic growth is "normal," then the latitude of beliefs is narrow. The belief in the dominant network over which institutions to implement will only vary on the margin, at least for those organizations that have more power.

To the extent that those in the dominant network get it right, then outcomes will be reasonably consistent with expectations.[14] The stability of the political system allows those in power to enjoy the economic and political rents that the system generates. Though they

---

[10] This is because popular pressures can play an important role in defining and redefining dominant networks, even in tightly elite-controlled societies.

[11] For example, from 1974 until 1987 in the United States, the maximum speed limit on interstate highways was 55 mph. Particularly in rural areas, the law was inconsistent with norms and compliance, and local enforcement low.

[12] This is one reason for the failure of the Washington Consensus in the 1990s to transform countries by following the World Bank/IMF recipe.

[13] The "beliefs" we describe are not all the beliefs at play in society. For example, societies have considerable disagreement as to the problematic nature of inequality, or the appropriate response to climate change. Nonetheless, we also share, by and large, a core set of beliefs across ideological differences. A window of opportunity is created when outcomes diverge significantly enough from the outcomes consistent with these beliefs.

[14] This does not imply a mechanism design view of the world, but simply that those in power generally change institutions marginally because they only seek marginal changes. Unanticipated outcomes certainly happen and are at the heart of our subsequent dynamic, but for now we are interested in explaining autopilot.

would like more (money or power), they are constrained by other organizations. Institutions change marginally. Countries pass laws, and issue decrees, which are interpreted by courts, and implemented through bureaucracies. The "new" laws influence behavior, as discussed in Parts I and II, but despite the sound and fury in the media, societies do not dramatically veer off in a new direction. Most of the time, it is more or less business as usual, or what we term autopilot on the same developmental trajectory. Autopilot reflects the comparative costs of institutional change. Refining existing governance structures on the margins is significantly less costly than a fundamental change to these structures. The costs of changing the constitutional-level beliefs in a given society are only outweighed by the anticipated benefits in cases where these beliefs are sufficiently out of line with expected outcomes.

This does not mean that ordinarily legislation and administrative rulemaking do not matter for organizations. They matter greatly to certain organizations in a financial sense, which is why there is so much lobbying.[15] This of course includes employees of organizations who at the very least value job security. But, for most citizens, life goes on more or less the same. More complex societies are more resilient with fewer economic and political fluctuations. Lower-income countries have fewer organizations and more economic and political fluctuations, but one can typify fluctuations as part of autopilot because these fluctuations can be anticipated as a general characteristic of these societies.

In Figure 8.2, we show the process of autopilot on the same developmental trajectory, which again does include regress for some countries. The dominant network operates under an overarching belief set that limits the degree of institutional changes that are in turn filtered through norms to produce outcomes. Societies can stay on this loop for a very long time, and it is the rare society that manages to change its trajectory significantly despite the well-intentioned efforts of multilateral organizations, donor countries, some societal organizations in the dominant network, and even some benevolent political heads of state.

---

[15] The legal transitions literature emphasizes the costs of legal change creating winners and losers as useful to understanding how and why legal change occurs (Kaplow, 1986). This understanding also underpins the public choice literature in economics treated in Chapter 4 of Part II.

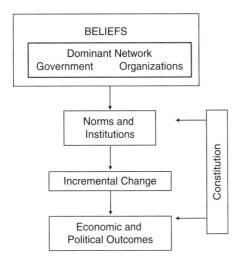

Figure 8.2 Development trajectories: Incremental change

Understanding a Critical Transition

To understand the process of a critical transition, we need to introduce some concepts to show the dynamic at work: windows of opportunity, leadership, and constitutional moments.[16] Organizations expect economic and political variance, but most fluctuations are not sufficiently large to produce a reactive window of opportunity for changing a country's overall trajectory, though such variance can have a very large impact in some policy areas. For example, the prohibition of alcohol in the United States with the implementation of the Twenty-First Amendment to the US Constitution resulted in an uptake in crime and violence. The law clearly went against norms in some regions and was laxly enforced. In short, over time there was a recognition that the amendment was a mistake. As a result, enough states voted to repeal Prohibition. This was a major change to the Constitution, but it did not affect the overall trajectory of the economy. Other examples abound: recognition that airline regulation was harmful to consumers, awareness of the health dangers of smoking, and awareness of the harm from polluted air and water all led to policy changes but did not significantly change the economic and political trajectory of US society.

[16] In this section, we draw upon and expand on the framework presented in Alston et al. (2016), who use the concepts to understand the developmental trajectory of Brazil from 1964 to 2016.

Windows of Opportunity

Here, we are concerned with *windows of opportunity* to change core beliefs. Windows of opportunity can be reactive or proactive.[17] If outcomes are sufficiently different from expectations, for example, an economic depression or a surprise electoral result, beliefs become malleable. In the face of a crisis, some of the organizations in power begin to question their belief in their mapping of institutions to outcomes; and some of the members of the dominant network exit and others enter. Most of the time, the dominant network is stable, but large deviations in outcomes can affect its composition and beliefs. Crises or large deviations in outcomes to expectations also affect the general public. When individuals across a given society see outcomes diverging from their expectations, this leads to demand for change through special interests and direct democratic mechanisms to "do something." Being able to draw upon this demand for change as a lever for coordination of the dominant network is one aspect of leadership, which we detail subsequently. These beliefs held by the population writ large often play a role in triggering a window of opportunity.

Windows of opportunity are periods of uncertainty and can only clearly be identified *ex post*,[18] although the right leader or organizations within the dominant network may perceive the possibility to

---

[17] The concept of windows of opportunity differs from a critical juncture (Acemoglu and Robinson, 2012). Critical junctures are exogenous events that change a trajectory of a country, but we delve deeper and ask why does change happen sometimes and other times societies drift back to the ex-ante status quo belief? A window of opportunity presents an opportunity for change, but for change to transpire, beliefs over institutions need to change, and the process is iterative such that belief deepening and institutional deepening take time.

[18] Defining exactly when a window of opportunity opens or closes is a specific example of the general boundary problem in identifying major events in the development trajectory of a given country. The more granular of a lens that one applies to a particular nation's history, the more difficult it becomes to say that this event or that event was the conclusive beginning or end of the process. Indeed, our definition of institutional deepening requires the operation of new institutions for an unspecified period before these institutions are sufficiently reinforced in core beliefs to where they become the new equilibrium from the perspective of our analysis. In Chapter 9, we use case studies to identify windows of opportunity. For example, the perceived failure of the Articles of Confederation by some of the US founding fathers gave them a window of opportunity that they seized/created to eventually deliver a new constitution. The window of opportunity was open for a long time, and it took leadership to mold the new beliefs behind the window.

change core beliefs and create a window of opportunity given extant conditions. Many windows of opportunity are not seized. During windows of opportunity, some organizations in the network want to stay the course while others advocate change.[19] The advocates of change are trying to seize a window of opportunity either for purely personal gain or for the public, though these are not mutually exclusive. With competing beliefs, a collective-action problem arises. What belief carries the day?

Leadership

This is where leadership matters. Much analysis of leadership takes the form of solving a principal-agent problem. This is true for much of the literature in business organizations and in military campaigns. But leadership of a different type is required to coordinate change to an overarching belief when there are many veto players to such change. Leadership is often embodied in a person, but more generally it is a group of people who exercise different dimensions of the leadership needed. The attributes of leadership in successfully coordinating belief change in the dominant network include: cognition of the problem to be solved and what to do; imagination or entrepreneurship; adaptability; and moral authority/legitimacy. Leadership can be reactive or proactive during windows of opportunity in coordinating a change in beliefs. In reacting to situations where there is a demand to "do something" because outcomes differed significantly from expectations, leadership recognizes which current institutions are insufficient to solve the current problem. Even though the head of an organization recognizes the problem and has a game plan, she must convince other heads of other organizations of the need to go along and take a chance. This can be accomplished through suasion or agenda control. The leader needs to be the most informed in the room and elicit information from others in a way that will bring others to her belief or convince others to adopt her belief as their own.[20]

---

[19]   Ginsburg and Huq (2018) characterize these competing demands as transformative and preservative in the context of the first period under a new constitution.

[20]   Riker (1984) has called this the art of policy making.

At times, leadership will require imagination or entrepreneurship.[21] This is more likely to be the case in proactive situations where a leader creates a window of opportunity for change over the extant status quo even when there is no immediate crisis. It may be seeing further down the decision tree than others or coming up with the unexpected. At times, imagination is spontaneous and other times deliberative. Adaptability is important because there are an infinite number of ways to encourage others to go along with a new belief. Side payments on a variety of margins are possible. Moral authority or legitimacy makes leadership easier. Having moral authority means that others will not question your motives for taking action. Some leaders come to power with moral authority, for example, George Washington, Nelson Mandela, or Vaclav Havel. Others can earn moral authority over time, for example, Winston Churchill and perhaps Harry Truman during the end of World War II. Legitimacy means that some power comes with the position; for example, the US president comes to the job as the commander in chief and has considerable latitude to act and sway beliefs.

Constitutions and Constitutional Moments

A constitutional moment occurs when a new belief, with the potential to change the trajectory of a country, is formally wrought into new institutions. Not all constitutional moments entail an amendment to a constitution or a new constitution. It could be a momentous law; for example, in the United States, the combined legislation of the Civil Rights and Voting Rights Act were a constitutional moment despite not changing the Constitution. The deliberations over a belief change are an important part of the process. For example, constitutional assemblies in deliberating a constitution shape beliefs prior to codifying beliefs (Alston et al., 2016). Lengthy deliberations in legislatures also shape beliefs and, as a result, the laws enacted.

Constitutionalism emerged in developed societies as an expression of a constitutional moment. Whether one considers the emergence of a constitution in France or the United States, the changes in each society's beliefs surrounding governance were fundamental and have

---

[21] On the role of imagination in breaking rules and getting away with it, see Shepsle (2017). Devising new rules can be as imaginative as breaking extant rules.

long been considered as creating a significant change in the country's trajectory of economic and political development. In these nations, the new constitution was an institutional articulation of a set of beliefs surrounding appropriate governance structures that implied a marked departure from those that came before. The various problems identified by some of the US founding fathers as systemic to a confederation of the states are indicative of the orchestration of a proactive window of opportunity. The Articles of Confederation initially appeared as a clear failure to some, but not a majority in the dominant networks across states. Ex post, we can see that those who saw the failures were looking forward in their mapping the impact of institutions to outcomes under two scenarios: the Articles of Confederation or states ceding power to the federal government in some domains.

The distinction between constitutional moments and the constitutional document of a nation itself is similar to the difference between a country's constitution and its constitutional document (Elkins, Ginsburg, and Melton, 2009). By the country's "constitution," we mean the beliefs surrounding how society should order and maintain the fundamental institutions of governance. The constitutional document contains the written rules of the game, in the shadow of which most incremental institutional change occurs. However, depending on the amendment rules of a given nation, changes to the constitutional document are more or less likely to represent a constitutional moment, where a major belief surrounding the institutions of governance has changed. In the United States, a constitutional amendment is relatively difficult, which makes it more likely that a given amendment represents a major change. The Bill of Rights and the Thirteenth, Fourteenth, and Fifteenth Amendments are ready examples.[22] However, other changes to the constitutional document in the United States, such as those surrounding Prohibition, did not change the fundamental trajectory of the nation in terms of political or economic development.

---

[22] The Thirteenth Amendment to the US Constitution officially abolished, and continues to prohibit, slavery to this day. The Fourteenth Amendment to the US Constitution declared that all persons born or naturalized in the United States are American citizens, including African Americans. The Fifteenth Amendment to the US Constitution prohibits each government in the United States from denying a citizen the right to vote based on that citizen's race, color, or previous condition of servitude.

The role of the judiciary in providing constitutional oversight means greater constitutional influence than other branches of government, but this explicit authority can come at the cost of scope. Even in the limited set of countries where the judiciary is granted the power to propose amendments for legislative or popular approval, though, they face the same high barriers to passage of actual constitutional changes (or changes in fundamental societal beliefs surrounding governance) as other powerful organizations. While the judiciary undoubtedly tinkers on the constitutional margins more so than other powerful organizations, any given judicial decision (and to a slightly lesser extent, any given decision of a nation's highest or constitutional court) does not carry a greater chance of creating a window of opportunity or a constitutional moment than do other functional outputs from the dominant network of society, be they the legislature, presidents, Wall Street, or populist movements. This is the distinction between the constitutional document, the desired output of the constitution (a form of constitutionalism specific to each country), and windows of opportunity/constitutional moments where fundamental beliefs surrounding governance are malleable. While the judiciary can play a primary or highly important role in such moments, their role is neither necessary nor sufficient. The same can be said for any other elite actor with the potential to create or seize a window of opportunity.

In countries such as Brazil, the constitution enacted in 1988 was lengthy and detailed from a comparative perspective.[23] Similarly, as a constitutional document, Brazil's Constitution is amended frequently.[24] This flexibility means that Brazil's critical transition in the phases since the constitutional document was enacted has not been limited to changes to the document itself – beliefs have also changed. For example, whether a society creates a credible enforcement structure that will penalize the most powerful for corruption, the constitutional document and the underlying criminal code typically prohibit such activity for all citizens. In Brazil's case, a major aspect of its modern

---

[23] While the average constitution in force worldwide has 16,000 words, the Brazilian Constitution at the time of enactment in 1988 stood at 65,000 words (Elkins, Ginsburg, and Melton, 2009).

[24] The recent constitution has been amended more than ninety times, and proposed amendments are much more numerous (Comparative Constitutions Project, 2016).

critical transition was bringing the de facto practices in society in line with the prohibitions against corruption expressed in its de jure institutions.

Despite this distinction between the law as specified and as enforced, the constitutional document of a nation is more likely to reflect the underlying set of constitutional beliefs surrounding governance than ordinary legislation resulting from most political processes. The costs of changing the constitution, either via amendment or wholesale redrafting, are significantly larger than the costs of ordinary lawmaking or executive action. Because of this link from the name of the legal document to the underlying belief set, changes to a constitutional document tend to have significantly more salience and gravity than ordinary legislation and rulemaking.

As the extent of change to the constitutional document increases, however, the likelihood that such change also reflects a constitutional moment increases. Modern nations that engage in wholesale drafting of a new constitution are at least engaged in significant change to their institutions of governance, with an accompanying adjustment to the set of powerful organizations/actors governing the country. This distinction holds whether the process by which a constitution is drafted is representative or tightly controlled by the dominant network. Comparative constitutional scholars have identified a range of functions that constitutions play in autocratic regimes, apart from the more traditional functions that constitutions have in the republics and democracies that initially developed them (Ginsburg and Simpser, 2013; Law and Versteeg, 2013).

Another way to understand changes to the written constitution reflecting a constitutional moment is to consider the widespread failure of the application of the US Constitution to emerging post-colonial systems in Latin America. Similar reasons underlie the underwhelming results of the rote application of the Washington Consensus. The US Constitution, to the extent that it got things right, did so because it reflected a period of intense renegotiation of the fundamental institutions of governance by the powerful actors across the states. This process, detailed in greater depth in Chapter 9, resulted in a document that reflected the demands of numerous powerful actors representing the interests of particular states, as well as their own beliefs surrounding the right balance of state and federal powers. To think that this specific balance, wrought over many years of coordination in the face of external powers and conflict over internal questions, would work when applied wholesale to another nation, misunderstands the nature of critical transitions and institutional deepening. The *process* resulting in a new constitutional document is more likely to determine the success of that document than the content of the document itself. This mirrors the difficulties in implementing beneficial institutions in environments that lack them; it may well be that these institutions need to emerge spontaneously from the conflict and coordination among the dominant network in a given country. As we repeatedly stressed in Parts I and II, context is paramount. When successfully coordinated by leadership, this process of conflict and coordination among the dominant network can result in a constitutional moment.

Constitutional moments entail significant institutional changes that in turn should change economic and political outcomes. To the extent they change outcomes in the expected direction, the cycle becomes virtuous, which feeds back and deepens beliefs in the dominant network and citizens at large on what to expect.[25] This in turn will generate more marginal changes in institutions, consistent with beliefs. The process of belief and institutional deepening is iterative and important to sustain a transition. Windows frequently open, or can be created, and yet many are not seized because of a failure of leadership.

Critical Transitions

We depict the process of moving to a critical transition in Figure 8.3. Windows of opportunity for a fundamental change in beliefs happen (1) reactively when outcomes fell short of expectations or (2) proactively by leaders envisioning downstream deleterious consequences to those in the dominant network. Situation 1 reflects the arrow in Figure 8.3 going from the window of opportunity to leadership, that is, leadership seizes the opportunity. Situation 2 reflects the arrow in Figure 8.3 going from leadership to the window of opportunity, that is, leadership creates the opportunity. Reacting to a situation where outcomes fall short of expectations will generally require some

---

[25] Critical transitions can lead to either better or worse economic and political outcomes.

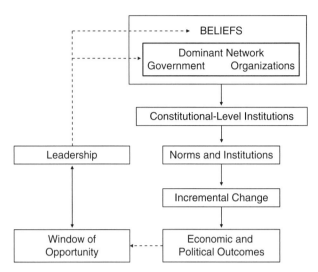

Figure 8.3 Development trajectories: Incremental change and critical transitions

coordination through leadership. There are situations where all organizations within the dominant network are like-minded with respect to how to react to outcomes far from expected. Think of 9/11 and the war on terror around the world. Western countries reacted similarly through incorporating an element of the politics of fear into their beliefs. Leadership can also be proactive to convince organizations within the dominant network to act now in order to avoid downstream consequences harmful to those in the dominant network. This may or may not be in the public interest.

A fundamental change in belief results in outcomes that we label constitutional moments. It may be a significant law, for example, Civil Rights/Voting Rights legislation in the United States in 1964 and 1965, or it could be a new constitution that codifies the changes in beliefs, for example, the Kenyan Constitution as described in Chapter 7 or US Constitution as discussed in length in Chapter 9. In Brazil in the 1990s, the leadership of President Fernando Henrique Cardoso tamed inflation through the *Plano Real*, a stabilization plan when Brazil was in the midst of a hyperinflation. We consider the *Plano Real* as a constitutional moment for Brazil. After the success of the *Plano Real*, Brazil (under the leadership of President Fernando Henrique Cardoso) then embarked on other institutional changes under the belief umbrella of fiscally sound social inclusion. The goals were lexico-graphic: first get their fiscal house in order, and then put institutions in place promoting inclusion. The constitutional moment results in new institutions whose goal is to incentivize behavior consistent with the new beliefs. Norms in society are sticky and not as amenable to public policy. As a result, institutions need to be compatible with norms or they may not be effective. For example, when the United States passed speed limits on interstate highways at 55 mph in 1974 in an effort to conserve oil, many western states simply did not enforce the law.

Belief changes do not instantaneously take root. They require an iterative process of institutional deepening. Institutions need to incentivize behavior to produce outcomes consistent with expectations. Moreover, institutional deepening requires more than a one-shot hit. Additional laws deepen the belief, provided the outcomes are consistent with expectations. For example, in the case of Brazil discussed in Chapter 9, President Cardoso's administration tightened controls on banks and established budget constraints on states, culminating in the Fiscal Responsibility Law of 2000. Following President Cardoso, President Lula da Silva further deepened beliefs in fiscally sound social inclusion, running fiscal surpluses in two terms while expanding social redistributive programs.

The entire period that makes change in a nation's fundamental beliefs and institutions surrounding governance is what we call a critical transition. Windows of opportunity open in response to significant changes in expected or actual outcomes that impact members of the dominant network. Windows of opportunity create the chance for a leader to successfully coordinate belief change in the dominant network. Through applying a blend of imagination, adaptability, and moral authority, a given leader can coordinate the costly move to a new set of beliefs, which are then formalized into institutions during a constitutional moment, and subsequently reinforced through institutional deepening on the country's new development trajectory.

A critical transition, as we define it, involves a fundamental change to beliefs surrounding governance institutions held by the dominant network. Whether this critical transition results in a positive or negative change to the country's development trajectory depends on the normative assumptions one applies to what makes development positive or negative. One such normative lens involves economic development, such that assuming economic development is desirable, a transition to an institutional set that better facilitates economic development is similarly positive. However, the explanatory value of our framework is broader, and does not rely on the application of a particular set of assumptions about what aspects of development are normatively preferable. Different countries at different time periods experienced fundamental changes to how their social institutions dealt with environmental problems, civil liberties, and positive rights, all of which enjoy considerable support in terms of their normative desirability.

In sum, when a *window of opportunity* opens, a *leader* may successfully coordinate the change to a new set of *beliefs*. These *beliefs*, expressed in the new *institutions* through a *constitutional moment*, can change the economic and political trajectory of society through a period of *institutional deepening*. This process in its entirety is a *critical transition*.

Dynamic of Institutional Deepening during a Virtuous Critical Transition

The application of leadership can result in a critical transition away from the status quo beliefs regarding the structure and purposes of government. As we have stressed, however, a critical transition need not be to a more positive state in terms of political or economic development.[26] What is clear, however, is that a virtuous critical transition needs to be in the perceived interests of a sufficient proportion of the dominant network whose support or acquiescence is needed to facilitate a transition. The potential benefits of belief and institutional change that a coordinating leader can hold out to members of the dominant network include enhanced commitment credibility, mutual self-reinforcement during the period of institutional deepening, and sustained periods of economic growth absent stagnation or decline. Furthermore, the extant institutions (and norms) can themselves determine whether a need is even present for leadership to coordinate

---

[26] In our case studies in Chapter 9, we illustrate that political development does not necessarily lead to more economic development. The belief change in Argentina following Perón did not sustain prosperity, but it did redistribute wealth.

belief change during a window of opportunity, or if the existing institutions are sufficiently resilient to weather the change through the ordinary operation of the political system. Our discussion in these subsections also displays the value of the analytical toolkit we laid out in Parts I and II, applied to questions surrounding the comparative levels of growth between nations worldwide.

A significant expected or actual departure from the status quo balance of power forces a reconsideration of fundamental beliefs surrounding governance. If a transition is successfully navigated by leadership among powerful organizations, a new constitution for a given nation often results. In cases where an entirely new constitutional document accompanies such a change in belief structures, such as the United States in 1787 or Kenya in 2010, the change in fundamental governance structures was comprehensive enough to warrant a similar change in the legal governance document that reflects the underlying belief structure. In other countries, such as Brazil in the past three decades, changes to discrete governance beliefs are more salient, such as accountability for corruption among the powerful organizations in society, as opposed to wholesale changes that would require a new constitutional document. In Brazil, it has been a matter of belief changes consistent with the constitution, as opposed to changes to the constitutional document itself.

In each case, the role for leadership is to successfully coordinate beliefs among the dominant organizations in a series of conflict/cooperation games. The constitutional document, if sufficiently likely to represent constitutional-level beliefs, serves as a focal point for constitutional changes, allowing opposing interests to gauge their expectations of each other, and defining government institutions in subsequent periods. If coordination by leadership is successful, powerful interests formerly in conflict may come to develop trust. In this case, powerful interests are more likely to adhere to the newly defined institutions throughout the period of critical transition. If it does not function well, and if mistrust remains high, the critical transition can break down. Importantly, the course-of-dealing facilitated by leadership in an initial period can increase the likelihood of successful cooperation in subsequent phases of the critical transition. Visible and costly coordination around a new set of core beliefs can serve as a form of mutual investments that bind agents in the dominant network so that agents have the incentive to mutually support one another in this period of institutional deepening.

For each side in the bargaining process, changes in core beliefs present potential benefits: the sum of these benefits is the progress to society that a window of opportunity makes possible. Nonetheless, the changes implicit to critical transitions do not exclusively present gains to coordination, and accordingly some potential changes are zero-sum, or even negative-sum, from the perspective of the players.

The question still remains, however, as to why a sufficient proportion of powerful organizations, especially organizations in conflict with one another in a given society, would agree to constrain their actions in future periods. Put differently, when do the predicted benefits from transitioning to the new order potentially trump defection at any stage? Oftentimes, the expected benefits do not exceed the gains from defecting, which is why many critical transitions flounder. Nonetheless, the connection between liberal constitutional orders and modern political and economic development shows that at least some transitions are virtuous. Further, the improvement in global economic and political measures, as well as measures of human rights in inequality, suggests that virtuous cycles may be increasing over time. This notion is supported by research treating institutional diffusion (Gilardi, 2005), and has been developed in the context of constitutional design choices in particular (Ginsburg and Versteeg, 2014).

Wallis (2018a) considers the question of why powerful interests in a given society would voluntarily bind themselves to a legal regime that constrains them more than the preceding one. This is one way to characterize the liberalization of a political system: powerful interests concede to an increased set of constraints on their behavior.[27] An answer to the paradox of why the institution of rule of law emerged in the first place lies in the problematic nature of commitments under illiberal regimes. Commitments are necessarily constrained under illiberal regimes because the extent and degree of a given individual's influence directly correlates with the unenforceability of contracts against them. Wallis terms this commitment

---

[27] North, Wallis, and Weingast (2009) describe this transition as a move from personal rule systems, in which outcomes under the law fundamentally depend upon the identity of the individual under question, to impersonal rule systems, where outcomes are significantly less dependent upon the personal identity of a given individual.

credibility defect the "paradox of privilege." This defect in commitments extends across the set of powerful groups whose identity affords them unique treatment under the rule set of a given regime. In any potential commitment where the level of power of the parties to the commitment is sufficiently different, the credibility of the more powerful party's commitment diminishes. In any regime where this dynamic has persisted, the norms of behavior and commitment that arise among powerful actors often dissipate significant rents in terms of defense of one's own interests and ensuring against defection from a given commitment. Under these types of arrangements, many transactions simply do not occur, because the credibility of the more powerful party's commitment is lacking. In the immediate phases of transition towards liberalization, these formerly rational norms of behavior can themselves prove an obstacle to the development of trust needed to ensure adherence to transition requirements by powerful interests.

The transition to a more liberal regime carries significant benefits in terms of facilitating new intradominant network commitments that were previously hindered by credibility issues. However, such a transition cannot occur overnight, and sheds light on the role of leadership. In providing a set of limited commitments to which powerful organizations must adhere, the initial phases of a critical transition can function as a signaling mechanism for later stages. This provides a way in which various opposing organizations can gauge the credibility, and hence, tenability of the first steps towards a more binding structure of impersonal commitment.

As applied to increasing the ratio of cooperative gains to conflict gains, this change in the credibility of commitments by powerful organizations is one way in which liberalization increases the size of the pie around which various organizations in society engage in the dynamic of cooperation/conflict we describe. Importantly, this is a set of gains that accrue directly to the types of groups who have the power to decide whether or not to commit to the institutional changes advocated by the leaders in a particular window of opportunity. However, these gains carry an additional benefit: by inducing parties to cooperate, as opposed to defect, the realization of a critical transition can provide a signaling function whose benefits accrue to other organizations in society, including the public as a whole.

These are the iterative mechanics of institutional deepening wherein different actors in society see the changes they anticipate from the critical transition being realized through the continued adherence of other actors, inducing their own continued commitment, and vice versa. The ways in which the rule of law facilitates commitment credibility are one example of the benefits that a critical transition to a new developmental trajectory can provide. Thus, the approach of Institutional and Organizational Analysis (IOA) provides valuable insights about the process by which institutions are iteratively reinforced. This process is closely tied to both our notions of institutional deepening and autopilot.

Potential Benefits of Critical Transitions: Institutions as Facilitating Complexity and Resilience

While the IOA can do much to explain the benefits that critical transitions hold out to members of the dominant network, these benefits are not limited to those we have discussed thus far. In this section, we examine additional contributions from scholars of the IOA to understanding what makes one institutional set preferable to another from the perspective of members of the dominant network, as well as society as a whole. We identify two beneficial effects that superior institutions can create. The first such benefits surround commitment credibility and increases in transactional magnitude and complexity;[28] these are each ways in which better institutions

---

[28] Economic systems have been characterized as complex, which is to say, they are a system composed of a large number of interacting components whose aggregate behavior is non-linear yet nonetheless subject to hierarchical sorting. Our analysis of societies stems in part from the recognition that specific pressures can result in observable regularities that are tractable to analysis. In our analysis, the specific pressures that create observable hierarchical regularities in economic and social systems are the differences in institutions, norms, and organizations from one society to another. Our framework for understanding the role of leadership in coordinating critical transitions in institutions is one example of this approach. More generally, we think institutions act as a scalar mechanism in allowing one social order to function productively at higher levels of complexity than another. Thus, while every economy is a complex system, institutions play an important role in determining the level of complexity that a given economy can sustain with its own specific underlying allocations of resources and culture, to the extent that these are determinants of productive capacity.

facilitate magnitude and complexity of transactions across societies. The second benefit surrounds resilience: a greater diversity of institutional forms, and a stock of faith in the institutions developed through iterative deepening, both lend themselves to a greater likelihood that the existing institutional set will prove sufficient to weather a shock.

The IOA is beginning to develop an underlying logic for comparatively beneficial institutions. This logic supports our argument that leaders, in order to successfully coordinate, must provide benefits in expectation to members of the dominant network that exceed the significant costs of major belief and institutional change. Nonetheless, the benefits that the IOA has identified are not exhaustive of those that a transition to a new institutional set can provide. Given the responsive or predictive nature of many applications of leadership, many benefits of institutional change are context-specific.

Importantly, the benefits of institutional deepening are not limited to those that follow a critical transition. Institutional change occurs on the margins in all societies, such that both stepwise and marginal institutional changes hold out the potential for benefits, whether or not the nation's entire developmental trajectory shifts. Put more simply, institutional changes can reduce potential transaction costs that otherwise impede actors in society from concluding beneficial transactions. These sustained institutional benefits serve as a means by which leaders coordinating belief change in the dominant network can present an institutional future that provides benefits in expectation to players who must undertake costly changes during a window of opportunity. This rationale does not diminish the role of leadership; instead, it provides a rational-interest-consistent explanation for why some institutions are "better" than others, even to members of the dominant network, and is an example of the logic underlying at least some of the coordinative moves or arguments presented by a leader in a window of opportunity.

These institutional changes begin during a constitutional moment where some organizations (and individuals within organizations) greatly benefit (Wallis, 2018a) to the extent that they take the lead in the critical transition. However, these institutional benefits continue during the period of institutional deepening and beyond, depending on the extent to which the critical transition resulted in a comparatively beneficial set of institutions. The increased set of commitments available to organizations in society under rules that treat participants anonymously and impersonally indicates one fundamental function of comparatively superior institutions: an increase in the potential number of transactions in a given economy given the same underlying set of resources. The commitments facilitated through an increase in the rule of law are now possible due to the reduction in transaction costs. This reduction operates on the *perceived* transaction costs any individual in society expects when considering a potential interaction.

This does not imply that the actual costs a given society expends to facilitate transactions and interactions is lower following a beneficial critical transition; the perceived (and likely, actual) benefits of an increased number and complexity of interactions is higher, which warrants undergoing potentially increased transaction costs in net. Under a less beneficial institutional set, many transactions are simply not occurring, so the associated transaction costs are never realized. A nation under such a comparatively inferior institutional set may expend less in total on transaction costs, but this does not mean they are better off. Put differently, more transactions are likely to occur under a comparatively superior institutional set, which necessarily implies greater transaction costs, but this increase through voluntary net beneficial exchanges means transactions that could not have occurred before because of associated costs are now possible. It is in this sense that transaction costs are minimized.

A focus on the transaction costs each institutional set creates takes us to the core of understanding economic, legal, and political development. What, if any, institutional structure writ large facilitates this development? Secure property rights and the rule of law have consistently been identified as integral to the development of modern prosperous societies (North, 1990; and many others). But the explanatory value of any one institution identified as beneficial is difficult to disentangle from the larger set of beliefs and the institutions and norms of which it is a part. Leaders are unlikely to have a precise understanding of exactly which institutional change during a constitutional moment will bring the benefits expected from the overall changes occurring during a critical transition. For example, the US Constitution changed considerably during the Constitutional Convention, yet the core belief on which it rested remained: shared federal and state power.

The wholesale contribution of an institutional set to economic development can be characterized as that of a scalar mechanism in ordering human behavior.[29] Scalar mechanisms are forces that allow social units to increase their size or magnitude. Whether firms or units of governance, these social units have been identified as constrained by ordered principles that determine the extent to which they can achieve a particular size or function. Through reducing the potential costs impeding any particular transaction, better institutions and norms (along with their enforcement) act as a scalar mechanism either by allowing or preventing an increase in the complexity, magnitude, frequency, and resilience of economic and political commitments, all of which are core inputs to sustainable development. Each individual's decisions as to how to allocate their time and resources can be characterized as decision making in the face of complexity (Ostrom, 2005: 4). The ability to productively assess and react to the diversity of individual decisions in complex modern economies is greatly influenced by the set of institutions and norms governing a particular nation. Similarly, coping with complexity has been characterized as a general problem that the institutions in a particular society can be more or less capable of resolving (Ostrom, 2005: 242, 256, 270; citing Herbert Simon). Organizations themselves can be seen as a response to the complexity of modern societies that minimize expected transaction costs as compared to available alternatives (Schenk, 2003: 2–7; Shirley, Wang, and Ménard, 2015: 229–30).

Throughout this book, we have emphasized norms and institutions and their accompanying transaction costs as significant determinants of economic and political performance. As transaction costs are better identified and specified, impediments to better economic and political performance are likewise clarified. Transaction costs prevent perfect representativeness in political institutions, which leads to the

---

[29] A variety of scholars have considered scalar institutions in a number of contexts. For a discussion of the factors that underlie the growth of cities around the world, see Bettencourt (2013). Xavier Gabaix (2016: 186–88) links the tightly defined relationship between the inverse of the population of a city and its rank within a country to a similar property underlying the size of firms in a given economy. The fact that the growth of cities and firms around the world is governed by "power laws" suggests that specific institutions are at play in ordering the behavior of economic actors as they scale into units defined either by geography or production. Aoki et al. (2012) also use the framework of facilitating decision making under complexity to explain institutions' contribution to economic development.

emergence of special interests. Transaction costs prevent universal use of individual contracting on the market, which leads to the emergence of firms. Transaction costs prevent a single central planner from optimally allocating capital and labor to maximize social welfare, which leads to the roles of federalism and decentralization in structuring government (Hirschman, 1970) as well as the relevance of local information to efficient economic and political decision making (Hayek, 1945). Each of these well-developed literatures indicates that an institutional set that better reduces transaction costs can sustain commitments and transactions of greater scale and complexity given the same set of resources. This is the very definition of a scalar mechanism facilitating a greater ability for a given system to sustain an increased level of complexity.

Central to this discussion has been a consideration of how a better institutional set facilitates a greater number of transactions given the same underlying set of resources. However, much of the research that has considered the emergence of institutions has instead focused on how institutions changed to better accommodate increases in the set of available resources. Put another way: specialization is limited by the extent of the market, but the extent of the market is limited by transaction costs. Scholars have long considered the development of property rights along frontiers as crucial to extracting the gains from trade (Alston, Harris, and Mueller, 2012; Anderson and Hill, 2004; Ellickson, 1991; Libecap, 1989; inter alia). Norms first emerged to govern transactions and disputes, followed by written codes, and finally norms codified into law.[30] The legal transition in property rules in frontier contexts fits a larger pattern associated with the development of law. As a given social group becomes larger and increasingly heterogeneous, the likelihood increases that the existing set of norms governing the group will require codification in order to prevent costly disputes as to the rules themselves (Hart, 2012: 89–90). These disputes create a deadweight loss as compared to circumstances where the rules have broad consensus. Law avoids the issue of consensus associated with norms.

---

[30] Of course, there are exceptions, and even though there may have been laws, the actors preferred their own norms. This can continue for a long time, provided the government opts out of enforcing their specified laws (e.g., see Ellickson, 1991; Ostrom, 1990).

Institutions frequently change in response to unanticipated demographic, technological, or market forces (e.g., inflows of immigration, inventions, discovery of new lands or resources, or invasions by a foreign power). In each case, the underlying set of resources changes, either in terms of the availability of labor for resource production or refinement, or the availability of resources given the underlying technological set. The extent to which institutional change in response to these unanticipated factors is positive can be a function of the extent to which leadership successfully coordinates this change.

The desire to reap the gains from trade fostered the development of institutions at a larger scale than the existing institutional solution could sustain.[31] As social groups change in size and purpose, the optimality of the set of institutions governing their behavior similarly changes. Oftentimes, the change in size, power, or purpose of a specific social group creates a window of opportunity to transition to a superior institutional set. In other cases, resilience in the face of unanticipated changes ensures continued economic and political performance.[32]

Absent secure title and contract enforcement that law can provide, an economy could not sustain the increasingly complex set of financial mechanisms that allow capital and resource reallocation with comparatively less friction. This iterative institutional development emphasizes another benefit of superior institutional sets: resilience to shocks. Credible commitment among organizations enhances resilience by facilitating the ability of the dominant network to coordinate in the face of unanticipated events. Resilience enables more developed societies to limit the economic stagnation or decline that prevents developing nations from achieving the sustainable economic and

---

[31]   One clear example comes from behavioral theory. Dunbar's number has been identified by behavioral theorists as the maximum number of people with whom a given individual can maintain stable social relationships based on personal identity (Dunbar, 1993: 724–25). Dunbar's research focused on the emergence of language to facilitate interactions beyond a single tightly knit social group where non-verbal communication was sufficient to govern potential interactions. Past such a point, other mechanisms become necessary to order conduct; in addition to language, customs and norms come into use. Hadfield (2016: 70) identifies human language and culture as generating "a quantum leap in the ability to adapt to changing novel environments."

[32]   This notion of institutional resilience draws upon Broadberry and Wallis (2016) and what they term "shrink theory."

political development that prosperous societies enjoy. What in one nation triggers a costly and uncertain window of opportunity (that may or may not be successfully coordinated by leadership into a critical transition) is in another merely a set of changes to be dealt with through the ordinary operation of the political system.

Institutional solutions to more specific resource allocation problems have also been characterized by their resilience in the face of complexity and uncertainty.[33] In an analysis of numerous field studies of resource allocation rules around the world, rule sets were characterized into broad groups such that the number of groups of rules and rules discovered in practice suggests a number of permutations of specific rules to govern resource allocations that is "potentially infinite" (Ostrom, 2005: 239). While Ostrom uses this sheer diversity of potential rules as evidence of the weakness of centrally planned solutions to resource allocation problems, it has a corollary implication: the need for local governance to resolve the complexity of resource allocation problems emphasizes the need for institutions to be able to adapt to the variety of local conditions, conditions that are themselves not static.

A component of resilience is the extent to which individuals can change institutions to better suit changing conditions. These emergent properties of institutions occur on the macroscale as well; law in the United States from 1800 to 2000 became increasingly specialized and standardized to match the increasingly complex nature of transactions occurring in the US economy (Hadfield, 2016: 121–22). In some instances, the benefits of institutions come from a reduction in complexity.[34] In others, institutions merely circumvent complexity, without reducing the level of complexity within which individuals and organizations interact (Schenk, 2003: 56–59).

---

[33] While a subset of potential outcomes facing any given society are known possibilities to members of the dominant network with the power to change institutions, not all outcomes can be characterized in this way. Thus, from the perspective of the set of outcomes as a whole that face any given society over time, this uncertainty is best thought of in Knightian terms, in which the scope and magnitude of potential outcomes is unknown.

[34] The dominance of fee simple over other types of interest in real property is an example of how institutions can evolve to reduce complexity that otherwise creates greater transaction costs. Hadfield (2016: 188–94) also argues that our current legal system has become too complex: too many rules that are too intricate are impeding the functionality of the legal system as a whole.

Sustainable development is one outcome of resilience that results from comparatively superior institutions. The nature of unanticipated events from drastic changes in commodity prices to the emergence of disruptive technology, or major demographic change, is that the status quo is unprepared for the shock.[35] Generally, the diversity of norms and institutions that developed societies display increases the likelihood that any one institution (or subset of institutions) will be sufficient to adapt to the unanticipated shock without provoking economic stagnation or decline.[36] If a "superior" set of institutions better facilitates the scale and complexity of transactions in a given society, these institutions themselves change and specialize to better accommodate this increased complexity.[37]

The notion of reduced transaction costs facing a particular individual has a more general extension in terms of resilience. Any shock, such as the aforementioned increases in scale and complexity, creates the need for individuals to decide whether or not to alter their behavior in light of the changed circumstances. The need for such a change is costly compared to the prior period when a given individual's affairs were arranged according to the existing resource allocation and transaction costs facing them. Institutions and norms that reduce these potential transaction costs facilitate resilience by increasing the likelihood a given individual will be able to reoptimize their decisions in light of the new shock. The more individuals across society who can update their behavior optimally to a new shock, the more optimally society as a whole can adapt to the shock.

---

[35]   Ostrom (2005: 272) identifies demographic changes in particular, and "rapid exogenous changes" more generally, as being shocks that can cause an existing set of resource governance institutions to become untenable.

[36]   Ostrom (2005: 8) uses the example of maps needed to locate her and her husband's vacation home in Ontario to emphasize the advantages a diversity of institutional forms can provide. A highly detailed map is necessary in order to drive to the home, which was located in a remote area. A larger, less detailed map, was more useful when describing to someone unfamiliar with Ontario where the home was located, but was less useful for actually reaching the home. A map that only showed major bodies of water across the North American continent was relatively useless for locating the vacation home, and would only be illustrative for someone with no geographic familiarity of the continent whatsoever. This simplified example emphasizes the value a diversity of institutional forms can have in terms of suiting the complexity of uses individual participants in society will have for them.

[37]   The institutions are superior to the extent that they avoid disruptive booms and busts.

Another way to frame the importance of resilience is in superior performance in the face of uncertainty. The specific realization of a shock is by definition unanticipated, and the current potential for future shocks is one way to view uncertainty. The confidence that existing institutions will prove sufficiently resilient to handle future shocks provides important benefits to individuals and organizations ordering their current decisions under these institutions. To expect otherwise requires costly precautions in the event shocks are likely to disrupt the entire institutional set, and in many cases, may prevent transactions and resource reallocations from occurring in the first place.

Institutions that reduce potential transaction costs provide the opportunity for a given society to engage in an increasingly complex set of interactions and transactions, allowing for a more optimal allocation of the same underlying resource set. The emergence of commitments to capital and labor allocations using increasingly specialized means highlights the mechanics of beneficial political and economic progress. This same process, especially when strengthened through institutional deepening following a critical transition, creates a robust institutional set that is more likely to be resilient in the face of the types of shocks that confront societies.[38] When the right leadership is applied to a window of opportunity, these benefits of scale and resilience are among the potential benefits to cooperation that a given leader offers to organizations in the dominant network, with potential spillovers to society more broadly.

The discussion has been about reacting to unexpected events, but in many cases more resilient societies look downstream and act preemptively to avoid the shock. This may be more important than reacting. As noted earlier, leadership can coordinate beliefs to avoid a crisis, thereby sustaining a developmental trajectory. Leadership may also be instrumental in rising to a developmental trajectory in the face of rapid technological change, which will necessitate new beliefs and institutions. The greater the benefits that the current institutional set provides

---

[38] Ostrom (2005: 30) noted that "the diversity of institutions and their resilience . . . require major attention." Hadfield (2016: 144) echoes the sentiment for a need for institutions (and institutional scholars) to better grapple with the complexity that the increasingly global digital age has introduced into societal transactions: "with yet another massive leap in the complexity of the economy, our legal infrastructure has yet to catch up."

to members of the dominant network, the greater the incentives are for incremental change that reinforces these institutions. These greater benefits under status quo institutions also facilitate resilience, that is, coordination in the face of unexpected change that would greatly impact societies governed by less beneficial institutional sets. In some cases, leadership is required to preempt the changes wrought by an unanticipated event, but in others, the comparative resilience of a given society's institutions provides all the incentives needed to coordinate the allocation of resources in light of unanticipated events.

Conclusion

We began with the observation that over the past 50 to 100 years, very few countries changed their development trajectories. Overall, most countries have grown, but there has not been convergence. Most countries remain as lower-, middle-, or upper-income countries. But some countries have risen and fallen from their historical trajectories. We presented a framework for understanding both the prevalence of persistence on the same trajectory as well as the factors necessary to move to a new trajectory. The concepts within the framework of a critical transition are: actual or expected outcomes, windows of opportunity, leadership, beliefs, power (dominant network), constitutional moments, and norms and institutions. Institutional change is embedded in beliefs held by the dominant network. Within the dominant network, beliefs are held on how institutions will affect expected economic and political outcomes. The dominant network is constrained in their choice set by other organizations inside and outside of the dominant network as well as by the judiciary in some countries. Most of the time, institutions produce outcomes that are more or less in line with expected outcomes. As a result, the institutional changes on the margin will deepen the extant belief in place.

At other times, however, the existing set of institutions creates a set of expectations that diverges sufficiently from outcomes. This is a window of opportunity where changes in rent streams, as a result of variance in economic or political outcomes, create the possibility for the expected benefits of major institutional change to exceed the costs. In such a window of opportunity, the core beliefs of the dominant network are malleable. Those in power begin to question their beliefs, and there is a sense that "something needs to be done" to address the

expected or actual divergence in outcomes from those originally anticipated. This is a window of opportunity during which organizations,
who likely hold different beliefs, jockey to champion their view of the
world. Leadership in these situations matters. Leadership entails coordinating others in the dominant network to adopt or go along with
a new belief on how new institutions can remedy the change in
the rental streams from the unanticipated outcome. If the new belief
produces outcomes consistent with those expected, it will deepen the
belief among more organizations in the dominant network with the
result that there will be more institutional change on the margin.
Iterative belief and institutional deepening can cause a critical transition to a new belief and, if significant institutional changes transpire,
countries may move significantly away from their status quo developmental trajectory.

In many instances, leaders foresee downstream events as a storm
approaching that can be avoided if the dominant network adopts
new beliefs and institutions to act preemptively. Leadership is especially critical in these situations because being proactive is more
difficult because of the heavy hand of the status quo. Those in
power enjoy the current rental streams, and downstream storms
are only imprecisely predicted. Depending upon the resilience of
institutions in a particular society, downstream events that create
a window of opportunity in one nation – due to these events'
expected impact on the rent streams of the dominant network –
may be nothing more than a bump in the road to which the ordinary
course of operation of the political system in another country
adjusts. Consider the role of natural disasters in countries' development trajectories depending on the strength of institutions within
that nation; Puerto Rico is still reeling from the effects of a hurricane
in 2017, while Houston and much of Florida – who also got
pounded by hurricanes in 2017 – rebounded quickly. While this
resilience is in great part the result of the comparative levels of
prosperity between states within the United States and the more
autonomous territory of Puerto Rico, our point is more specific:
what came as a great shock in terms of the deaths and destruction
to property triggered chaos in Puerto Rico, but not in Houston or
Florida. While each was a human tragedy in its own right, for Puerto
Rico it will take years to recover whereas in Florida and Houston,
the effects were not devastating.

In the next chapter, we discuss four illustrative cases of critical transitions where leadership played a role, both reacting to events as well as proactively changing beliefs. The cases emphasize the explanatory value of our framework, and they are not limited to transitions deemed positive by traditional definitions of economic and political development. Nonetheless, our framework has applicability for transitions that have resulted in increases in welfare associated with modern development. The dynamics of virtuous institutional deepening surrounding the emergence of the rule of the law, discussed earlier in the chapter, display generalizable benefits surrounding the ability of a given economy and government to sustain transactions of increasing complexity and magnitude given the same underlying resource allocation. The benefits result in greater resilience to exogenous shocks based upon the diversity of organizations and institutions, and the decreased costs of adjusting behavior to suit new circumstances created by a given shock. With development, societies must solve the paradox of time (a "catch-22"): longer periods of belief and institutional deepening beget more development and resilience in part due to increased confidence in institutions by the organizations in society.

9 | Case Studies of Critical Transitions
Argentina, Brazil, Ecuador, and the United States

In this chapter, we apply the framework from Chapter 8 in an illustrative fashion to four critical transitions. All transitions are contextual with their own nuances. But transitions have common features: window of opportunity, leadership, change in beliefs, and a new dominant network followed by new institutions. Our examples also display how a critical transition should not be assumed to be inherently positive or negative; such a characterization depends upon one viewing economic or political development as normatively preferable as compared to other outcomes. Furthermore, the transition to a new set of core beliefs might be highly detrimental to a nation's trajectory, given these same traditional notions of economic and political development. From the founding of the United States, to Argentina's notable decline during the twentieth century, to two recent examples of Latin American development, our examples of critical transitions display the explanatory value of the framework applied to specific national contexts.

United States, 1783–1789: Transitioning from "States Rule" to the United States of America

The rebellious colonies fought a war for independence from Great Britain from 1776 to 1783. Prior to the French and Indian War, Britain allowed the colonies considerable autonomy. They could pass any law that was not repugnant to the Crown (Hughes, 1976). Following the end of the French and Indian War in 1763, policies towards the North American colonies changed. The French and Indian War was costly, and Britain decided to increase the tax burden on the colonies, which previously had been negligible.

Some of the colonists, particularly those in New England, felt that rule from afar was arbitrary and no longer tolerable. This was the initial rationale for the Revolutionary War. Taxation without representation was one of the issues, but not the sole complaint. Calls for action increased. Initially, the calls for action by the colonists were not centrally organized within or across colonies. The overall climate changed following the British retaliatory actions against the colony of Massachusetts after the Boston Tea Party. The colonists termed Britain's policies the Intolerable Acts. Britain shut the Port of Boston, closed the Massachusetts legislature, mandated that British offences be tried in Britain – not in the colonies – and stated that British troops could be quartered in homes. These actions fed a belief by some that Britain was taking away the liberties of the colonies (Rakove, Ruttan, and Weingast, 2004). The fear spread: if it could happen in Massachusetts, it could happen in Pennsylvania or Virginia. The dominant network consisted of the colonies and special interests within the colonies, most importantly merchants and others in the upper class. Members of the network identified with colonies not as a unified body. However, as the belief spread that the perceived arbitrary actions of Britain could hit any colony, there was an incentive to act collectively. Increasingly, more players in the dominant network felt that British rule was intolerable. Twelve of the thirteen colonies sent delegates to a convention in Philadelphia in fall of 1774 to discuss a response to Parliament, and it became known as the First Continental Congress.

The colonists agreed that the Intolerable Acts warranted a response. The beliefs over what to do varied. The Conservatives carried the day, and Congress agreed to petition the Crown for a repeal of the Intolerable Acts. To put some teeth into their request, Congress called for a boycott of British goods beginning in December of 1774. The appeal to the Crown was not successful, and hostilities between the British and colonists broke out on April 19, 1775, in the "shot heard round the world." War of some sort now seemed inevitable. The Second Continental Congress convened in May 1775 and managed the war effort. Congress appointed George Washington as general of the war. Despite a seemingly centralized, organized effort, early on the fighting was mostly local, entailing state militias as the combatants. The state of affairs reached a tipping point and Congress voted for independence from Britain on July 2, 1776.

The United States became "united" to defeat the British. In November 1777, Congress passed the Articles of Confederation with each state having one vote. But, importantly, it took until 1781 for all states to ratify, some fearing too much centralization. Large states and small states would be on equal footing, signifying the importance that the sovereign unit of governance was at the state level. The war demanded collective coordination, but the prevailing belief was that each state was autonomous and participated when they saw it in their interest. States united to defeat the British, but the Articles of Confederation left them without the central power to tax to fund the war. Washington repeatedly asked for more funding from Congress, but there was the free-rider problem in that states not directly involved in hostilities did not see much need to pay for the war. In part because of a lack of funding, Washington fought a large part of the war by avoiding the better-funded British army.

Hostilities ended in 1781, but it took until 1783 to sign the Treaty of Paris, which was the official settlement of the war. Following the conclusion of the war, many states found that the loose cooperation under the Articles of Confederation suited their needs. States as colonies had been autonomous governing bodies as colonies, and the belief was that this should continue. States did realize that they needed some form of cooperation in the case of attack by a foreign nation, but they won the war and many felt that the Articles of Confederation were sufficient to organize their collective interests. A stronger alliance was not deemed necessary by most states and the heterogeneity across states made cooperation difficult. The Continental Congress continued to meet, and some early Federalists clearly saw the weaknesses of the Confederation and started talking and writing that the states needed a stronger union. Weaknesses included: the unanimity rule to change provisions in the Articles; a lack of consensus on how to pay the debt from the war; an inability to credibly engage in foreign affairs; and a fear that the new nation could not defend its borders from threats in the future. George Washington and Alexander Hamilton were the earliest proponents of a stronger union, with Hamilton being the most outspoken. Washington and Hamilton early on worked on creating a window of opportunity.

The weaknesses of the Articles of Confederation provided the window of opportunity for leadership to change a belief in a loose confederation of states to a federal United States. Increasingly so, beliefs that some reform was necessary became more apparent, especially among members of the Continental Congress. Within states, governors and their allies remained more pro states' rights because they naturally saw sharing power as diminishing the power of states. The window of opportunity for change was forward-looking and centered on both the downstream weaknesses as well as the advantages from a United States. Alexander Hamilton, more than any of the Founding Fathers, created the window of opportunity. In January 1786, Congress agreed to hold a convention in Annapolis in September to discuss the rules regulating interstate trade. It was not meant to entail sweeping changes, but the hope of some was that it could limit tariffs across state lines. Madison, who supported it, saw it as an incremental experiment, which if successful could lead to other reforms. The convention itself was a failure because only five states sent delegates, so no reform was possible. At the conclusion of the convention, Hamilton – displaying amazing imagination – rose and announced that there was unanimous agreement that states should send delegates to a Constitutional Convention in Philadelphia on the second Sunday in May 1787 to address all the weaknesses of the Confederation.

This was Hamilton's out-front brand of leadership in its most flamboyant form. A convention called to address the modest matter of commercial reform had just failed to attract even a quorum, and now Hamilton was using this grim occasion to announce the date for another convention that would tackle all the problems affecting the confederation at once. It was as if a prizefighter, having just been knocked out by a journeyman boxer, declared his intention to challenge the heavyweight champion of the world. Given the overwhelming indifference that had suffocated all previous attempts at comprehensive reform of the Articles, no one with any semblance of sanity could possibly believe that Hamilton's proposal enjoyed even the slightest chance of success. (Ellis, 2015: 100)

Surprisingly, Congress in late 1786 agreed that states should send delegates to Philadelphia to discuss reforms. Now the most pressing issue – as seen by Hamilton, Jay, Madison, and others – was to convince George Washington to attend.[1] Washington was comfortably retired at Mount Vernon and believed that things had to get even worse before they could get better. Washington was beseeched that without his presence, the Constitution would fail, but with his presence it stood a chance of succeeding. The rationale for the importance of

---

[1] Henry Knox, a confidante of Washington, at first counseled Washington not to attend, but changed his mind when Madison convinced Knox that all states would send delegates. Knox subsequently lobbied Washington by arguing that success in Philadelphia would assure Washington the epithet of "Father of our Country" (Ellis, 2015: 112).

Washington was his moral authority. Having suffered so greatly during the war, no one distrusted the motives of George Washington in wanting to make the nation strong. To the resounding approval of the Federalists, Washington agreed to be a Virginia delegate.

The next step was to set the agenda at the convention. Normally, debate ensues over the status quo. Madison strategized with others to change the agenda. Madison, along with others, conceived of the Virginia Plan, which was a major departure from the Articles of Confederation and called for three branches of government and equal representation by population in the House and the Senate. The details are not important, but it was crucial that this plan became the focal point around which debate ensued. Madison not only convinced his fellow Virginians to support the Virginia Plan, but he convinced other key players, notably Gouverneur Morris of Pennsylvania. On May 30, a majority of the delegates approved a proposal by Morris calling for a national government along the lines of the Virginia Plan. A new focal point was set, thanks to the coordinative skills of Madison, who did his homework prior to the convention, unlike most of the delegates. The new focal point of the Virginia Plan was endorsed prior to most of the New England delegates arriving, though several were already strong Federalists. The second order of business for the Federalists was to install Washington as the chair of the convention. The vote was unanimous. Though Washington said little at the convention, his presence and silent endorsement of the views of the Federalists had a huge impact on the delegates and the overall tone of the convention.

Though there was much tinkering on the margin with the Virginia Plan, especially that each state received two senators, the essence of a tripartite system with strong checks and balances emerged from the convention.[2] With the Constitution having been drafted in Philadelphia, it now needed to be ratified by two-thirds of the states, that is, nine states. Almost immediately, Hamilton, Jay, and Madison went to work to sway public opinion with the Federalist Papers, exhibiting clear entrepreneurship, an attribute of leadership.

---

[2] For an excellent quantitative analysis of voting at the convention, see McGuire (2003).

Of most concern to the proponents was the fate of New York, which seemed reluctant to sign on. For this reason, Hamilton, Jay, and Madison published eighty-five essays in New York newspapers. A majority of the Federalist Papers discussed issues of national defense. Having just fought a war that the United States barely won, the issue of collective defense resonated in the minds of a large segment of the population. The essays also sought to justify the proper alignment of shared power, with the majority of decision making residing in states. Only those decisions transcending boundaries should be the province of the national government, for example, the ability to tax to maintain a standing army, the right to negotiate international treaties, and the right to regulate interstate commerce.[3] The vote by states was a simple yes or no, though many states suggested amendments to the Constitution. The numerous suggested amendments to the Constitution largely concerned issues of personal freedoms, which the leaders already presumed citizens had through their state constitutions. Nonetheless, to assuage states and solidify a belief in nationhood, Jay convinced Madison of the need for a Bill of Rights. Madison once again exhibited leadership through agenda control by writing a draft of the Bill of Rights as amendments to the Constitution and submitting it to Congress. Though not accepted in its entirety, it set the focal point for bargaining.

The passage of the Constitution and Bill of Rights represented a constitutional moment in codifying the new belief in the United States with a sharing of power between states and the central government. The new nascent belief was federalism. It established a credible commitment for the dominant network of states to be able to tax themselves when necessary, negotiate international treaties, and defend themselves against foreign powers. The Constitution was seen at home and abroad as a commitment mechanism for ensuring credibility as a nation and demonstrating the ability to raise money for national defense. Was there a complete critical transition to a belief in nationhood? No, there will always be a tension between states' rights and central power. Belief deepening requires institutional deepening, and

---

[3] Though no one can definitively quantify the impact on voters, the essays remain an incredible repository of the thoughts of three of the leaders of the rationale for federalism.

there were clearly some short-run institutional changes that deepened beliefs. Between 1790 and 1794, largely under the leadership of Hamilton with staunch support from Washington, the United States: funded the National Debt, an issue of contestation under the Articles of Confederation; established a National Bank; and put down the Whiskey Rebellion, demonstrating the power of the federal government over taxation. Equally important, the federal government did not interfere in the designated rights of states.

Over time, there was more institutional deepening, further solidifying the belief in the United States as the sovereign entity over the states in various domains. On the judicial side, the John Marshall Court in *Marbury* v. *Madison* established judicial review of the legislation of states as being under the umbrella of the Supreme Court, though this took time to solidify.[4] The United States expanded its territory tremendously under the Louisiana Purchase in 1803. With so much more territory to govern and defend, defense was a concern hearkening back to one of the key issues uniting the country as the United States. This was followed by the War of 1812 with Britain, which demonstrated the role for National Defense. Though slavery remained an area of disagreement across the states, the states agreed to take slavery off the legislative agenda through the balance rule, whereby free and slave states were admitted to the union in pairs (Weingast, 1998). As long as the total number of slave and free states were equal, the Senate could veto any move to restrict slavery. As a result, the tariff was the most contentious issue in the antebellum years. The balance rule held for quite a while until slavery split the nation apart. But even here, Lincoln asserted that it was a matter of nationhood, not slavery per se, that drove his actions.

If there be those who would not save the Union, unless they could at the same time *save* slavery, I do not agree with them. If there be those who would not save the Union unless they could at the same time *destroy* slavery, I do not agree with them. My paramount object in this struggle *is* to save the Union, and is *not* either to save or to destroy slavery. If I could save the Union without freeing *any* slave I would do it, and if I could save it by freeing *all* the slaves I would do it; and if I could save it by freeing some and leaving others alone I would also do that. What I do about slavery, and the colored race, I do because I believe it helps to save the Union; and what I forbear, I forbear

---

[4] See Chapter 7 for a discussion of *Marbury* v. *Madison*.

because I do *not* believe it would help to save the Union. (Letter to Horace Greeley, August 22, 1862; emphasis in original)

The existing institutions in the United States at the time of independence did not themselves create a crisis. Nonetheless, a variety of concerns emerged surrounding the resilience of the Articles of Confederation in the face of likely future events, such as the need to pay the war debt and defend against foreign aggressors. In addition to their perceived inability to adapt to uncertain future outcomes, the Articles of Confederation also suffered from general problems in institutional design, such as the holdout problem that the unanimity rule created. Hamilton, Jay, Madison, and Washington anticipated the negative consequences the defects of the Articles of Confederation would create. Through a variety of adaptive and imaginative political maneuvers, Hamilton, Jay, and Madison created a window of opportunity to coordinate fundamental belief change upon a large part of the dominant network. Their leadership coordinated the movement to the belief in a stronger federal system with the *United States* as the sovereign unit. This belief was formalized in perhaps the most famous constitutional moment in history. The United States Constitution was necessary but not sufficient to ensure continued economic and political development, and considerable belief and institutional deepening ensued.

Argentina, 1912–1955: Budding Belief in Checks and Balances to Redistributive Populism

From the late nineteenth until the mid-twentieth century, Argentina was generally in the top richest GDP per capita countries in the world, but in 2015, its GDP per capita ranked 53rd, having steadily lost ground to the highest-income countries.[5] In the narrative that follows, we propose that its fall from an upper-income country to a middle-income country was due to a shift from a budding belief in the dominant network in checks and balances to a belief in redistributive populism. In 1912, Argentina passed the Sáenz Peña law. Prior to the Sáenz Peña law, the dominant network consisted of an oligarchic conservative elite in the Pampas, the richest part of the country, and

---

[5] This section draws heavily from Alston and Gallo (2010) and Alston et al. (2016) and sources cited therein. We thank Gustavo Torrens for extensive comments.

the dominant exporters. Named after the conservative president who spearheaded the initiative, the Sáenz Peña law established the secret ballot as well as stricter monitoring for fraud, the naturalization of immigrants, and citizenship to the children of immigrants. This was a constitutional moment because it had the potential to put Argentina on a new political trajectory of checks and balances. By changing the rules governing citizenship, the Sáenz Peña law dramatically changed the electorate. It is ironic that a completely conservative-run tight dominant network would pass such a law. Its motivation is unclear, though in part it was spurred by labor and citizen unrest over the lack of voice of many people in politics. We speculate that it was also motivated by Argentina's desire to demonstrate to the other rich countries that Argentina had advanced sufficiently to establish a more open electoral system. Argentina considered itself culturally, socially, and economically ahead of the rest of South America, and on a par with Europe and the United States. It was now time to catch up politically.

The first year that the Sáenz Peña law affected a national presidential election was 1916. The belief of the dominant network mirrored that of the developed countries: a system of checks and balances coupled with export-driven growth. Hipólito Yrigoyen from the Radical Party won the presidency, and the Radicals also won a majority in the Deputies chamber. The Radicals derived the majority of support among the urban middle class. The Conservatives held onto the Senate. Divided governance remained in force over the next sixteen years. The dominant network widened to include not just the military and the conservative landowners from the Pampas and their elite urban allies, but many rural and urban workers.[6] The dominant network established institutions under the umbrella of a budding belief in checks and balances, including a role for the judiciary, and maintenance of export-driven growth. With divided government, the legislature became more competitive and they proposed legislation favoring urban and rural workers. The Chamber of Deputies proposed laws to control rural rents as well as other pro-labor legislation. Not all the

---

[6] The majority of rural workers did not vote, but nonetheless the Radical Party represented their interests through attempts at reforms of tenancy law.
The military always sided with the Conservatives and did not change their belief, but the dominant network played (for the most part) by the new rules of the Sáenz Peña law.

legislation passed, but the number of votes that went for a roll call over a voice vote increased considerably. The political system worked better for most workers. There were still labor protest movements, sometimes brutally put down by the military, but there was considerably more political voice compared to previously. The lower classes still did not vote in large numbers, but some of the legislation proposed during this period related to tenants in the rural sector by the Radical Party. This gave the rural lower-to-middle classes in the countryside some limited voice. By proposing favorable legislation for tenants, the Radical party hoped to woo the rural workers into being more active in the Radical Party. On the economic side, export-led growth continued to deliver benefits for all of the classes, though income inequality remained high. GDP per capita growth from World War I through the 1920s exceeded 4 percent, one of the highest in the world. The political and economic systems were still relatively closed, and some fraud at the ballot boxes remained, but the period following the constitutional moment of the Sáenz Peña law represents a relatively sharp break from the past. A critical transition was in its infancy, and beliefs and institutions needed to deepen.

Unfortunately, before the system could mature, the Great Depression rocked the world economy. Argentina relied on its exports of agricultural commodities, and the prices of commodities tanked in 1930. From December 1929 to December 1930, the price of wheat was halved and the price of beef fell by almost as much (US Department of Agriculture, 1936: 21, 216). Congress acted from both sides of the aisle with legislation to "do something," but the legislation never received the approval of the aging President Yrigoyen.[7] At the behest of the Conservatives and as countenanced by the Radicals, the military acted to remove Yrigoyen. It was a bloodless coup, though not done according to the rules. Argentina could have initiated impeachment proceedings, though the Conservatives felt that they could not wait. The decline in prices was too great and misery was mounting along with unemployment.

The Supreme Court should have protested the abandonment of the rule of law, but most called it a "triumphant revolution," though one justice resigned in protest (Alston and Gallo, 2010: 182). The military

---

[7] We could not find any definitive account of the reasons behind the inaction of Yrigoyen. Most accounts simply cite his age and decline in cognitive functioning.

sided with the Conservatives and put them in power. The plan of the military was to move quickly back to elections and the former system of checks and balances. The military presumed that the public would recognize that policies to combat the Great Depression needed the Conservatives in power. They misread public opinion. In the first free election in April 1931 in the province of Buenos Aires, the Radicals won the election. Surprised, the military annulled the results.

The Military/Conservatives learned their lesson. In the National Election of 1932, the military forbade any Radical politicians who had been in office during Yrigoyen's last term. This represents a further departure from a belief in checks and balances. The Conservatives were willing to share some power with the Radicals, but not during an economic emergency. The military had never believed in checks and balances. In protest, no Radical Party members ran for office. Naturally, the Conservatives came back to power. The dominant network now consisted of the Conservatives, the military, agricultural producers – particularly in the Pampas – and other exporters. The dominant network justified their actions by arguing that the Great Depression required emergency measures and that the economy could not be in the hands of the Radicals. Ironically, economic historians have given Argentina high grades for managing the economy during the Great Depression (Della Paolera and Taylor, 1998, 1999, 2001). The Conservatives resorted to fraud throughout the 1930s to stay in control and proudly labeled it "Patriotic Fraud" (Alston and Gallo, 2010).

The urban middle classes lost faith that checks and balances could ever return.[8] Ten years is a long departure from a political voice. We will never know the counterfactual, but Argentina may have managed the economy well, albeit at huge social cost.

The conservative regimes of the 1930s, in spite of their flirtations with fascist reformism, brought to a halt the modest momentum for political and social reform started by the Radical governments. Their failure to buttress the relative healthy economic structure with social and political arrangements

---

[8] The urban middle class represented the interests of rural tenants, yet the vote by rural tenants was very low because of their economic dependency on their landlords. The Radical Party attempted to encourage the rural workers to join and vote for the Radical Party, but their hope never materialized.

allowing for growing security and political participation for rural and urban masses contributed to the creation of revolutionary possibilities. (Diaz Alejandro, 1970: 107–108)

In short, the Conservatives appeared to have won the battle by fraud, but lost the war by abandoning the rule of law.

Finally, in 1940, the electorate saw a ray of hope. President Roberto Ortiz promised a return to fair elections in 1942, which would have expanded the dominant network to re-include the Radical Party and had the potential to return to the path departed in 1929. Regrettably, we will never know if he could have implemented an honest election. Ortiz died in office on June 27, 1942. His successor, President Ramón Castillo, did not live up to the promise of Ortiz. Fraud again riddled the elections of 1942. Fraud reached a tipping point, which a nationalistic faction of the military resented. The military staged a coup in 1943, vowing to return to elections shortly. The power went to their heads and they waited until 1946 to announce an election with Juan Perón as their candidate. Perón campaigned on a populist platform, especially reaching out to labor. The election was clean and Perón won with 52 percent of the vote. Perón appealed to those who lost their political voice in the 1930s.[9]

Throughout the 1930s, fraud, coupled with military rule from 1943, opened a window of opportunity. After the election, Perón seized the window of opportunity. He did this skillfully as a leader. Perón created a new dominant network through coordinating a move to a belief in redistributive populism. The new dominant network consisted of urban and rural workers as well as the governors in outlying provinces. The dominant network no longer included the interests in the Pampas. Perón created the new dominant network and shaped belief on redistributive populism through subsidies to labor, both rural and urban, and by drawing in rural governors from outlying provinces with transfers. He accomplished this through extracting rents from agricultural landowners in the Pampas. In order to extract rents, Perón relied on price controls on wheat, which may have been ruled unconstitutional.

---

[9] In a counterfactual regression analysis, Alston and Gallo (2010) found that if fraud had not occurred, Perón would not have won the election. Perón's vote was greatest in those areas where fraud prevailed. The experience in the province of Cordoba also supports this view. Cordoba did not engage in fraud in the 1930s and the Radicals stayed in power. In the election of 1946, only a minority voted for Perón in Cordoba.

Perón saw the court as an obstacle to populist policies and believed that he had the answer: impeach the court on the grounds of their countenance of fraud in the 1930s.

> In my opinion, I put the spirit of justice above the Judicial Power, as this is the principal requirement for the future of the Nation. But I understand that justice, besides being independent has to be effective, and it cannot be effective if its ideas and concepts are not with the public sentiment. Many praise the conservative sentiment of the Justices, believing that they defend traditional beliefs. I consider that a dangerous mistake, because it can put justice in opposition to the popular feeling, and because in the long run it produces a rusty organism. Justice, in its doctrines, has to be dynamic instead of static. Otherwise respectable popular yearnings are frustrated and the social development is delayed, producing severe damage to the working classes when these classes, which are naturally the less conservative, in the usual sense of the word, see the justice procedures closed they have no other choice than to put their faith in violence. (Diario de Sesiones del Honorable Senado de la Nacion Constitutido en tribunal, T. VI, December 5, 1946: 89; quoted in Alston and Gallo, 2010: 192)

Perón's allies in Congress moved swiftly and impeached all but one of the Supreme Court justices. We see this as a constitutional moment because with the court out of the way, it enabled Perón to solidify the belief in redistributive populism. He nationalized several public utilities and kept prices low for their services (water, telephone, and railroads). He also reached out to rural workers by controlling rents. He accomplished this by taxing the landowners in the Pampas through his monopoly purchasing power at below-market prices. The new Constitution of 1949 codified the belief in redistributive populism.

The majority of citizens approved of the redistribution, but it was not sustainable because he subsidized and spent more than he taxed the agricultural interests in the Pampas. Also, landowners in the Pampas reduced their investments in light of the rent extraction by Perón. When revenues started to fall below expenditures, Perón leaned on the Central Bank to monetize debts. They did, but at the cost of starting inflation. Both the fiscal and monetary situation began to worsen over time. Perón remained popular with the masses who never abandoned their belief in redistributive populism. He would not lose an election. However, the military realized that the trajectory of Argentina was unsustainable, especially in the face of declining foreign and domestic investment as well as a loss of international credit. The military, with the political backing of the landowners in the Pampas and the Catholic Church, staged a coup in 1955. The military reversed some of the redistributive populist policies of Perón, but redistributive populism as a belief never disappeared.

For the past century, Argentina has gone through several belief mechanisms. The Sáenz Peña law in 1912 ushered in a new belief in a transition to checks and balances, though never held by the military and fragile with the Conservatives. The Great Depression in 1929 and a subsequent military coup in 1930 installed the Conservatives in power. The Conservatives stayed in power through electoral fraud in the 1930s, which eroded belief in checks and balances. A nationalistic military coup in 1943 ended the rule of the Conservatives and ushered in Juan Perón, who won the fair election of 1946. Military rule, coupled with electoral fraud, created a window of opportunity. Perón seized it, and through his leadership created a new dominant network under the belief of redistributive populism. The Conservatives, who were taxed to pay for redistribution, never adopted belief in redistributive populism. They always held to belief in fiscal and monetary orthodoxy along with export-driven growth. In the face of inflation, declining foreign and domestic investment, as well as a lack of international credit, the military ousted Perón in 1955. The belief in redistributive populism did not die in 1955; the dominant network simply changed with the military and conservatives in power. But, when democracy returned, so too did belief in redistributive populism. Over the latter part of the twentieth century and into the twenty-first century, the dominant network oscillated between redistributive populism and fiscal and monetary orthodoxy, though even the parties on the right have become more inclusive and favor some redistribution.

Brazil, 1985–2014: Belief in Social Inclusion to Fiscally Sound Social Inclusion

Developmentalism was the overarching belief during the military dictatorship in Brazil from 1964 to 1985. Developmentalism was top-down state planning and, as a military government, limited political rights.[10] Under this belief, this period saw tremendous growth and modernization up to 1974, but then economic stagnation with increasing political oppression and inequality. Following the military period where citizens, intellectuals, and many on the left had no voice, the redemocratization brought many voices to the table. As such, the dominant network was quite diffuse and included most organizations in society except for the military, though they played a strong hand in opening up to democracy. The belief that swept over society was social inclusion, born of revulsion at the previous authoritarian period. Social inclusion was a belief that societal welfare could best be enhanced through being more inclusive in politics and economics. All interests get something. On the political front, many political parties emerged. Land reform was on the agenda. The Constitution passed in 1988 explicitly granted many rights. For economic organizations, all interest groups received benefits from policies. Businesses received subsidies. High tariff walls remained. Unions received rights to strike. Illiterates received the right to vote, despite not actively petitioning for the vote. In a sense, it was democracy without real checks and balances. Social inclusion without constraints could never fully reach a critical transition because of its unsustainable macroeconomic implications. Hyperinflation became the norm, with yearly inflation rates from 1988 until 1994 in the hundreds to thousands of percent. Brazil initiated five major stabilization plans between 1986 and 1993. Each stabilization plan was a window of opportunity, but no administration was able to seize the opportunity with a successful plan. At the time of the impeachment proceedings of President Fernando Collor de Melo, inflation raged at more than 3,000 percent per year. Clearly, this was an incredible shock to the economic and political system. Naturally, it hurt the lower- and middle-income classes most because they could not hedge their savings.

Amid the macroeconomic chaos, President Collor was under impeachment proceedings on allegations of corruption. Collor resigned on December 30, 1992, and Vice President Itamar Franco took over as president of Brazil. The first order of business was to stabilize the economy. President Franco appointed Fernando Henrique Cardoso as foreign minister and then in May 1993 appointed Cardoso as finance minister. At first blush, Cardoso was an unlikely candidate for finance

---

[10] Our account draws heavily on Alston et al. (2016).

minister, having been a former professor of sociology at the University of São Paulo and known for his work on dependency theory. But, by 1993, Cardoso had changed his political and economic views, moving from the left to the center. Taming hyperinflation had been a window of opportunity for all presidents and their finance ministers, but it took the leadership of Cardoso to coordinate the dominant network of political and economic organizations to take the costly steps necessary to rein in their currency.

Cardoso recruited an economic team mostly from PUC-Rio (Pontifical Catholic University of Rio de Janeiro). The team crafted the *Real Plan*. Most of the team received their PhDs in economics from prestigious schools in the United States. Gustavo Franco, one of the architects, wrote his PhD dissertation at Harvard on hyperinflation and its solution in Germany. Despite expectations of the market and the IMF, the *Real Plan* tamed inflation, though not with a big bang. In part, it was the design and in part it was the messenger, Cardoso. Unlike some earlier plans, the new currency was not forced on anyone and, indeed at first, was not a medium of exchange but simply a unit of account floating against the Cruzeiro, which floated against the dollar. Cardoso was a great spokesman, stressing the transparency of the plan as well as encouraging organizations to start using the *Real* as a unit of account. Cardoso, a former senator, also interacted skillfully with Congress as well as with President Franco. Naturally, the political interests hoped for success. The economic team insisted on independence from Congress, and Cardoso guaranteed his economic team protection from interference.

The success of the *Real Plan* and its approval was a constitutional moment because it set in motion restraints on social inclusion. Largely due to taming inflation, Cardoso ran for president in 1994 and won. He brought several of the members of his economic team to his administration. Pedro Malan became the minister of finance for both of Cardoso's terms, and Gustavo Franco became head of the Central Bank. Quelling inflation was a necessary but not sufficient condition to change beliefs from social inclusion to fiscally sound social inclusion. Brazil needed institutional deepening that, if yielding the right outcomes, would strengthen beliefs. After inflation, Cardoso had to act on the fiscal side. He did so with budget stabilization. This entailed reining in spending by state governments and necessitated reforming state banks so that the debts held by state governments would not be monetized by the Central Bank, the extant practice. The national budget also needed to be stabilized. On this front, Cardoso reformed pension laws requiring several constitutional amendments. The hallmark of the success for Cardoso was the Fiscal Responsibility Law in 2000, which made states more fiscally sound and transferred power to the central government.

To succeed, Cardoso needed support among powerful business organizations in the dominant network. He also needed the broad support of members of Congress, which, given his coalition management, he achieved. His supporters increased over time across private businesses as well as in the political coalition. His success was testimony to his leadership skills in coordination and adaptability. Despite the success of Cardoso's two terms, there were critics on the left in the Workers' Party (PT). Luís Inácio "Lula" da Silva ran for presidency in 2002 and won. Prior to taking office, the *Real* depreciated, suggesting that the public and outside investors had doubts about the extent to which the belief in fiscally sound social inclusion was firmly embedded. Lula fooled the markets. In part thanks to high commodity prices, Lula expanded social programs, such as *Bolsa Familia*, while maintaining a budget surplus.[11] Lula proudly announced to the world that Brazil was immune to the financial crisis that shook the world's richest countries in 2008. Lula's approval ratings went through the roof during his two terms. Two terms of Lula sustaining fiscally sound social inclusion did much to complete the critical transition.

On his coattails, Dilma Rousseff, Lula's anointed successor, ran for the presidency in 2010 and won. In her acceptance speech, she reaffirmed a commitment to fiscally sound social inclusion: "the Brazilian people do not accept that governments spend more than is sustainable." Her actions did not match her words. She increased state intervention in public companies at the same time that commodity prices declined. As a result, her revenues declined. Despite the decline in revenues, she managed to run budget surpluses during her first term. Rousseff was reelected in 2014 in a runoff, indicating that her popularity had declined over her first term. Public opinion started to turn against Rousseff because of the declining economy and the *Petrobrás*

---

[11] By 2006, *Bolsa Familia* was one of the largest targeted welfare programs in the world, covering more than forty million people.

scandal, the largest corruption scandal in history.[12] In 2015, the General Accounting Office of Brazil unanimously voted that Rousseff overstated the budget surplus figures in the 2014 election year. Based on the ruling by the accounting office, Congress began impeachment proceedings against Rousseff in the spring of 2016. In August 2016, the Senate voted to impeach Rousseff. Vice President Michel Temer assumed the presidency.

An impeachment could, in theory, signal a window of opportunity and abandonment of the belief in fiscally sound social inclusion. Yet, there is evidence, such as ongoing investigations and prosecutions for corruption, that institutions supporting fiscally sound social inclusion may be robust. But, as of December 2017, the jury is still out as to whether the current belief will hold. President Temer is not a popular president, and the corruption scandal continues to erode public confidence in government. Only time will tell whether the current belief will hold or be replaced by a new belief most likely ushered in by new leadership, not currently visible in the wings as of 2017.

Ecuador, 1998–2017: From a Neoliberal Belief to a Belief in Inclusive Politics

Ecuador's experience in the past two decades provides an example of a critical transition that changed the political development trajectory, without yet significantly altering the economic growth trajectory of the nation.[13] The enactment of a new constitution in 2008, and its initial phases of implementation, required a significant adjustment to the balance of power, a transition coordinated by the leadership of President Rafael Correa, and his party, *Alianza País*. Correa

---

[12] *Petrobrás* is Brazil's publicly owned oil company.

[13] Until the administration of Correa, the perception on the part of the population writ large surrounding their benefiting from economic growth did not materialize. This perception existed despite GDP per capita within the country more than doubling between 2000 and 2007. Since Correa's tenure in power began, the country has experienced periods of strong GDP growth, although not as much in the preceding years (World Bank, 2017). The country's dependence on natural resource revenues suggests that this growth is due to a commodities price boom that occurred during much of the same period. What is clear, however, is that the Correa administration translated the natural resource-driven growth into government policies that significantly decreased poverty within the country.

coordinated a major change in the dominant network within the country by exploiting a window of opportunity: widespread popular dissatisfaction with the government, based on the failure of previous administrations and the prior constitution to restrain corruption and distribute rents from natural resource wealth. The recognition by Correa of the widespread, latent popular demand for progressive and environmentalist ideals led to a sufficient level of electoral success for *Alianza País* and subsequent redrafting of the constitution. Correa reshaped the dominant network by campaigning on a rejection of the political establishment. More than eight years after the enactment of the 2008 Constitution, the program of the government displayed a marked change in public service provision, as well as an increased recognition of indigenous and environmental concerns.

In many nations, the emergence of a new constitution occurs because of the perceived failures of the preceding one. In Ecuador, the 1998 Constitution was borne from a political crisis and resulted in neoliberal policy reforms while simultaneously facilitating the rise of new citizen and indigenous movements. Although driven by a desire for more inclusive democracy, the Constitution of 1998 did not accomplish enough to avoid the political turnover that ultimately led to the rise of Correa, and subsequently, the 2008 Constitution (Ortiz Crespo, 2008: 14). Although the decentralized governance contemplated by the 1998 Constitution led to more inclusive democratic outcomes at the subnational level, it did not create the opportunity for reform at the national level. The dominant network that benefited from the status quo at the national level remained unaffected by indigenous rights movements at the provincial and local level, movements nonetheless empowered by the 1998 Constitution.

Seven different administrations governed between 1996 and 2006, each emphasizing market liberalization and reduction of the state. Each administration fell under distinct circumstances, but corruption plagued each turnover of administrations (Paz y Miño Cepeda, 2009: 74). Inequality rose considerably over the period, along with high unemployment and underemployment. The beliefs in the dominant network consisting of banking, oil, and other export interests (e.g., fruit and flowers) did not respond quickly enough to the change in the economic and political outcomes. Decentralization created the opportunity for movements previously excluded from the political process to experience newfound political success. The inflexibility on the part of the dominant network led directly to the arrival of *Alianza País*, the party that largely drove the development of the 2008 Constitution and since enjoyed a near unbroken hegemony in the legislative and executive branches. The sources of constitutional reform led to a popular view of the constitutional process as embodying the right to political participation, correcting the abuses of rights within the country, and creating altogether new rights that better represented the fundamental beliefs of the new dominant network, including newly enfranchised groups (Ortiz Crespo, 2008). The previous dominant network failed to adjust their beliefs in the window of opportunity following the 1998 Constitution (Salvador Tamayo, 2014: 44), which created the opening for Correa and his party.

Prior to the rise of President Rafael Correa and *Alianza País*, a majority of the population increasingly began to question the legitimacy of the government. The decline of legitimacy led to the rise of the movements of workers and indigenous peoples that crystallized into a broad citizen's movement that supported Correa's party. The post-constitutional electoral results in 2009 highlight the extent of disillusionment with the traditional parties, with only 9 of 124 seats in the National Assembly retained by members of the former dominant network prior to 2008 (Pachano, 2010: 308). Moreover, none of the former parties fielded a presidential candidate in the 2009 elections (Bowen, 2010: 187). This stands as a clear indication of the extent to which Correa's party leveraged high levels of disillusionment with the previous system to coordinate successfully a major transition regarding the beliefs in the dominant network.

The political turnover preceding Correa's administration resulted in the unification of diverse indigenous movements. The newly unified movements were instrumental in protests against the corruption and inequality that characterized the seven administrations preceding that of *Alianza País*. By one estimate, the political process excluded 80 percent of the Ecuadorian population, and this was the base that Correa effectively tapped for his rise to power and reframing of the Ecuadorian social contract (Becker, 2011: 48). Correa's party dominated the constituent assembly, "a very loose and diverse grouping of social-movement activists, academics, and nongovernmental organization leaders," as well as notable indigenous leaders (Becker, 2011: 49). Many community and indigenous activists made the calculated bet that the best chance of seeing their interests represented lay with working within the new dominant network, as opposed to on the margins to which they had been relegated during preceding administrations. Correa first tapped into widespread and persistent popular disillusionment with the political elite writ large, and then subsequently orchestrated a referendum calling for a new constitutional document (Salvador Tamayo, 2014). This produced a focal point for coordination between the demands of citizens and the interests of the dominant network. The positive vote on a referendum on whether to have a new constitution clearly indicates the broad levels of support for a fundamental change to the social contract; *Alianza País's* position of yes received 82 percent of the vote, which firmly delivered them the mandate to elect a constituent assembly. The leaders of indigenous political coalitions, who achieved representation in the constituent assembly, valued both the highly progressive environmental ideals of "*Pachamama*"[14] and "*sumak kawsay*,"[15] as well as the more traditional leftist development ideals of rights to health care, education, and social security. Another indigenous objective that became a contentious issue in the constituent assembly was the official recognition of indigenous languages as equal to Spanish. This move failed in the assembly, which led to a significant backlash against Correa and the assembly itself, including being denounced as racist (Becker, 2011: 56). Perhaps in response to the public outcry, the languages of Kichwa and Shuar eventually received formal recognition, although this recognition did not grant official government status like that of Spanish.[16] Certainly, in terms of actual cost, and the diverse objectives the collective indigenous movements sought from the 2008 Constitution, the nominal inclusion, as opposed to formal imposition, was the less costly of the two. Such a compromise highlights the trade-offs between consensus and compromise that leadership during a critical transition entails.

On September 28, 2008, Ecuadorian citizens approved the new constitution by a wide margin, receiving 64 percent of the vote

---

[14] This term can loosely be thought of as "Mother Earth," with an emphasis on the nurturing role nature and a clean environment play on achieving sustainable public health outcomes.

[15] This is an indigenous term whose equivalent in Spanish is "buen vivir," which loosely translates to "good living," which more broadly translates in a policy sense to sustainable development outcomes, from the perspective of health, education, and economic well-being.

[16] 2008 Constitution of the Republic of Ecuador, Art. 2.

(Gudynas, 2009: 38). The 2008 Constitution treats social rights in detail, which range from health care (articulated as a broad concept of health, in addition to that contemplated in reference to *"sumak kawsay"*),[17] to social security,[18] to education,[19] to specific care for the elderly[20] and youth,[21] to rights of the disabled to non-discrimination and adequate care,[22] among others.

By 2008, the Correa administration came under criticism for the extent of centralized authority that it claimed was needed to provide rights to health care and education, as opposed to the promise of decentralized representative democracy that *Alianza País* had held out to its coalition of supporters (Ortiz Crespo, 2008). Inclusion of previously marginalized groups in a new constitutional moment necessarily results in compromises. As the number of different groups represented within a single coalition increases, the level of compromise from ideal points similarly increases. Drastically increasing the level of public services enjoyed across the nation, while simultaneously creating and enforcing new rights to environmental protection, is a social contract that is quite difficult to satisfy in the short term. However, the maintenance of such a social contract does not require immediate adherence to every provision articulated in a given constitution; rather, it requires satisfying a sufficient base of constituents such that the continued implementation of the social contract is possible in subsequent electoral periods. This is the dynamic of institutional deepening, where sufficient progress towards new aims of governance creates the very faith needed to maintain progress in the medium term.

Although the term *"sumak kawsay"* is indigenous in origin, it has taken on a broader significance, to indicate a rejection of all that came before in terms of chronic poverty and underemployment. However, as a term is adopted by a wider range of political groups, it is likely to experience changes in meaning as it is adjusted to fit the specific demands of each group. For example, the National Planning and Development Secretariat, SENPLADES, labeled the concept of *sumak*

---

[17] 2008 Constitution of the Republic of Ecuador, Art. 32.
[18] 2008 Constitution of the Republic of Ecuador, Art. 34.
[19] 2008 Constitution of the Republic of Ecuador, Art. 32.
[20] 2008 Constitution of the Republic of Ecuador, Arts. 36–38.
[21] 2008 Constitution of the Republic of Ecuador, Arts. 39, 44–46.
[22] 2008 Constitution of the Republic of Ecuador, Arts. 47–49.

kawsay as a social pact (SENPLADES, 2010: 6). This is more than coincidental, and likely indicates how a social pact requires compromises from the groups that are party to it. There was widespread popular demand for the Ecuadorian government to secure the rights of individuals as well as groups, but this demand did not extend as cleanly to the rights of nature. This has led to the government focusing on economic development and positive rights provenance, especially in terms of health care and education. Such a tension in meaning directly results from the trade-offs that the formalization of constitutional-level beliefs in society requires (Alston, 2018). Any constitutional document that accurately reflects the diversity of core beliefs within a given nation faces this tension.

The tension over interpretation and implementation of the constitution led to a significant political divide within the country regarding how *sumak kawsay* should best be understood and translated into public policy. Supporters of *Alianza País* see "the good life" as composed of both increases in standards of living as well as reasonable amounts of environmental protection (Guardiola and Garcia-Quero, 2014: 177–78). In contrast, indigenous groups conceive of the *sumak kawsay* as inextricably linked to the notion of every individual being part of the larger natural environment in which they are situated; absent good environmental protections, *sumak kawsay* cannot be achieved (Guardiola and Garcia-Quero, 2014: 177–78). This difference in meaning has increasingly placed indigenous groups in opposition to the government's goals for economic development and social welfare provenance. Furthermore, revenues for implementation of government programs are not the only reason *Alianza País* has prioritized natural resource development. Resource extraction projects are often in the poorest and most remote parts of Ecuador. These are the areas that would most benefit from reductions in unemployment and infrastructural development. The benefits of natural resource extraction highlight a tension within the constitution itself, where strong environmental rights appear alongside a guarantee of benefits to citizens from the development of natural resources. Somewhat ironically, both conceptions of *sumak kawsay* enjoy significant support within the country (Guardiola and Garcia-Quero, 2014: 182).

Constitutional implementation also entailed substantial structural changes to the economy, beginning with the government repudiating external debts. The repudiation of the debt reduced the national debt as a percentage of GDP from 23.2 percent and 18.3 percent in 2007 and 2008, to a level of 14.3 percent of GDP in 2009 (Pachano, 2010: 303). The repudiation was not due to fiscal insolvency so much as making a political statement that reflected popular sentiment towards powerful foreign nations (Becker, 2013: 47). This reflects the importance of reasserting national sovereignty as a salient topic surrounding the change in government that led to the 2008 Constitution; National Sovereignty received its own committee within the constitutional drafting body. *Alianza País* would have faced significant political recriminations if they had not done something of a significant magnitude to signal to the population that sovereignty was alive and well. Balancing these types of demands, while ensuring sufficient revenue to implement rights to education and health care, embodies the coordinative aspects of leadership during a critical transition.

The government coupled repudiation with significant increases in government expenditure on infrastructure, health care, and education. Previously, privatized enterprises fell under state control as the nation weathered the global economic downturn. Ecuador also experienced a decline in investment domestically, likely due to the nationalization of major industries. This restructuring in the face of a global downturn resulted in several years of economic contraction.

High commodity prices, especially oil, financed the government's development policies, especially given the contraction of the economy during the first years under the new constitution. Repudiating external debts led to a lack of international financing available to the country, and so Correa's administration turned to China for a loan backed by future petroleum revenues (Pachano, 2010: 303). The initial years of adjustment stand in stark contrast, at least numerically, to the subsequent years where public spending greatly contributed to a growth rate of 8 percent in 2011, a significant boost to the 3.6 percent growth in the year before (Becker, 2013: 43). The electoral success of *Alianza País* in 2013 is likely due to this economic growth, which both increased employment and allowed the government to continue providing increases in the positive social rights enshrined in the 2008 Constitution.

Current political leaders in Ecuador share the initially optimistic conclusions of many scholars as to the long-run impact from the 2008 Constitution's environmental and indigenous rights.

The *Alianza País* government argues that creating new rights, even given imperfect enforcement during initial phases of implementation, does not necessarily entail the destruction of more classical rights. The emergence of a new system of government within the shadow of the 2008 Constitution creates a process necessarily constrained by political realities. The political realities include Ecuador's economic reliance on natural resource revenues to finance its development program, and the rights to health care and education guaranteed in the constitution. Although tax revenues also support these social welfare programs, Ecuador's relatively low levels of economic development before Correa's rise indicate that no single tax policy could achieve the changes contemplated by the more than one hundred rights found in the 2008 Constitution (Radcliffe, 2012: 242).

As we noted in Chapter 8, the framework for judging critical transitions is inherently normative, and so any interpretation of the beneficial or detrimental nature of a transition depends upon the normative lens one chooses to apply. In regards to civil and political liberties within Ecuador, scholars and journalists identified several ways in which the concentration of power in the executive branch resulted in problematic governance outcomes. In particular, the legislature amended the constitution to extend presidential term limits in December 2015, although the specific terms of the law prevented Correa from running in the 2017 presidential election. *Alianza País* nonetheless narrowly prevailed in the electoral contest. Furthermore, a number of different outlets criticized the troubling stance of *Alianza País* and the freedom of press. From severely sanctioning a newspaper critical of the government's handling of a police officer's protest, to shutting down dissident activist groups, the actions of the Correa administration came under considerable criticism from international groups such as the United Nations and the Organization of American States (OAS). All of this suggests that the critical transition the country has undergone, while undeniably institutionally transformative, has not been without significant blemishes from the perspective of civil and political liberties (Alston, 2018).

Ultimately, Ecuador's modern political development displays all the characteristics of our explanatory framework. After a decade of administrative turnover, corruption, and economic crisis, popular support for the dominant network was extremely weak, which Correa capitalized upon to create a window of opportunity for change in the dominant network. Correa's political leadership allowed him to successfully coordinate political leaders and popular demands into a new vision for the nation. The 2008 Constitution enshrined the vision that displays the formalization of the belief changes within a constitutional moment into a fixed constitutional document. Subsequently, the nation entered a nascent period of institutional deepening, where political institutions better reflect the beliefs of society. Although implementation has not been without hiccoughs, the endurance of the administration and the provenance of social rights stand as clear examples of the new political trajectory the nation has embarked upon under the leadership of Correa.

Conclusion

The examples in this chapter are illustrative uses of our framework to better understand the process of economic and political development.[23] All our examples confront a society at a time when "something is not working." Beliefs during such times become malleable, and there is a difference of opinion across organizations on the belief about how potential institutions will solve the problem. There were many failed attempts at a transition before leadership seized the latent window of opportunity. This highlights the point that our framework for understanding the role of leadership in coordinating changes in a nation's fundamental institutions is more readily suited to understanding major outcomes *ex post*, than to predicting major change *ex ante*. This has a related implication: until a critical transition has been subject to several iterative periods of institutional deepening, the ultimate outcomes are uncertain. Thus, while our framework has great explanatory value in the instances we highlight, it is not as illustrative in those cases where a transition was unsuccessful, or a window of opportunity was not seized, or a leader was unsuccessful in coordinating belief change in the dominant network following such a window. Each of these, absent a high level of expertise in a given nation's history and political order, is quite difficult to distinguish from the ordinary operation of the political

---

[23]   See Alston et al. (2016) for a book-length treatment of the transition in Brazil. We encourage readers to further pursue the examples here or, ideally, other countries with a fuller treatment.

system that we label "autopilot." This is not to say that our concepts do not have explanatory value until they are realized in a particular context; instead, we caution the uninitiated reader from applying the concepts to any given window for political change in a country, because the coordinative moves of leadership in a window of opportunity are not certain to be successful.

In the United States, Hamilton, Jay, Madison, and Washington understood the defects of the Articles of Confederation and coordinated the movement to a new Constitution under a stronger federal system with the belief of the *United States* as the sovereign unit. The Constitution was necessary but not sufficient, and considerable belief and institutional deepening ensued, which we document briefly.

Argentina had suffered a decade of electoral fraud that eroded the budding belief in the 1920s in a system of checks and balances. Conservative elites took control of the government and held on to power through fraud, which was brought to a close first with a military coup followed by the election of Juan Perón in 1945, who led Argentina to a new belief in redistributive populism that entailed a dominant network of rural and urban workers, along with provincial governments. Redistributive populism grew as a belief, but fell because it was not fiscally sustainable. In the 1950s, inflation mounted; domestic and foreign investment declined; and international credit dried up. The military stepped in and ousted Perón in 1955 and changed by fiat the dominant network. Yet the belief in redistributive populism did not die, and even parties to the right have moved towards more inclusion and redistribution over time, especially as the power of the military declined in the latter part of the twentieth century.

Following the opening up of the country after the twenty years of military rule, Brazil exploded with economic and political inclusion, but without a budget constraint. Hyperinflation ensued. After several failed stabilization plans, Fernando Henrique Cardoso in 1994 led Brazil to first tame inflation and then deepen a belief in fiscally sound social inclusion over two administrations. This entailed restricting spending at the state and local levels through the historic Fiscal Responsibility Law in 2000, along with only expanding social programs if Brazil could afford them. Somewhat surprisingly, Lula stayed the course, or so it seemed.

In Ecuador, the country had historically been ruled by an elite dominant network associated with the oil, banking, and fruit companies. This was an extractive society and not inclusive. In the late 1990s, attempts at neoliberal reforms failed, though there was increased political inclusion of indigenous groups on the subnational level. It took until the leadership of Rafael Correa under a new party to enfranchise more of the country under the belief of inclusion. Although Correa did not maintain approval ratings at the levels he enjoyed at the time of constitutional enactment, he secured the levels of support needed politically through expenditure on social programs, a program that was largely financed by oil revenues derived from a commodities price boom.

Conclusion

We had three goals in writing this book: (1) to present a set of concepts, for example, institutions, norms, property rights, and transaction costs, used in Institutional and Organizational Analysis (IOA) that link institutions and norms to economic performance; (2) to use the same set of concepts to better understand political organizations and performance; and (3) to build a framework based on those concepts for understanding divergent developmental trajectories of nations around the world. In Parts I and II, we defined the concepts needed to understand how economic activity is organized and how economic and political outcomes are shaped by institutions and norms. In Part III, we add to our framework the comparatively recent work on beliefs and leadership to better understand the fundamental question of why there has not been convergence in economic and political performance across countries. This discussion is followed by illustrative examples to understand both the stability of economic and political trajectories as well as those critical transitions when leaders coordinate a change in a given nation's beliefs and fundamental institutions, enabling a movement to a new economic and political trajectory.

To accomplish our goals, we stood on the shoulders of many renowned scholars. Instead of attempting the impossible task of listing them all, we single out the Nobel Laureates who most influenced our work: Ronald Coase, James Buchanan, Douglass North, Elinor Ostrom, and Oliver Williamson. Our book is a tribute to their pioneering work. Coase was foundational, though much of his work on transaction costs (1937) and property rights (1960) went unrecognized by the profession until the 1970s. Buchanan was one of the founders of Public Choice theory in the 1960s. Public choice was a departure from most of political science and economics where scholars presumed that government officials and their agents acted in the public interest. Buchanan and his coauthors and followers imbued the government actors with rational self-interest. Buchanan also pushed out the frontier of the importance of constitutions versus legislation.

The question of why some countries are rich and others are poor drove the research of Douglass North throughout his career. North was first interested in measurement – the Cliometric Revolution; then transaction costs and property rights and their impact on economic development followed by the impact of institutions on development. North then moved to understanding mental models and cognition for why societies did not adopt the same institutions or develop the same norms. He finished his career by analyzing the role of violence on development. Elinor Ostrom is best known for her work on understanding the organization known as the commons. She sought to understand why some groups organize and establish rules to manage a commons while other groups dissipate the resource. Towards the end of her career, issues of institutional design and complexity also featured on her research agenda. Oliver Williamson extended the research of Coase and went beyond the question of why do firms exist to examine the myriad of organizations and contracts designed to minimize transaction costs. It is an honor to follow in the wake of such illustrious scholars, and we fully realize that we have neglected many scholars who equally contributed to our concepts and frameworks. We anticipate that others whose work influenced us will someday be in Stockholm and similarly recognized for their contributions to IOA. This is a conclusion, but in many ways our intellectual journey has just begun. Our book is a call for other scholars to continue to expand the frontiers of IOA.

Our exposition throughout the book surrounds a simple intuition: the rules matter for understanding economic and political outcomes. When these rules are the output of a recognized enforcement authority, they are properly understood as institutions; when the rules instead emerge as the result of individual beliefs and preferences expressed in the aggregate across society, they are properly understood as norms. From the simple intuition that the rules matter has sprung a wealth of analytical insights for understanding the emergence and development of political and economic institutions around the world. Our fundamental argument throughout this text has been that anyone interested in understanding causal influences and outcomes of complex social systems should carefully consider the institutions and norms specific to a given context.

In Part I, we provide an overview of some of the most foundational tools and concepts used in the IOA. Part of the purpose of Part I is to define terms that are then usable in a consistent way throughout the book and by other scholars. For instance, a definition of institutions as rules, created and enforced by recognized authorities, and norms as long-standing patterns of behavior that are shared by a group of people highlights the different ways that institutions and norms arise, are perceived, and are enforced. Taking institutions and norms as given, we link the institutions of a society to de jure and de facto property rights, transaction costs, and the organization of economic activity. Defining transaction costs as the costs of establishing and maintaining property rights enables us to discuss contemporary theories of the firm along with other organizations and contracts. Economic activity can be organized in myriad ways, and the literature associated with the IOA has provided a host of models to explain the tremendous organizational diversity. We discuss some of the models, including the incentives for work effort, the vertical and horizontal boundaries of the firm, and the financing of the activities of a firm.

There is much in the literature that we did not address. Important contributions from personnel economics, social psychology, and management are almost entirely absent from our discussion. Similarly, we do not specifically address financial organizations and the incentives they have on property rights, transaction costs, and other organizational and contractual arrangements. Scholars will continue to hone the definitions of institutions, norms, and transaction costs to improve and combine our current frameworks. While we covered a few of the important models of organizational choice, we just scratched the surface of this rich literature. Current research on culture, authority, and leadership will shed additional light on the internal workings of organizations. Research on the links between organization and innovation will provide guidance on how to manage research and development. And additional research on hybrids will provide new explanations for the great variety of organizational forms. Relatedly, research on networks and relational contracting will provide new models for understanding the emergence of organizations and contracts in societies.

In Part II, we took the level of economic development and the constitutional level rules-for-making-rules as given, and analyzed the interaction of players in the process through which societies create laws and policies that determine outcomes, intermediated by norms. Institutions determine the property rights and transaction costs in political organizations that in turn affect political outcomes. The relevant property rights here are the political property rights that affect which proposals for laws and legislation get initiated and how they shape their final de jure and de facto form and implementation.

Any given case typically involves a large number of interacting players, each with their own powers, preferences, and sets of information. For expositional clarity, however, we organized Part II of the book in four chapters to focus on four main subsets of players. In Chapter 4, we analyzed what we loosely called the "demand" for policies, where interest groups and citizens use a large variety of strategies to try to influence those who have the power to shape the laws of society. In the three following chapters, we focused on different organizations that "supply" the laws out of which ultimately emerges political performance. By political performance, we have in mind outcomes such as political competition and equity (e.g., gender outcomes). We addressed Executive-Legislative relations in Chapter 5; the Bureaucracy in Chapter 6; and the Judiciary in Chapter 7. These chapters showed that different forms of political organization can have decisive impacts on political outcomes and performance. Institutions matter in contextual and complex ways.

Although these four chapters covered many of the political institutions, norms, and organizations that determine the laws of societies, we left out many specific themes and strands of the literature because of space constraints. For example, we did not explicitly address the roles of important organizations in the process such as the military, police, press, unions, central banks, and public prosecutors, among others. Another shortcoming is that most of the literature has been developed specifically to understand American political institutions, so there is much scope to explore how the theories and results fare in the context of different countries and societies. Additionally, we anticipate that advances in empirical research, from bigger and better data sets, new methods in network theory, and more rigorous treatments of causality, will confirm or improve our discussion. Behavioral approaches will also undoubtedly bring new insights to our understanding of the interaction among political players. Finally, in Part II, we did not consider the role of beliefs and culture, which we took as exogenous, and yet they drive the goals and objectives of individuals in organizations in their quests to shape outcomes.

In Part III, we describe an additional contribution of the IOA to understanding economic and political outcomes: the great divergence in economic and political performance across countries around the world. Most contributions have focused on explanations consistent with rational interest theories of the emergence of institutions that determine economic and political development for better or worse. More recent contributions in the literature focus on the role of culture. Closely linked to the concept of culture and derivative from it are the underlying beliefs associated within a country. We take up the role of beliefs. We outline in detail a framework for understanding the role of leadership coordinating a move to a new belief that in turn generates major institutional changes and outcomes in a country. The benefits that institutional change can offer in expectation create an opportunity for specific individuals and organizations to coordinate the costly steps towards a different set of fundamental institutions. New institutional sets create transactional possibilities of greater magnitude and complexity while simultaneously enhancing the resilience of a given institutional set in the face of exogenous and endogenous shocks. A successful critical transition towards a "virtuous" institutional cycle necessarily involves a period of institutional deepening, where the benefits from the new institutions iteratively reinforce the faith of participants under the new belief and institutions. Better outcomes enhance the legitimacy and effectiveness of the new institutions in subsequent periods. Our examples highlight that although major institutional change is highly contextual, a critical transition to a new core belief can be understood using a framework that includes windows of opportunity, leadership, constitutional moments, and institutional deepening.

Much of our exposition in Part III references the underlying belief structure surrounding institutions in a given society. This is an area of the literature that has only recently been subject to examination with the analytical toolkit that we introduce. We provide historical examples from Argentina, Brazil, Ecuador, and the United States for the simple reason that they are most familiar to the authors. Our hope is that other scholars will use our framework in Part III to examine critical transitions and "autopilot" in other countries. Our framework is consonant with rational-interest-consistent explanations for the emergence of institutions, a topic that has consistently inspired scholars in the IOA, but where more remains to be done. Other promising developments at this level of analysis surround the increasing ability to granularly measure institutional change, from constitutions to ordinary legislation to rules in bureaucracies and the judiciary. Finally, our explanations of the benefits that "superior" political and economic institutions provide rely integrally on the study of complex systems (including networks) and their properties like resilience. This is a final area of analysis that is likely to prove fruitful in contributing to our understanding of the emergence and evolution of complex rule sets.

References

Abdal-Haqq, Irshad. 2002. "Islamic Law: An Overview of Its Origin and Elements." *Journal of Islamic Law and Culture* 7(1): 27–82.

Acemoglu, Daron. 2003. "Why Not a Political Coase Theorem? Social Conflict, Commitment, and Politics." *Journal of Comparative Economics* 31(4): 620–52.

Acemoglu, Daron and James A. Robinson. 2006. *Economic Origins of Dictatorship and Democracy*. New York, NY: Cambridge University Press.

2012. *Why Nations Fail: The Origins of Power, Prosperity, and Poverty*. New York, NY: Crown Business.

Ahmed, Dawood I. and Tom Ginsburg. 2014. "Constitutional Islamization and Human Rights: The Surprising Origin and Spread of Islamic Supremacy in Constitutions." *Virginia Journal of International Law* 54(3): 616–95.

Akerlof, George A. 1970. "The Market for 'Lemons': Quality Uncertainty and the Market Mechanism." *Quarterly Journal of Economics* 84(3): 488–500.

Alchian, Armen A. 1965. "Some Economics of Property Rights." *Il Politico* 30: 816–29.

1977. *Economic Forces at Work*. Indianapolis, IN: Liberty Press.

Alchian, Armen A. and Harold Demsetz. 1972. "Production, Information Costs, and Economic Organization." *American Economic Review* 62(5): 777–95.

Alesina, Alberto and Paola Giuliano. 2015. "Culture and Institutions." *Journal of Economic Literature* 53(4): 898–944.

Allen, Douglas W. 1991. "What Are Transaction Costs?" *Research in Law and Economics* 14: 1–18.

1998. "Property Rights, Transaction Costs and Coase: One More Time." In *Coasean Economics: Law and Economics and the New Institutional Economics*, edited by Steven G. Medema, 105–18. Boston, MA: Kluwer.

2000. "Transaction Costs." In *Encyclopedia of Law and Economics*, edited by Boudewijn Bouckaert and Gerrit De Geest, 893–926. Cheltenham, UK: Edward Elgar.

2006. "Theoretical Difficulties with Transaction Cost Measurement." *Division of Labour and Transaction Costs* 2(1): 1–14.

2014. "The Coase Theorem: Coherent, Logical, and Not Disproved." *Journal of Institutional Economics* 11(2): 1–12.

Allen, Douglas W. and Dean Lueck. 2003. *The Nature of the Farm: Contracts, Risk, and Organization in Agriculture*. Cambridge, MA: MIT Press.

Almendares, Nicholas and Patrick Le Bihan. 2015. "Increasing Leverage: Judicial Review as a Democracy-Enhancing Institution." *Quarterly Journal of Political Science* 10: 357–90.

Alston, Eric. 2018. "Ecuador's 2008 Constitution: The Political Economy of Securing an Aspirational Social Contract." *Constitutional Studies* 3 (June).

Alston, Lee J., Thráinn Eggertson, and Douglass C. North, eds. 1996. *Empirical Studies in Institutional Change*. New York, NY: Cambridge University Press.

Alston, Lee J. and Joseph P. Ferrie. 1993. "Paternalism in Agricultural Labor Contracts in the U.S. South: Implications for the Growth of the Welfare State." *American Economic Review* 83(4): 852–76.

1999. *Southern Paternalism and the American Welfare State: Economics, Politics, and Institutions in the South, 1865–1965*. New York, NY: Cambridge University Press.

Alston, Lee J. and Andres A. Gallo. 2010. "Electoral Fraud, the Rise of Peron and Demise of Checks and Balances in Argentina." *Explorations in Economic History* 47(2): 179–97.

Alston, Lee J. and William Gillespie. 1989. "Resource Coordination and Transaction Costs: A Framework for Analyzing the Firm/Market Boundary." *Journal of Economic Behavior and Organization* 11(2): 191–212.

Alston, Lee J., Edwyna Harris, and Bernardo Mueller. 2012. "The Development of Property Rights on Frontiers: Endowments, Norms, and Politics." *Journal of Economic History* 72(3): 741–70.

Alston, Lee J. and Robert Higgs. 1982. "Contractual Mix in Southern Agriculture since the Civil War: Facts, Hypotheses, and Tests." *Journal of Economic History* 42(2): 327–53.

Alston, Lee J., Gary D. Libecap, and Bernardo Mueller. 1999a. "A Model of Rural Conflict: Violence and Land Reform Policy in Brazil." *Environment and Development Economics* 4: 135–60.

1999b. *Titles, Conflict, and Land Use: The Development of Property Rights and Land Reform on the Brazilian Amazon Frontier*. Ann Arbor, MI: University of Michigan Press.

2000. "Land Reform Policies, the Sources of Violent Conflict, and Implications for Deforestation in the Brazilian Amazon." *Journal of Environmental Economics and Management* 39(2): 162–88.

2010. "Interest Groups, Information Manipulation in the Media, and Public Policy: The Case of the Landless Peasants Movement in Brazil." NBER Working Paper No. 15865, www.nber.org/papers/w15865.

Alston, Lee J., Shannan Mattiace, and Tomas Nonnenmacher. 2009. "Coercion, Culture, and Contracts: Labor and Debt on Henequen Haciendas in Yucatán, Mexico, 1870–1915." *The Journal of Economic History* 69(1): 104–37.

Alston, Lee J., Marcus André Melo, Bernardo Mueller, and Carlos Pereira. 2006. "Political Institutions, Policymaking Processes and Policy Outcomes in Brazil." Latin American Research Network Working Paper R–509. Washington, DC: Research Division, Inter-American Development Bank.

2016. *Brazil in Transition: Beliefs, Leadership, and Institutional Change.* Princeton, NJ: Princeton University Press.

Alston, Lee J. and Bernardo Mueller. 2006. "Pork for Policy: Executive and Legislative Exchange in Brazil." *Journal of Law, Economics, and Organization* 22(1): 87–114.

Alt, James E. and David D. Lassen. 2008. "Political and Judicial Checks on Corruption: Evidence from American State Governments." *Economics and Politics* 20(1): 33–61.

Amar, Akhil Reed. 1989. "Marbury, Section 13, and the Original Jurisdiction of the Supreme Court." *University of Chicago Law Review* 56(2): 443–99.

Ames, B. 1995. "Electoral Rules, Constituency Pressures, and Pork Barrel: Bases of Voting in the Brazilian Congress." *The Journal of Politics* 57(2): 324–43.

2001. *The Deadlock of Democracy in Brazil.* Ann Arbor, MI: University of Michigan Press.

Anderson, Erin and David C. Schmittlein. 1984. "Integration of the Sales Force: An Empirical Examination." *The Rand Journal of Economics* 15(3): 385–95.

Anderson, Terry L. and Peter J. Hill. 1975. "The Evolution of Property Rights: A Study of the American West." *Journal of Law and Economics* 18(1): 163–79.

2004. *The Not So Wild, Wild West: Property Rights on the Frontier.* Redwood City, CA: Stanford University Press.

Aoki, Masahiko, Kenneth Binmore, Simon Deakin, and Herbert Gintis, eds. 2012. *Complexity and Institutions: Markets, Norms and Corporations.* London: Palgrave Macmillan.

Argersinger, Peter H. 1980. "'A Place on the Ballot': Fusion Politics and Antifusion Laws." *The American Historical Review* 85(2) (April): 287–306.

1991. *Structure, Process, and Party*. Armonk, NY: M. E. Sharpe.

Arrow, Kenneth J. 1951. *Social Choice and Individual Values*. New York, NY: Wiley.

1963. *Social Choice and Individual Values*. 2nd edn. New Haven, CT: Yale University Press.

1968. "The Economics of Moral Hazard: Further Comment." *American Economic Review* 58(3): 537–39.

1985. "The Economics of Agency." In *Principals and Agents: The Structure of Business*, edited by John W. Pratt and Richard J. Zeckhauser, 37–51. Cambridge, MA: Harvard Business School Press.

Arruñada, Benito. 2012. "Property as an Economic Concept: Reconciling Legal and Economic Conceptions of Property Rights in a Coasean Framework." *International Review of Economics* 59(2): 121–44.

Arruñada, Benito, and Veneta Andonova. 2005. "Market Institutions and Judicial Rulemaking." In *Handbook of New Institutional Economics*, edited by Claude Ménard and Mary Shirley, 229–50. New York, NY: Springer.

Austen-Smith, D. and William H. Riker. 1987. "Asymmetric Information and the Coherence of Legislation." *American Political Science Review* 81(3): 897–918.

Backhouse, Roger E. and Steven G. Medema. 2009. "Retrospectives: On the Definition of Economics." *Journal of Economic Perspectives* 23(1): 221–34.

Baker, George P., Robert Gibbons, and Kevin J. Murphy. 2008. "Strategic Alliances: Bridges between 'Islands of Conscious Power.'" *Journal of the Japanese and International Economies* 22(2): 146–63.

Banks, Jeffrey S. 1991. *Signaling Games in Political Science*. Chur, Switzerland: Harwood Academic Publishers.

Barbera, S. and M. O. Jackson. 2004. "Choosing How to Choose: Self-Stable Majority Rules and Constitutions." *Quarterly Journal of Economics* 119(3): 1011–48.

Baron, David P. 1989. "Service-Induced Campaign Contributions and the Electoral Equilibrium." *Quarterly Journal of Economics* 104(1): 45–72.

1994. "Electoral Competition with Informed and Uninformed Voters." *American Political Science Review* 88(1): 33–47.

2002. "Review of Grossman and Helpman's *Special Interest Politics*." *Journal of Economic Literature* 40 (December): 1221–29.

2005. "Competing for the Public through the News Media." *Journal of Economics and Management Strategy* 14(2): 339–76.

Barzel, Yoram. 1989. *Economic Analysis of Property Rights*. Cambridge: Cambridge University Press.

1997. *Economic Analysis of Property Rights*. 2nd edn. Cambridge: Cambridge University Press.

Baum, Lawrence. 2009. *Judges and Their Audiences: A Perspective on Judicial Behavior*. Princeton, NJ: Princeton University Press.

Baumgartner, F. R., B. D. Jones, and P. B. Mortensen. 2014. "Punctuated Equilibrium Theory: Explaining Stability and Change in Public Policy Making." In *Theories of the Policy Process*, edited by P. A. Sabatier and C. M. Weible, 59–104. Boulder, CO: Westview Press.

Becker, Gary S. 1983. "A Theory of Competition among Pressure Groups for Political Influence." *Quarterly Journal of Economics* 98(3): 371–400.

Becker, Marc. 2011. "Correa, Indigenous Movements, and the Writing of a New Constitution in Ecuador." *Latin American Perspectives* 38(1): 47–62.

2013. "The Stormy Relations between Rafael Correa and Social Movements in Ecuador." *Latin American Perspectives* 40(3): 43–62.

Bentley, Arthur F. 1908. *The Process of Government*. Chicago, IL: University of Chicago Press.

Bernheim, B. Douglas and Michael D. Whinston. 1986. "Common Agency." *Econometrica* 54(4): 923–42.

Bernstein, Lisa. 1992. "Opting Out of the Legal System: Extralegal Contractual Relations in the Diamond Industry." *Journal of Legal Studies* 21(1): 115–57.

2015. "Beyond Relational Contracts: Social Capital and Network Governance in Procurement Contracts." *Journal of Legal Analysis* 7(2): 561–621.

Bertrand, Elodie. 2006. "The Coasean Analysis of Lighthouse Financing: Myths and Realities." *Cambridge Journal of Economics* 30(3): 389–402.

Besley, Timothy and Robin Burgess. 2001. "Political Agency, Government Responsiveness and the Role of the Media." *European Economic Review* 45(4–6): 629–40.

Besley, Timothy, Robin Burgess, and Andrea Prat. 2002. "Mass Media and Political Accountability." In *The Right to Tell: The Role of Mass Media in Economic Development*, edited by Roumeen Islam, 45–60. Washington, DC: World Bank Institute.

Bettencourt, Luis M. A. 2013. "The Origins of Scaling in Cities." *Science* 340: 1438–41.

Bird, R. M. 1992. *Tax Policy and Economic Development*. Baltimore, MD: John Hopkins University Press.

Black, D. 1958. *The Theory of Committees and Elections*. Cambridge: Cambridge University Press.

Bolt, J. and J. L. van Zanden. 2014. "The Maddison Project: Collaborative Research on Historical National Accounts." *The Economic History Review* 67(3): 627–51.

Borjas, George J. 1978. "Discrimination in HEW: Is the Doctor Sick or Are the Patients Healthy?" *Journal of Law and Economics* 21(1): 97–110.

Botero, Juan C. and Alejandro Ponce. 2010. "Measuring the Rule of Law." The World Justice Project – Working Paper Series WPS No. 001, Washington, DC.

Boudreaux, Donald J. 2014. "Liberty Matters: Deirdre McCloskey and Economists' Ideas about Ideas." Liberty Fund. http://oll.libertyfund .org/titles/2628.

Bowen, James D. 2010. "Ecuador's 2009 Presidential and Legislative Elections." *Electoral Studies* 29(1): 186–89.

Bresnahan, Timothy and Jonathan Levin. 2013. "Vertical Integration and Market Structure." In *The Handbook of Organizational Economics*, edited by Robert Gibbons and John Roberts, 853–90. Princeton, NJ: Princeton University Press.

Broadberry, Stephen and John Joseph Wallis. 2016. "Growing, Shrinking and Long Run Economic Performance: Historical Perspectives on Economic Development." Working Paper.

Brousseau, Eric and Jean-Michel Glachant, eds. 2002. *The Economics of Contracts: Theories and Applications*. New York, NY: Cambridge University Press.

eds. 2008. *New Institutional Economics: A Guidebook*. New York, NY: Cambridge University Press.

Buchanan, James M. 1985. "The Moral Dimension of Debt Financing." *Economic Inquiry* 23 (January): 1–6.

Buchanan, James M. and Gordon Tullock. 1962. *The Calculus of Consent: Logical Foundations of Constitutional Democracy*. Ann Arbor, MI: University of Michigan Press.

Calabresi, Guido. 1965. "The Decision for Accidents: An Approach to Nonfault Allocation of Costs." *Harvard Law Review* 78(4): 713–45.

Caldeira, Gregory A., and John R. Wright. 1998. "Lobbying for Justice: Organized Interests, Supreme Court Nominations, and the United States Senate." *American Journal of Political Science* 42(2): 499–523.

Canes-Wrone, B. 2003. "Bureaucratic Decisions and the Composition of the Lower Courts." *American Journal of Political Science* 47(2): 205–14.

Cappelletti, Mauro. 1989. *The Judicial Process in Comparative Perspective.* New York, NY: Oxford University Press.

Carugati, Federica. 2018. "Constitution and Consensus: The Institutional Foundations of Democratic Stability." Working Paper, Ostrom Workshop, Indiana University.

Center for Constitutional Transitions. 2013. "Justice Albie Sachs Discusses His Role 'Judging the Judges after Transition' in Kenya." April 16. http://constitutionaltransitions.org/albie-sachs-summary/.

Cheibub, J. A. 2006. *Presidentialism, Parliamentarism, and Democracy.* New York, NY: Cambridge University Press.

Cheibub, J. A., Z. Elkins, and T. Ginsburg. 2013. "Beyond Presidentialism and Parliamentarism." *British Journal of Political Science* 44(3): 515–44.

Cheung, Steven. 1983. "The Contractual Nature of the Firm." *Journal of Law and Economics* 26(1): 1–21.

1989. "Economic Organization and Transaction Costs." In *Allocation, Information and Markets*, edited by John Eatwell, Murray Milgate, and Peter Newman, 77–82. London: MacMillan.

Choi, Stephen J., G. Mitu Gulati, and Eric A. Posner. 2010. "Professionals or Politicians: The Uncertain Empirical Case for an Elected rather than Appointed Judiciary." *Journal of Law, Economics, and Organization* 26(2): 290–336.

Clark, Tom S. 2011. "The Public and Judicial Independence." In *The Politics of Judicial Independence*, edited by Bruce Peabody, 123–46. Baltimore, MD: Johns Hopkins University Press.

Coase, Ronald H. 1937. "The Nature of the Firm." *Economica* 4: 386–405.

1960. "The Problem of Social Cost." *Journal of Law and Economics* 3 (October): 1–44.

1974. "The Lighthouse in Economics." *Journal of Law and Economics* 17 (24): 357–76.

1988. *The Firm, the Market, and the Law.* Chicago, IL: University of Chicago Press.

1992. "The Institutional Structure of Production." *American Economic Review* 82(4): 713–19.

Coate, Stephen and Stephen Morris. 1995. "On the Form of Transfers to Special Interest." *Journal of Political Economy* 106(6): 1210–35.

Comparative Constitutions Project. 2016. http://comparativeconstitutionsproject.org/.

Constitution of Kenya Review Commission. 2005. "*The Final Report of the Constitution of Kenya Review Commission.*" Nairobi: Government Printer.

Constitution of the Republic of Kenya, 1963 (as amended to 2008), art. 61, par. 2.

Cooter, Robert D. and Thomas Ulen. 2011. *Law and Economics*. 6th edn. Boston, MA: Addison Wesley.

Costello, George. 2005. "The Supreme Court's Overruling of Constitutional Precedent: An Overview." Congressional Research Service Report for Congress.

Cox, Gary W. 1997. *Making Votes Count: Strategic Coordination in the World's Electoral Systems*. New York, NY: Cambridge University Press.

Cox, Gary W. and Matthew D. McCubbins. 2000. "The Institutional Determinants of Economic Policy Outcomes." In *Presidents, Parliaments, and Policy*, edited by Stephan Haggard and Mathew McCubbins, 21–63. New York, NY: Cambridge University Press.

2005. *Setting the Agenda: Responsible Party Government in the U.S. House of Representatives*. New York, NY: Cambridge University Press.

2007. *Legislative Leviathan: Party Government in the House*. 2nd edn. New York, NY: Cambridge University Press.

Crawford, Sue E. S. and Elinor Ostrom. 1995. "A Grammar of Institutions." *American Political Science Review* 89(3): 582–600.

Cross, H. L. 1953. *The People's Right to Know: Legal Access to Public Records and Proceedings*. New York, NY: Columbia University Press.

Crouch, Melissa and Tim Lindsey, eds. 2014. *Law, Society and Transition in Myanmar*. London: Bloomsbury Publishing.

CRP (Center for Responsive Politics). 2015. "Money in Marijuana." November. www.opensecrets.org/news/issues/marijuana/.

Culp, Peter W., Robert Jerome Glennon, and Gary Libecap. 2014. *Shopping for Water: How the Market Can Mitigate Water Shortages in the American West*. Washington, DC: Island Press.

Dahlman, Carl J. 1979. "The Problem of Externality." *Journal of Law and Economics* 22(1): 141–62.

Daly, Yvonne M. 2011. "Judicial Oversight of Policing: Investigations, Evidence and the Exclusionary Rule." *Crime, Law and Social Change* 55(2): 199–215.

Danziger, Shai, Jonathan Levav, and Liora Avnaim-Pesso. 2011. "Extraneous Factors in Judicial Decisions." *Proceedings of the National Academy of Sciences* 108(17): 6889–92.

Della Paolera, Gerardo and Alan M. Taylor. 1998. "Finance and Development in an Emerging Market: Argentina in the Interwar Period." In *Latin America and the World Economy since 1800*, edited by John H. Coatsworth and Alan M. Taylor, 139–70. Series on Latin American Studies. Cambridge, MA: David Rockefeller Center for Latin American Studies; distributed by Harvard University Press.

1999. "Economic Recovery from the Argentine Great Depression: Institutions, Expectations, and the Change of Macroeconomic Regime." *Journal of Economic History* 59(3): 567–99.

2001. "Bailing Out: Internal versus External Convertibility." In *Straining at the Anchor: The Argentine Currency Board and the Search for Macroeconomic Stability, 1880–1935*, edited by Gerardo della Paolera and Alan M. Taylor, 165–87. National Bureau of Economic Research Series on Long-Term Factors in Economic Development. Chicago, IL: University of Chicago Press.

Del Rosal, Ignacio. 2011. "The Empirical Measurement of Rent-Seeking Costs." *Journal of Economic Surveys* 25(2): 298–325.

Demsetz, Harold. 1967. "Toward a Theory of Property Rights." *American Economic Review* 57 (May): 347–59.

Denzau, Arthur T. and Michael C. Munger. 1986. "Legislators and Interest Groups: How Unorganized Interests Get Represented." *American Political Science Review* 80(1): 89–106.

De Soto, Hernando. 1989. *The Other Path: The Invisible Revolution in the Third World*. New York, NY: HarperCollins.

2000. *The Mystery of Capital: Why Capitalism Triumphs in the West and Fails Everywhere Else*. New York, NY: Basic Books.

Diaz Alejandro, Carlos F. 1970. *Essays on the Economic History of the Argentine Republic*. New Haven, CT: Yale University Press.

Dixit, Avinash. 1996. *The Making of Economic Policy: A Transaction-Cost Politics Perspective*. Cambridge, MA: MIT Press.

Downs, Anthony. 1957. "An Economic Theory of Political Action in a Democracy." *Journal of Political Economy* 65(2): 135–50.

1967. *Inside Bureaucracy*. Boston, MA: Little, Brown.

Drobak, John N. and John V. C. Nye, eds. 1997. *The Frontiers of the New Institutional Economics*. Cambridge, MA: Academic Press.

Dunbar, R. I. M. 1993. "Coevolution of Neocortical Size, Group Size and Language in Humans." *Behavioral and Brain Sciences* 16(4): 681–735.

Dunleavy, P. 2012. "Duverger's Law Is a Dead Parrot. Outside the USA, First-Past-the-Post Voting Has No Tendency At All to Produce Two Party Politics." http://blogs.lse.ac.uk/politicsandpolicy/duvergers-law-dead-parrot-dunleavy/.

Dunleavy, P. and R. Diwakar. 2013. "Analysing Multiparty Competition in Plurality Rule Elections." *Party Politics* 19(6): 855–86.

Duverger, Maurice. 1963. *Political Parties: Their Organization and Activity in the Modern State*. New York, NY: Wiley.

Eggertsson, Thráinn. 1990. *Economic Behavior and Institutions*. Cambridge: Cambridge University Press.

2005. *Imperfect Institutions: Possibilities and Limits of Reform.* Ann Arbor, MI: University of Michigan Press.

Elkins, Zachary, Tom Ginsburg, and James Melton. 2009. *The Endurance of National Constitutions.* New York, NY: Cambridge University Press.

Ellickson, Robert C. 1991. *Order without Law: How Neighbors Settle Disputes.* Cambridge, MA: Harvard University Press.

Elliott, Mark. 2001. *The Constitutional Foundations of Judicial Review.* Oxford: Hart Publishing.

Ellis, Joseph J. 2015. *The Quartet: Orchestrating the Second American Revolution, 1783–1789.* New York, NY: Knopf.

Elster, Jon. 2007. *Explaining Social Behavior: More Nuts and Bolts for the Social Sciences.* New York, NY: Cambridge University Press.

Engdahl, David E. 1992. "John Marshall's 'Jeffersonian' Concept of Judicial Review." *Duke Law Journal* 42: 279–339.

Engerman, Stanley L. and Kenneth L. Sokoloff. 2012. *Economic Development in the Americas since 1500: Endowments and Institutions.* New York, NY: Cambridge University Press.

Engstrom, Erik J. and Samuel Kernell. 2005. "Manufactured Responsiveness: The Impact of State Electoral Laws on Unified Party Control of the Presidency and House of Representatives, 1840–1940." *American Journal of Political Science* 49(3): 531–49.

Epstein, D. and S. O'Halloran. 2001. "Legislative Organization under Separate Powers." *Journal of Law, Economics, and Organization* 17(2): 373–96.

Epstein, L., W. M. Landes, and R. A. Posner. 2013. *The Behavior of Federal Judges.* Cambridge, MA: Harvard University Press.

Epstein, Richard. 1990. "The Independence of Judges: The Uses and Limitations of Public Choice Theory." *Brigham Young University Law Review* 1990(3): 827–55.

Eskridge, William N. 1991. "Overriding Supreme Court Statutory Interpretation Decisions." *Yale Law Journal* 101: 331–455.

Fehr, Ernst and Herbert Gintis. 2007. "Human Motivation and Social Cooperation: Experimental and Analytical Foundations." *Annual Review of Sociology* 33: 43–64.

Ferejohn, John A. 1995. "Foreword." In *Positive Theories of Congressional Institutions*, edited by Kenneth A. Shepsle and Barry R. Weingast, ix–xiii. Ann Arbor, MI: University of Michigan Press.

Figueiredo, A. C. and F. Limongi. 1996. "Congresso Nacional: Organização, Processo Legislativo e Produção Legal." *Cadernos de Pesquisa 5.*

2000. "Presidential Power, Legislative Organization and Party Behavior in Brazil." *Comparative Politics* 32: 151–70.

Flyvbjerg, Bent. 2014. "What You Should Know about Megaprojects and Why: An Overview." *Project Management Journal* 45(2): 6–19.

Fon, Vincy and Francesco Parisi. 2006. "Judicial Precedents in Civil Law Systems: A Dynamic Analysis." *International Review of Law and Economics* 26(4): 519–35.

Foss, Nicolai J., Henrik Lando, and Steen Thomsen. 2000. "The Theory of the Firm." In *Encyclopedia of Law and Economics, Volume 3: The Regulation of Contracts*, edited by Boudewijn Bouckaert and Gerrit De Geest, 631–58. Cheltenham, UK: Edward Elgar.

Frisman, P. 2008. "Connecticut's Littering Law." OLR Research Report, May 20, 2008, www.cga.ct.gov/2008/rpt/2008-R-0314.htm.

Fuller, Lon L. 1977. *The Morality of Law*. New Haven, CT: Yale University Press.

Furubotn, Eirik G. and Rudolf Richter, eds. 1991. *The New Institutional Economics: A Collection of Articles from the Journal of Institutional and Theoretical Economics*. Heidelberg, Germany: Mohr Siebeck.

Furubotn, Eirik G. and Rudolf Richter. 2005. *Institutions and Economic Theory: The Contribution of the New Institutional Economics*. 2nd edn. Ann Arbor, MI: University of Michigan Press.

Gabaix, Xavier. 2016. "Power Laws in Economics: An Introduction." *Journal of Economic Perspectives* 30(1): 185–206.

Gainer, Maya. 2016. "Transforming the Courts: Judicial Sector Reforms in Kenya, 2011–2015." OGP-ISS Case Study. https://successfulsocieties .princeton.edu/sites/successfulsocieties/files/MG_OGP_Kenya.pdf.

Galiani, Sebastian and Itai Sened, eds. 2014. *Institutions, Property Rights, and Economic Growth: The Legacy of Douglass North*. New York, NY: Cambridge University Press.

Gardbaum, Stephen. 2014. "Separation of Powers and the Growth of Judicial Review in Established Democracies." *American Journal of Comparative Law* 62(3): 613–39.

Gardner, Bruce. 1983. "Efficient Redistribution through Commodity Markets." *American Journal of Agricultural Economics* 65(2) (May): 225–34.

Garlicki, Lech. 2007. "Constitutional Courts versus Supreme Courts." *International Journal of Constitutional Law* 5(1): 44–68.

Garoupa, Nuno and Tom Ginsburg. 2015. *Judicial Reputation: A Comparative Theory*. Chicago, IL: University of Chicago Press.

Gathii, James Thuo. 2016. *The Contested Empowerment of Kenya's Judiciary, 2010–2015: A Historical Institutional Analysis*. Sheria Publishing House.

Gely, Rafael and Pablo T. Spiller. 1990. "A Rational Choice Theory of Supreme Court Statutory Decisions with Applications to the 'State Farm' and 'Grove City Cases'." *Journal of Law, Economics, and Organization* 6(2): 263–300.

Gerken, H. K. 2013. "Exit, Voice, and Disloyalty." *Duke Law Journal* 62: 1349–86.

Gibbons, Robert. 2005. "Four Formal(Izable) Theories of the Firm?" *Journal of Economic Behavior and Organization* 58(2): 200–45.

Gibbons, Robert and Rebecca Henderson. 2012. "What Do Managers Do?" In *The Handbook of Organizational Economics*, edited by Robert Gibbons and John Roberts, 680–731. Princeton, NJ: Princeton University Press.

Gibbons, Robert and John Roberts, eds. 2013. *The Handbook of Organizational Economics*. Princeton, NJ: Princeton University Press.

Gilardi, Fabrizio. 2005. "The Institutional Foundations of Regulatory Capitalism: The Diffusion of Independent Regulatory Agencies in Western Europe." *Annals of the American Academy of Political and Social Science* 598(1): 84–101.

Gilligan, T. W. and K. Krehbiel. 1987. "Collective Decisionmaking and Standing Committees: An Informational Rationale for Restrictive Amendment Procedures." *Journal of Law, Economics, and Organization* 3(2): 287–335.

Ginsburg, Tom. 2003. *Judicial Review in New Democracies: Constitutional Courts in Asian Cases*. New York, NY: Cambridge University Press.

2010. "Public Choice and Constitutional Design." In *Research Handbook on Public Choice and Public Law*, edited by Daniel Farber and Anne Joseph O'Connell, 261–82. Cheltenham, UK: Edward Elgar.

2011. "Pitfalls of Measuring the Rule of Law." *Hague Journal on the Rule of Law* 3(2): 269–80.

Ginsburg, Tom and Aziz Huq. 2018. "The Theory and Practice of Constitutional Implementation." In *From Parchment to Practice*. New York, NY: Cambridge University Press.

Ginsburg, Tom and Alberto Simpser, eds. 2013. *Constitutions in Authoritarian Regimes*. New York, NY: Cambridge University Press.

Ginsburg, Tom and Mila Versteeg. 2014. "Why Do Countries Adopt Constitutional Review?" *Journal of Law, Economics, and Organization* 30(3): 587–622.

Glaeser, Edward L. and Andrei Shleifer. 2003. "The Rise of the Regulatory State." *Journal of Economic Literature* 41(2): 401–25.

Glynn, Adam and Maya Sen. 2015. "Identifying Judicial Empathy: Does Having Daughters Cause Judges to Rule for Women's Issues?" *American Journal of Political Science* 59(1): 37–54.

Gode, Dhananjay K. and Shyam Sunder. 1997. "What Makes Markets Allocationally Efficient?" *Quarterly Journal of Economics* 112(2): 603–30.

Godinho, Vitorino M. 1965. *Os Descobrimentos e a Economia Mundial.* Vols. I, II, III. Lisbon: Editora Arcádia.

Goldberg, Victor P. and John R. Erickson. 1987. "Quantity and Price Adjustment in Long-Term Contracts: A Case Study of Petroleum Coke." *Journal of Law and Economics* 30(2): 369–98.

Greif, Avner. 1993. "Contract Enforceability and Economic Institutions in Early Trade: The Maghribi Traders' Coalition." *American Economic Review* 83(3): 525–48.

2006. *Institutions and the Path to the Modern Economy: Lessons from Medieval Trade.* New York, NY: Cambridge University Press.

Greif, Avner and Christopher Kingston. 2011. "Institutions: Rules or Equilibria?" In *Political Economy of Institutions, Democracy, and Voting*, edited by N. Schofield and G. Caballero, 13–43. Berlin: Springer-Verlag.

Groseclose, T. 1994. "Testing Committee Composition Hypotheses for the U.S. Congress." *The Journal of Politics* 56(2): 440–58.

Groseclose, T. and D. C. King. 2001. "Committee Theories Reconsidered." In *Congress Reconsidered*, 7th edn., edited by L. C. Dodd and B. I. Oppenheimer. Washington, DC: CQ Press.

Grossman, Gene M. and Elhanan Helpman. 2001. *Special Interest Politics.* Cambridge, MA: MIT Press.

Grossman, Sanford J. and Oliver D. Hart. 1986. "The Costs and Benefits of Ownership: A Theory of Vertical and Lateral Integration." *Journal of Political Economy* 94(4): 691–719.

Guardiola, Jorge and Fernando Garcia-Quero. 2014. "Buen Vivir (living well) in Ecuador: Community and Environmental Satisfaction without Household Material Prosperity?" *Ecological Economics* 107: 177–84.

Gudynas, Eduardo. 2009. "The Political Ecology of the Biocentric Turn in Ecuador's New Constitution." *Revista de Estudios Sociales* no. 32 (January/April): 34–46.

Guerra, Kristine. 2016. "'Intolerable': Judge Reprimanded After She 'Berated and Belittled' Domestic-Violence Victim." *Washington Post*, September 1.

Hadfield, Gillian K. 2005. "The Many Legal Institutions that Support Contractual Commitments." In *Handbook of New Institutional Economics*, edited by Claude Ménard and Mary Shirley, 175–203. New York, NY: Springer.

2016. *Rules for a Flat World.* New York, NY: Oxford University Press.

Hadfield, Gillian K. and Barry R. Weingast. 2012. "What Is Law? A Coordination Model of the Characteristics of Legal Order." *Journal of Legal Analysis* 4(2) (December): 471–514.

2013. "Law without the State: Legal Attributes and the Coordination of Decentralized Collective Punishment." *Journal of Law and Courts* 1(1): 3–34.

Haidt, Jonathan. 2012. *The Righteous Mind: Why Good People Are Divided by Politics and Religion.* New York, NY: Pantheon Books.

Hall, J. A. 1985. *Powers and Liberties: The Causes and Consequences of the Rise of the West.* Oxford: Blackwell.

Hallerberg, M. and P. Marier. 2001. "Executive Authority, the Personal Vote, and Budget Discipline in Latin American and Caribbean Countries." ZEI Working Paper. ZEI – Center for European Integration Studies.

Hammond, T. H. and J. H. Knott. 1996. "Who Controls the Bureaucracy?: Presidential Power, Congressional Dominance, Legal Constraints, and Bureaucratic Autonomy in a Model of Multi-Institutional Policy-Making." *Journal of Law, Economics, and Organization* 12(1): 119–66.

Handelsman Shugerman, Jed. 2012. *The People's Courts: Pursuing Judicial Independence in America.* Cambridge, MA: Harvard University Press.

Hansmann, Henry. 1988. "Ownership of the Firm." *Journal of Law, Economics, and Organization* 4(2): 267–304.

1996. *The Ownership of Enterprise.* Cambridge, MA: Harvard University Press.

2013a. "All Firms Are Cooperatives – and So Are Governments." *Journal of Entrepreneurial and Organizational Diversity* 2(2): 1–10.

2013b. "Ownership and Organizational Form." In *The Handbook of Organizational Economics*, edited by Robert Gibbons and John Roberts, 891–917. Princeton, NJ: Princeton University Press.

2016. "Firm Ownership: The Legacy of Grossman and Hart." In *The Impact of Incomplete Contracts on Economics*, edited by Phillipe Aghion, Mathias Dewatripont, Patrick Legros, and Luigi Zingales, 307–14. Oxford: Oxford University Press.

Hanssen, F. Andrew. 2004. "Is There a Politically Optimal Level of Judicial Independence?" *American Economic Review* 94(3): 712–29.

Hart, H. L. A. 2012. *The Concept of Law.* New York, NY: Oxford University Press.

Hart, Oliver D. 1995. *Firms, Contracts, and Financial Structure.* Oxford: Oxford University Press.

Hart, Oliver D. and John Moore. 1990. "Property Rights and the Nature of the Firm." *Journal of Political Economy* 98(6): 1119–58.

Hayek, Friedrich A. 1945. "The Use of Knowledge in Society." *American Economic Review* 35: 519–30.

1978. *The Constitution of Liberty.* Chicago, IL: University of Chicago Press.

Hayes, Thomas C. 1990. "Confrontation in the Gulf: The Oilfield Lying Below the Iraq-Kuwait Dispute." *New York Times*, September 3.

Helmholz, Richard. 2009. "Bonham's Case, Judicial Review, and the Law of Nature." *Journal of Legal Analysis* 1(1): 325–26.

Helper, Susan and Rebecca Henderson. 2014. "Management Practices, Relational Contracts, and the Decline of General Motors." *Journal of Economic Perspectives* 28(1): 49–72.

Hennart, Jean-Francois. 1993. "Explaining the Swollen Middle: Why Most Transactions Are a Mix of 'Market' and 'Hierarchy'." *Organization Science* 4(4): 529–47.

Higgs, Robert. 1996. "Legally Induced Technical Regress in the Washington Salmon Fishery." In *Empirical Studies in Institutional Change*, edited by Lee J. Alston, Thráinn Eggertsson, and Douglass C. North, 247–79. New York, NY: Cambridge University Press.

Hirschl, Ran. 2009. *Towards Juristocracy: The Origins and Consequences of the New Constitutionalism*. Cambridge, MA: Harvard University Press.

Hirschman, Albert O. 1970. *Exit, Voice, and Loyalty: Responses to Decline in Firms, Organizations and States*. Cambridge, MA: Harvard University Press.

    1984. "Against Parsimony: Three Easy Ways of Complicating Some Categories of Economic Discourse." *American Economic Review* 74 (2): 89–96.

Hochfelder, David. 1999. "Taming the Lightning: American Telegraphy as a Revolutionary Technology, 1832–1860." PhD diss., Case Western Reserve University.

Hodgson, Geoffrey M. 1988. *Economics and Institutions: A Manifesto for a Modern Institutional Economics*. Cambridge: Polity Press.

    2003. *Recent Developments in Institutional Economics*. Cheltenham, UK: Edward Elgar.

    2007. "Meanings of Methodological Individualism." *Journal of Economic Methodology* 12(2): 211–26.

Hoekstra, V. and N. LaRowe. 2013. "Judging Nominees: An Experimental Test of the Impact of Qualifications and Divisiveness on Public Support for Nominees to the Federal Courts." *Justice System Journal* 34(1): 38–61.

Hohfeld, Wesley Newcomb. 1913. "Some Fundamental Legal Conceptions as Applied in Judicial Reasoning." *The Yale Law Journal* 23(1): 16–59.

    1917. "Fundamental Legal Conceptions as Applied in Judicial Reasoning." *The Yale Law Journal* 26(8): 710–70.

Holmström, Bengt and Paul Milgrom. 1991. "Multitask Principal-Agent Analysis: Incentive Contracts, Asset Ownership, and Job Design." Special issue, *Journal of Law, Economics, and Organization* 7: 24–51.

1994. "The Firm as an Incentive System." *American Economic Review* 84 (4): 972–91.

Howard, R. M. and D. C. Nixon. 2002. "Regional Court Influence over Bureaucratic Policymaking: Courts, Ideological Preferences, and the Internal Revenue Service." *Political Research Quarterly* 55(4): 907–22.

2003. "Local Control of the Bureaucracy: Federal Appeals Courts, Ideology, and the Internal Revenue Service." *Washington University Journal of Law and Policy* 13: 233–56.

Howell, William G. 2003. *Power without Persuasion: The Politics of Direct Presidential Action*. Princeton, NJ: Princeton University Press.

Huber, J. D. and C. R. Shipan. 2002. *Deliberate Discretion?* New York, NY: Cambridge University Press.

Hughes, Jonathan R.T. 1976. *Social Control in the Colonial Economy*. Charlottesville: University Press of Virginia.

Inman, R. and M. Fitts. 1990. "Political Institutions and Fiscal Policy: Evidence from the US Historical Record." *Journal of Law, Economics, and Organization* 6: 79–132.

Iyigun, Murat and Jared Rubin. 2017. "The Ideological Roots of Institutional Change." IZA Working Paper No. 10703, April. Bonn, Germany: IZA – Institute of Labor Economics.

Jackson, Vicki. 2012. "Judicial Independence: Structure, Context, Attitude." In *Judicial Independence in Transition: Strengthening the Rule of Law in the OSCE Region*, edited by Anja Seibert-Fohr, 19–86. New York, NY: Springer.

Jacob, Brian A. and Steven D. Levitt. 2003. "Rotten Apples: An Investigation of the Prevalence and Predictors of Teacher Cheating." *Quarterly Journal of Economics* 118(3): 843–77.

Jarrell, Gregg A. 1978. "The Demand for State Regulation of the Electric Utility Industry." *Journal of Law and Economics* 21(2) (October): 269–95.

Jefferson, Thomas. 1904–1905. "To William Charles Jarvis [September 28, 1820]." In *The Works of Thomas Jefferson*, Federal Edition, vol. 12. New York and London: G. P. Putnam's Sons.

Jensen, Michael C. and William H. Meckling. 1976. "Theory of the Firm: Managerial Behavior, Agency Costs and Ownership Structure." *Journal of Financial Economics* 3(4): 305–60.

Johnson, R. N. and G. D. Libecap. 1994. *The Federal Civil Service System and the Problem of Bureaucracy: The Economics and Politics of Institutional Change*. Chicago, IL: University of Chicago Press.

Jones, Bryan D. and Frank R. Baumgartner. 2005. *The Politics of Attention: How Government Prioritizes Problems*. Chicago, IL: University of Chicago Press.

Jones, E. L. 1981. *The European Miracle: Environments, Economies, and Geopolitics in the History of Europe and Asia*. New York, NY: Cambridge University Press.

Joskow, Paul L. 1985. "Vertical Integration and Long-Term Contracts: The Case of Coal-Burning Electric Generating Plants." *Journal of Law, Economics, and Organization* 1(1): 33–80.

   1987. "Contract Duration and Relationship-Specific Investments: Empirical Evidence from Coal Markets." *American Economic Review* 77(1): 168–85.

Joskow, Paul L. and Roger G. Noll. 1981. "Regulation in Theory and Practice: An Overview." In *Studies in Public Regulation*, edited by Gary Fromm, 1–78. Cambridge, MA: MIT Press.

Judges and Magistrates Vetting Board. 2016. "Vetting of Judges and Magistrates in Kenya: Final Report." www.jmvb.or.ke/?wpdmdl=1270.

"Judiciary Transformation Framework: 2012–2016." 2012. Registrar of the Judiciary. www.judiciary.go.ke/portal/assets/downloads/reports/Judiciary's%20Tranformation%20Framework-fv.pdf.

Kalt, Joseph P. and Mark A. Zupan. 1984. "Capture and Ideology in the Economic Theory of Politics." *American Economic Review* 74(3) (June): 279–300.

   1990. "The Apparent Ideological Behavior of Legislators: Testing for Principal-Agent Slack in Political Institutions." *Journal of Law and Economics* 33(1) (April): 103–31.

Kaplow, Louis. 1986. "An Economic Analysis of Legal Transitions." *Harvard Law Review* 99(3): 517–19.

Kastellec, Jonathan P., Jeffrey R. Lax, and Justin H. Phillips. 2010. "Public Opinion and Senate Confirmation of Supreme Court Nominees." *The Journal of Politics* 72(3): 767–84.

Kaufmann, Patrick J. and Francine Lafontaine. 1994. "Costs of Control: The Source of Economic Rents for McDonald's Franchisees." *Journal of Law and Economics* 37(2): 417–53.

Keele, Denise M., Robert W. Malmsheimer, Donald W. Floyd, and Lianjun Zhang. 2009. "An Analysis of Ideological Effects in Published versus Unpublished Judicial Opinions." *Journal of Empirical Legal Studies* 6(1): 213–39.

Kennedy, J. B. 2015. "'Do This! Do That!' and Nothing Will Happen: Executive Orders and Bureaucratic Responsiveness." *American Politics Research* 43(1): 59–82.

Khan, Zorina. 2005. *The Democratization of Invention: Patents and Copyrights in American Economic Development, 1790–1920*. Cambridge: Cambridge University Press.

Khan, Zorina and Kenneth L. Sokoloff. 2001. "The Early Development of Intellectual Property Institutions in the United States." *Journal of Economic Perspectives* 15(3): 233–46.

Kiewiet, R. D. and M. D. McCubbins. 1994. *The Logic of Delegation: Congressional Parties and the Appropriations Process.* Chicago, IL: University of Chicago Press.

Kim, Jongwook and Joseph T. Mahoney. 2005. "Property Rights Theory, Transaction Costs Theory, and Agency Theory: An Organizational Economics Approach to Strategic Management." *Managerial and Decision Economics* 26(4): 223–42.

King, The Honourable L. J., AQ CQ. 2002–2003. "Removal of Judges." *Flinders Journal of Law Reform* 6(2): 169–83.

Kiser, Edgar and Yoram Barzel. 1991. "The Origins of Democracy in England." *Rationality and Society* 3(4): 396–422.

Klein, Benjamin. 1980. "Transaction Cost Determinants of 'Unfair' Contractual Arrangements." *American Economic Review* 70(2): 356–62.

Klein, Benjamin, Robert G. Crawford, and Armen A. Alchian. 1978. "Vertical Integration, Appropriable Rents, and the Competitive Contracting Process." *Journal of Law and Economics* 21(2) (October): 297–326.

Klein, Peter G. 2005. "The Make-Or-Buy Decision: Lessons from Empirical Studies." In *Handbook of New Institutional Economics*, edited by Claude Ménard and Mary M. Shirley, 435–64. New York, NY: Springer.

Klein, Peter G. and Michael E. Sykuta. 2010. *The Edward Elgar Companion to Transaction Cost Economics.* Cheltenham, UK: Edgar Elgar.

Kosová, Renatá and Francine Lafontaine. 2012. "Much Ado about Chains: A Research Agenda." *International Journal of Industrial Organization* 30(3): 303–8.

Krehbiel, K. 1992. *Information and Legislative Organization.* Ann Arbor, MI: University of Michigan Press.

Kuran, Timur. 2011. *The Long Divergence: How Islamic Law Held Back the Middle East.* Princeton, NJ: Princeton University Press.

Lakner, Christoph and Branko Milanovic. 2016. "Global Income Distribution: From the Fall of the Berlin Wall to the Great Recession." *World Bank Economic Review* 30(2): 203–32.

Landes, D. S. 1998. *The Wealth and Poverty of Nations: Why Some Are So Rich and Some So Poor.* New York, NY: Norton.

Landes, Elisabeth M. 1982. "Insurance, Liability, and Accidents: A Theoretical and Empirical Investigation of the Effect of No-Fault Accidents." *Journal of Law and Economics* 25(1) (April): 49–65.

La Porta, Rafael, Florencio Lopez-de-Silanes, Cristian Pop-Eleches, and Andrei Shleifer. 2004. "Judicial Checks and Balances." *Journal of Political Economy* 112 (April): 445–70.

La Porta, Rafael, Florencio Lopez-de-Silanes, and Andrei Shleifer. 2008. "The Economic Consequences of Legal Origins." *Journal of Economic Literature* 46(2): 285–332.

Law, David S. and Mila Versteeg. 2011. "The Evolution and Ideology of Global Constitutionalism." *California Law Review* 99: 1163–257.

2013. "Sham Constitutions." *California Law Review* 101(4): 863–952.

Leflar, Robert A. 1961. "Some Observations Concerning Judicial Opinions." *Columbia Law Review* 61(5): 810–20.

Levy, Brian and Pablo T. Spiller. 1996. *Regulations, Institutions, and Commitment: Comparative Studies of Telecommunications*. New York, NY: Cambridge University Press.

Lewis, David K. 1969. *Convention: A Philosophical Study*. Cambridge, MA: Harvard University Press.

Libecap, Gary D. 1989. *Contracting for Property Rights*. New York, NY: Cambridge University Press.

1992. "The Rise of the Chicago Packers and the Origins of Meat Inspection and Antitrust." *Economic Inquiry* 30(2): 242–62.

2007. "The Assignment of Property Rights on the Western Frontier: Lessons for Contemporary Environmental and Resource Policy." *The Journal of Economic History* 67(2): 257–91.

Lijphart, Arend. 1977. *Democracy in Plural Societies: A Comparative Exploration*. New Haven, CT: Yale University Press.

1999. *Patterns of Democracy: Government Forms and Performance in Thirty-Six Countries*. New Haven, CT: Yale University Press.

Lim, Claire S. H. 2013. "Preferences and Incentives of Appointed and Elected Public Officials: Evidence from State Trial Court Judges." *American Economic Review* 103(4): 1360–97.

Linneman, Peter. 1980. "The Effects of Consumer Safety Standards: The 1973 Mattress Flammability Standard." *Journal of Law and Economics* 23(2) (October): 461–79.

Linz, J. 1990. "The Perils of Presidentialism." *Journal of Democracy* 1(1) (Winter): 51–69.

Lott, John R., Jr. 1997. "Does Political Reform Increase Wealth?: Or, Why the Difference between the Chicago and Virginia Schools Is Really an Elasticity Question." *Public Choice* 91(3/4): 219–27.

Ludington, Arthur C. 1911. *American Ballot Laws, 1888–1910*. Albany: New York State Library.

Lueck, Dean and Thomas Miceli. 2007. "Property Law." In *Handbook of Law and Economics*, edited by A. Mitchell Polinsky and Steven Shavell, 183–257. Amsterdam: Elsevier.

Maddison Project. 2013. www.ggdc.net/maddison/maddison-project/home.htm.

Mainwaring, Scott. 1993. "Presidentialism, Multipartism, and Democracy: The Difficult Combination." *Comparative Political Studies* 26(2): 198–228.

 1999. *Rethinking Party Systems in the Third Wave of Democratization: The Case of Brazil*. Stanford, CA: Stanford University Press.

Mainwaring, Scott and Matthew S. Shugart. 1997. *Presidentialism and Democracy in Latin America*. New York, NY: Cambridge University Press.

Makadok, Richard and Russell Coff. 2009. "Both Market and Hierarchy: An Incentive-System Theory of Hybrid Governance Forms." *The Academy of Management Review* 34(2): 297–319.

Maliti, Tom. 2012. "Four Kenyan Appeals Court Judges Declared Unfit for Office." *International Justice Monitor*. www.ijmonitor.org/2012/04/fo ur-kenyan-appeals-court-judges-declared-unfit-for-office/.

Manne, Henry. 1997. "The Judiciary and Free Markets." *Harvard Journal of Law and Public Policy* 21(1): 11–37.

Marchand, James R. and Keith P. Russell. 1973. "Externalities, Liability, Separability, and Resource Allocation." *American Economic Review* 63 (4): 611–20.

Martimort, D. 1996. "Exclusive Dealing, Common Agency, and Multiprincipals Incentive Theory." *RAND Journal of Economics* 27(1): 1–31.

Masten, Scott E. 1988. "A Legal Basis for the Firm." *Journal of Law, Economics, and Organization* 4(1): 181–98.

Masten, Scott E. and Edward A. Snyder. 1993. "United States versus United Shoe Machinery Corporation: On the Merits." *Journal of Law and Economics* 36(1): 33–70.

Mattiace, Shannan and Tomas Nonnenmacher. 2014. "The Organization of Hacienda Labor during the Mexican Revolution: Evidence from Yucatán." *Mexican Studies-Estudios Mexicanos* 30(2): 366–96.

McCarty, Nolan. 2004. "The Appointments Dilemma." *American Journal of Political Science* 48(3): 413–28.

McCloskey, Deidre. 1998. "The So-Called Coase Theorem." *Eastern Economic Journal* 24(3): 367–71.

 2006. *The Bourgeois Virtues: Ethics for an Age of Commerce*. Chicago, IL: University of Chicago Press.

 2010. *Bourgeois Dignity: Why Economics Can't Explain the Modern World*. Chicago, IL: University of Chicago Press.

 2016. *Bourgeois Equality: How Ideas, Not Capital or Institutions, Enriched the World*. Chicago, IL: University of Chicago Press.

McCubbins, Matthew D., Roger G. Noll, and Barry R. Weingast. 1987. "Administrative Procedures as Instruments of Control." *Journal of Law, Economics, and Organization* 8(2): 243–77.

1989. "Structure and Process, Politics and Policy: Administrative Arrangements and the Political Control of Agencies." *Virginia Law Review* 75(2): 431–82.

McCubbins, Mathew D. and Thomas Schwartz. 1984. "Congressional Oversight Overlooked: Police Patrols versus Fire Alarms." *American Journal of Political Science* 28(1): 165–79.

McGuire, Robert A. 2003. *To Form a More Perfect Union: A New Economic Interpretation of the United States Constitution.* Oxford: Oxford University Press.

McKelvey, Richard D. 1976. "Intransitivities in Multidimensional Voting Bodies." *Journal of Economic Theory* 12: 472–82.

1979. "General Conditions for Global Intransitivities in Formal Voting Models." *Econometrica* 47(5): 1085–112.

McNamara, Paul. 2006. "Deontic Logic." In *The Handbook of the History of Logic, vol. 7: Logic and the Modalities in the Twentieth Century*, edited by Dov Gabbay and John Woods, 197–288. Amsterdam, Netherlands: Elsevier Press.

Medema, Steven G. 1999. "Legal Fiction: The Place of the Coase Theorem in Law and Economics." *Economics and Philosophy* 15(2): 209–33.

Medema, Steven G. and Richard O. Zerbe Jr. 2000. "The Coase Theorem." In *Encyclopedia of Law and Economics, Volume 1: The History and Methodology of Law and Economics*, edited by Boudewijn Bouckaert and Gerrit De Geest, 836–92: Cheltenham, UK: Edward Elgar.

Ménard, Claude. 2013. "Hybrid Modes of Organization: Alliances, Joint Ventures, Networks, and Other Strange Animals." In *The Handbook of Organizational Economics*, edited by Robert Gibbons and John Roberts, 1066–1108. Princeton, NJ: Princeton University Press.

Ménard, Claude and Emmanuel Raynaud. 2010. "Ulysses and the Sirens: Hands-Tying Governance in Hybrid Forms." Working Paper, Centre d'Economie de la Sorbonne.

Ménard, Claude and Mary M. Shirley, eds. 2005. *Handbook of New Institutional Economics.* New York, NY: Springer.

Merrill, Thomas W. and Henry E. Smith. 2011. "Making Coasean Property More Coasean." *Journal of Law and Economics* 54(4): S77–S104.

Milgrom, Paul and John Roberts. 1990. "Bargaining Costs, Influence Costs, and the Organization of Economic Activity." In *Perspectives on Positive Political Economy*, edited by James E. Alt and Kenneth A. Shepsle, 57–89. New York, NY: Cambridge University Press.

Miller, Gary J. 2005. "The Political Evolution of Principal-Agent Models." *Annual Review of Political Science* 8: 203–25.

Mishan, E. J. 1967. "Pareto Optimality and the Law." *Oxford Economic Papers* 19(3): 255–87.

Moe, Terry M. 1985. "Control and Feedback in Economic Regulation: The Case of the NLRB." *American Political Science Review* 79(4): 1094–116.

    1987. "An Assessment of the Positive Theory of 'Congressional Dominance'." *Legislative Studies Quarterly* 12(4): 475–520.

    2013. "Delegation, Control, and the Study of Public Bureaucracy." In *The Handbook of Organizational Economics*, edited by Robert Gibbons and John Roberts, 1148–81. Princeton, NJ: Princeton University Press.

Moe, Terry M. and William G. Howell. 1999a. "The Presidential Power of Unilateral Action." *Journal of Law, Economics, and Organization* 15(1): 132–79.

    1999b. "Unilateral Action and Presidential Power: A Theory." *Presidential Studies Quarterly* 29(4): 850–73.

Moe, Terry M. and S. Wilson. 1994. "Presidents and the Politics of Structure." *Law and Contemporary Problems* 57 (Spring): 1–44.

Mokyr, Joel. 2012. *The Enlightened Economy: An Economic History of Britain 1700–1850*. New Haven, CT: Yale University Press.

    2017. *A Culture of Growth: The Origins of the Modern Economy*. Princeton, NJ: Princeton University Press.

Moser, Petra. 2005. "How Do Patent Laws Influence Innovation? Evidence from Nineteenth-Century World's Fairs." *American Economic Review* 95(4): 1214–36.

Mossoff, Adam. 2014. "O'Reilly v. Morse." George Mason University Law and Economics Research Paper no. 14–22. www.law.gmu.edu/assets/files/publications/working_papers/1422.pdf.

Mueller, Bernardo. 1998. "The Economic Theory of Regulation: The Case of Agrarian Reform Legislation in Brazil." *Revista Brasileira de Economia* 52(1) (January/March): 83–110.

Mueller, Bernardo and João Gabriel Ayello Leite. 2016. "Coevolution of Institutions and Culture in 16th Century Portuguese Empire." Working Paper, University of Brasilia.

Mueller, Dennis C. 2003. *Public Choice III*. Cambridge: Cambridge University Press.

Muris, T. J. 1986. "Regulatory Policymaking at the Federal Trade Commission: The Extent of Congressional Control." *Journal of Political Economy* 94(4): 884–89.

Myerson, R. B. 2008. "Perspectives on Mechanism Design in Economic Theory." *American Economic Review* 98(3): 586–603.

Neustadt, R. E. 1990. *Presidential Power and the Modern Presidents*. New York, NY: Free Press.

Nichols, Lionel. 2015. *The International Criminal Court and the End of Impunity in Kenya.* New York, NY: Springer.

Niskanen, William A. 1971. *Bureaucracy and Representative Government.* New York, NY: Aldine-Atherton.

⎯⎯⎯ 1975. "Bureaucrats and Politicians." *Journal of Law and Economics* 18 (December): 617–43.

"Nobel Prize in Economic Sciences, 1991 – Press Release." Nobel Media. www.nobelprize.org/nobel_prizes/economic-sciences/laureates/1991/press.html.

Noll, Roger G. 1989a. "Comments on Peltzman's: 'The Economic Theory of Regulation after a Decade of Deregulation'." Special issue, *Brookings Papers on Economic Activity*: 48–58.

⎯⎯⎯ 1989b. "Economic Perspectives on the Politics of Regulation." In *Handbook of Industrial Organization*, Volume 2, edited by R. Schmalensee and R. D. Willig, 1253–87. Amsterdam: Elsevier Science.

Noonan, John Thomas. 2005. *A Church that Can and Cannot Change: The Development of Catholic Moral Teaching.* Notre Dame, IN: University of Notre Dame Press.

North, Douglass C. 1989. "Institutions and Economic Growth: An Historical Introduction." *World Development* 17(9): 1319–32.

⎯⎯⎯ 1990. *Institutions, Institutional Change, and Economic Performance.* New York, NY: Cambridge University Press.

⎯⎯⎯ 1992. "Institutions and Economic Theory." *The American Economist* 36(1) (Spring): 3–6.

⎯⎯⎯ 2005. *Understanding the Process of Economic Change.* Princeton, NJ: Princeton University Press.

North, Douglass C. and Robert P. Thomas. 1973. *The Rise of the Western World: A New Economic History.* New York, NY: Cambridge University Press.

North, Douglass C., John Joseph Wallis, and Barry R. Weingast. 2009. *Violence and Social Orders: A Conceptual Framework for Interpreting Recorded Human History.* New York, NY: Cambridge University Press.

North, Douglass C. and Barry R. Weingast. 1989. "Constitutions and Commitment: The Evolution of Institutions Governing Public Choice in Seventeenth-Century England." *The Journal of Economic History* 49(4): 803–32.

Ober, Josiah. 2017. *Demopolis: Democracy before Liberalism in Theory and Practice.* New York, NY: Cambridge University Press.

Olson, Mancur. 1965. *The Logic of Collective Action.* Cambridge, MA: Harvard University Press.

Ordeshook, Peter C. and Olga V. Shvetsova. 1994. "Ethnic Heterogeneity, District Magnitude, and the Number of Parties." *American Journal of Political Science* 38(1): 100–23.

Ortiz Crespo, Santiago. 2008. "Citizen Participation: The Constitution of 1998 and the New Constitutional Project." *Revista de Ciencias Sociales* 32 (September): 13–17.

Ostrom, Elinor. 1990. *Governing the Commons: The Evolution of Institutions for Collective Action*. New York, NY: Cambridge University Press.

   2005. *Understanding Institutional Diversity*. Princeton, NJ: Princeton University Press.

Ostrom, Vincent. 1991. *The Meaning of American Federalism: Constituting a Self-Governing Society*. San Francisco, CA: ICS Press.

Overby, L. M., B. M. Henschen, M. H. Walsh, and J. Strauss. 1992. "Courting Constituents? An Analysis of the Senate Confirmation Vote on Justice Clarence Thomas." *American Political Science Review* 86(4): 997–1003.

Owens, Ryan J., Daniel E. Walters, Ryan C. Black, and Anthony Madonna. 2014. "Ideology, Qualifications, and Covert Senate Obstruction of Federal Court Nominations." *University of Illinois Law Review* 2014(2): 347–88.

Ozielo, Ojonnia. 2010. "Judicial Integrity and the Vetting Process in Kenya." *Amani Papers* 1(6). UNDP Kenya. www.ke.undp.org/content/dam/ken ya/docs/Amani%20Papers/AP_Volume1_n6_Sept2010.pdf.

Pachano, Simón. 2010. "Ecuador: New Political System into Operation." *Revista de Ciencia Política* 30(2): 297–317.

Parisi, Francesco and Vincy Fon. 2009. *The Economics of Lawmaking*. New York, NY: Oxford University Press.

Parliament of Australia. 2012. "Completed Inquiries 2010–2013: Chapter 1." Senate Standing Committees on Legal and Constitutional Affairs. www.aph.gov.au/Parliamentary_Business/Committees/Senate/Legal_and_Constitutional_Affairs/Completed_inquiries/2010–13/judi cialcomplaints/report/c01.

Pashigian, Peter P. 1976. "Consequences and Causes of Public Ownership of Urban Transit Facilities." *The Journal of Political Economy* 84(6) (August): 1239–59.

   1985. "Environmental Regulation: Whose Self-Interests Are Being Protected?" *Economic Inquiry* 23 (October): 551–84.

Pauly, Mark V. 1968. "The Economics of Moral Hazard: Comment." *American Economic Review* 58(3): 531–37.

Paz y Miño Cepeda, Juan. 2009. "El Gobierno de Rafael Correa: Un nuevo ciclo en la historia de Ecuador" [The government of Rafael Correa: A new cycle in the history of Ecuador]. *Metapolítica* 65: 71–76.

Peabody, Bruce. 2011. *The Politics of Judicial Independence*. Baltimore, MD: Johns Hopkins University Press.

Peltzman, Sam. 1973. "An Evaluation of Consumer Protection Legislation: The 1962 Drug Amendments." *Journal of Political Economy* 81(5): 1049–91.

1975. "The Effects of Automobile Safety Regulation." *Journal of Political Economy* 83(4): 677–726.

1976. "Toward a More General Theory of Regulation." *Journal of Law and Economics* 19 (August): 211–40.

1989. "The Economic Theory of Regulation after a Decade of Deregulation." Special issue, *Brookings Papers on Economic Activity*: 1–59.

Pereira, Carlos and Bernardo Mueller. 2000. "Uma teoria da preponderância do poder Executivo: O sistema de comissões no Legislativo brasileiro." *Revista Brasileira de Ciências Sociais* 15(43): 45–67.

2004. "The Cost of Governing Strategic Behavior of the President and Legislators in Brazil's Budgetary Process." *Comparative Political Studies* 37(7): 781–815.

Peretti, Terri Jennings. 2002. "Does Judicial Independence Exist?: The Lessons of Social Science Research." In *Judicial Independence at the Crossroads: An Interdisciplinary Approach*, edited by Stephen B. Burbank and Barry Friedman, 103–33. Thousand Oaks, CA: Sage.

Pinker, Steven. 2011. *The Better Angels of Our Nature: Why Violence Has Declined*. New York, NY: Viking.

Plott, Charles R. 1967. "A Notion of Equilibrium and Its Possibility under Majority Rule." *American Economic Review* 57: 787–806.

Plum Book. 2012. *Policy and Supporting Positions*. Washington, DC: Committee on Oversight and Government Reform.

Popper, Karl. 1963. *Conjectures and Refutations: The Growth of Scientific Knowledge*. London: Routledge.

Posin, Daniel Q. 1990. "The Coase Theorem: If Pigs Could Fly." *Wayne Law Review* 37(1): 89–120.

Posner, Richard A. 1974. "Theories of Economic Regulation." *The Bell Journal of Economics and Management Science* 5(2): 335–58.

1998. "Rational Choice, Behavioral Economics, and the Law." *Stanford Law Review* 50: 1551–75.

2005. "Judicial Behavior and Performance: An Economic Approach." *Florida State University Law Review* 32: 1259–79.

Posner, Richard A. and Francesco Parisi, eds. 1997. *Law and Economics, Volume 1: Theoretical and Methodological Issues*. Cheltenham, UK: Edgar Elgar.

Posner, Richard A. and Eric Rasmusen. 1999. "Creating and Enforcing Norms, with Special Reference to Sanctions." *International Review of Law and Economics* 19: 369–82.

Poterba, J. M. 1994. "State Responses to Fiscal Crises: The Effects of Budgetary Institutions and Politics." *Journal of Political Economy* 102(4): 799–821.

Prendergast, Canice. 2007. "The Motivation and Bias of Bureaucrats." *American Economic Review* 97(1): 180–96.

Przeworski, A., M. E. Alvarez, J. A. Cheibub, and F. Limongi. 2000. *Democracy and Development: Political Institutions and Well-Being in the World*. New York, NY: Cambridge University Press.

Radcliffe, Sarah A. 2012. "Development for a Postneoliberal Era? Sumak Kawsay, Living Well and the Limits to Decolonisation in Ecuador." *Geoforum* 43: 240–49.

Rakove, Jack, Andrew Ruttan, and Barry R. Weingast. 2004. "Ideas, Interests, and Credible Commitments in the American Revolution." Working Paper, Hoover Institution, Stanford University, August.

Report of the Committee of the Administration of Justice. 1998. Nairobi: Government Printer.

Report of the Integrity and Anticorruption Committee. 2003. Nairobi: Government Printer.

Richter, Rudolf. 2015. *Essays on New Institutional Economics*. New York, NY: Springer.

Riker, William H. 1980. "Implications from the Disequilibrium of Majority Rule for the Study of Institutions." *American Political Science Review* 74(2): 432–46.

1982. "The Two-Party System and Duverger's Law: An Essay on the History of Political Science." *American Political Science Review* 76(4): 753–66.

1984. "The Heresthetics of Constitution-Making: The Presidency in 1787, with Comments on Determinism and Rational Choice." *American Political Science Review* 78(1) (March): 1–16.

Robinson, David T. and Toby E. Stuart. 2006. "Network Effects in the Governance of Strategic Alliances." *Journal of Law, Economics, and Organization* 23(1): 242–73.

Robinson, J. A. and R. Torvik. 2011. "Institutional Comparative Statics." National Bureau of Economic Research Working Paper Series No. 17106.

Rodrik, Dani, Arvind Subramanian, and Francesco Trebbi. 2009. "Institutions Rule: The Primacy of Institutions over Geography and Integration in Economic Development." National Bureau of Economic Research Working Paper Series No. 9305.

Rothbard, Murray. 1995. *Economic Thought before Adam Smith: An Austrian Perspective on the History of Economic Thought, Volume I*. Brookville, VT: Ashgate.

Roubini, N. and J. D. Sachs. 1989. "Political and Economic Determinants of Budget Deficits in the Industrial Democracies." *European Economic Review* 33 (April): 903–38.

Rourke, Francis E. 1984. *Bureaucracy, Politics, and Public Policy.* New York, NY: Harper Collins.

Rowley, Charles K. and Friedrich Schneider, eds. 2004. *The Encyclopedia of Public Choice.* 2 vols. Boston, MA: Kluwer.

Rubin, Paul H. 2005. "Legal Systems as Frameworks for Market Exchanges." In *Handbook of New Institutional Economics,* edited by Claude Ménard and Mary Shirley, 205–28. New York, NY: Springer.

Rudalevige, A. 2012. "The Contemporary Presidency: Executive Orders and Presidential Unilateralism." *Presidential Studies Quarterly* 42: 138–60.

Rutherford, Malcolm. 1994. *Institutions in Economics: The Old and the New Institutionalism.* Cambridge: Cambridge University Press.

Salvador Tamayo, Estefanía. 2014. "*The Understanding of Development in Ecuador through Institutions and Beliefs, 1950–2014.*" Masters Economics Thesis, Lund University.

Scarrow, Howard A. 1986. "Duverger's Law, Fusion, and the Decline of American 'Third' Parties." *Western Political Quarterly* 39(4) (December): 634–47.

Scartascini, C., and W. M. Crain. 2002. "The Size and Composition of Government Spending in Multi-Party Systems." *SSRN Electronic Journal* (April).

Schelling, Thomas C. 1960. *The Strategy of Conflict.* Cambridge, MA: Harvard University Press.

Schenk, Karl-Ernst. 2003. *Economic Institutions and Complexity.* Northampton, MA: Edward Elgar.

Schlag, Pierre. 2015. "How to Do Things with Hohfeld." *Law and Contemporary Problems* 78(1–2): 185–234.

Schofield, Norman. 1993. "Political Competition and Multiparty Coalition Governments." *European Journal of Political Research* 23: 1–33.

   2006. *Architects of Political Change: Constitutional Quandaries and Social Choice Theory.* New York, NY: Cambridge University Press.

   2008. *The Spatial Model of Politics.* London: Routledge.

Schultz, P. Wesley, and Steven R. Stein. 2009. "Litter in America: National Findings and Recommendations." *Keep America Beautiful.*

Schumpeter, Joseph A. 1942. *Capitalism, Socialism, and Democracy.* New York, NY: Harper & Brothers.

Scott, James C. 1985. *Weapons of the Weak: Everyday Forms of Peasant Resistance.* New Haven, CT: Yale University Press.

Segal, Jeffrey A., Charles M. Cameron, and Albert D. Cover. 1992. "A Spatial Model of Roll Call Voting: Senators, Constituents, Presidents, and Interest Groups in Supreme Court Confirmations." *American Journal of Political Science* 36(1): 96–121.

Segal, Jeffrey A. and H. J. Spaeth. 2002. *The Supreme Court and the Attitudinal Model Revisited*. Cambridge: Cambridge University Press.

SENPLADES. 2010. "*Los nuevos retos de América Latina: Socialismo y Sumak Kawsay*" [The new challenges of Latin America: Socialism and Sumak Kawsay]. Quito: SENPLADES.

Shear, Michael D. 2016. "Ruth Bader Ginsburg Expresses Regret for Criticizing Donald Trump." *New York Times*, July 14.

Shepsle, Kenneth A. 2008. "Old Questions and New Answers about Institutions: The Riker Objection Revisited." In *The Oxford Handbook of Political Economy*, edited by Barry R. Weingast and Donald A. Wittman, 1031–49. New York, NY: Oxford University Press.

  2010. *Analyzing Politics: Rationality, Behavior, and Institutions*. 2nd edn. New York, NY: Norton.

  2017. *Rule Breaking and Political Imagination*. Chicago, IL: University of Chicago Press.

Shepsle, Kenneth A. and Barry R. Weingast. 1981. "Structure-Induced Equilibrium and Legislative Choice." *Public Choice* 37(3): 503–19.

  1987. "The Institutional Foundations of Committee Power." *American Political Science Review* 81(1): 85–104.

  1995a. "Positive Theories of Congressional Institutions." In *Positive Theories of Congressional Institutions*, edited by Kenneth A. Shepsle and Barry R. Weingast, 5–35. Ann Arbor, MI: University of Michigan Press.

  eds. 1995b. *Positive Theories of Congressional Institutions*. Ann Arbor, MI: University of Michigan Press.

Shipan, Charles R. 1997. *Designing Judicial Review: Interest Groups, Congress, and Communications Policy*. Ann Arbor, MI: University of Michigan Press.

Shirley, Mary M., Ning Wang, and Claude Ménard. 2015. "Ronald Coase's Impact on Economics." *Journal of Institutional Economics* 11(2): 227–44.

Shugart, M. and J. Carey. 1992. *Presidents and Assemblies: Constitutional Design and Electoral Dynamics*. New York, NY: Cambridge University Press.

Siaroff, A. 2009. *Comparing Political Regimes: A Thematic Introduction to Comparative Politics*. Toronto, Canada: University of Toronto Press.

Simon, Herbert A. 1957. *Models of Man*. New York, NY: Wiley.

  1961. *Administrative Behavior: A Study of Decision-Making Processes in Administrative Organization*. 2nd edn. New York, NY: Macmillan.

  1991. "Organizations and Markets." *Journal of Economic Perspectives* 5(2): 25–44.

Skaaning, Svend-Erik. 2010. "Measuring the Rule of Law." *Political Research Quarterly* 63(2): 449–60.

Smith, Adam. [1776] 2007. *An Inquiry into the Nature and Causes of the Wealth of Nations*. Edited by S. M. Soares. MetaLibri Digital Library. www.ibiblio.org/ml/libri/s/SmithA_WealthNations_p.pdf.

Smith, Henry E. 2000. "Semicommon Property Rights and Scattering in the Open Fields." *Journal of Legal Studies* 29(1) (January): 131–69.

Smith, J. Allen. 1914. "Effect of State Regulation of Public Utilities upon Municipal Home Rule." *Annals of the American Academy of Political and Social Science* 53: 85–93.

Sobbrio, Francesco. 2011. "Indirect Lobbying and Media Bias." *Quarterly Journal of Political Science* 6(3–4): 235–74.

Sokoloff, Kenneth L. and Stanley L. Engerman. 2000. "Institutions, Factor Endowments, and Paths of Development in the New World." *Journal of Economic Perspectives* 14(3): 217–32.

Spence, Michael. 1973. "Job Market Signaling." *Quarterly Journal of Economics* 87(3): 355–74.

Spiller, Pablo T. 1990. "Politicians, Interest Groups, and Regulators: A Multiple-Principals Agency Theory of Regulation, or 'Let Them Be Bribed.'" *Journal of Law and Economics* 33(1): 65–101.

Spiller, Pablo T. and Rafael Gely. 1992. "Congressional Control or Judicial Independence: The Determinants of U.S. Supreme Court Labor Relations Decisions, 1949–1988." *Rand Journal of Economics* 23: 463–92.

2009. "Strategic Judicial Decision-Making." Oxford Handbooks Online. www.oxfordhandbooks.com/view/10.1093/oxfordhb/978019920842 5.001.0001/oxfordhb-9780199208425-e-3.

Spiller, Pablo T. and Sanny Liao. 2008. "Buy, Lobby or Sue: Interest Groups' Participation in Policy Making: A Selective Survey." In *New Institutional Economics: A Guidebook*, edited by Eric Brousseau and Jean-Michel Glachant, 307–27. New York, NY: Cambridge University Press.

Starrett, David A. 1972. "Fundamental Nonconvexities in the Theory of Externalities." *Journal of Economic Theory* 4(2): 180–99.

Steensgaard, Niels. 1974. *The Asian Trade Revolution of the Seventeenth Century: The East India Companies and the Decline of the Caravan Trade*. Chicago, IL: University of Chicago Press.

Stevens, John Paul. 1986. "The Third Branch of Liberty." *University of Miami Law Review* 41(2): 277–93.

Stigler, George J. 1971. "The Theory of Economic Regulation." *The Bell Journal of Economics and Management Science* 2(1): 3–21.

ed. 1988. *Chicago Studies in Political Economy*. Chicago, IL: University of Chicago Press.

Stigler, George J. and Claire Friedland. 1962. "What Can Regulators Regulate? The Case of Electricity." *Journal of Law and Economics* 5 (October): 1–16.

Stiglitz, Joseph E. 1975. "The Theory of 'Screening,' Education, and the Distribution of Income." *American Economic Review* 65(3): 283–300.

Stromberg, David. 2004. "Mass Media Competition, Political Competition, and Public Policy." *Review of Economic Studies* 71: 265–84.

Sunstein, Cass R. 1989. "On the Costs and Benefits of Aggressive Judicial Review of Agency Action." *Duke Law Journal* 1989(3): 522–37.

Tadelis, Steven and Oliver E. Williamson. 2013. "Transaction Cost Economics." In *The Handbook of Organizational Economics*, edited by Robert Gibbons and John Roberts, 159–89. Princeton, NJ: Princeton University Press.

Tridimas, George. 2005. "Judges and Taxes: Judicial Review, Judicial Independence and the Size of Government." *Constitutional Political Economy* 16: 5–30.

Tullock, Gordon. 1965. *The Politics of Bureaucracy*. Washington, DC: Public Affairs Press.

1967. *Toward a Mathematics of Politics*. Ann Arbor, MI: University of Michigan Press.

Tullock, Gordon and Geoffrey Brennan. 1981. "Why So Much Stability." *Public Choice* 37(2): 189–204.

Tushnet, Mark V. 2003. *Slave Law in the American South: State v. Mann in History and Literature*. Lawrence: University Press of Kansas.

Umbeck, John. 1981. "Might Makes Rights: A Theory of the Formation and Initial Distribution of Property Rights." *Economic Inquiry* 19(1): 38–59.

US Department of Agriculture. 1936. *Agricultural Statistics 1936*. Washington, DC: US Department of Agriculture.

van der Schyff, Gerhard. 2010. *Judicial Review of Legislation: A Comparative Review of the United Kingdom, the Netherlands, and South Africa*. New York, NY: Springer.

van Zandt, David E. 1993. "The Lessons of the Lighthouse: 'Government' or 'Private' Provision of Goods." *Journal of Legal Studies* 22(1): 47–72.

Viscusi, Kip W., Joseph E. Harrington Jr., and John M. Vernon. 2005. *Economics of Regulation and Antitrust*. Cambridge, MA: MIT Press.

Voigt, Stefan. 1997. "Positive Constitutional Economics: A Survey." *Public Choice* 90(1/4): 11–53.

2008. "The Economic Effects of Judicial Accountability: Cross-Country Evidence." *European Journal of Law and Economics* 25(2) (April): 95–123.

2011. "Positive Constitutional Economics II – A Survey of Recent Developments." *Public Choice* 146(1–2) (January): 205–56.

Volden, C. 2002. "A Formal Model of the Politics of Delegation in a Separation of Powers System." *American Journal of Political Science* 46(1): 111–33.

Wallis, John Joseph. 2018a. "Leviathan Denied: Rules, Governments, and Social Dynamics." Unpublished book manuscript.

2018b. "What Institutions Are: The Difference between Norms and Institutions, Rules and Enforcement." Working Paper, University of Maryland, January.

Weingast, Barry R. 1979. "A Rational Choice Perspective on Congressional Norms." *American Journal of Political Science* 23(2) (May): 245–62.

1998. "Political Stability and Civil War: Institutions, Commitment, and American Democracy." In *Analytic Narratives*, edited by Robert Bates et al., 148–93. Princeton, NJ: Princeton University Press.

2015. "Capitalism, Democracy, and Countermajoritarian Institutions." Working Paper, Stanford University. https://papers.ssrn.com/sol3/pape rs.cfm?abstract_id=2639793.

2016. "Exposing the Neoclassical Fallacy: McCloskey on Ideas and the Great Enrichment." *Scandinavian Economic History Review* 64(3): 189–201.

Weingast, Barry R. and W. J. Marshall. 1988. "The Industrial Organization of Congress; Or, Why Legislatures, Like Firms, Are Not Organized as Markets." *Journal of Political Economy* 96(1): 132–63.

Weingast, Barry R. and Mark J. Moran. 1983. "Bureaucratic Discretion or Congressional Control? Regulatory Policymaking by the Federal Trade Commission." *Journal of Political Economy* 91(5): 765–800.

Wellisz, Stanislaw. 1964. "On External Diseconomies and the Government-Assisted Invisible Hand." *Economica* 31(124): 345–62.

Whinston, Michael. 2003. "On the Transaction Cost Determinants of Vertical Integration." *Journal of Law, Economics, and Organization* 19(1): 1–23.

Wiggins, Steven N. and Gary D. Libecap. 1985. "Oil Field Unitization: Contractual Failure in the Presence of Imperfect Information." *American Economic Review* 75(3): 368–85.

Williamson, Oliver E. 1971. "The Vertical Integration of Production: Market Failure Considerations." *American Economic Review* 61(2): 112–23.

1975. *Markets and Hierarchies: Analysis and Antitrust Implications.* New York, NY: Free Press.

1985. *The Economic Institutions of Capitalism: Firms, Markets, Relational Contracting.* New York, NY: Free Press.

1990. "The Firm as a Nexus of Treaties: An Introduction." In *The Firm as a Nexus of Treaties*, edited by Masahiko Aoki, Bo Gustafsson, and Oliver E. Williamson, 1–25. London: Sage.

1996. *The Mechanisms of Governance*. Oxford: Oxford University Press.

2000. "The New Institutional Economics: Taking Stock, Looking Ahead." *Journal of Economic Literature* 38(3): 595–613.

2002. "The Theory of the Firm as Governance Structure: From Choice to Contract." *Journal of Economic Perspectives* 16(3): 171–95.

Wilson, James Q. 1980. *The Politics of Regulation*. New York, NY: Basic Books.

1989. *Bureaucracy: What Government Agencies Do and Why They Do It*. New York, NY: Basic Books.

Wittman, Donald A. 1989. "Why Democracies Produce Efficient Results." *Journal of Political Economy* 97(6): 1395–424.

World Bank. 2017. *World Databank*. http://databank.worldbank.org/data/home.aspx.

Yandle, Bruce. 1983. "Bootleggers and Baptists: The Education of a Regulatory Economist." *Regulation* 7(3): 12–16.

Young, H. Peyton. 1996. "The Economics of Convention." *Journal of Economic Perspectives* 10(2): 105–23.

Yu, Zhihao. 2005. "Environmental Protection: A Theory of Direct and Indirect Competition for Political Influence." *Review of Economic Studies* 72: 269–86.

Zelder, Martin. 1998. "The Cost of Accosting Coase: A Reconciliatory Survey of Proofs and Disproofs of the Coase Theorem." In *Coasean Economics: Law and Economics and the New Institutional Economics*, edited by Steven G. Medema, 30–94. New York, NY: Springer Science.

Index

academic context *see* Institutional and
   Organizational Analysis
accountability, judicial system 235–38
adherent organizations 46–47
ADICO (grammar of institutions)
   34–37, 41–42
adverse selection 69–70, 88–91
agency theory, firms 88–91
agents *see* principal-agent models
Alianza País, Ecuador 336–44
Amazonian land conflict 76–79
anti-fusion laws 201–4
Argentina 1912–1955 transition
   326–32, 345
Articles of Confederation 297, 320–26
asset specificity 93–96
assets, hybrids 102–5
authority, judicial system 241–45
autopilot, development trajectories
   285–88, 292

Becker, Gary 143–45, 151
behavioral beliefs 13
behaviors
   enforcement vs. equilibrium 47–50
   individuals 44–46
   judiciary 246–48
   littering decline 3–4
   political liberalization 305–7
   rules, institutions and norms 36
   transaction costs 26–27
beliefs
   behavioral 13
   constitutional moments 22–23,
      296–300
   core 13, 20–21, 277–78
   critical transitions 288–89, 301–3
   development trajectories 290–91
   government 21–22

individuals 44–46
institutional deepening 302–3, 304–6
institutions 278–82, 351–52
littering decline 3–4
Portugal's decline in the Sixteenth
   Century 7–11
see also norms
bilateral governance 95–96
bilateral relationships 95
bonded rationality 44–46, 68–69
Brazil
   1985–2014 transition 332–36, 345
   Amazon land conflict 76–79
   constitutional documents 298–99,
      304
   constitutional moments 167
   land reform 4–7, 167, 168–69
   multiple-party system 195, 196
   presidential control of bureaucratic
      agencies 222
Buchanan, James 347–48
bureaucracies 207–9, 228
   book overview 110
   congressional dominance 207–9,
      213–16
   controllers of 209–13, 224–28
   and delegation in a multiple-principal
      context 211, 219, 224–28
   discretion and autonomous agencies
      216–19
   institutions, commitment, and
      performance 121
   interest groups 157–63
   legal constraints on bureaucratic
      action 222–24
   presidential control of bureaucratic
      agencies 219–22
   US political system 18–19
   see also executive and legislative
      government

385